THIS I CANNOT FORGET

This
I Cannot Forget

THE MEMOIRS OF
NIKOLAI BUKHARIN'S WIDOW

Anna Larina

Introduction by
STEPHEN F. COHEN

Translated from the Russian by
GARY KERN

W·W·NORTON & COMPANY
New York · London

Printed in the United States of America.

The text of this book is composed in Plantin Light 118,
with the display set in Plantin Light 118.
Composition and manufacturing by the Haddon Craftsmen, Inc.
Book design by Jacques Chazaud.

Library of Congress Cataloging in Publication Data

Larina, Anna.
[Nezabyvaemoe. English]
This I cannot forget : the memoirs of Nikolai Bukharin's widow / by Anna Larina ;
introduction by Stephen F. Cohen ; translated from the Russian by Gary Kern.
p.   cm.
Translation of Nezabyvaemoe.
Includes index.
1. Larina, Anna.   2. Bukharin, Nikolai Ivanovich, 1888–1938.
3. Revolutionaries—Soviet Union—Biography.   4. Soviet Union—Politics and
government—1917–1936.   5. Wives—Soviet Union—Biography.   I. Title.
DK268.B76N4913   1991
947.084′092—dc20   91-12739

ISBN 0-393-03025-3

W.W. Norton & Company, Inc., 500 Fifth Avenue, New York, N.Y. 10110
W.W. Norton & Company Ltd., 10 Coptic Street, London WC1A 1PU

1 2 3 4 5 6 7 8 9 0

This book
is dedicated
to the two men
closest and dearest to me:

my father and my husband

CONTENTS

Photographs appear following page 192.

INTRODUCTION

The Afterlife of
Nikolai Bukharin

by

S T E P H E N   F.   C O H E N

> "If you want to live, then shut up about Bukharin!"
> —Lavrenty Beria to Anna Larina, 1939

Readers are opening a book unlike any other in the long and agonized history of Soviet literature. Circumstantially, it belongs to the large volume of personal testimony by survivors of Stalin's twenty-five-year terror and Gulag Archipelago, as Aleksandr Solzhenitsyn once and forever named that far-flung system of interrogation cells, transit prisons, forced-labor camps, and remote exile populated by millions of lost souls and brutally obedient guards. Here, again, we journey into the lower depths of a debased world "covered in the shame of unbridled terror, awash in the blood of the innocent" and particularly "the tears of women . . . torn from their children and husbands." Gulag literature, much of it written secretly decades ago and only recently freed from censorship, continues to appear. It may be, with its counterpart from the other defining holocaust of modern times, the most characteristic writing of the twentieth century.

But Anna Mikhailovna Larina's book is different, indeed unique. It is not primarily the story of her twenty years of suffering and survival in the Gulag—that, too, would make an astonishing volume—but of her previous life as a daughter and wife among the founding fathers of the Soviet Union. Except for Leon Trotsky's autobiography and fragmentary reminiscences of a later period by Stalin's daughter, Larina's book is the only uncensored memoir ever to appear from inside the highest levels of that historic and doomed world.[1] At once a family tale, love story, and quest for political justice, it is unprecedented in Soviet literature. Nor is anything similar likely ever to emerge from still closed archives; everyone who might have written a comparable account seems to have perished in the terror before putting pen to paper.

Born in 1914, Anna Larina grew up among self-proclaimed professional revolutionaries who set out to create a virtuous new civilization for the entire world and ended up instead with a monopoly of power—the Bolsheviks (later known as Communists) who took power in 1917, directed the Red victory in the Russian civil war from 1918 to 1921, and formed the nucleus of the original Soviet elite that ruled the country until most were swept away by Stalin's blood purges in the second half of the 1930s. As the adopted daughter of Yury Larin, a leading Bolshevik intellectual close to Lenin's inner circle, Anna was a child of their doomed revolution. She lived in a regal hotel set aside for the founders' families and later in the Kremlin itself, sat on Lenin's knee, vacationed at the leadership's dachas, was sternly lectured on revolutionary etiquette by Trotsky, watched her father buried with honor in the Kremlin wall, and sent girlish love notes through an unwitting, and yet unmenacing, Stalin.

In 1934, at the age of twenty, Anna tied her personal fate forever in marriage to the man who would soon be the most contagious political "leper" in Stalin's Russia—Nikolai Ivanovich Bukharin. Despite having been ousted from the inner circle of leadership by Stalin in 1929, the forty-five-year-old Bukharin, whom Lenin had called the "golden boy of the revolution" and the "favorite of the entire Party," remained the most genuinely revered of all the living Soviet founders. In late 1936, a few months before Bukharin's arrest in February 1937, she gave birth to his only son, Yury. Their courtship and marriage, told in flashbacks as Anna falls ever deeper into Gulagland, is the core of her memoir, though it can also be read, across a chasm of fifty years, as the death agony of an entire revolutionary elite.

Above all, *This I Cannot Forget* is the book of a political widow who survived to carry out a sacred mission.[2] Written secretly in the 1970s

1. Lenin's widow, Nadezhda Krupskaya, published "memoirs," but they were exceedingly elliptical and heavily censored.

2. An analogy might be drawn with Russia's literary widows who survived to restore the reputations of martyred writers. See Carl R. Proffer, *The Widows of Russia* (Ann Arbor, 1987). The greatest example was Nadezhda Mandelstam, widow of the poet Osip Mandelstam, and particularly the first volume of her memoirs, *Hope against Hope* (New York, 1970). The example is doubly appropriate

and early 1980s, when her husband's name was still a taboo in the Soviet Union, it is essentially about Bukharin—his personality, role in history, and martyrdom. Larina saw him for the last time the day he knew he would be arrested and would never return, and she learned nothing more about him until the news of his trial and execution in March 1938. As we might expect of a founding father,[3] he implored her to memorize, for "a future generation of Party leaders," a letter-testament denying all the criminal charges being heaped on him by Stalin, and to raise their infant son "as a Bolshevik."

Larina fulfilled the first bequest, silently reciting the letter from memory "like a prayer" throughout her years of imprisonment, though she had to endure five decades before being able to publish it in the Soviet Union. Their son, however, was beyond her reach. Eleven months old when his mother was arrested in June 1937, he grew up under another name in foster homes and orphanages. They met again only in 1956.

Not surprisingly, Larina's memoirs were a political sensation when they were finally published in Moscow, under Mikhail Gorbachev, in 1988. Issued in 650,000 copies, first in a monthly journal and then as a book,[4] they were the centerpiece in Bukharin's official exoneration and elevation to a special place of honor in Soviet history. At seventy-four, Anna Mikhailovna—I have always called her that with the respect shown to an older person in Russia—began yet another life, now as a best-selling author and celebrated figure of "living history." But the widow's real work was done.

All of the Soviet founders falsely charged and executed by Stalin were rehabilitated under Gorbachev, but only Nikolai Bukharin became the subject of a "dialogue with the dead" and even a fledgling political cult.[5] His official restoration to honor was one of the most fiercely resisted,

---

because, as she recorded, Bukharin "very actively" protected the poet for as long as he could: "He simply saved us." Nadezhda Mandelshtam, *Moe zaveshchanie i drugie esse,* 2d ed. (New York, 1982), pp. 126–27.

3. If this term seems odd in the Soviet context, see Yevgeny Yevtushenko's poem "Bukharin's Widow" (*Izvestiia,* March 20, 1988), which puts Bukharin among the "real fathers of the revolution."

4. They were serialized in the popular journal *Znamia,* nos. 10–12, 1988, which had a print run at that time of just over 500,000 copies. The book —*Nezabyvaemoe* (Moscow, 1989)—appeared in a printing of 150,000 copies, which quickly sold out.

5. For this expression, see *Voprosy istorii KPSS,* no. 3, 1991, p. 151. For the

long-awaited, and important decisions taken during the decades following Stalin's death in 1953, but perhaps inexorable. As a Western scholar wrote rhetorically many years ago, "Why is it that [Bukharin's] heresy, so often condemned, so often refuted, so often punished, is so often resurrected? Why does this ghost not keep to his grave, though the stake is driven into his corpse again and again?"[6]

The personally appealing Bukharin who emerges from Larina's memoirs is only a small part of the answer. A zestful man with boyish charm and passionate enthusiasms for everything from politics, ideas, and science to sports, nature, and culture, he was, according to Soviet and foreign contemporaries, the best-liked leader of the Bolshevik Revolution. Bukharin's personal popularity helps explain why his show trial and execution as a criminal "enemy of the people" seemed particularly unjust and his martyrdom doubly tragic. So too does his reputation, almost singular in the dictatorial Party leadership, as a man who formed friendly personal relations with the regime's ideological opponents and even defended them. Larina mentions the iconoclastic poet Boris Pasternak in this respect, but she could also have noted her husband's remarkable relationship with the anti-Bolshevik physiologist Ivan Pavlov and especially with the doomed poet Osip Mandelstam, whom Bukharin protected for more than a decade.[7]

But the real source of Bukharin's enduring importance was political—or more precisely, programmatic—and is to be found in the Soviet 1920s. Fighting a merciless civil war in the aftermath of the 1917 revolution, the Bolsheviks resorted to extremist measures that imposed a draconian state monopoly over much of the economy and dictatorial, often terror-backed Party control over political life. In 1921, with the civil war won but the economy in ruins and even the Party's own constituencies in growing rebellion, Lenin introduced a fundamental change of course known as the New Economic Policy, or simply NEP. Until Stalin abolished NEP in 1929, it was, to use language popularized later in Soviet history, the first era of Communist liberalization, the first Moscow Spring, or, as was said during Gorbachev's reforms, the first perestroika.

"Bukharinist Boom," see G. A. Bordiugov and V. A. Kozlov, *Istoriia i koniunktura* (Moscow, 1992), chap. 2.

6. Bertram D. Wolfe, *Khrushchev and Stalin's Ghost* (New York, 1957), pp. 135, 139.

7. See above, note 2; and Mandelstam, *Hope against Hope*, pp. 22–23, 112–18, 136, 145. Bukharin's efforts to save the poet are also documented in a contemporary investigation of Mandelstam's death. See *Izvestiia,* May 25–29, 1992.

Though the NEP 1920s were far from democratic, compared to the decades of despotic terror and heavy-handed bureaucratic tyranny that followed, they were for most citizens a "golden era" in Soviet history. Market relations and private enterprise were officially encouraged in economic life, especially in peasant agriculture and retail trade, so a large independent sector developed alongside the state-owned industrial one. The Communist Party maintained its political monopoly, but while exercising far more tolerance and permitting much more social, intellectual, and cultural diversity than would ever again be the case until the Gorbachev years. That is why Stalin's renunciation of NEP as "rotten liberalism" destroyed a historical model of Communist rule in which, decades later, anti-Stalinists from the Soviet Union and Eastern Europe to China would find a lost and legitimate alternative to Stalinism.

Lenin created NEP, but after the leader's death in 1924, as his heirs on the ruling Politburo and Central Committee split into factions warring over power and policy, Bukharin became its greatest interpreter and defender—the "Pushkin of NEP," as one opponent contemptuously dubbed him. He did so first in alliance with Stalin against a series of oppositions inside the Communist Party—the Trotskyist Left, then a group headed by Grigory Zinoviev and Lev Kamenev, then a united opposition of Trotsky, Zinoviev, and Kamenev. And he did so finally, with the support of his Politburo allies Aleksei Rykov and Mikhail Tomsky, against Stalin in 1928 and 1929.[8]

Defending NEP as the only acceptable road to modernization and socialism in backward peasant Russia, Bukharin developed programmatic ideas and policies that anticipated those of anti-Stalinist reformers decades later. Regretting his own extremist views during the civil war, he now warned repeatedly against the abuses of power inherent in the Party's political monopoly and ideological zealotry—great leaps beyond the people's wishes, warfare actions against society, administrative hypercentralization and rampant bureaucracy, elite privilege and economic decay. He advocated instead conciliatory, evolutionary policies that would encourage both the private and the state sectors to "grow into socialism" in mutually beneficial conditions of market relations and civil peace.

Bukharin called his program "socialist humanism." Like all Bolsheviks, he believed in the need for state planning, industrialization, and

8. For Bukharin's role in the 1920s, and the material I use here, see my *Bukharin and the Bolshevik Revolution: A Political Biography, 1888–1938* (New York, 1973 and 1980), chaps. 5–9; and, for a summary version, my *Rethinking the Soviet Experience: Politics and History since 1917* (New York, 1985; exp. ed., 1993), chap. 3.

some kind of large-scale collective farming, but insisted that "our economy exist for the consumer, not the consumer for the economy"—or as he put it elsewhere, "the bureaucrat for the people, not the people for the bureaucrat." He continued to defend the Party's political dictatorship, but wanted it based on "Soviet law, and not Soviet arbitrariness moderated by a 'bureau of complaints' whose whereabouts is unknown." As the Communist Party's leading theorist, he hoped Marxism would prevail everywhere in intellectual and cultural life, but only on the "principle of free, anarchistic competition" rather than "squeezing everybody into one fist."

In short, Bukharinism was not only an alternative for Soviet Russia's development after the revolution but a premonition of Stalinism, which during the next two decades tried to squeeze everybody and everything into the state's mailed fist. When Stalin broke with NEP at the end of the 1920s, for a draconian kind of industrialization based on forcing the country's 125 million peasants into state-run collective farms, Bukharin's protests put him at the head of the so-called Right Opposition inside the Party. Even before the general secretary's measures of 1929–33 had left perhaps ten million peasants dead or imprisoned in a vastly swollen Gulag, Bukharin understood their "monstrously one-sided" intent—and their consequences. "Stalin's policy is leading to civil war. He will have to drown the revolts in blood." The outcome, he warned, "will be a police state."

That prophetic opposition sealed Bukharin's fate. In late 1929, the new Stalinist majority stripped him of all his leadership positions—member of the Politburo, editor of the Party's newspaper *Pravda*, and head of the Moscow-based Communist International. Once the Soviet Party's coleader and acknowledged ideologist, Bukharin saw his ideas and programs anathematized as "anti-Leninist Right deviationism." For the first time since the Bolshevik Revolution, he had no real power or influence over events, though he remained a nominal member of the Party Central Committee until his arrest at its fateful meeting on February 27, 1937.

At this point in his life, in 1930, Bukharin began the courtship of Anna, and thus comes to dominate her memoirs. As readers will learn, he continued to play significant political roles, especially during a short-lived thaw in Stalin's policies from 1934 to mid-1936, as editor of the government newspaper *Izvestiya*, author of sections of a new Soviet constitution, and advocate of pro-Western alliances against the growing threat of Nazi Germany. All this was, however, prelude to a macabre kind of martyrdom, as readers will also discover.

Exactly when Stalin decided to destroy the old Bolshevik Party, including the men who had been part of Lenin's original leadership, is not known. Probably, it was in the early 1930s, when he had already acquired enormous power and was becoming the subject of a cult of personal infallibility. The catastrophe of collectivization, with its terrible toll in peasant lives and calamitous impact on agriculture, redoubled Stalin's need to prove that his leadership and policies were the only legitimate outcome of the revolution. And small clandestine groups of lower-ranking Bolsheviks were calling for his removal, including one headed by a former Bukharin supporter, Martemyan Ryutin.

The assassination of Sergei Kirov, head of the Leningrad Party organization, on December 1, 1934, gave Stalin the pretext, and indeed almost certainly was arranged by him. Claiming that the killing was part of a vast conspiracy inside the Communist Party, he used the secret police, once known as the Cheka and, under Stalin, as the NKVD, to plot a mass terror against Party officials throughout the country. About a million Communists were arrested during the worst years, from 1936 to 1939, about a third of the Party's members and the majority of those who had joined before Stalin's victory over Bukharin. Most of them were executed. (Communists were, however, only part of the millions of citizens taken during the great terror.)

All of Lenin's coleaders were falsely condemned as lifelong covert criminals, but special defamation was reserved for Bukharin, whose NEP program and popularity remained the greatest reproach to Stalin's cult. He was forced to play the role of chief defendant—twenty-one sat in the dock, including his erstwhile ally Rykov—in the third and most ambitiously staged Moscow trial of old Bolsheviks. Stalin's press set the tone after the opening day on March 2, 1938: "Bukharin sits there with his head bowed low, a treacherous, two-faced, whimpering, evil nonentity who has been exposed . . . as leader of a gang of spies, terrorists, and thieves, as instigator of assassination. . . . This filthy little Bukharin." As the trial moved toward its preordained outcome, Stalin, through his mouthpiece-prosecutor Andrei Vyshinsky, leveled an exceptional accusation against Bukharin: "The hypocrisy and perfidy of this man exceed the most perfidious and monstrous crimes known to the history of mankind."[9]

On the surface, Bukharin's trial remains, as it was at the time, a great political mystery: Why did he—indeed, all the illustrious Bolsheviks put in the dock—confess to hideously false charges? (Bukharin's eleven-day trial captured worldwide attention, though news of his exe-

9. *Pravda,* March 3, 1938; and *The Case of the Anti-Soviet "Bloc of Rights and Trotskyists": Report of Court Proceedings* (Moscow, 1938), pp. 656–57.

cution, on March 15, was overshadowed by Hitler's march into Austria.) Formally, the proceedings were public, held before some three hundred handpicked observers in the same aristocratic building where Lenin had lain in state, and published in several languages as a thick official stenograph.[10] That outward decorum misled most Western commentators into taking the trial at face value, and to the prevailing view, elaborated in Arthur Koestler's famous novel *Darkness at Noon*, that Bukharin, sincerely repentant for his past opposition, willingly confessed as a "last service" to Stalin's Communist Party. In fact, nothing supports such an interpretation of Bukharin's behavior.

Separated forever by his arrest, Larina can shed no new light on her husband's conduct in the courtroom or, equally important, during his year-long pretrial imprisonment. In these memoirs, she suggests that he confessed because he was "morally broken," though in a later interview she points to a different explanation—she and their infant son were "hostages" in a terror system that routinely, and murderously, victimized wives and children as well. My own view, developed in detail elsewhere, is that Bukharin did not actually confess to any of the criminal accusations leveled against him. Instead, he was astonishingly defiant throughout the proceedings, as a few observant Western spectators noted at the time and some Russian experts now agree.[11]

After holding out in prison for three months and knowing he would be executed anyway, Bukharin finally agreed to go through Stalin's show trial for two compelling reasons. (Unlike so many other victims, he seems not to have been brutally tortured.) He hoped to save Anna and their son but also his previous wife and their thirteen-year-old daughter, Svetlana, as well as other members of his large extended family—if not their freedom, at least their lives.[12] And taking on his assigned role as the representative of a martyred Bolshevik movement, he wanted to turn his

10. The English-language edition is cited in the preceding note.

11. I present the evidence, including commentary at the time, in my *Bukharin and the Bolshevik Revolution*, pp. 372–81. For the first scholarly analysis of Bukharin's real conduct at the trial, see Robert C. Tucker's introduction to our jointly edited book *The Great Purge Trial* (New York, 1965); also his *Stalin in Power* (New York, 1990), chap. 18. According to the Soviet Supreme Court judge who reviewed Bukharin's trial and exonerated him in 1988, he "was a fighter to the end, despite the conditions in which he found himself." *Izvestiia*, February 7, 1988.

12. In addition to Anna, several family members eventually were arrested but survived the terror, including Bukharin's brother, Vladimir; second wife, Esfir Gurvich; and daughter, Svetlana. For evidence that Svetlana was used as a hostage, see *Moscow News*, October 9–16, 1988. Bukharin's first wife, Nadezhda Lukina, however, was treated brutally and executed. See Aleksandr Borin, "Ritual," *Literaturnaia gazeta*, November 23, 1988.

last public appearance into a countertrial (a well-known practice of Russian revolutionaries)—to defend his reputation and Bolshevism's any way he could against the Stalinist regime. Bukharin knew that the court's verdict had already been determined, but he went on trial before a higher court of history and the "future generation" addressed in the letter he had entrusted to Larina.

Briefly explained, Bukharin's strategy was simple but exceedingly difficult to carry out. To satisfy Stalin's minimum demands and save his family, he accepted personal responsibility for the entire criminal indictment while denying all of its specific charges. "I plead guilty to . . . the sum total of crimes committed by this counterrevolutionary organization, irrespective of whether or not I knew of, or whether or not I took a direct part in, any particular act." Lest anyone fail to understand that the second part of the statement negated the first, Bukharin later discredited his whole "confession" with a simple aside: "The confession of the accused is a medieval principle of jurisprudence." As for the outlandish charges featured in Stalin's witch-hunt, he flatly and repeatedly rejected them: "I do not plead guilty. . . . I do not know of this. . . . I deny it. . . . I categorically deny any complicity."

Already condemned and without any legal protection, Bukharin's last struggle was to indict Stalin's regime by showing that its criminal accusations were political falsifications, and that the original Bolsheviks had never been a "counterrevolutionary organization" but the revolution's true leaders with different visions of the Soviet future. Despite a bullying Stalinist prosecutor and judge, he did so with a tenacious display of double-talk, code words, evasion, and digressions. The prosecutor and judge, panicked by his "acrobatics" and refusal to follow Stalin's jailhouse script, tried to frighten him from "following definite tactics . . . hiding behind a flood of words . . . making digressions into the sphere of politics." But Bukharin persevered day after day in the face of Vyshinsky's threatening examination. In his final statement, he again "confessed" to the indictment but then, according to a foreign reporter in the courtroom, "proceeded, uninterrupted this time, to tear it to bits, while Vyshinsky, powerless to intervene, sat uneasily in his place."

Three decades later, a Western historian would conclude that Bukharin's trial, "degrading as it was in many respects, may fairly be called his finest hour."[13] Bukharin no doubt hoped that this would be history's judgment. In the Soviet Union, however, it took fifty years, and three post-Stalin leaderships, just to overturn the court's verdict.

13. Anonymous reviewer of George Katkov's *The Trial of Bukharin* (New York, 1969), in *Times Literary Supplement*, January 29, 1970.

The saga of Bukharin's political afterlife spanned the entire history of post-Stalin communism. A struggle to clear his name—"rehabilitation," as the process was called—stretched from Anna Larina's Siberian exile, where in 1956 she first wrote down Bukharin's testament and finally reunited with their son, to Communist parties in Western and Eastern Europe, and even China. For different reasons and in different ways, it eventually involved very diverse kinds of people, many of them long unknown to each other, including the widow and son, Communist officials, Soviet dissidents, European socialists, and American university scholars with no political stake in the outcome. Until the end, official Moscow's willingness to respond favorably always lagged far behind the resurgence of Bukharin's reputation elsewhere.[14]

Embattled reformers in ruling Communist parties had the biggest stake in his rehabilitation. After Stalin's death in 1953, as the impulse grew to expose his crimes, reject his legacy, and change the system he had forged in the Soviet Union in the 1930s and imposed on Eastern Europe after World War II, Communist reformers sought inspiration and legitimacy in Lenin's NEP and the Soviet 1920s. There, of course, they rediscovered Bukharin's ideas and policies, which, as a Czech reformer remarked during the Prague Spring of 1967–68, "make themselves heard, so to speak, in the language of the contemporary era."

The martyred Bukharin thus became an important ancestral symbol—the most essential one after the Lenin of NEP—for anti-Stalinist Communist movements in several countries. From the 1950s to the 1980s, the struggle to reform Stalin's system of monopolistic Party-state control over society, particularly the economy, spread across Eastern Europe to other Communist parties, with partial successes and traumatic setbacks, sometimes inflicted by Soviet tanks. Wherever and whenever reformers managed to score substantial victories over entrenched Stalinist and conservative leaderships, a rediscovery of Bukharin usually was under way. Thus, by the early 1980s, the most sustained political and intellectual interest in his role in Soviet history had developed in China, where a major reenactment of NEP was unfolding.[15]

In the Soviet Communist Party, however, the ban on Bukharin remained in force, and thus the prohibition against his policy ideas in the country where they mattered most. Some kind of political battle—we still do not know the full story—was fought in Moscow over his rehabili-

14. For the story up to 1985, see my *Rethinking the Soviet Experience,* chap. 3; and, for after 1985, the expanded edition (1993), chaps. 3, 6.

15. Ibid., chap. 3; and James D. White, "Chinese Studies of Bukharin," *Soviet Studies,* no. 4, 1991, pp. 733–47.

tation during the reforms of Nikita Khrushchev from 1953 to 1964. Khrushchev began the historic process of Soviet de-Stalinization, later embraced far more boldly by Gorbachev, at a closed session of the Twentieth Party Congress, in 1956, where he attacked Stalin's cult and exposed some of his crimes. During the next few years, millions of Gulag prisoners and exiles, like Larina, were set free. Case by case, some 700,000 victims of Stalin's terror were juridically rehabilitated, including many lesser Communist officials and even secondary defendants in the show trials, but not Bukharin or the other major Bolshevik leaders.

Bukharin posed a special problem for the always conflicted Khrushchev, who had risen to high office during Stalin's terror. For political and personal reasons, he often seemed inclined to press for Bukharin's exoneration. Party commissions that he set up to investigate the Kirov assassination and show trials reported to him privately on Stalin's complicity and Bukharin's innocence. In 1962, not long after Khrushchev assaulted Stalin's reputation more publicly at another party congress and had his body removed from the Lenin Mausoleum, he even authorized a spokesman to tell a little-publicized scholarly conference, "Neither Bukharin nor Rykov was, of course, a spy or a terrorist."[16]

But that 1962 remark, the only official one of its kind until the Gorbachev years, lacked juridical and political force. High-level opposition to Bukharin's rehabilitation was too great, or Khrushchev's resolve too weak. Legions of Party neo-Stalinists and conservatives understood the grave danger inherent in relegitimating this founding father, and thus his conception of Soviet socialism. It could only unleash a torrent of pent-up resentment against Stalinist pillars of the existing system, including the still unproductive collective farms, wasteful state-planning bureaucracy, and oppressive censorship.

Not surprisingly, Bukharin's rehabilitation became a casualty of Khrushchev's overthrow by his own colleagues in October 1964. The new Soviet leadership headed by Leonid Brezhnev and Aleksei Kosygin grew into a broad conservative reaction against Khrushchev's reforms, which required the rehabilitation not of Stalin's victims but of important aspects of the late dictator's own reputation. Any lingering hope that Bukharin's case might be reconsidered ended with the Soviet invasion of Communist Czechoslovakia in 1968. For the Moscow leadership, the heretical Prague Spring provided contemporary proof of Stalin's axiom,

16. *Vsesoiuznoe soveshchanie o merakh uluchsheniia podgotovki nauchno-pedagogicheskikh kadrov po istoricheskim naukam, 18 dekabria 1962 g.* (Moscow, 1964), p. 298.

first set out in the late 1920s against Bukharin, that the "Right deviation is the main danger."[17] As the Soviet Union under Brezhnev sank deeper into what Gorbachev later termed an "era of stagnation," the Central Committee apparatus even informed Bukharin's family, in 1977, that the 1938 criminal charges, which had rarely been mentioned since the 1950s in favor of simply "anti-Leninist" ones, "have not been removed."

And yet, Moscow's official attitude hardly reflected Bukharin's real reputation in the world, or even inside the Soviet Union. Khrushchev's de-Stalinization policies gave birth to a larger, more radical reform movement that survived him inside the Soviet Communist Party, particularly among intellectuals. Finding safe havens in various Party, state, and academic institutions, those forerunners of Gorbachev's perestroika continued to develop, guardedly and at some risk, far-reaching criticisms of the existing system and to call for more economic and social freedom and less state control. Without mentioning Bukharin's name, they too were echoing his forbidden ideas of the NEP 1920s. As a Western scholar of the Brezhnev era concluded, "It was astonishing to discover how many ideas of Bukharin . . . were adopted by current reformers as their own and how much of their critique of past practices followed his strictures and prophecies even in their expression."[18]

Bolder Soviet intellectuals of the 1970s defied the authorities and openly embraced Bukharin. The reimposition of heavy-handed censorship under Brezhnev generated a flood of samizdat, or typed and privately circulated, writings about the country's Stalinist past and historical alternatives. In those uncensored article and book manuscripts, Bukharin was quickly rehabilitated—portrayed warmly by memoirists and admired by nonconformist historians for his programmatic opposition to Stalinism. They, too, concluded that his ideas "have not lost their acuteness to this day." Dissident Marxists, who hoped to liberalize or even democratize Soviet socialism, naturally were especially eager to restore his political legitimacy, but some anti-Marxist dissidents also were effusive. Emphasizing Bukharin's opposition to Stalin's collectivization war against the peasant majority, one called his defeat "Russia's greatest tragedy."[19]

17. See, for example, F. M. Vaganov, *Pravyi uklon VKP(b) i ego razgrom,* 2d ed. (Moscow, 1977).
18. Moshe Lewin, *Political Undercurrents in Soviet Economic Debates: From Bukharin to the Modern Reformers* (Princeton, 1974), p. xiii.
19. Boris Shragin, "Nikolai Ivanovich Bukharin," Radio Liberty Seminar Broadcast, no. 38 012-R (1978). For the leading dissident Marxist historian, see Roy A. Medvedev, *Nikolai Bukharin: The Last Years* (New York, 1980).

Outside the Soviet Union, two disparate developments during the Brezhnev years further enhanced Bukharin's reputation. One was, of course, the ongoing struggle for reform inside other ruling and nonruling Communist parties, which persisted despite Moscow's disapproval and thus continued to increase Bukharin's status as a political symbol. Indeed, in 1978, the ninetieth anniversary of his birth and fortieth anniversary of his execution, he became the focus of an unusual international campaign. Spurred by an unexpected appeal from his son, Yury Larin, to the Italian Communist Party, the Bertrand Russell Peace Foundation in England organized a joint petition of prominent Western Communists and normally anti-Communist socialists calling for Bukharin's rehabilitation in Moscow. The petition attracted worldwide publicity and gathered many signatures.[20] Moscow ignored it.

The other development was Bukharin's belated emergence as a major subject of research by non-Communist Western scholars remote from politics. Until the early 1970s, most Anglo-American Sovietologists had viewed Stalinism as the only possible outcome of the Bolshevik Revolution. When that consensus finally broke down, a growing number of them began to study the NEP experience, and particularly Bukharin's policies, as a Bolshevik alternative.[21] No consensus emerged on this large interpretative question, but there no longer was scholarly neglect of Bukharin's role in history except, of course, in the Soviet Union. He was the subject of a major international conference in Rome in 1980, and studies of his ideas continue to appear in the West today.[22]

Except for Yury Larin's uncharacteristic public appeal in 1978, almost all of these international developments unfolded without any connections and often unknown to the Bukharin family. Indeed, most Western observers were surprised to learn that Bukharin's widow and son had survived Stalin's terror, as were many Soviet citizens when she

20. See Ken Coates, *The Case of Nikolai Bukharin* (Nottingham, 1978); Bertrand Russell Peace Foundation, *Dossier on Bukharin* (Nottingham, 1978); and Yannick Blanc and David Kaisergruber, *L'affaire Boukharine: au, Le recours de la mémoire* (Paris, 1979).

21. See, for example, my *Bukharin and the Bolshevik Revolution* (1973) and Lewin's *Political Undercurrents in Soviet Economic Debates*. The pioneer was, however, Alexander Erlich, *The Soviet Industrialization Debate* (Cambridge, Mass., 1960).

22. Istituto Gramsci, *Bucharin tra rivoluzione e riforme* (Rome, 1982). For more recent studies, see Miklòs Kun, *Buharin* (Budapest, 1988); Theodor Bergmann and Gert Schäfer, eds., *"Liebling der Partei": Bucharin—Theoretiker des Sozialismus* (Hamburg, 1989); and Nicholas N. Kozlov and Eric D. Weitz, eds., *Nikolai Ivanovich Bukharin: A Centenary Appraisal* (New York, 1990).

gave her first interview in Moscow in 1987. Larina's own ordeal "as the wife of a husband . . . cursed by the entire nation" is told only fragmentarily in these memoirs, so readers learn little about what happened to her after her dramatic confrontation with Lavrenty Beria, head of the NKVD, in Moscow's Lubyanka prison in 1939.

In the winter of wartime 1941, after almost three years in an underground Lubyanka cell, Larina was dispatched back to a Siberian labor camp to serve out her eight-year sentence. Technically "free" in September 1945, she was sentenced to what the Stalinist regime intended to be external banishment in Siberia. She lived there in various towns and villages, closely watched and constantly harassed, with her two younger children, Nadezhda and Mikhail, by her second husband, Fyodor Fadeyev. (Photographs from that time show a still remarkably beautiful woman but no traces of the innocent "Anyutka" of the 1930s.) Larina had met Fadeyev in the camp. An agronomist and high-ranking agricultural official in Soviet Kazakhstan, he too had been arrested on fraudulent political charges in 1937. He served out his full term in 1945, but he refused to desert Larina and for that was rearrested three times. In broken health, Fadeyev was finally released in 1953, after Stalin's death, yet another casualty of the Bukharin family's tragedy.

Readers meet Larina again in 1956, a few months after Khrushchev's revelations about Stalin's crimes, when Yury, now twenty years old, arrives at the Siberian settlement to see his mother for the first time since 1937. Raised in an orphanage near Stalingrad, he had become a hydraulic-engineering student in Novocherkassk after misunderstanding a guarded letter from his foster father, a Gulag forced laborer arrested in 1946, about the pleasures of working on a dam project. Yury had written to his mother two years earlier, at the beginning of their correspondence, "I don't understand everything in my life. Why did I leave my own home? Where is my papa? . . . Mama, I'm already grown up. If I am not mistaken, I'll be eighteen on May 8. I beg you to answer all these questions." Their reunion and Larina's explanations, which climax her story, are a special moment in this book and in Russian memoir literature.

In 1959, after three years of refusing to leave Siberia until the post-Stalin authorities fully exonerated her, Larina finally returned to Moscow with her new family. Fadeyev died three months later. Yury joined her in the capital in 1960. For the next twenty-five years, apart from a clandestine celebrity among a narrow circle of friends, the family lived quietly and anonymously, in cramped apartments and with barely enough money, under the same ban that still proscribed Bukharin. Anna Mikhailovna's children came of age, made and lost marriages, and gave her three grandchildren, including Yury's own son, Nikolai, named after Bukharin. Surviving tuberculosis and a major brain tumor operation, Yury gradually pursued his real calling as an artist. Eventually, his watercolor and oil paintings were exhibited in New York and Moscow, and acquired by museums and private collectors in several countries.

Larina's own thirty-year crusade to have Bukharin rehabilitated, known only to a few relatives and friends, persisted through all the joys and sorrows of Moscow family life—and all the hopes raised and disappointed by Soviet politics. She privately petitioned every entrenched Soviet leadership from Khrushchev's to Gorbachev's. Some of the documents she wrote were short appeals; others were long, meticulously researched treatises on Bukharin's role as a founder. On one occasion, a handful of surviving old Bolsheviks sent a letter supporting her appeal. All of her petitions asked for Bukharin's full exoneration and posthumous restoration to Communist Party membership.

None of them were directly answered, except for the 1977 reaffirmation of the criminal charges. Her expectations raised enormously by Khrushchev's anti-Stalinism, Larina in 1961 gave a text of Bukharin's own appeal, "To a Future Generation of Party Leaders," to the Central Committee apparatus. It was buried. Her hopes dashed by neo-Stalinist developments under Brezhnev, she began in the early 1970s the slow process of writing these memoirs. She wrote when she could, amid matriarchal duties, sometimes in the dimly lit, overoccupied apartment on Krzhizhanovsky Street, sometimes at a borrowed ramshackle summer dacha.

Our paths now crossed. In May 1975, seventeen months after my biography of Bukharin was published in New York, I received a smuggled note of introduction from Yury, with a photograph of his year-and-a-half-old son. A copy of my book had slowly found its way to the family. We met for the first time in Moscow three months later. Given the danger felt by both Anna Mikhailovna and Yury, it was a daring step on their part. As our relationship grew into a special friendship—readers will note that it does not exclude some disagreements about Bukharin's biography—I was entrusted with two large secrets.

Larina's memoirs were well under way, but she was certain that they could never be published in the Soviet Union, at least not in her lifetime, and that even her concealed carbon copy was not safe. I was more optimistic about eventual publication—or perhaps I just made the argument so that she would not become discouraged—but I fully shared her other concern. KGB searches were common among dissidents and even aged remnants of Bolshevik families. Both of us had such friends, and some raids had already affected us. We decided that I would find a way to take a copy of the manuscript, chapter by chapter, to the United States for safekeeping. I did so well into the early 1980s, when she finished.

The other secret bore fruit faster. Determined to learn more about his father, Yury had begun the huge work of translating my long book on Bukharin into Russian. He was helped by a remarkable family friend, Yevgeny Aleksandrovich Gnedin. (Specialists will be amazed to discover that he was the son of Parvus, the pre–World War I "merchant of revolution.") A Soviet journalist and diplomat who had worked under Bukharin at *Izvestiya* in the 1930s, and served later in Berlin, Gnedin had been arrested in 1939 and also survived many years in Stalinist camps and exile. A wonderful man and important writer in his late seventies, he lent his good reading knowledge of English to Yury's undertaking.[23] Working secretly every Thursday for several years, they made good progress, but by the late 1970s could do no more. I took their completed chapters to the United States, where the rest were translated and the first Russian-language edition published in 1980.[24] Clandestine copies soon began to circulate rather widely in Moscow and other Soviet cities.

Outwardly, Yury's translation of my book only worsened the situation. Confiscated copies were seized as evidence in KGB raids. Some Soviet officials hinted darkly that I had written this "bourgeois falsification" about Bukharin at the bidding of the CIA.[25] And from 1982 to 1985, I was refused a visa to visit the Soviet Union. Everything was much worse, of course, for the Bukharin family.

The only heartening news for Larina was an astonishing development in the provincial city of Brezhnev (now Naberezhnye Chelny), site of the massive Kamaz truck plant. In early 1983, a twenty-five-year-old

---

23. Gnedin died in 1983, at the age of eighty-four. For an appreciation of his life, see Stephen F. Cohen, *Sovieticus: American Perceptions and Soviet Realities*, exp. ed. (New York, 1986), pp. 104–7. His own memoirs, *Catastrophe and Rebirth* and *Exit from the Labyrinth*, which were published only abroad in Russian before his death, are scheduled for publication in Moscow, along with selections of his other writings, in 1993.

24. It was first published by Strathcona, a small press affiliated with Ardis Publishers in Michigan, and then in a second printing by Ardis in 1986. A Soviet edition was published in April 1989, despite the misleading date on the title page, as Stiven Koen, *Bukharin: politicheskaia biografiia 1888–1938* (Moscow: Progress, 1988). The translators listed as E. Thursday and Iu. Thursday were, of course, Gnedin and Larin, who worked on the translation every Thursday.

25. Not surprisingly, this charge resurfaced in Soviet anti-Bukharin, anti-Gorbachev writings after Bukharin's rehabilitation. See, for example, Iu. V. Emelianov, *Zametki o Bukharine* (Moscow, 1989).

worker and Young Communist, Valery Pisigin, formed an unofficial organization that soon became the Bukharin Political Club. Having discovered Bukharin's ideas through their own surreptitious reading, Pisigin and his fellow idealists located Larina in Moscow and vowed to support her struggle. At the time, their growing activities seemed both doomed and dangerous. But great changes were gathering strength behind the scenes. Thus, while the KGB was "arresting" Yury's translation, some highly placed Soviet officials were privately reading it, among them Mikhail Gorbachev.[26]

Though Anna Mikhailovna refused to hope again, strong indications already existed when Gorbachev came to power, in March 1985, that he wanted to rehabilitate Bukharin. Politically, he had to do so. NEP's liberalizing ideas and market-oriented policies, "Lenin's real conception of socialism," were at the heart of Gorbachev's proposed Soviet reformation, or perestroika—at least until the process later led him well beyond Leninism. But the fifty-year-old ban on Bukharin as an "enemy of the people" was also a ban on any full rediscovery of NEP and return to its principles. Still more, in order to overcome widespread ideological and bureaucratic opposition deeply rooted in the system inherited from Stalin, to protect his reforms and himself from Khrushchev's fate, Gorbachev had to destroy enduring Stalinist myths left over from the 1930s. That meant exposing all of Stalin's crimes, from the slaughter of peasants during collectivization to the falsified charges behind the terror against the old Bolshevik Party.

Gorbachev understood all this from the beginning, but so did the powerful enemies of reform throughout the Communist Party and state bureaucracies. For two years, he could do little more than tacitly enable a few prominent writers to reintroduce Bukharin elliptically as a political rather than a criminal figure. Only on November 2, 1987, speaking on the seventieth anniversary of the Bolshevik Revolution, could Gorbachev himself utter even a few public words mildly in praise of Bukharin.[27] They were more than enough. Western observers mistook Gorbachev's reticence for a lack of radicalism, but Soviet reformers

26. As I was told later by several Gorbachev aides and by Gorbachev himself.

27. M. S. Gorbachev, *Oktiabr i perestroika* (Moscow, 1987), pp. 16–17. The most important writers who reintroduced Bukharin prior to Gorbachev's speech were Mikhail Shatrov, in his film *Shtrikhi k portretu V. I. Lenina* and play *Brestskii mir,* and Fyodor Burlatsky in his very bold article "Politicheskoe zaveshchanie." See, respectively, *Literaturnaia gazeta,* January 28, 1987; *Novyi mir,* no. 4, 1987, pp. 3–51; and *Literaturnaia gazeta,* July 22, 1987. Yevgeny Yevtushenko's poem "Bukharin's Widow" was written in July 1987 and being read publicly that summer, but it could be published only later, in *Izvestiia,* March 26, 1988.

immediately understood that their leader had deliberately opened the door.

Three weeks later, the country's most popular magazine published a long, emotional interview with Larina. Full of startling revelations— she also recited Bukharin's own appeal for rehabilitation—it was a sensation. Two other influential weeklies quickly followed with articles eulogizing Bukharin, and in January 1988 the leading pro-Gorbachev Party journal reprinted Bukharin's last great protest against Stalin's policies, which he had entitled "Lenin's Political Testament."[28] On television, most Soviet citizens began to see Bukharin's face for the first time. As always, officialdom lumbered behind. On February 5, 1988, fifty years after his trial and execution, the Soviet Supreme Court announced Bukharin's full exoneration, striking down all the criminal charges. Official political rehabilitation came four months later, when a top-level commission restored his name to the ranks of the Communist Party.[29]

What followed was, in the words of two Russian historians, a "Bukharinist Boom"[30]—an avalanche of writings and other Bukhariniana that peaked around October 1988, the centenary of his birth, but continued until the end of the Soviet Union in 1991. In addition to multiple commentaries in virtually every significant newspaper, magazine, journal, and broadcast, it included two full-scale biographies, a score or more of other books featuring Bukharin, three films, a dozen or so major conferences (at sites ranging from Naberezhnye Chelny to Moscow), a full-length novel, a long poem by Yevgeny Yevtushenko, a stage play, many new editions of Bukharin's own writings and speeches, and a year-long exhibition about his life in the Central Museum of the Revolution.[31]

Several large factors drove the Bukharin phenomenon, in addition to genuine and long-repressed admiration for his historical role. (In a

28. See, respectively, *Ogonek*, no. 48 (November), 1987; *Moskovskie novosti*, December 6, 1987; *Nedelia*, no. 51 (December), 1987; and *Kommunist*, no. 1 (January), 1988.

29. *Pravda*, February 5, 1988, and July 10, 1988.

30. Bordiugov and Kozlov, *Istoriia i koniunktura*, chap. 2.

31. For many, but far from all, of the serious historical publications, see ibid. The biographies were mine and I. E. Gorelov, *Nikolai Bukharin* (Moscow, 1988). The films were *Caro Gorbaciov*, a 1988 theatrical film about Larina and Bukharin made in Italy and shown in Moscow; Yelena Andrikanes's documentary *Bukharin* (1989); and another theatrical film, *Enemy of the People—Bukharin Accused* (1991), by Viktor Dyomin and Leonid Maryagin. For the poem, see above, note 27; for the novel, Leonid Likhodeev, *Pole brani, na kotorom ne bylo ranenykh* (Moscow, 1990); and for the play, *Sovetskaia kultura*, July 16, 1988. Other items, including Bukharin's own writings, are too numerous to list here.

1988 Moscow survey poll, he had by far the highest positive and lowest negative rating of five former Soviet leaders.) An outpouring of hatred for Stalin played a major part, as did an ongoing process of political "repentance" by once conformist political figures and intellectuals. And, of course, Bukharin now was an important ancestor in Gorbachev's own de-Stalinization movement, which was becoming ever more radical. Some of the "Bukharinist Boom" approached a new canonization, but much of it underlay a serious and much belated reexamination of Soviet history, of roads taken and not taken. "Bukharin as a person, the problem of an alternative in our postrevolutionary development," a historian wrote in 1990, "now clearly is the focus of public attention."[32]

Larina's memoirs, serialized in late 1988 and published in book form in 1989, were at the epicenter of that attention. Suddenly, she became a lionized author, a sought-after presence at somber conferences and raucous public *mitingi* then sweeping Moscow, and probably Russia's most famous living widow. Publication soon followed in Europe and elsewhere, with personal tours to Italy, Germany, and, most sentimentally, Paris, where the young, pregnant Anna and Bukharin had spent a last (and politically fateful) vacation in 1936. In the aftermath, the whole family emerged from the shadows. Yury at last received the major Moscow exhibition that his paintings deserved. And even his teenage son, Nikolai ("Kolya"), now an acknowledged founder's grandson,[33] changed. After indifferent school years, at college he took up the study of Soviet history, though, as also befit the new times, soccer remained his only real passion.

Western readers will naturally react differently to Larina's book than did Soviet citizens, for whom it was an emotional excursion into their long forbidden past. Some will judge it as a political morality tale and regret Larina's loyalty to the Bolshevik Revolution of her childhood. But most will read it, I think, as a deeply moving human saga. Specialists, on the other hand, will find here unique historical information, and thus be doubly grateful for Larina's scrupulous distinctions between what she actually observed and what she learned secondhand, as well as

32. *Nedelia*, no. 6 (February), 1990. For the poll, see *New York Times*, May 27, 1988. One taken two years later had Bukharin rated third among eleven historical figures in "sympathy," behind Lenin and Dzezhinsky, but with the lowest "antipathy" rating. See *Moscow News*, no. 44, 1990. For examples of Bukharin as an ancestor in the history of the Party's anti-Stalinist movement, see *Reabilitirovan posmertno*, 2 vols. (Moscow, 1988); *Vozvrazhchennye imena*, 2 vols. (Moscow, 1989); *Est u otechestva proroki* (Petrozavodsk, 1989); and V. M. Podugolnikov, ed., *Oni ne molchali* (Moscow, 1991).

33. See, for example, *Vechernii komsomolets*, no. 3 (November), 1991.

her refusal, rare among memoirists of any time and place, to "view things from the present" and thus seem "wiser than you were."

Certainly, Larina's inside account will stand as a basic source on the Bolshevik era and its descent into a monstrous terror. But there is also a wealth of information about lesser-known events and people. Larina's loving portrait of her remarkable adoptive father (the senior Yury Larin) will make this unduly neglected figure more accessible to historians. Other portraits are fleeting but also significant. Readers may want to know, for example, that the defiant boy Pyotr Yakir, son of an executed army commander, thirty years later helped found the Soviet dissident movement, but then finally succumbed to the effects of a brutalized childhood in Stalin's Gulag and recanted. And that Andrei Sverdlov, the son of another Bolshevik founder and once Anna's childhood friend, who reappears before her in NKVD uniform as one of Beria's men, eventually was disgraced by those same dissidents.

Given my own involvement, it is not for me to say more about the value of Anna Mikhailovna's book, though I am certain it will long be read as an essential memoir of the Soviet experience. As a biographer, however, I can say that Larina brings Bukharin to life as has no one else. Even more, her portrait of this historical figure, with all his appealing qualities and human weaknesses, is the most intimately drawn picture we now have of any of the Bolshevik founders who, as was said then, shook the world. One important question does remain, though: Was the forty-five-year-old Bukharin she married in 1934 really as blind to Stalin's worst nature and his own doom as Larina insists?

In fairness, I will only repeat briefly what I have said to Anna Mikhailovna over the years. A veteran of tsarist prisons, revolutionary violence, and twelve traumatic years in power, Bukharin almost certainly understood more about Stalin's real intentions in the 1930s, or had darker forebodings, than he was willing to tell his very young wife. No doubt, he did hope for the best, but to have told her everything he knew or suspected would have been cruel and unwise, casting clouds over their few years together much earlier and putting her in even graver danger. As Bukharin probably guessed would happen, and readers will learn from this book, older wives and children of Stalin's victims often paid the supreme penalty.

Anna Mikhailovna cannot believe that the husband for whom she suffered so much did not confide fully in her. She is entitled to this cherished belief, but she inadvertently gives us some counterevidence. If Bukharin thought Stalin capable of murdering his own wife in 1932, as Larina reports, could he have had any illusions about the despot's character? When Bukharin refused to discuss Kirov's assassination with

Larina, did it not mean he knew or suspected more than he wanted to tell her? And even as the inexorable end approached, did Bukharin really believe that his boyhood friend Grigory Sokolnikov had been arrested by the NKVD for some "financial impropriety," as he told her?

The widow's conviction about her husband's political naïveté also informs two long episodes in her memoirs, both somewhat abridged in this edition. Anna Mikhailovna believes passionately that Bukharin's private discussion with the Bolshevik oppositionist Kamenev in 1928, and particularly his Paris encounters with the Menshevik émigré Boris Nicolaevsky in 1936, were falsified by those people in ways that did him grievous harm. Despite having no personal connection with the first event, and having arrived in Paris a month after the second would have occurred, she is adamant. Though mysteries remain and much of the evidence is circumstantial, most of it does not support Larina's arguments.[34] Why, then, did she allow herself these digressions and thus the only sections in her memoirs about which readers might have doubts? Partly, I think, out of her old-fashioned widow's notion that a loyal Bolshevik would not have broken "Party discipline," as Bukharin was charged with having done. But mainly to maintain her image of a Bukharin without any political guile, even in the best of causes.

Viewed in the context of his whole life, Bukharin was a complex figure, politically and personally. Larina's portrait of a man vulnerable to "nervous overloads" is convincing, but it is also true that, while never an able politician, he demonstrated considerable resolve and even toughness during his years in power, before she really knew him. It is not likely that he so completely lacked those traits in the 1930s. Indeed, substantial evidence suggests that Bukharin went on struggling for his own ideas and policies in the Stalin years, though necessarily in more guarded ways, even while managing to save his family's life—that he was, as the Soviet judge who reviewed his trial reported in 1988, "a fighter to the end."[35] If so, it only further enhances the man whom Anna Mikhailovna loved and still admires so much.

The actor who played Bukharin in a 1991 film explained his role in characteristic Russian fashion: "In Russia, there are no happy end-

---

34. See, for example, Iu. G. Felshtinskii, "Dva epizoda iz istorii vnutripartiinoi borby: konfidentsialnye besedy Bukharina," *Voprosy istorii*, nos. 2–3 (1991), pp. 182–203; and the commentaries on this question by André Liebich and Robert C. Tucker in *Slavic Review*, Fall 1992.

35. See above, note 11.

ings."[36] Bukharin's rehabilitation and Larina's triumph in 1988 seemed
to belie that adage, but none of the planned memorials to him were ever
unveiled. Three years later, the Soviet Union collapsed and Communists turned anti-Communists came to power in Moscow. Professing
disdain for the entire Soviet experience, from the era of Lenin to that of
Gorbachev, they had nothing good to say about any of the revolutionary
founding fathers. An opinion even emerged in the post-Communist
media that all the Bolsheviks, including Bukharin, really had been enemies of Russia's progress. Anna Mikhailovna's world turned upside
down again.

Is this new historical perspective likely to prevail in Russia, again
condemning Bukharin to oblivion or disgrace? A case could be made
that he has no positive role to play in the historical memory of post-
Soviet Russia. Even at the peak of his rehabilitation under Gorbachev,
right-wing nationalists (not unlike unrepentant Party neo-Stalinists) angrily protested the Bukharin revival as part of a campaign by reform
Communists and democrats to Westernize Russia and thus destroy the
nation's best traditions and special destiny.[37] On the other side of the
political spectrum, Western-style liberals were right in arguing that Bukharin, a founder and defender of the one-party dictatorship, had not
been a democrat; they, too, lamented the "euphoria" associated with his
rehabilitation.[38]

Much depends, however, on our understanding of Russia's past
and present. If we take the view, now popular among Western and
Russian commentators, that communism was something alien to and
imposed upon Russia, we might expect the country, freed at last from
the Party's rule, to escape quickly from its Soviet past and move toward
Western-style capitalism and democracy. In that case, Bukharin is
scarcely relevant. But if Soviet communism actually grew out of and
perpetuated much older and deeper Russian traditions, as many scholars there and here believe, we cannot assume that the country will easily
or willingly shed almost a century of historical experience and memory.
In that case, the Soviet past still has important lessons to teach and lost
alternatives to ponder.

36. *New York Times,* August 13, 1990.

37. See, for example, the nationalist journals *Nash sovremennik* and *Molodaia
gvardiia;* Emelianov, *Zametki o Bukharine;* Vadim Kozhinov, *Sudba Rossii* (Moscow, 1990); and the views reported by Vladimir Semeniuk in *Ogonek,* no. 15 (April),
1991.

38. See, for example, Viacheslav Kondratev in *Literaturnaia gazeta,* May 24,
1989; and the retrospective views in Bordiugov and Kozlov, *Istoriia i koniunktura,*
chap. 2.

The latter view is, I think, closer to the truth. If so, Bukharin will be a subject of large interest in post-Communist Russia as well—and, if viewed in the context of his own times, perhaps even admiration. (Is it significant, for example, that in mid-1992 Larina's memoirs, though out of print, are still widely sought and read; or that Valery Pisigin, now head of an expanded Bukharin Foundation, sits on one of President Boris Yeltsin's advisory councils?) Even an anti-Bukharin Russian nationalist, who nonetheless saw him as "a son and victim of his time," concluded, "Historians will continue to argue about Bukharin and his role in history and the revolution as long as people have a lively interest in the past, which is linked inseparably to the future."[39]

Rethinking Russia's fate in the twentieth century, right-wing nationalists and liberal democrats alike will find it hard to bypass a political figure whose life intersected with three of the most abiding tragedies. It was Bukharin, after all, who opposed Stalin's destruction of the country's rural and urban markets, which have yet to revive; whose antifascism in the 1930s offered an alternative to Stalin's pact with Hitler, which left the country unprepared for a war that cost thirty million Soviet lives; and whose show trial symbolized a terror that engulfed the nation. The full truth about those fateful turning points, particularly about Bukharin's foreign policy and trial, is still buried in post-Communist archives, but neither it nor his full role can stay there forever.[40]

Even more important, Russia has yet to escape its most tenacious tsarist and Soviet tradition—that of a society overwhelmed and abused, politically and economically, by a dominant state. Bukharinism has little if anything to say about Russia's democratic exit from this tradition, if there is to be one, but Bukharin's defense of NEP against Stalin's latter-day Leviathan hardly has lost its relevance. If nothing else, Bukharin's defense of society against bureaucracy, markets against state monopolies, consumers against producers, and law against administrative caprice still remains only an aspiration in Russia. Indeed, a modern-day NEP would virtually be the post-Communist revolution that is often lauded but has not yet actually taken place.

Moscow
June 1992

39. Emelianov, *Zametki o Bukharine*, p. 315.

40. I have in mind, for example, documents from Bukharin's pretrial year in prison, including the full record of his interrogation; a film record of the trial proceedings made by Soviet cameramen in the courtroom; and the unedited courtroom transcript. Documents by Stalin, Vyshinsky, and others indicating what was being demanded of Bukharin at the trial also seem to exist.

A WORD ON THE TRANSLATION

Chapter headings and comments in brackets were supplied by the translator. All parenthetical statements belong to the author. These are set within brackets when inside quotations.

G.K.

AUTHOR'S PREFACE

I lived with Nikolai Ivanovich Bukharin, my husband, through what were both the happiest and the most exciting days of our lives. But our last six months together were made so difficult, so painful, that each day felt like a century. This memoir of that time was written over the many years since, set down in fragments whenever I found relief from family worries and cares. Yet, not for a moment did I forget the disastrous events of my youth. Not for a single day did terrible memories fail to trouble my mind and shake my very soul.

You must understand that, from childhood, I lived among people who were totally dedicated to the cause of socialist revolution. First, of course, was my father, Yury Larin (Mikhail Aleksandrovich Lurye). Amazingly brilliant and astonishingly courageous, he probably played the decisive role in the formation of my character and convictions. In addition, since he was a steadfast friend of Bukharin, it was as a young girl that I first came to know the man to whom I would later be linked by destiny.

Today, the names of their many associates and colleagues, rendered "nonpersons" for half a century and literally expunged from the genealogy of our fatherland, are being revived for the Soviet people, for our history. Then, however, I watched as most of the idealistic, selfless people I had known since I was a little girl succumbed to fate's merciless blows. Many of them, like Grigory Zinoviev, Lev Kamenev, Grigory Sokolnikov, Karl Radek, Yury Pyatakov, and other prominent Communist Party and state officials, gave false testimony against both themselves and Bukharin—for reasons that today need no explanation. Sadly, my husband, Nikolai Ivanovich, could not himself escape this bitter disgrace. Nor did Aleksei Rykov. These two friends, morally broken, impeached each other in the infamous trial of the so-called Anti-Soviet Bloc of Rightists and Trotskyists in 1938.

Such was the nature of the time.

Memoirs cannot fail to be subjective, yet I have worked hard to tell the truth here as completely as possible. Nikolai Ivanovich would approve of that aim, I believe, for his nature, though complex, did not include deception. Forgive me, therefore, for the abundance of detail, for I have included each fact, each fine point, in pursuit of the complete truth. Forgive me, too, for any jumps in my account. They are involuntary, dictated by the caprices of memory. In short, I have never withheld information just because it might discomfit or dismay someone, but I have also kept in mind this wise saying: "Don't expect more from the truth than it actually contains."

Now that Nikolai Ivanovich's name has been rightfully restored, I am happy that my voice was among those that counted. I have fought long and hard for his rehabilitation.

Through those difficult decades, my dear friends and many others gave me moral support. I am grateful to them all.

THIS I CANNOT FORGET

Who jealously conceals the past
can hardly be on good terms
with the future. . . .

—Aleksandr Tvardovsky

In December 1938, I was returning to an "investigative prison" in Moscow following a year and a half of arrests and imprisonments. First came exile in Astrakhan, then arrest and imprisonment there; next, I was sent to a camp in Tomsk for family members of so-called enemies of the people; on the way, I was held in transit cells in Saratov and Sverdlovsk; after several months in Tomsk, I was arested a second time and sent to an isolation prison in Novosibirsk; from Novosibirsk, I was transferred to a prison near Kemerovo, where after three months I was taken out and put on the train for Moscow.

At this time, the wives of many major military and political figures were being recalled from the camps and prisons and returned to Moscow. The purpose was not to lighten their sentence but, on the contrary, to lengthen it—or even to dispose of the ones who had witnessed real crimes, in contrast to the false crimes attached to them. Among the women I chanced to meet in these years were the wives of three generals—Yan Gamarnik, Mikhail Tukhachevsky, and Iyeronim Uborevich—as well as Lyudmila Shaposhnikova, wife of Mikhail Chudov, second secretary of the Leningrad District Party Committee, who had worked under Sergei Kirov.

[The Tomsk Camp, December 1937–March 1938]

I spent only a few months in the Tomsk camp, but it was there I had to endure from afar my husband's ordeal—the infamous "Bukharin trial"—and his execution. There, too, I began to feel sharply the tragedy of that time and came to perceive it, quite apart from the horrors I personally experienced, as the tragedy of the entire Soviet nation. In our camp alone, there were some four thousand wives of the men now known as traitors to the motherland. Far from being unique, the Tomsk camp of confinement was one of many.

The only males there were the prison guards in their black overcoats, counting and recounting us every morning, and a latrine cleaner, Uncle Kaka—so dubbed by Yura, a two-year-old boy confined to the camp with his mother.

We wives were quite diverse in terms of moral and intellectual qualities, as well as the levels of our husbands' former positions and political careers, but a common denominator had marked us out for this camp. Among us were the wives of such old revolutionaries as Aleksandr Shlyapnikov and Béla Kun, the wives of such military men as Iona Yakir and his younger brother (both shot), the wives of the directors of the Party and the soviets in the union republics, the wives of collective farm chairmen and of ordinary collective farm workers, the wives of the chairmen of village soviets and of NKVD personnel from Genrikh Yagoda's tenure as chief, as well as the sisters of Tukhachevsky. In common, we were all confined for our associations with "enemies of the people," though not one of our husbands or brothers had ever been any such thing. Each of us was officially labeled a *chesir*, or "family member of a traitor to the motherland."

In the mind of the camp command, I suppose, most of us *chesirs* had a kind of abstract "enemy" quality, because they themselves had no idea what was actually going on in the country. They merely saw a continuing flow of transports of prisoners, one after the other. The people had become their own enemy.

And when the command—for the most part, a drab, poorly educated lot—encountered the wives of their famous former leaders, they felt they were dealing with special enemies. One incident proving this is burned into my memory. On my second day in camp, our jailers made the "ordinary" *chesirs* form a circle in front of the barracks and put me and Yakir's wife, Sarra Lazarevna, in the center. A red-cheeked commandant who had come from the Gulag administration shouted at the top of his voice:

"See these women? They're the wives of the most vicious enemies of the people. They helped our enemies in their traitorous acts, yet here, just look at them, they still turn up their noses. Nothing pleases them, nothing seems right to *them.*"

It would have been odd to be "pleased" at being confined in a camp, but in fact, we had not had time to turn up our noses and were even relatively happy. After a long, tormenting forced journey that included stops at transit prisons, we had finally (or so we thought) reached our destinations, and no physical labor was required of us at the Tomsk camp.

Having shouted out these terrible words with great passion, the hardy, self-satisfied officer headed for the prison gates. Horrified, the convicts began to disperse. Although some began to shy away from Sarra Lazarevna and me, most were disgusted with this performance. We ourselves were in shock. It felt as if we had run the gauntlet. Unable to move, we stood stock still in the bitter frost until someone led us back into the barracks, to our cold corner by a window encrusted with snow. Around the walls, the two levels of bed boards were completely packed with women. The previous night had been real torture. No one could find a comfortable position. Almost every woman lay on her side, and when someone wanted to shift her position, she had to wake her neighbor so that they could turn over together, thus initiating a chain reaction of awakenings down the line.

Now the barracks was like a cracked beehive. Everyone was buzzing about what had happened. Some got nasty: "The Bukharins and Yakirs have messed everything up, and now we and our husbands must suffer because of them." But the rest cursed the Gulag commandant, and many advised us to write a complaint to Moscow. Of course, Sarra Lazarevna and I understood that this would be pointless. That night, we sat on the edge of the plank bed, wide awake. Our places filled instantly with sleeping bodies, but neither of us felt like sleeping, or even living, at that moment. We conversed softly amid the sweet snoring of slumbering women.

General Yakir had been shot on June 11, 1937. On September 20, his wife and fourteen-year-old son were arrested in Astrakhan, where they had been living in exile. (I had been arrested in Astrakhan on the same day.) Even before this latest disaster befell her, Sarra Lazarevna Yakir had been barely hanging on to life.

Now it was December. I had yet to endure the execution of my husband and awaited it with foreboding and in ignorance. No correspondence was allowed. (Later, we would be permitted to write a single, solitary letter to ask for warm things and inform the recipient that we could receive packages of food once a month. We would not even be permitted to write a letter confirming the receipt of such packages.) Toward morning, Sarra Lazarevna and I woke up our neighbors so that they would make room for us, but no sooner did we finally drop off to sleep than it was time for the morning count.

We lined up in a row, and the duty officer, a young lad, began the roll call: "Las' name, firs', middle, year of birth, article, term. . . . Las' name, firs', middle, year of birth, article, term. . . ."

Obediently, the women gave their name and date of birth. For the article under which they had been sentenced and the term of imprisonment, they recited like this:

"*Chesir* . . . eight years."

"*Chesir* . . . eight years." (Now and then, only "five years.")

Chesir sounded less derogatory than "family member of a traitor to the motherland." And for the few among us who had little schooling, it meant nothing at all. They had trouble memorizing the full phrase for their official stigma.

When he came up to me, the duty officer shouted out with special emphasis, "Aha! Las' name?"

"Larina," I answered. Only that name was written on my documents, but, though I did not know it yet, both Larina and Bukharina were set down as surnames in my dossier. For some reason, no one had ever asked my surname during transport. Here, my married name had apparently been entered on the roll.

"Larina!" he screamed. "What, keeping your spy name silent?"

It was not hard to guess his meaning, so I answered, "Bukharina. Only if it's a spy name, then your name is Chinese."

Everyone froze in fear. Sarra Lazarevna, standing beside me, poked me in the side.

"Want to go to the cooler, do you? To the cooler? You haven't been yet, but you'll go."

I was not sent to the cooler, but you can see how I spent my first days in the Tomsk camp.

That morning, Sarra Lazarevna and I left the stuffy barracks and walked through the compound for fresh air and distraction from our thoughts. In the frosty haze, we could see the Siberian sun shining blood-red. ("A sun fit for war," said the women.) It lightly tinted the snow, which was still free from footprints, virginally pure right up to the fence, since it was forbidden to walk there. At the corners of the fence, hastily thrown together with wooden beams, stood the watchtowers

from which the guards (still called marksmen) followed our every movement. Should anyone edge just slightly toward the fence, there would be
the cry "Halt! Who goes there?" For this reason, the path leading from
the dismal barracks to the kitchen became our only thoroughfare. It was
always packed with women, many of whose faces were stamped with
suffering, confusion, and fright. In jest, we named this walkway after
Leningrad's grand boulevard, Nevsky Prospekt (there were a lot of
Leningraders among us), or "Main Street in a fit of panic." To keep
from freezing, the crowds of unfortunates hurried along the Nevsky at a
fast clip. Most of us were dressed in torn, quilted jackets and cold boots.
Those arrested during the summer wrapped themselves in the cloth
blankets of the camp, replacing their lightweight skirts and scarves.

Catching sight of me in the crowd, Lyudmila Kuzminichna Shaposhnikova called out from afar. A friend of my parents, she had known
me since I was a child. Blond with greenish eyes and a winning, big-
hearted smile, she had not lost her charm in the camp. Belying a pam-
pered look, which concealed her already advanced years, Lyudmila
Kuzminichna was strong-willed and faced her new misfortunes with
equanimity. An old Party member, "risen from the ranks of the workers" (as we used to say back then), she had managed a perfume business
in Leningrad. Once, together with Vyacheslav Molotov's wife, Polina
Zhemchuzhina, she had gone to America and been received by President Franklin Roosevelt. Because few Russians traveled abroad in those
years, this event stuck in my mind. Lyudmila Kuzminichna was a camp
favorite. She naturally commanded authority among the *chesirs* and had
been chosen for the most responsible post, that of running the kitchen.

She had a warning for me, "Be very careful . . . don't talk openly
about what goes on in the camp . . . keep quiet about Nikolai Ivanovich.
The situation here is rotten, as you saw for yourself with that Gulag
officer yesterday. The spy network is well developed. A lot of low-life
women will try to win their freedom by getting you to talk about dangerous subjects, and you can be dragged off to Section Three for interrogation. You have to be extra careful; this is a hard time. And you must
survive! As for myself, my days are numbered. They won't let me
live . . ."

"What do you mean 'numbered'?" I naively objected. "You got
eight years, just like the rest of us."

"There will be more. The eight years will be extended."

Shaposhnikova explained that she was being taken to interrogations
in the camp and would most likely be sent back to Moscow. I could
make no sense of this.

"But why?" I asked. "Why?"

"I know a lot, that's why."

As she spoke, she glanced around to see if anyone was nearby, but we were alone.

"A Leningrader," I thought, "close to people who worked with Sergei Kirov. She herself says she knows a lot. How do the closest comrades of Kirov explain his assassination?"

I couldn't miss a chance like this.

"Lyudmila Kuzminichna! What actually happened to Sergei Mironovich? What do you know about it? They must have talked with you about it there in Leningrad. How much do they really know?"

"Ah, so that's what you'd like to know!"

She looked at me for a long time, her face reddened, nervous and distraught. Finally, she exclaimed, "What questions you put to me! Can one really talk about this?"

"I think we can, Lyudmila Kuzminichna. *We* can!"

"Yes, yes, I'm going to die anyway, but you must go on living. I'm not afraid for myself, but for you. However . . . can you keep as silent as the grave?"

Naturally, I insisted I could. She was persuaded.

"Zinoviev didn't need to get Kirov. This came down from the very top, on orders from the Boss. [That's exactly how she put it.] After Kirov was shot, many Leningraders understood this. Chudov did, too."

By this time, I already understood that Zinoviev had not needed Kirov's death, but a variety of scenarios still seemed possible to me. When Kirov was murdered, in December 1934, I was not able to think my way through to a conclusion. But after my arrest, while in the Astrakhan prison, I found myself entertaining the most terrible thoughts. Even so, now that my rising suspicions were confirmed, I could only gasp, "How horrible!"

"Horrible? And why is the murder of Kirov any more horrible than all the other murders? His was an easy death, murder from around the corner. Sergei Mironovich didn't die as an 'enemy of the people,' as a 'spy.' He suffered no tortures. Will the murder of Bukharin be any less horrible? Better not think about it. . . . You have a lot of horrible experiences ahead of you."

"But whom did the Boss rely on?"

"I won't tell you. Time will tell."

Having said this, Lyudmila Kuzminichna changed the subject, reminiscing about a summer we had spent together in Mukhalatka, in the Crimea—she with her husband, Mikhail Semyonovich Chudov, I with my father. To my surprise, she recalled some juvenile lines of verse I had written then for Chudov [whose name derived from the word for "wonder" or "miracle"]. He was a tall, powerful man with broad shoulders. At age fifteen, I facetiously called him Ilya Muromets, the great bogatyr (or hero) of the old Russian epics.

> *What a miracle, what a miracle,*
> *To us has come Uncle Miraculous.*
> *Uncle is a worker of wonders,*
> *A Leningrader bogatyr.*

"A bogatyr like that," Lyudmila Kuzminichna mused, "a bogatyr, and he was blown away like a piece of straw." Mikhail Semyonovich had been executed a few months before. She rubbed away a tear, and we parted quickly, before drawing too much attention from the other strollers on Nevsky Prospekt.

Shaposhnikova would indeed be sentenced a second time and shot.

We were all sapped of energy both by the oppressive conditions in the camp and by the lack of anything to do. There was no work. No books or magazines. Later, many inmates were sent packages of yarn and began knitting and embroidering. The Ukrainians, who excelled in this art, produced handicrafts good enough to be put on display.

The liveliest spot in camp was the clearing outside the kitchen. Here, there was the hustle and bustle of women carrying out barrels of gruel and kasha, sawing and chopping wood. The saw buzzed; the ax clunked. In the frost, the logs fell to the ground with a crunch. Especially adept at this work was vivacious, sharp-eyed Tanya Izvekova. Her former husband, Lazar Shatskin, organizer of the Komsomol [Communist Youth League], had been much admired during the first years of the revolution as an authoritative, intellectual leader. As she and the other workers bent to their tasks, a crowd always gathered around to lend support. The optimists bore good news, or "sweet buckets," as we called the camp scuttlebutt. They might report that there was going to be an amnesty on New Year's Day, then on May 1, then most definitely on Stalin's birthday.

I will never forget Dina, who worked in the kitchen. Her case was exceptional, for she had suffered a double injustice. Far from being wife to a "traitor to the motherland," she was not actually married. A sturdy woman, she had been a dockworker in Odessa, loading and unloading ships. She had met and married a stevedore, but they were later separated, years before her arrest. She heard nothing from him, did not seek him out, and, being a proud woman, raised her children without a penny of support from their father. Unfortunately, she did not bother to get a formal divorce, a particular that did her in. At her interrogation, she learned that her former husband had attained a high post in some other city. Her interrogators accepted none of her explanations.

In Tomsk, Dina served as a beast of burden, literally taking the place of a horse. Our supplies came from the prison nearby. It was Dina's job to load them onto a cart and drag them to the kitchen. She hauled potatoes, cabbages, groats, and carcasses of meat so scrawny that we thought the miserable creatures must have been bred specially for us.

These foodstuffs sorely tested Lyudmila Kuzminichna's ingenuity. How could she feed us with frozen potatoes and cabbages? Yet, somehow, her organizational skills always won out. Once, she came to us in the barracks and said:

"Girls!"—as she addressed all of us, regardless of age—"I've got an idea. Nothing can be done with this meat as it is. It'll be cooked into the gruel with frozen potatoes and won't make the slightest bit of fat. Let's do it this way instead. . . . Since it's freezing, we can store the carcasses we get each day for a week and then make a real meat soup on Sunday. Maybe there'll even be enough left over for a cutlet apiece. What do you say?"

"We agree, we agree!" we shouted in unison. All of the other barracks (a total of eight, I think) went along. On Sunday, it actually happened: we got good soup and a cutlet each besides. But in the preparation it became obvious that it was very difficult to make a meal in this way. There was no lack of extra hands to do the work, only a lack of room in the kitchen; it couldn't hold all these "cooks." And so the experiment was not repeated, at least during my time in the camp.

Whenever we saw Dina pulling the loaded cart by its shafts, we would cry out, "Dina's coming! Dina's coming!"—and run to the gate to help by pushing the cart from behind. To compensate Dina for her extra expenditure of energy, the camp command saw fit to allot her a double ration. Unfortunately, the caloric content of one ration was so low that even a triple portion would not have saved our "horse," and she didn't eat oats. Lyudmila Kuzminichna rescued her, feeding her on the sly in the kitchen.

Dina had one misadventure. There was a young woman in camp named Zhilina, but nicknamed Carmen for her singing. She did not sing very well, but it was good enough to give pleasure to people deprived of positive emotions and overloaded with negative ones. Rumors began to go around—and rumors were highly prized in camp—that Carmen was bald and wore a wig. I can't say the matter particularly interested most of us, but Dina was quite taken with it. Our Dina was very inquisitive, and an inquisitive nature only gets worse with idleness. So as Carmen was walking one day along Nevsky Prospekt in her camp attire of boots and patchwork jacket, Dina suddenly swooped down on her and snatched the wig—for such it was—right off. Carmen's head was as glossily smooth, as glabrous as that of Governor Plyushch in Saltykov-Shchedrin's novel *History of a Town*. With one hand, Dina easily hoisted Carmen, bald as an egg and crying, up over her shoulder, while with the other hand she waved the wig around like a trophy as she dashed up and down the walkway, laughing loudly. A guard ran up at once and ordered her to let Carmen go.

For her prank, Dina was sentenced to five days and nights in the cooler on a ration of bread and water. However, she used her great strength to resist the puny little guard who tried to convey her to the punishment cell. When he tried to twist her arm behind her back, he instantly found himself thrown up on that back. Thus Dina carried him off to the cooler, as we all laughed. On her first day inside, the absence of any other hauling force in camp was keenly felt. So she was let out the next day and again harnessed to her cart.

Aside from the fact that Dina was not married to either "enemy" or indeed "friend of the people," she differed from us in actually liking the camp. So wretched was her existence in freedom, so full of cares for her children and her daily bread, so heavy was her work in port, so joyless was her whole life that in camp Dina did not feel deprivation of freedom so much as liberation from everyday burdens. This made us feel sorry for her, but she felt the joy of carefree days.

Dina always rested her cart with its fallen shafts under three birches that stood beside the kitchen. They were the only birches in camp and would be cut down later. That year, 1938, spring came unusually early; in all my twenty years to come in Siberia, there would never be another like it. The birch branches not only bristled with little buds but here and there produced a tender lace of barely opened pale green leaves. How good these birches were, with crowds of gloomy women in threadbare clothing milling around them, some tossing off their dirty gray quilted jackets! How good they looked against the background of dilapidated low barracks and trampled-down earth, the compound it seemed you would never leave! Every day, after finishing a stint of work, Dina would lie down in her cart beneath the birches. She stretched out in her full camp apparel—a woman's jacket so soiled you could not make out its color, a black chintz skirt, pigskin shoes without socks. Beneath her head, she placed her new quilted jacket, folded once or twice; it was a rare item in the camp. Alongside lay her cloth cap with ear flaps. With the sun beaming down so warmly, it was unnecessary, but Dina looked to the future. Winter lay ahead. Not just one winter but eight more. "Who knows what they'll do, those intellectuals and nonintellectuals?" she would say in disgust. "They swiped my bread ration, didn't they?" Someone had apparently taken her ration, knowing she would not go hungry; Dina could always get an extra serving in the kitchen. But caps were not handed out by Lyudmila Kuzminichna, so Dina always carried hers around, just in case. Thus, she lay in the cart, with all of her possessions beside her. In camp it's true that things only weigh you down; when a transfer comes up, you have to carry them with you. But without them life is no picnic.

Sometimes, I would sit down next to Dina in the cart. I was drawn to the birches. Fortunately, Dina remained silent and never asked my opinion about my husband's trial, which had just taken place in March. In other words, I did not have to worry whether or not her conversation would be a provocation. Traps had been laid everywhere after Bukharin's conviction. . . . How was I to make out who was who? It was impossible to be on the alert with everyone, but with Dina there was no problem.

Nevertheless, she did speak up once: "Why're you coming here, huh? You feel sorry for me, is that it? There's no reason to. Feel sorry for your own life, because I'm not doing bad here." With her right hand, she folded one finger on her left. "For one, my kids are in the children's home. They're well fed." She folded a second finger. "Second, they've got clothes." And a third. "Third, they've got shoes."

"All right, Dina, you don't even miss your children. But what about freedom. . . . Aren't you sorry to lose it?"

"What kind of freedom did I have, working from morning to night in the port? Fact is, I almost never saw the children."

"Why didn't you ever study, Dina?"

"Why didn't I study? Because Soviet power didn't give me the head for it," she snorted. "I gave it a try, but it didn't work out. I'll tell you one more time. . . . Don't worry about someone else's freedom; worry about your own. And don't worry about someone else's children. If you have any, worry about them. Anyway, why did such a pretty young thing like yourself choose an enemy for your husband? And they say he's a real enemy—eeyuu, a bitter enemy!"

She might as well have tossed scalding water on me. All along I had been thinking she did not know who I was. There was no way to answer her. I jumped out of the cart to run away, but Dina caught me firmly with her big, strong hand and held me in place. Instantly, her tone changed.

"You know, they gab a lot about him. They say he was real smart, and it's death to be too smart. A little smarter than me is enough. They even say he worked with Lenin himself; I heard it. Well, maybe that's an old wives' tale, but he probably did see him. At least once, huh?" She couldn't contain her curiosity. For the first time in a long while, I broke into a smile.

"Maybe he did see Lenin one time. He didn't tell me about it. . . . But who has been gabbing with you, Dina? Gab too much, and you'll get into trouble!"

"With me? Now, who would bother to talk to little old me? I just lie here and hear all sorts of chitchat about this, about that."

That was my last conversation with Dina, but I remember every word and gesture, as if it were only yesterday.

[Transit Prisons]

I decided to relate this conversation to a close friend, Viktoriya Aleksandrovna Rudina, whom Sarra Lazarevna and I had met in the Sverdlovsk transit camp. Viktoriya Aleksandrovna had been sent there from Moscow's Butyrka prison. We had been transported from the Astrakhan prison after a stop in the Saratov holding cells.

The long corridor at Saratov, so filled with smoke that the musty air lost its transparency, had seemed to me the very bowels of hell, even more terrible than the infamous Peter and Paul Fortress, in Leningrad. Back in the 1920s, my father, Yury Larin, had taken me to the fortress to see the very cell he had occupied before the 1905 revolution. (The museum there had not yet opened then, but he was let in as a former inmate.) At Saratov, sounds from the other cells barely penetrated the thick doors. One could hear only the keys rattling on the guards' belts— that and the clank of the bolts being opened. For some reason, the guards were especially cruel. No matter how overcrowded the holding cells, they still managed to shove us in. Still, it was easier to bear the transit centers than the investigative prisons, for one reason: mistakenly, we assumed our fate had been finally decided, and the agony of waiting vanished.

The next stop, Sverdlovsk, differed from the other transit prisons in that prisoners could no longer be given a place on, under, or even in between the bed boards. Consequently, they put us in the corridor. It was narrow but bright, because the windows had no louvers, or muzzles, as they were called. It was also very cold. That afternoon, Sarra Lazarevna and I made a place for ourselves on the floor by spreading out a flannel blanket Bukharin had given me and laying on top of it a warmer woolen one that had belonged to Yakir.

An insane woman from Leningrad lay beside me. One moment she would sit up and rip her black coat into thin strips, picking out the wadding, and the next she would unexpectedly send a cry ringing down the corridor: "We killed Sergei Mironovich. We killed him, we all killed him, that's why we're all in jail!" Then she leapt up and ran with eccentric motions to the window, which was completely covered with hoar frost. Like Pushkin's Tatyana, though not with a delicate finger but rather with a fat and dirty one swollen from the cold, she scratched out her own "cherished monogram": SMK. The initials stood for Sergei Mironovich Kirov. During these few minutes of calm, she managed to inscribe all of the windows with Kirov's initials, then began screaming hysterically again:

"Monsters, monsters, monsters. . . . We're the ones who killed Comrade Kirov, our dear Mironych! Every one of us! Save him, save him!"

By nightfall, she had quieted down, but then she found something else to do—pick lice out of her hair. This required no great skill, since they swarmed over her in vast numbers. Lay your hand on her head, and you would be sure to make a catch. Eventually, she sprinkled some lice on my head with the words "Share and share alike; we're marching toward communism."

Despite this constant disturbance, my attention was drawn to an ancient crone who sat quietly eyeing us all from the vantage point of her aged wisdom. Mottled and wrinkled like a baked apple, dried up and diminutive, unaccountably clean for prison conditions, with a snow-white lace bonnet nicely set upon her head, she occupied the least space of all. I heard her voice for the first time when she stopped the medic. (In prison, the medical assistant was usually one of the common criminals, or nonpoliticals, who had found a soft spot for himself. He would know nothing about medicine but could perform some simple procedures. His fellow criminals often called him *lepkom* [a meaningless word suggesting "sculpture commissar," if anything] rather than the appropriate *lekpom*, or medical assistant, simply because it was easier to pronounce.)

"Sonny," the old lady said, "you should give me something for my lower back."

"Like what? You're 110 years old. What could help you?"

We all gasped. Could she really be 110?

"Any little pill would help me. Give me one," the old woman begged.

"Here's an aspirin. Swallow it, but a lot of good it will do you."

I had to ask. "Is it true, Granny, that you're 110?"

"That's right, that's right," the medic said. "I saw her dossier. Born in 1827."

"What's true is true," the old granny agreed.

"So you lived in Pushkin's time?"

"You mean the one who wrote verses? That's what they say. . . . I was alive then."

"Then what did they put you in prison for, Granny?"

"I don't know. The investigator said that I read the Gospels, that bad things about Lenin are written there."

"No, Granny, you must have mixed something up. That can't be."

"It's not me who mixed things up, but him."

Grandmother got ten years in the camps for reading about Lenin in the Gospels.

The gruel at Sverdlovsk always had cockroaches. Without fail you could find at least a couple in your bowl. It was because of this cockroach gruel and the mad Leningrader that I met and became friends with Viktoriya Rudina. The first time I saw her, she was picking her way down the corridor through the bodies packed tightly on the floor. When she reached the locked door, she began banging away with fierce energy, demanding to see the prison warden. Finally, he made an appearance. Viktoriya Rudina, who was the wife of a military man and had taught Russian language and literature in primary school, gave him a disdainful look. To me, it seemed that she ran her eyes over him from head to toe with displeasure, then in a tone fit only for a subordinate, she gave orders.

"First, take this crazy woman out of here. She needs treatment, but in here she is only spreading lice and preventing others from sleeping. Second, stop cooking gruel with cockroaches in it, since it has yet to be proved that these insects are of value to the human organism. Got it?"

The warden heard her out but retired without a word. Toward evening, the madwoman was taken away. At supper, there were fewer cockroaches. They floated still in some bowls, but far from all. Evidently, they were being fished out of the serving kettle.

The very next day, Viktoriya, Sarra, and I were transferred to the Tomsk camp. This former schoolteacher soon took up cobbling, obtaining the necessary tools from the camp command. She lived in a barracks right across from the kitchen, our most popular gathering place. When it warmed up that spring, she came outside and set up her shoe-mending business by the wall opposite the birches. Tall, thin, and pale, her eyes inflamed by malnutrition and the intensely visual work of cobbling, Viktoriya sat bent over in her old overcoat. Suitable for spring or fall, this fair-weather coat, once cherry colored, had faded and wrinkled on the prison bed slats. Viktoriya had frozen in it through the long Siberian winter. Placing a rag on her knees, she deftly handled the awl and stitching cord. Soon, she started a school for cobblers. Perhaps it was her pedagogical talent that enabled her to train a number of women to cobble in a short time, but it was not her superb knowledge of literature that enabled her to master this trade. She simply knew how to give herself to people. Even so, her mastery as chief cobbler remained unsurpassed. Everyone asked that she herself do their repairs. In the conditions in which we were living, such work was vital to her comrades in misfortune. And everything went along well, for her *shkola* [school] was not labeled a *shkolka* [coterie] and disbanded as a counterrevolutionary organization.

Later, when Viktoriya had been exiled to the Tatar Republic and was teaching Russian language and literature, one of her most capable students completed school with excellent marks and took the entrance exams to Kazan University. Because he fell short of the cut-off level by one point, however, he was not allowed to enroll. Viktoriya believed that this was an unfair quirk of fate. At great personal risk, since she could be rearrested for violating exile, she went to Kazan to see the university rector.

"How tiresome you have become, Mommie!" With just such words, the rector greeted her.

"I'm not your Mommie, I'm his teacher," she retorted. "He's my most outstanding pupil. But if I've become too tiresome for you, just pick up the phone and call you-know-who. I'm an exile. Tell them I'm in Kazan, and they'll arrest me again."

The rector stood up, shook her hand, and said, "Don't worry. Your pupil will be accepted."

And he kept his promise.

[*Mothers and Babies in Prison*]

When I found Viktoriya after my disturbing conversation with Dina, she was surrounded by women.

"Viktoriya, dearest, sew up my shoes," asked the wife of a collective farm worker, herself formerly a collective farmer in Ryazan oblast. "They belonged to my father. He said they might come in handy here, and boy did they ever! I would have been lost without them. Oh, it's so hard." She sighed. "First they arrested my husband; then they came that night for me and took me away to the Ryazan prison. They opened the lock, put me in the cell, and right then and there I knew: He doesn't exist. God, that is."

Vanka's mama went up to Viktoriya next. Sixty of the women in camp had been arrested with their newborn babies. Yura was the only one two years old. I often went to see him and his mother in the "mamas" barracks. He reminded me of my own Yura. He was the same age and even somewhat similar in appearance. The babies were growing. Lyudmila Kuzminichna succeeded in getting us flannel, which we sewed into clothing for them. We called the mothers by their babies' names: Lyubochka's mama, Vaska's mama, Vanka's mama. As I waited, Vanka's mama was baring her soul.

"Viktoriya, just think," she began. "Lady Telman—her nickname for the chief woman guard—comes up to me and says, 'You see how Soviet power cares for children. You sit in prison, but over there they sew your Vanka such a nice little outfit.' And what do you think I answered her? 'As far as I'm concerned,' I said, 'if they'd give me just a mat, I'd wrap my Vanka up in it and take him home with me, and then I wouldn't need any nice little outfit from you.' There were eleven members in our family—myself, my husband, eight children, and my mama, who lived with us. I took only Vanya with me; the rest were left with the old woman and Dunka, the eldest. She's sixteen. Lady Telman thinks we've never seen a good life. But my man used to drive into town himself and buy a kilo of sugar for a week, and you could eat as much as you liked."

Moved by this tale, Viktoriya responded in verse:

> *Grief, grief—it surrounds you,*
> *So deep the grief of those around you,*
> *You feel ashamed to think of your own.*

But should one really feel ashamed? Not in those times! I had no qualms about thinking of my own grief. Besides, even if you do banish your "own material" from yourself, your thoughts will not leave you alone. They will torment you.

[Wives of Political Prisoners]

Nikolai Nekrasov, the nineteenth-century poet, wrote this of the cruel practices of serf-owning Russia:

And on this side and that—
The bones of Russians,
How many there are!
Vanechka, do you know how many?

But were those bones so many in comparison with our own? Innumerable pyramids could be built with the bones of those fallen by execution, famine, and cold in our day. What are the tears of times past in comparison with the tears of the women in our prison camps, torn from their children and husbands, humiliated and destroyed though innocent? Consider the "Russian women," Princess Trubetskaya and Princess Volkonskaya, abandoning their lives of luxury in Petersburg and riding post chaise to join their Decembrist husbands in Siberia. There's no denying it; that was a heroic deed! A subject fit for a poet! But how did they travel? Behind a team of six horses, wrapped in furs, enclosed in a marvelously furnished carriage. "The count himself fluffed up their pillows and spread the bearskin warmer over their legs." Also, they were riding to their husbands! Our women, Russians and non-Russians—Ukrainians, Byelorussians, Georgians,* Jews, Poles, Volga Germans, and Communist exiles from fascist Germany, along with Comintern officials and various others (Stalin, after all, was an internationalist)—were transported in cattle cars or in prison "Stolypin cars," and on arrival we had to line up and walk from the station to the camp, drained of strength, barely able to haul our miserable belongings in suitcases or bundles, guarded by police dogs, and terrorized by the shouts of the convoy: "Anyone steps to the side, and I'll fire without warning!" or "Sit!" Even in snow or muck, just sit! And we were not going to our husbands, though some dreamers among us naively hoped that in that camp over in the other world they would be united with their men—men who had been sentenced to ten years without any mail or, in other words, men who had been shot. Ah, how different that road would have been to me, if I could have believed that it led to Nikolai Ivanovich!

But I was unable to hope.

---

*Stalin did not spare the Georgians, either; he cannot be accused of national spirit or familial feeling on their account. His relatives in the Svanidze and Alliluyev families he doomed to suicide, execution, and camp. Accustomed to an easy, warm climate, the Georgians were the first to perish in Siberia. Georgians were also shot in great numbers. They probably claim first place among the nationalities in percentage of people persecuted.

[Mothers of Disgraced Sons]

The poet Nekrasov also wrote about "Orina, a soldier's mother," whose son died of tuberculosis during a long, hard term of tsarist military service. And he wrote truly: "Few are her words, but of grief a small river!" In the grim years of war, our own sons also died at the front, and their mothers' grief was immeasurable. But these sons died as heroes defending the homeland, not as prisoners wrongly cursed by their own people. What can be said about the mother whose son was taken away at night in a "Black Maria"? And even this poor soul can be envied by the mother whose son just yesterday not only was respected by acquaintances, fellow workers, and neighbors but was the pride of the entire nation, yet today is held up for universal scorn. The poem to her endless spiritual pain, her measureless devotion, her eternal questioning, could be read in eyes that said, "Can it be true? How could this happen?" Such grief fell to many, but not for long. They could not endure bearing the heavy cross of their disgraced and destroyed sons.

Fate brought me into contact with just such a mother. Her son had been honored by the whole country, which then turned around and cursed him with one voice. I knew what this was like, as the wife of a husband also cursed by the entire nation. Condemnation by all of the people, ridicule from everyone. What can be worse? Death alone brings salvation from such torment!

My acquaintance, though not "Orina, a soldier's mother," but Mavra Tukhachevsky, a marshal's mother, was also a simple peasant woman. We met on June 11, 1937, on the train taking us from Moscow into exile in Astrakhan. A NKVD [People's Commissariat of Internal Affairs, predecessor of the KGB] officer had driven me to the station and put me in a coach—unreserved, but free of charge. Ironically, he made a point of politely bidding me farewell and wishing me the best. At station stops all along the line, passengers got off to grab newspapers with the latest sensational announcement beginning, "The Military Collegium of the Supreme Court of the USSR in a closed session has examined . . ." Inevitably, each story went on, "All of the accused admitted their guilt" and "The sentence has been carried out." On that very first day of my transport, every one of the USSR's major military commanders perished: Mikhail Tukhachevsky, Iona Yakir, Iyeronim Uborevich, Avgust Kork, Robert Eideman, Boris Feldman, Vitovt Putna, and Vitaly Primakov.

The chief of the Red Army Political Administration, Yan Gamarnik, had already committed suicide on May 31. I learned about the circumstances from his wife, who shared a cell with me in the Astrakhan prison. Gamarnik was visited that day by a very agitated Marshal Vasily Blyukher, who acquainted him with the incriminating materials brought against him and, apparently, against the military commanders who were later executed. Immediately after Blyukher left, two other officials showed up to seal Gamarnik's office safe: Smorodinov, director of affairs for the People's Commissariat of Defense, and Bulin, one of the chief's own assistants. Before they were done, the shot was heard.

You would think these events could no longer amaze me and I would accept them as yet another inexplicable turn of fate. Two Bolshevik trials had already taken place: the Zinoviev-Kamenev trial in 1936, the Radek-Pyatakov trial in 1937. Mikhail Tomsky, chairman of the trade unions, had killed himself in 1936. Rykov and Bukharin, my husband, had already been arrested. I need not mention some of the earlier trials, for they had not raised doubts in my mind at the time. The exception was the censure of Nikolai Sukhanov at the trial of the Mensheviks in March 1931, which had made me wonder.

Sukhanov, a famous revolutionary, publicist, economist, and man of letters, had been a Menshevik before the revolution. His multivolume work *Notes on the Revolution,* published in Berlin in 1922–23, was avidly read by the Bolshevik upper crust. His views were, of course, considered incorrect from their standpoint but inspired many debates and were accorded a certain historical value. Sukhanov had visited my father's apartment rather often, and their talks went on for hours—not incidentally, I suspect, because he was attracted to my mother. For this reason, I developed a dislike for him and zealously guarded the interests of my father, who was not well. Actually, my feelings toward Sukhanov were at first ambivalent, for he was a fascinating man, but antipathy won the day. His refined manners, European appearance, gabardine coat, gray felt cap, and pince-nez all irritated me. By contrast during the same period, I was delighted when Bukharin, bubbling with life, would dash around the apartment, his cloth coat tossed carelessly in a heap in my father's study. As for Sukhanov, the most interesting thing about him then, in my view, was the story he told about his mother's sensational divorce case. He recounted all the fine details of the scandal, but, unfortunately, I have forgotten them. I do recall that she had been sentenced to a term in a tsarist prison, an incident Lev Tolstoi used, according to Sukhanov, as the basis for his play *The Living Corpse.*

Because of my personal animus, I tried to spite Sukhanov, to sting him, every time he visited. Once, when I observed him listening less to my father, who was waxing enthusiastic about the new architecture and cities of the future, and attending more to my mother, I tried to distract his gaze from her by breaking into song at the top of my voice. "Higher and higher and higher we urge the flight of our birds," I sang, a phrase from a very popular march of the day. This ruse merely amused Sukhanov, who understood everything, and angered my father, who understood nothing. "You are tactless," he said. "Leave the study." Afterward, Sukhanov always announced his arrival with that march.

Another time, I stung him painfully by playing on a well-known historical fact. Because he was a prominent Menshevik, the Bolsheviks had chosen his apartment (shared with his Bolshevik wife, Galina Flakserman) as a safe place to decide the question of the armed uprising in 1917.

"You know, Nikolai Nikolayevich," I said casually to him, "the Bolsheviks really pulled one over on you in October 1917, when they decided on the uprising in your apartment and in your presence."

Taking offense, he snapped, "No one could ever pull one over on me, for your and your parents' information! I left on purpose to give them an opportunity to decide the matter."

Sukhanov always expressed his views openly, even when he did not support Bolshevik politics. But not long before his arrest in 1931, I heard his statement that he had recently come to support the Bolshevik Party and planned to join it. Therefore, he planted a seed of doubt in my mind about the trial of the Union Bureau of Mensheviks that year. His conviction there did not make sense to me. After the Bolshevik trials, this doubt grew into a full certainty that the pre-Menshevik trials had been fabrications, too.

But apparently it is human nature not to cease to be amazed. On the train toward Astrakhan, I was astonished yet again, to put it mildly, by the news about this latest trial. I glanced over the shoulder of my neighbor to read the newspaper report with my own eyes, but the letters jumped up and down. I could make out only the conclusion: "The sentence has been carried out." This execution of the entire military command shook me, and I began to seek explanations of any kind.

The charge that the commanders had conspired against the Soviet state, in league with Hitler, simply could not be believed. But since repressions had reached the level of a national catastrophe, I speculated that they had indeed decided to remove Stalin in order to bring the horrors to an end. They had failed in a noble mission. But later, in September 1939, one of my interrogators in Lubyanka prison, a certain Matusov, inadvertently suggested the truth of the matter:

"You thought that Yakir and Tukhachevsky would save your Bukharin! But we do good work. That's why the commanders didn't succeed!"

So, even though no such conspiracy against Stalin actually existed, it seems that he and his henchmen feared it. In my view, that was the real reason for the death of our military leaders.

For now, I could only look out the train window and wipe away my tears. It was a warm day. Through the glass, I could see the expansive steppes, the green thickets, and the bright sky, clear as clear as could be. Only on the horizon was it obscured by feathery clouds. Nature alone seemed eternal and pure, while all around me people were being lined up and shot to death. The execution of the commanders was all the more painful because I had been acquainted with Tukhachevsky, Yakir, Kork, and Uborevich. Now the train was whisking me away to unknown Astrakhan, each minute taking me farther and farther from my native Moscow, and from my year-old son. Among these uninvolved people on the train who did not understand my tragedy, I felt utterly alone.

Suddenly, in the opposite window, I took note of an old lady, a woman of about thirty-five, and an adolescent girl, because like me they were listening closely to the conversation of newspaper readers and to the reactions of people around them. I felt magnetically drawn to the trio. The facial features of the old one reminded me of someone. I left my place and asked the passenger sitting across from them if he would trade seats with me. He agreed. Now I needed to explain myself. In such a situation, I knew that the women would not identify themselves until I did so. But how to say it? I might be mistaken in assuming that they were in the same category as I, a category now closer than that of blood relative. I went straight over to the younger woman and said very quietly, "I am the wife of Nikolai Ivanovich." I had decided not to state the surname right away, since Bukharin's given name and patronymic were as famous as his family name. Should she fail to understand, I would use the surname. But her answer came back in a flash: "And I, of Mikhail Nikolayevich."

Thus, I made the acquaintance of Tukhachevsky's family: his mother, Mavra Petrovna, his wife, Nina Yevgeniyevna, and his daughter, Svetlana.

Meanwhile, the passengers were loudly venting their hatred for "the traitors."

"They wouldn't be tried for nothing."

"Just look at the harm they did. . . . Don't worry about the reason."

Yes, indeed, just spit on reason, as long as "they" are removed. . . . How could the people have guessed that this was exactly the way the chief murderer thought? They had to assume that Stalin must have had a reason for his actions. After all, he acted so boldly and confidently, without fear of failure. No one surpassed him in despotism, treachery, evil, or deceit.

"They themselves confessed; they did! You can't hide from the evidence."

Excitedly, the people tried in vain to figure it all out.

"But look who tried them, commanders like Blyukher, Budyonny, and Dybenko! What are they doing trying people when they themselves should be tried!"*

An argument to be reckoned with. At that moment, the people could hardly guess that a bit later Blyukher, too, would become a "spy" and be shot, or that Kliment Voroshilov, marshal of the Soviet Union, would be denounced as an English spy and would be barred from meetings of the Politburo (as Khrushchev would reveal to a closed session of the Twentieth Party Congress in 1956) without special permission to attend.

"What more did they need? They had fame and position!"

"And foreign money, besides," muttered one woman.

But then a passenger in an embroidered Ukrainian shirt declared with sudden boldness, "I don't believe what they say about Yakir!" Sitting not far from me, he was flushed with agitation. "You can write a hundred pages in that paper, and still I won't believe it! I knew Iona and fought under him in the civil war, so I know what kind of man he is. A fascist hireling? That's absurd, a filthy lie! He's Jewish, you know, so like hell he needs fascists! Think what military maneuvers he carried out near Kiev. The world has never seen the like! That was to strengthen our readiness for battle, not to—"

"Say, look who piped up!" someone interrupted. "He defends Yakir, because he fought along with Yakir, but maybe I fought under Tukhachevsky, and someone else under Kork or Uborevich, so does that mean it's all lies, it's all 'made up'? Then tell me why it's necessary to kill off such military commanders, if they're innocent? That would only strengthen the enemy's hand!"

Another strong argument, but Yakir's defender did not back down.

---

*Members of the court were also military leaders: Army Commanders Boris Shaposhnikov, Ivan Belov, Yakov Alksnis, and Nikolai Kashirin and Corps Commander Yelisei Goryachov, in addition to those named above. Of them, only Shaposhnikov and Semyon Budyonny remained alive. Goryachov committed suicide on the day of the military trial. All the other members of the court were shot. Whether these military commanders actually presided at the trial or whether their names were simply used to show that the court had consisted of authoritative people, I do not know.

"Yakir is not Tukhachevsky, a landowner's little boy. Most likely, Tukhachevsky dragged them in, and Yakir got mixed up in it."

And so it was that those who had stood in awe of the commanders' military prowess, their brilliant strategic abilities, their heroism and courage, and those who had fought under their command for the Soviet aims in the fire of the civil war and had put down the interventionist armies, and those who had applauded them and shouted "Hurrah!" now, bewildered and feeling deceived, passionately cursed them. The authority of the military heroes had vanished, their credibility had collapsed, their shining ideals were tarnished.

"Monsters, hirelings, traitors. . . . A bullet's too good for 'em. They should've been drawn and quartered! Hanged! They got off with too easy a death!"

Petrified with grief and horror, the mother of Marshal Tukhachevsky sat in the midst of these infuriated people. How merciless proved her son's fate, but how generous had nature been to him! His exceptional talent, rare leadership abilities, and his spiritual beauty were combined with striking physical features. When, in my childhood, I first beheld the man, I could not take my eyes off him. My mouth hanging open, I stared at him so hard it made the people around me start laughing and his mother give me a warm-hearted smile. "Children love what is beautiful, too," observed his father.

Now I was looking at his mother. Her deathly pale face and big trembling hands, which had worked hard in their time, revealed her agitation. Traces of her former beauty remained, and I could pick out the features transmitted from her to her son. She was sizable and seemed still strong and surprisingly proud, even in her suffering and humiliation. Yes, Nekrasov could have been looking right at her when he wrote:

> There are women in our Russian hamlets
> With a calm and dignity of face,
> With a beautiful strength in their movements,
> With a tsaritsa's gait, and with her gaze.

Anyone who saw Mavra Petrovna just once will certainly agree with me. Though the anger and curses directed at her son pierced her maternal heart like poisoned arrows, she shed not a single tear in the presence of onlookers. She did not wail, as peasant women usually do when their children die, whether from wounds at the front or from illness at home. I have seen the grief of many such women in my life, most recently the mother of Vasily Shukshin, the popular writer who died in 1974. Out of her mind with grief at his grave, her face puffy from crying, clutching at the mound of wreaths and flowers, she wailed, "I'm the guilty one, I'm the guilty one, I didn't pray enough for you, I didn't pray enough for you, I'm the guilty one."

Mavra Petrovna, however, could not let out her grief this way. Who would have commiserated with her, if she had? Grief burned her from within. On that very day, when the tragic events of 1937 brought us together, she had received the certificate of death for her son, and it was the worst kind possible.

Yet, I would one day see Mavra Petrovna crying. She came to me in Astrakhan after the arrest of her daughter-in-law, Nina Yevgeniyevna. (Yakir's wife and I would be arrested two weeks later.) She wanted to send a package to Nina Yevgeniyevna in the Astrakhan prison. "I write bad," she told me and asked that I write what she said. "Write, 'Ninochka, I am sending you onions, herring, and a loaf of bread.' " I wrote this down. Unexpectedly, Mavra Petrovna began sobbing and placed her head on my shoulder, repeating again and again, "Mishenka! Mishenka! My little boy Mishenka! You are no more, you are no more!"

She did not know then, and perhaps never did, that her other two sons, Aleksandr and Nikolai, were also shot—and only because they were born of the same mother who had given birth to Mikhail. Nor did she know then that her four daughters had also been arrested and sentenced to eight years in the camps. Two of them, Olga Nikolayevna and Maria Nikolayevna, would be with me in the Tomsk camp. The third, Sofia Nikolayevna, was also subjected to persecution; she was sent out of Moscow and disappeared without a trace. Yelizaveta Nikolayevna, the fourth, suffered no less misery.

Mavra Petrovna died in exile. I want to believe that the time will come when she will touch the poet's heart, and we will read of Mavra Petrovna as of "Orina, a soldier's mother."

Look how far my reflections on Nekrasov have carried me! It is no accident that precisely his verses came to mind so often: my father brought me up on them, for Nekrasov was the favorite poet of many revolutionaries.

[How Stalin Toyed with Bukharin—The Bukharin Trial]

If it is possible to rate life's experiences in order of difficulty, then without doubt the months of interrogation preceding my husband's arrest, more than the trial itself, were the most unbearable for me. At the time, early in 1937, my mind had not yet become accustomed to the horrendous accusations against him: plotting a "palace revolution," planning terror against Stalin (and against Lenin, too, back in 1918). Nor had I, or Bukharin either, adjusted to the inexplicable and terrible cross-examining of several defendants at once. I will never forget that February night when a snowstorm raged as I accompanied Bukharin, enfeebled by a hunger strike, to the Kremlin for the famous meeting of the Party's Central Committee, the February–March plenum of 1937. His trial there was the logical culmination of what had obviously begun for Nikolai Ivanovich back in August 1936, when his name was mentioned along with those of Tomsky, Rykov, Radek, and others at the trial of Zinoviev.

Today, we understand that, immediately after the death of Lenin, Stalin had begun preparing his traps very carefully, but in those days it would have been considered the wildest fantasy to imagine that differing ideological views within the Party would one day be represented as the acts of criminals and bandits. I say this even though the so-called Bukharinist Right Opposition had been routed after 1929 and Nikolai Ivanovich ceased to occupy a leading position in the Party, and even though he felt oppressed at always being in Stalin's sights and under his fire. For example, Stalin baited Bukharin by suggesting to him that his former young political protégés, who had been denigrated with the term *shkolka* and driven away, many to work outside Moscow, had turned into counterrevolutionaries. He also set the Press Department of the Central Committee against Bukharin, as well as the editor of *Pravda*, Lev Mekhlis, with whom Nikolai Ivanovich had frequent run-ins. After my husband was appointed chief editor of *Izvestiya*, in 1934, Stalin telephoned from time to time to hand down various directives. For example, Bukharin and Radek were ordered to write "destructing" articles ("destructing" is exactly how he put it) about the late Bolshevik historian and revolutionary Mikhail Pokrovsky.

Once, Stalin called Bukharin and chewed him out because the author of some article, gushing with priase, had written that Stalin's mother called him Soso [the Georgian equivalent of Joe or Joey].

"What's this 'Soso' business?" demanded the enraged Stalin. It was impossible to understand what had set him off. Was it the mention of his mother, to whom (as I had heard) he never paid the slightest attention, or did he believe that his mother, like everyone else, should call her son the "Father of All the Peoples" and the "Corypheus of Science"?

Yet, simultaneously, Stalin "petted" my husband. In the spring of 1935, at a banquet for graduates of the military academies, he gave this toast: "Let us drink, comrades, to Nikolai Ivanovich, and let bygones be bygones!" At a banquet for young officers, this was a toast not to a military leader but to the disgraced, but still beloved, Bukharin! The audience drank and burst into stormy applause, which swelled, as we are accustomed to say, into an ovation. Nikolai Ivanovich was completely taken by surprise. This was Stalin's way of testing the people's attitude. With him, everything was calculated, every step—no, every inch of every step. Of course, this is obvious *now,* but then no one, including my husband himself, suspected a thing. The toast was considered a sincere expression of Stalin's attitude toward Bukharin.

To take another example, Stalin phoned in the summer of 1934 to congratulate Nikolai Ivanovich on a speech about poetry he had given at the First Congress of Soviet Writers. Stalin was especially pleased by Bukharin's analysis that the poet Demyan Bedny was in danger of falling behind the times. Another time, Stalin phoned in the dead of night, waking us up. When I went to the telephone, I heard three words: "Stalin. Call Nikolai!" Nikolai Ivanovich said to me, "More trouble again," and uneasily took the receiver. But there was no trouble. Stalin, not sober, had called to wish us well on our marriage. "Nikolai, I congratulate you! You outspit me this time, too!" Nikolai Ivanovich did not ask about the phrase "this time, too," but did want to know how he had "outspit" Stalin, who replied, "A good wife, a beautiful wife, a young one . . . younger than my Nadya!" This is the way he talked, even though by then she was no longer among the living. After pranks of this kind, we had learned to expect trouble the next day. Nikolai Ivanovich became accustomed to this nerve-racking business, to a certain degree, and up until August 1936 was able to master it with his natural joie de vivre. But beginning at that point—that is, with the Zinoviev trial—the accusations against him became so terrible that his life-sustaining forces dried up before my very eyes.

I had been waiting for Bukharin's trial for a whole year, but I was sent to the camp before it began. I knew the sentence would be death; I prayed for the quickest possible end so that my husband's sufferings would be over. And I nourished the feeble hope that Nikolai Ivanovich would leave life proudly, declaring loudly (as he had at the February–March 1937 plenum), "No, no, no! I will not lie about myself!" This hope was born entirely of my great love for him.

But it was unfounded. I already understood very well that any of the accused brought to trial would confess to crimes they could not have committed.

Usually, we got no newspapers in camp, but in the first days of March 1938 a guard brought in papers reporting the trial of Bukharin and those charged with him. Giving me a mean, contemptuous look, he shouted, "Read, read who you are!," handed the papers to the barracks *starosta* [head woman], and left, slamming the door. The *starosta,* Zemskaya by name, always reminded me in both appearance and name of a snake [*zmeya*]. She was also, of course, someone's wife. In Leningrad, she had been a public prosecutor; in camp, she was an informer. She once caused me trouble by reporting that I had in my possession a book stamped "Library of N. I. Bukharin" with the very suspicious title *Dangerous Liaisons.* This was, of course, the lively and witty novel about high-society libertines written by Choderlos de Laclos, the eighteenth-century French author and political activist. An excellent edition of the Russian translation had been released in the early 1930s by Academia, the Soviet publishing house. I cannot recall now why I had that particular book with me. After Zemskaya snitched, my things were searched and this world-famous classic was confiscated and declared "counter-revolutionary."

Now, instead of passing out the newspapers to us prisoners, the *starosta* sat on the upper bed boards, right across from me, and read them aloud. When she read the prosecution's charges against Bukharin specifically, she sometimes broke off and glanced in my direction so that she could later report my reactions. She had complete coverage of the trial of the accused men, except for the newspaper reporting Nikolai Ivanovich's concluding statement. I was very interested to know whether this was mere coincidence or whether something was being withheld.

Before my husband's trial, I thought I had more or less prepared myself psychologically for it by reading the initial evidence against him. The documents had been sent to him before his arrest, when he was still under investigation. But the accusations leveled at the trial surpassed all expectations in vulgarity and monstrosity. In them, the criminal fantasies of Stalin (those reading the charges were his pawns) reached their apogee. The sheer mass of crimes alleged against Bukharin could not possibly have been committed by only one criminal in his entire lifetime—not just because one lifetime would have been insufficient, but because he would certainly have failed after the first few.

Nikolai Ivanovich was supposedly guilty of spying and wrecking; the attempted dismemberment of the USSR; the organization of kulak uprisings; conspiratorial ties with German fascists, as well as German and Japanese intelligence; terrorist hopes of murdering Stalin; the murder of Kirov; a terrorist act against Lenin in 1918 previously attributed solely to the Right Social Revolutionary Fanny Kaplan, but her hand now shown to be Bukharin's hand; the executions of the long ailing, nonfunctioning Vyacheslav Menzhinsky [nominal chief of the political police from 1926 to 1934], Valerian Kuibyshev [chief of the Party's

Central Control Commission], and the writer Maxim Gorky; and even an attempt to poison Nikolai Yezhov [then chief of the NKVD]. As if to say, "Well, how could you fail to take care of an old pal?"

After the recitation of charges against all of the accused, Vasily Ulrikh, the chairman of the Military Collegium of the Supreme Court, asked whether or not they admitted their guilt. Only one, Nikolai Krestinsky, was able to declare, "I do not."

Tears shot from my eyes at these words. This was a moment of transcendence and pride in him. It seemed to me that I could actually see Krestinsky's kindly face with his myopic eyes peering through thick glasses. His denial of guilt would not endure. He was soon forced to "confess"—that is, to lie—but this moment put a considerable dent in the progress of the trial.

I had been sitting as the *starosta* began her reading, but finally, in order to avoid the stares of curious women, I lay down on the bed boards and pulled the cover over my head. Blood was flowing from my nose; I had a terrible headache. Sarra Yakir, inseparable from me, moistened a towel with cold water, put it under my nose, and said softly, "Deaden yourself, deaden yourself. You have to try not to notice anything. Follow my example. . . . I am already dead to everything!"

Suddenly, Zemskaya broke off her reading and shouted in a commanding voice, "Bukharina! Come here and wash the corridor! It's your turn today!"

In fact, it was not my turn; moreover, the *starosta* could see my condition. She knew I could not wash the corridor. She simply wanted to report my refusal, which would be added to my characterization as a counterrevolutionary.

Sarra spoke up. "Don't you worry, Zemskaya. I'll wash it for her."

And, though exhausted herself, she went off to wash the dirty and interminable corridor.

In my condition at that moment, in a barracks where no fewer than a hundred women fixed their stares upon me, and when I could not take a newspaper into my own hands and reflect upon what had just been read, could not make even the most elementary analysis of that squalid travesty of justice, all of the accused seemed to have the same face. Except for Krestinsky. In fact, in my imagination, Nikolai Ivanovich looked much more abject than when, many years later, I was able to read the account of the trial and his final words for myself. As the *starosta* read on, I even began to have doubts that the man in the dock was really Bukharin and not some stand-in made up to look like him. His admissions were so monstrous that if he had made them to me in private I would have thought him insane. Indeed, many people at the time did think that there were stand-ins at the trial, that this Bukharin was not Bukharin. But as the reading continued, my initial doubts rapidly dissolved. I knew Nikolai Ivanovich too well not to recognize his style and character. Besides, using imposters would have been too crude and risky a subterfuge in general, and with Bukharin in particular. Indeed, the very events of the trial, which included an altercation with the chief prosecutor, Andrei Vyshinsky, made the supposition of a stand-in untenable.

Many years afterward, when I had returned to Moscow, the writer Ilya Ehrenburg confirmed that it was definitely Nikolai Ivanovich in the dock. He told me that he had attended one of the court sessions and sat near the accused men. At certain intervals, he recalled, a bailiff would come over to Bukharin and lead him out, then bring him back a few minutes later. No one else was taken out like this. Ehrenburg suspected that Nikolai Ivanovich was being given injections to weaken his willpower.

"Maybe," he said, "it was because they feared him more than the rest."

Ehrenburg had been given his ticket to the trial by the satirist Mikhail Koltsov, editor of the satiric paper *Krokodil*. "Go, Ilya Grigoriyevich, and take a look at your buddy!" he had said in a hostile tone. But Koltsov, too, would suffer Bukharin's fate.

The composition of the group of accused at Bukharin's trial left me incredulous, even though two earlier political trials also included defendants who were not connected by political activity, mutual aims, or oppositional inclinations with the principal defendants Kamenev and Zinoviev, in the first instance, or Pyatakov, Radek, and Sokolnikov, in the second. But there was an even larger number of extraneous figures at this third trial.

Many of the accused in the preceding two trials had held senior positions in various establishments, had then been expelled from the Party, and then readmitted; they were former Trotskyists who had long ago broken with Trotsky. In Bukharin's trial, only one member of this "Right Opposition," Aleksei Ivanovich Rykov, was among the accused. Another Right Oppositionist, Mikhail Tomsky, had understood right away that you could not prove your innocence in a court that did not want such proof. With his firm worker's hand, he had put a bullet through his head. Whenever I thought of him, I recalled his broad, powerful hands, imprinted in my memory when he carried the urn of my father's ashes to the Kremlin Wall in 1932.

Naturally, I had assumed that adherents of Bukharin's political views would be brought to trial with him: Dmitry Maretsky, Aleksandr

Slepkov, Yan Sten, Aleksandr Zaitsev, Valentin Astrov, Aleksandr Aikhenvald, Ivan Kraval, Yefim Tsetlin, and others like them. All of them had been smeared with the word *shkolka,* a word Bukharin, like a robot, repeated again and again at his trial. Back in the late 1920s, these men had been attacked by Kamenev but defended by, of all people, Molotov! He had said, archly, "Such a fine 'democrat' as Comrade Kamenev refers to these young people only with contempt as Maretskies and Stetskies. He can find no other way to speak of those who are beginning to grow up within the Party and its ruling organs, who are proving to be of the most enormous value to our Party."*

But these adherents of Bukharin's views were not in the dock. Nor was Moshe Frumkin, whom Stalin considered to be to the right of Nikolai Ivanovich, or Nikolai Uglanov, who had supported Bukharin in 1928. Valerian Osinsky (Obolensky) and Varvara Yakovleva, both of whom had backed my husband during the debates over the Brest-Litovsk treaty in 1918 and had supposedly participated in his crimes, appeared as witnesses, not among the accused. No, the ones on trial with Bukharin were the so-called doctor poisoners, men completely unconnected with politics. All of them were skilled physicians, including Professor Dmitry Pletnyov, a heart specialist known widely at home and abroad. It had become necessary to manufacture Rightists for the trial. Who fit the bill? Preposterously, one of the central figures among the accused was Yagoda, NKVD chief during the Zinoviev-Kamenev trial and during the earlier trials of non-Bolsheviks. For Yagoda, my husband had felt nothing but contempt during these last days, believing that he had degenerated, forgotten his revolutionary past, and become an adventurist, careerist, and functionary. Yagoda, in fact, was never Rightist or Leftist; he simply held on to his post, carrying out the Boss's directives precisely, never guessing how he would be "repaid"! Ironically, not one word was said at the trial about any of Yagoda's real crimes against the people. He was as misrepresented and maligned as his victims.

But at least one incident Yagoda testified to at the trial, and confirmed by Rykov and Bukharin, really did occur. When peasants in the countryside began rebelling against Stalin's collectivization measures in 1928 and the bad news came in from the provinces to Rykov and Nikolai Ivanovich, one of them apparently initiated a contact with Yagoda, then people's commissar of internal affairs, for precise numerical data on the disturbances. The aim was to make a report either to the Polit-

*XIV s"ezd VKP(b): Stenograficheskii otchet [Stenographic Record, Fourteenth Congress of the VKP(b)—All-Union Communist Party (Bolsheviks)] (Moscow, 1926), p. 472.

buro or, possibly, the plenum of the Central Committee that would both help prevent the spread of the disorders and affirm the author's position. No one would have more accurate statistical information than Yagoda. And it was his duty to provide the data, though he had never been part of the Right Opposition, when the go-between Rykov, chairman of the Council of People's Commissars, contacted him. At the Bukharin trial, Yagoda's cooperation in providing the numbers became a point of contention. Evidently, he had not accurately weighed his options. The correct move was to refuse to provide the information, and Stalin could not forgive him the blunder. I heard Bukharin and Larin discuss this incident, so I know that it actually happened.

The second man changed into a Rightist was Akmal Ikramov, secretary of the Uzbekistan Communist Party's Central Committee. Not only had he never belonged to the Right Opposition, he had come out against it. Still, it is possible that he was a silent adherent of my husband's views, and it is in fact difficult to determine exactly who supported Nikolai Ivanovich in 1928–29. Mikhail Kalinin, for example, once encountered Bukharin in the Kremlin, just before the Sixteenth Party Congress, in 1930, and said, "You, Nikolai Ivanovich, are 200 percent right, but there is nothing more effective than a monolithic party. We have missed our chance, Stalin has too much power. . . . The rest you understand yourself." In the same vein, Nikolai Shvernik also expressed sympathy for Bukharin's position, but only face to face with him. In any event, at the trial, Ikramov was convenient for the falsifiers, as was Faizulla Khodzhayev, formerly head of the Kazakh Communist Party. While on vacation in the Pamir Mountains, my husband had stopped at Ikramov's place in Tashkent and had encountered Khodzhayev there.

Yes, wherever Bukharin stepped, his foot of necessity carried "counterrevolution." But the Tashkent meeting was not enough "proof"; other proofs had to be made up. And they were. (Later, I will discuss this in more detail.) The notion that Bukharin "recruited" Ikramov is no less incredible than the latter's false testimony about himself, that he was involved in wrecking activities and so on. Unquestionably, his interrogators had demanded before the trial that he lie about himself as well as about Bukharin.

In addition, others mentioned during the trial had never been Rightists—Yan Rudzutak, Avel Yenukidze, and many more—and had not shared the views of Bukharin, Rykov, and Tomsky in 1928–29.

Vyshinsky's interrogation produced a terrible impression about the years Bukharin spent abroad before the revolution. It appeared that he had not lived in western Europe and America as a political émigré fleeing the persecutions of the tsarist government, though this was when many revolutionaries had fallen to the agent provocateur of the tsarist secret police, Roman Malinovsky. No, he had gone abroad to establish ties with the police agencies of the U.S. and European countries.

I knew that, apart from his political participation in the workers' movement abroad and his association with Lenin in exile, Nikolai Ivanovich had studied a lot in those years. For example, he attended lectures by Eugen von Böhm-Bawerk and Friedrich Wieser, bourgeois economists of the so-called Austrian school of political economy. He published articles criticizing the theory of value and profit and defending the orthodox Marxist point of view. In Vienna, he wrote *The Economic Theory of the Leisure Class,* a fierce attack upon the anti-Marxist positions of Böhm-Bawerk and Mikhail Tugan-Baranovsky. This book, published in Soviet Russia in the first years after the revolution, was read with as much enthusiasm by economics students and experts as his *The ABCs of Communism* was read in workers' schools. In America, where Bukharin participated actively in the workers' movement and edited the left socialist newspaper *New World,* he was much admired by workers. They wrote him letters now and then after the October Revolution, and representatives of New York typesetters sent him a gift on his fortieth birthday, in 1928. Wrapped in a long red ribbon imprinted with English verses dedicated to him was a pen, at that time called an automatic fountain pen, set in a golden stand of very fine craftsmanship. It was inscribed with tiny Russian letters: "N. I. Bukharin. Use this pen, Nikolai, to beat the enemies of the working class!"

When he was abroad, Bukharin was more than once arrested for his participation in the workers' movement—for example, in Sweden, where he was drawn into the affair of the left socialist Karl Zeth Höglund. The assumed name that Nikolai used in Stockholm, Moisha-Abe-Pinkus Dovgolevsky, was hilarious to us all and remains firmly fixed in my memory because he used it whenever he visited my father, right up to the very end. He would ring at the door, but before you could open it you would hear his infectious laughter: "Open up! Moisha-Abe-Pinkus Dovgolevsky has come!"

Also in Austria, which had joined Germany in the war against Russia, he was arrested on suspicion of espionage and sabotage. This was logical from the point of view of the Austrian police, who did not understand that a Russian Bolshevik would never work on behalf of the tsarist government. Stalin, too, was in Vienna, as I would learn later, and Nikolai Ivanovich helped him write a book on the nationalities problem, since he did not know German.

In camp, as I listened to how Vyshinsky had questioned Bukharin about his alleged ties to foreign police agencies, I knew I had to hear it all clearly. I threw off the cover and sat down next to Sayechka (my nickname for Sarra Lazarevna, who had been called this by the family she had lost). I no longer cared about the curious stares of the other women. I listened attentively to the examination, so humiliating to my husband. Perhaps, in fact, it was no more horrible than others like it, but it seared into my memory because I could sense his protest. Nonetheless, in the interest of complete accuracy, I am citing the stenographic record of this episode:

VYSHINSKY: Perhaps, as a preface, I could ask you two or three questions of a biographical nature.
BUKHARIN: Please.
VYSHINSKY: You lived in Austria?
BUKHARIN: I did.
VYSHINSKY: A long time?
BUKHARIN: 1912 and 1913.
VYSHINSKY: You had no connection with the Austrian police?
BUKHARIN: None.
VYSHINSKY: You lived in America?
BUKHARIN: Yes.
VYSHINSKY: A long time?
BUKHARIN: A long time.
VYSHINSKY: How many months?
BUKHARIN: About seven months.
VYSHINSKY: Were you connected with the police in America?
BUKHARIN: Absolutely not.
VYSHINSKY: From America, you traveled to Russia by way of . . .
BUKHARIN: By way of Japan.
VYSHINSKY: Did you stay there a long time?
BUKHARIN: A week.
VYSHINSKY: During that week, you were not recruited?
BUKHARIN: If you must ask such questions.* . . . My connection with the Austrian police consisted in being locked up in the fortress in Austria. . . . I spent time in a Swedish jail, twice in a Russian jail, and in a German jail.†

*Sudebnyi otchet po delu antisovetskogo "pravo-trotskiskogo bloka" [Court Record in the Case of the Anti-Soviet "Bloc of Rightists and Trotskyists"] (Moscow, 1938), pp. 342–43.
†Ibid., p. 344.

By asking these derisive questions, Vyshinsky counted on a cheap effect, their ability to influence the assumptions of the uninformed: There, you see? It's clear he's a spy; he flitted this way and that.

Striving only to debase Bukharin even more and paralyze his will, Vyshinksy was not restrained by the fact that, from the standpoint of elementary logic, such questions cannot withstand scrutiny. If Nikolai Ivanovich had wanted to overthrow Soviet power in order to restore capitalism, why would he have needed to contact the Austrian police to help in the fight against tsarist Russia? . . . or enlist the aid of the American and Japanese police in February 1917 in a struggle against the provisional Russian government of Aleksandr Kerensky? In both instances, Russia was already capitalist without any help from Bukharin.

In the trial reportage, a reference by Bukharin to supposedly counterrevolutionary talks with the Menshevik émigré Boris Nicolaevsky in Paris, in 1936, chagrined me. In fact, Nikolai Ivanovich, who was in the French capital on a government assignment, met with Nicolaevsky at the Politburo's specific request. I was present and can attest that the conversation was confined entirely to official business, as I will explain in detail later.

Some pages back, I wrote how I could imagine the trial only from the perspective of the Tomsk camp, how my nerves were then strained to the utmost, and how difficult it was to catch everything by ear, in part because my reason was at times clouded, because I did not yet know of Bukharin's concluding statement, and because I purposely began to deaden myself to the endless stream of information about the "crimes" of Nikolai Ivanovich and his codefendants, "crimes" having nothing to do with their actual political activities. The whole thing was like a cheap thriller.

The death sentence itself was anticlimactic. I had already made up my mind that, as far as I was concerned, Nikolai Ivanovich had been shot on the day of his arrest. Indeed, he had himself prepared me for this when he was being investigated. When the *starosta* read out the verdict, the anxiety of waiting vanished and, terrible as it may seem to others, my awareness that his sufferings had finally come to an end brought a certain relief, even as I simultaneously fell into a state of depression. Everything around me grew dim and became one huge and spiritless zone of gray. It was scarcely credible that life, human happiness, and mundane joys existed anywhere on earth. And that, somehow, we wives too lived and breathed here, crowded together in dark masses behind this fence with watchtowers, and our multitude of feet tramped down the short, solitary walkway, our "Nevsky Prospekt."

[A Nightmare]

The trial ended on March 13, 1938. Afterward, I did little but lie on the bed boards, shocked by the horrifying travesty of justice and more than usually debilitated by malnutrition, since I had stopped taking even a piece of bread into my mouth. When I recovered a bit, I began to go outside the confines of the barracks into the compound. At the Tomsk camp, I was the only woman whose husband had gone through an open trial. Aside from me, only one other, Yakir's wife, was also fully aware of her husband's tragic fate. The overwhelming majority of the women knew nothing about their husbands and continued to hope that they were still alive.

Therefore, in those days, I was a person of special interest to the women around me. They reacted toward me in a variety of ways, depending upon their political development, their intellectual level, their attitude toward my husband before his trial, or their knowledge of him and his codefendants. On the one hand, then, I felt the hateful gaze of those who accepted the confessions of the accused at face value, and, unfortunately, they were not few in number. Yet I also saw the pained eyes of those who understood everything, along with the suffering of many who had known Bukharin—and, indeed, not him alone.

The wife of a Ukrainian Party worker came up to me. "Why are you moping? History will vindicate Bukharin, but no one will ever know about our husbands."

Just two days before my rearrest in camp, I had a terrifying dream. As a boa constrictor wrapped itself around my neck and strangled me, I could see in his maw the head of my little son just about to be swallowed out of sight. I woke up because Sayechka Yakir was poking me in the side, if not because I heard my own scream.

"Wake up! What's wrong with you?" I heard Sayechka saying. I told her my dream. "The horror in the world of awakeness," she said, "is already like a terrible dream. Yet you have such nightmares besides. I see that something new is going to happen, but what more *could* happen? It seems that everything has already happened."

The next morning, I managed to tell my nightmare to Viktoriya, too. And then, in the afternoon, the supervisor came and took me and Sayechka to the cooler for a search. This time, he decided to confiscate the photograph of my son, which had not been confiscated the first time I was searched here.

"Who's this?" he asked spitefully, as if discovering still another "conspirator." The little eyes of my eleven-month-old baby, Yura, shined from the photo, which I had snapped after his father's arrest in hopes of sending it to Nikolai Ivanovich in prison.

"My child," I said with foreboding.

"You bitch!" he yelled, "still dragging a Bukharinist pup around with you!"

Before my very eyes, he snatched the photograph of my son, the last remaining joy in my life, and spit on it and stamped on it with his filthy boots.

"What are you doing!" Sayechka screamed in indignation.

"Shut up, you Yakirian swine, you defender!"

I was so shaken I could not say a word.

After the search, they left us in the cooler for the rest of the day and night, then sent us back to barracks.

"There's your boa constrictor," said Sarra Lazarevna. "There, right in front of your face, is your dream."

We were back no more than an hour before the supervisor reappeared.

"Bukharina, collect your things and get ready!"

"To go where?" I asked.

"Where? Where? When you get there, you'll find out where!"

Instantly, the news that I was being taken away spread throughout the entire camp, and many of the women came out into the compound to see me off. I saw a saddened Lyudmila Kuzminichna Shaposhnikova standing at a distance, the huge Dina, and Viktoriya. My Sayechka walked with me to the very gates leading out of our compound and into the prison, sobbing. She kissed me, I was led away, and the gates closed.

So it was I took my leave of the Tomsk camp for wives of "traitors to the motherland."

[The Fate of Her Child and Memories of a Happier Siberian Journey]

In May, I was taken to the investigative prison in Novosibirsk, traveling by rail third-class with a plainclothes escort. At the time, the Third Investigative Department of the NKVD Siblag [the Siberian camps] was located there. Its mandate was to investigate cases that were still open or had recently arisen in the camps. The results for prisoners, as a rule, were not happy: either extension of one's term or execution.

I had been held for a long time in the Tomsk prison before boarding the train and being warned that mixing with passengers was forbidden. This prohibition did not bother me. Indeed, I felt no desire to converse with anyone in the coach, for a great divide lay between us, that gulf that always separates the world behind bars from the world outside. Such, at least, was my impression.

None of the passengers understood my situation; they were all busy chatting and paid me no mind, except for one old longbeard. He persistently stared my way, at my pale wasted face, at the out-of-season fur coat lying beside me (which had nearly been burned up in the disinfecting rooms of the transit prisons), and at my leather suitcase, quite stylish for those times, which Nikolai Ivanovich had brought back from London in 1931 after an international congress on science and art.

No doubt, the old fellow was perplexed by my silence. Throughout the long trip, I did not exchange a single word with my traveling companion (the guard). Oddly enough, the latter had a refined, even intellectual appearance; he could easily be taken for my friend, or my relative, or my husband, though he remained completely indifferent to my presence and also said nothing. The old man kept on staring, never taking his eyes off me, which eventually began to get on my nerves. Yet, since I could not escape his persistent gaze, I involuntarily glanced back. Choosing a convenient moment, when my escort went off briefly, he hastened to ask me where I was going. I knew my answer would confirm his suspicions and replied quite unambiguously, "I go wherever they take me." Back at the Tomsk prison, when I had asked where I was being transported, the officer registering my passport had answered, "You'll wind up wherever they take you!" This tactic of concealing more than even the investigative process required was purposely used by the camp and prison administration to insult the human dignity of prisoners.

Convinced that I was a prisoner, the old man proffered me a piece of white bread, cheese, and some eggs. Because of extreme nervous excitement, I was not feeling at all hungry. The food not seen for so long gave me only aesthetic pleasure. How blindingly white that bread seemed, as if I had never seen its like; through the smooth, clean little shell of the egg, I could see its contents, the golden yolk hidden in a thick mass of egg white; the porous Swiss cheese, as creamy white as a tea-room rose, shedding tears, begged to be taken into my mouth. But I declined. I looked at this food with complete indifference, as at a masterfully painted still life.

If the old man knew who I was, I thought, he might not offer me a single piece of bread. Or, on the contrary, he might share with me his last morsel. Who can tell? All sorts of unexpected things have happened in my life!

Later, my strange traveling companion, not actually a convoy guard but an NKVD Siblag official assigned specially to me for this trip, also decided to feed me. Without a word, he placed on a crumpled newspaper—better to say, tossed, as if to a dog—a ration of bread, some salted fish, and even a piece of cucumber, which was never part of prison fare. This food sat next to me on the seat. It, too, I did not touch.

Two months had passed since Bukharin was shot. I didn't expect anything good for myself, either. At first, it had seemed improbable enough that I could survive eight years in a camp, but now I knew that a more severe sentence was imminent. Occasionally, I was overcome by the desire to leave this life. It seemed the best way out of the hopeless situation in which I found myself. I could not shake the feeling that the dreadful turn of events was sucking me deeper and deeper into its bloody funnel. Yet, at the same time, I had a strong incentive to prevail: I was duty bound to fulfill my husband's last testament, to convey his letter-address, carefully preserved in my memory, "To a Future Generation of Party Leaders." When I considered that the likelihood of realizing his last desire was very slim, though, I could be thrown into despair.

I had come to love going to sleep so as not to feel anything. Consequently, when I awoke, the catastrophe would rush back in on me all the more forcefully.

I was further disheartened by what I had learned about my mother from Nataliya Grigoriyevna, Georgy Lomov's wife, who had been brought to the Tomsk camp after me. Before my exile to Astrakhan a year earlier, I had left Yura with his grandmother, who was already over fifty years old and was sickly, suffering from a severe form of pulmonary tuberculosis. Now it turned out that she had been arrested just months earlier, in January, and my baby, then twenty months old, had been put in a children's home. Like many people persecuted in Stalin's time, my mother had participated in the revolutionary movement as early as 1907. Before the revolution, she had been arrested more than once and had been locked up in Butyrka prison in 1911. Now, in 1938, she found herself there again. (She would survive almost two decades of incarceration but remain so physically broken after her release and rehabilitation that her life became one long ordeal of pain. Chained to her bed, she endured her torments heroically for the eighteen years until her end, in 1973.) My friend Nataliya Grigoriyevna had received this depressing news from my husband's father, Ivan Gavrilovich, whom she'd run into by accident. He told her that he'd located Yura only with difficulty and had not been able, despite repeated requests and a letter to Stalin, to have his grandson turned over to him. Ultimately, the authorities did give Yura to him, but only after my son had fallen seriously ill and was apparently beyond hope. As for Ivan Gavrilovich, he was old and weak and had taken the execution of his son badly. I knew that he was in no condition to look after the boy, nor could he materially support his grandson, since his pension had been taken away immediately upon Nikolai Ivanovich's arrest. Whether Ivan Gavrilovich was still alive now and where my son was, I did not know.

Only one thought brought me emotional relief. I was happy that my father had died at the right time—early, indeed, at age forty-nine, but not killed by one of Stalin's bullets, as was Nikolai Ivanovich at exactly the same age.

Never before could I have imagined that the moment would come when I would look on the early death of my beloved father as a blessing, or that I would think, This is the single piece of good fortune in my life. Thus do the grimaces of history change our view of the world.

In the coach to Novosibirsk, there were many children; from all sides one heard the cries of "Mama" and "Papa." These voices stirred within me the maternal instincts I was trying in every way to suppress. I recalled that my own child had parted from his father when he was ten and a half months old. The month before, he had consciously (and very early) called Nikolai Ivanovich "Papa." That was his first word: "Papa."

"He's had to hurry," my husband had remarked. "Soon, he won't have anyone to call Papa."

After Bukharin's arrest, the little tyke crawled around searching for his father, looking under his writing desk, under the cabinet, and calling, "Papa, Papa."

"We are no longer in life, neither I nor my son," I kept telling myself. "We died along with Nikolai Ivanovich." Though I could still feel the beating of my heart, only a mysterious shadow of me remained, reminding me of the past and also, alas, giving me the ability to keep thinking. But my thoughts were terrible. "I think, therefore I am," Descartes said, proposing that thinking is the essential feature of human life. But for me the distinction between "life" and "existence" had lost all meaning. I thought but did not live. I only led a miserable existence.

In the morning, the train arrived in Novosibirsk.

"Prepare to get off," my escort ordered brusquely. I tossed on my rumpled fur coat; he, uncharacteristically, took my suitcase. We got out on the platform and walked through a little station. The air was warm, but a spring rain poured down. Thunder clapped powerfully, and zigzag flashes of lightning cut through the low clouds. As always, the phenomena of nature lifted my spirits and inspired impossible dreams: "Nikolai

Ivanovich is still alive; he wasn't shot, after all!" The thought flashed through my mind with the speed of lightning and just as swiftly died.

We walked over to a rather small, dirty-olive car with a tarpaulin top. "You know where to go?" my escort asked the driver. "I know, I know." "Then take her yourself. I'm busy." The driver got out of the car, and only then could I get a good look at his face. I was shocked: this man had worked as chauffeur for Robert Eikhe, once secretary of the West Siberian District Party Committee and a candidate member of the Politburo. I knew, because Eikhe used to send his car around to pick up Nikolai Ivanovich.

Because this unexpected, unpleasant encounter with a chauffeur of previous acquaintance crossed my trying path, I shall digress somewhat from the main subject of my narrative and tell about a previous trip to Siberia, a voluntary one—the happy trip Nikolai Ivanovich and I took for his vacation in August 1935.

Our month-long Siberian trek had two aims. First, my dissertation for the Economic Planning Institute, "The Technical and Economic Basis of the Kuznetsk Metallurgical Combine," had to do with the region. Nikolai Ivanovich wanted to introduce me to our country's foremost metallurgist, Academician Ivan Bardin, who had supervised the construction of the Kuznetsk Metallurgical Combine and now served as its technical director. When we visited, Bardin acquainted us with the huge combine and provided extensive material for my work. Then we traveled to Leninsk and Prokopiyevsk, the chief mining towns in the Kuznetsk coal basin of Kuzbass. My husband went down in the mines with me and talked with the workers, who greeted him with applause.

Second, we wanted to see the Altai region, having heard much about its great beauty. Indeed, this picturesque landscape lives in my memory today. The unharnessed Katun River hurled its emerald waters headlong against the barriers of moss-covered rocks piled up in the river Biya, there to merge with it and form the mighty Ob. The precipitous cliffs bordering the banks of the Katun stood like trusty watchmen, directing its flow down the course conceived by nature. The snow-capped peak of two-headed Belukha Mountain glinted in the sun, while alongside, velvet in the distance, dark green mountains covered with cedars formed a striking contrast with Belukha's glacial, humpbacked whiteness.

I do not know about the present, but back then there was no paved road to Teletskoye Lake. Somehow, we made our way within hiking distance in our car. As we passed remote villages, packs of little children, hearing our engine, would race out into the road. There were blond Russians with flaxen little heads and Altaians with jet black hair, like little jackdaws, all shouting, "Give me a ride, give me a ride, uncle!"

Nikolai Ivanovich would always ask the driver to stop. We would get out, and the kids, hollering and screaming, shoving each other aside to find room, would scramble in and take our places. After letting them have their fun, we would get back in and continue on to the next village, where the same thing would happen all over again. It was nightfall before we finally reached the last settlement, where we had to spend the night on the floor, on the filthy rags provided by our hosts. The bedbug attacks made it impossible to sleep.

Early the next morning, we resumed our journey on the backs of sturdy little mountain horses. As these agile creatures scuttled up and down the perpendicular cliffs, we could barely hold on to our saddles.

The rays of the setting sun painted huge Teletskoye Lake golden and lilac. Its steep forest banks were riddled with a multitude of gorges with plummeting waterfalls that formed little rivulets winding into the lake. Here we remained about a week, sheltered by some Leningrad ornithologists on a scientific expedition. They offered us one of their two rooms, and our party—I, Nikolai Ivanovich, and the two bodyguards assigned to him—made sleeping places on the floor by spreading out bearskins.

Once, when Nikolai Ivanovich was discussing ornithological matters with the scientists, surprising them with his knowledge, the door suddenly opened and in walked an aged Altaian wearing a patched padded jacket and ragged footwear, holding a small sack in one hand. He looked us all over carefully, trying to determine which was Bukharin.

"What can we do for you?" one of the ornithologists asked.

Turning to the one who wore a black felt hat with a broad brim, the Altaian replied in faltering Russian, "Me come yours to see." The old man had taken the scientist for Bukharin, assuming that a famed leader would definitely be wearing a hat. "Yes, yours to see," the Altaian repeated, looking at the ornithologist. "I heard she came and in this hut lives."

He used only the feminine gender and could not decline nouns or conjugate verbs.

"Well, if it's 'yours' you want to see, I am not 'she,'" said the ornithologist with a laugh. "Why don't you guess who 'she' is?"

"Not she?" smiled the Altaian, completely disconcerted because no one else was wearing a hat. He thought a moment, considered the other ornithologist, who was smoking a pipe off to the side, and pointed to him.

"Again not 'she,'" laughed the one with the hat. Including the bodyguards, there were only three men left. The ornithologist decided to help.

"Look at that one over there!" He nodded toward Bukharin.

"That's she?" the old fellow marveled. "Your truth are telling?"

Nikolai Ivanovich, short in stature, wearing boots, a sports shirt, and a little cap that was by no means a hat, failed to meet the Altaian's expectations.

"Bukharin is big, beautiful . . . but what's this?"

This set off a deafening roar. The bodyguards laughed longest of all. At last, Nikolai Ivanovich spoke up.

"Why did you come to see me? I'm not a bride, and, as you see, I'm not big and beautiful. Complete disenchantment!"

What "disenchantment" meant, the Altaian had no idea, but he understood everything about the "bride."

"Me not need a bride, me have a woman. She baked you a cake."

And he held out for Nikolai Ivanovich his little sack, which was filled with flat cakes. They were baked from first-class wheat flour and were, I must say, done superbly. Nikolai Ivanovich began to share them with us, but the Altaian took offense.

"My woman only for you guest baked. Little flour."

"But to what do I owe such an honor?" Bukharin asked.

"What? Me not understand."

"Why, I ask, did your woman bake flat cakes only for me?"

"Me said: bake cakes for guest Bukharin because she loves persons."

"The people," one of the ornithologists suggested.

"Loves the people, the people, yes, yes, yes," repeated the Altaian.

"Well, tell me," said Bukharin, "how are you getting along now on the collective farm?"

The old man hesitated. "I would tell you, but persons here many."

"Tell me, tell me. Don't be afraid."

"Me already said everything, so understand, listen how we live! I say, persons many, no way to talk."

The Altaian made for the exit. We all accompanied him down to the shore of the lake, where he had tied up his homemade boat, a thick, sawed-off tree trunk with a hollowed-out seat. He bid farewell to Bukharin (and to no one else)—"Be healthy, my dear!"—and paddled away.

Evening was approaching, the gentle splashes from his paddle could be heard clearly in the silence, and his departing silhouette could be seen for some time.

Nikolai Ivanovich spent his vacation, as usual, immersed in nature, asserting his love of life to the full. He swam in cold mountain streams with floating chunks of ice and hunted for wild duck from rafts bobbing down the rapids of the Katun, which was certainly not without risk. A good shot, he jumped for joy as the ducks fell one by one on the raft. When we took a car up the Chuisky road to the Mongolian border, he hunted roe deer. We stayed with the border patrol, who were skillful in smoking meat. In the evening, after a successful hunt, all of us—the two bodyguards, the border patrol, my husband and I—had our supper by the campfire.

Nikolai Ivanovich also spent a lot of time painting in Altai. Of the canvases he brought back to Moscow, I particularly liked three, and therefore remember them quite well: *Waterfall in the Mountain Gorge, Teletskoye Lake,* and *Katun River.* All were exhibited at the Tretyakovsky Gallery from the end of 1935 through the first months of 1936. When we visited the show, the artist Konstantin Yuon was standing in front of Bukharin's works. He liked them so much that he told Nikolai Ivanovich, "Give up politics. Politics promises nothing good in the future. Take up painting. Landscapes, that's your calling!" The advice came too late.

In the Siberian resort town of Chemal, we checked into an exclusive government rest home but traveled around more than we rested. Toward the end of our vacation, however, an "exceptional circumstance" forced Nikolai Ivanovich to remain in town. The watchman for the Chemal chicken coop gave him a magnificent gift, a huge horned owl. Chickens had been disappearing from the coop, so one night the watchman kept a vigil and nabbed this thief. The owl's unusually large size, beautiful plumage, big brick-colored eyes, and remarkably powerful clucking won my husband's heart. He decided to take the owl back to Moscow no matter what. He himself built an enclosure for it, learned to cluck, and teased the bird by imitating its calls. This duet drove the owl into a fury, making it cluck all the more loudly, and Nikolai Ivanovich laughed uproariously. The watchman wove a big basket out of branches for the bird, and we carried it in our compartment on the international train. In Moscow, the owl did not stay with us long. We had no place to keep it and no time to care for it. Eventually, Nikolai Ivanovich gave it to Anastas Mikoyan's children, but he thought of it frequently afterward.

In Novosibirsk, both before our trip to Kuzbass and Altai and upon our return, we stayed several days with Robert Indrikovich Eikhe in his apartment and also at his dacha outside town. Fate had driven this famous revolutionary to Siberia back in the 1920s. Even now, I can clearly see this lanky, haggard Latvian, looking like Don Quixote. At times, his permanently exhausted and severe-looking face would break out in a surprisingly pleasant, kindhearted smile. How wrapped up he was in the building then going on in Siberia, and how popular and beloved he was! I want to share just one episode that occurred toward the end of Robert Indrikovich's life.

Imprisoned, he wrote Stalin a remarkable letter. It was found in the tyrant's archives after his death and quoted by Khrushchev in his famous confidential report to the Twentieth Party Congress. In this letter, Eikhe pleaded innocence of the charges brought against him and explained that he had confessed only because of the horrible tortures inflicted upon him. His interrogators had beaten him on the spine, where it was excruciatingly painful. I particularly recall that Eikhe reminded Stalin, hoping to prove his innocence, that he had never belonged to any opposition. Even on the threshold of his death, Eikhe did not understand that he was appealing to his murderer, or that actual involvement with any opposition was not necessary as proof of one's criminal activities.

Alas, Eikhe was not alone in his delusions. So many other people also believed in Stalin and also thought that their lack of membership in an opposition group would vindicate them in the eyes of the executioner.

But when we were in Novosibirsk, Eikhe was not at all terrified by Nikolai Ivanovich, who really had been in the opposition more than once. Our host traveled around the city with us, pointing out the new construction on the central street, Krasny Prospekt, with its modern, multistory buildings. We clambered with him up to the flat roof of the unfinished Theater of Opera and Ballet, which gave a panoramic view of the whole town. Later, when Eikhe offered us a parlor car, Nikolai Ivanovich steadfastly resisted; he had not used a private coach even when he was a member of the Politburo, considering it an extravagant luxury. Robert Indrikovich eventually convinced him, however, that we would not cramp anybody by traveling in a private coach. In Kuzbass, because it was so hard to get apartments then, we would actually live in the coach, parked in the station on a dead-end track.

The two bodyguards I mentioned earlier and their police dog had set out with us in the coach from Novosibirsk. Despite every effort during our vacation trip, Nikolai Ivanovich could not get free of them. He had not had a personal guard in Moscow for some years. Previously, his only bodyguard had been Rogov, assigned in 1919 after a Left Socialist Revolutionary bomb went off in the Moscow Party Committee

building on Leontiev Lane just as Bukharin was supposed to be giving a
report. Ten years later, in 1929, Nikolai Ivanovich was removed from
the Politburo and Rogov was relieved of duty.

Eikhe had explained that the bodyguards were necessary to restrain
Nikolai Ivanovich's enthusiasm out in the provinces. "You can't play
around with Altaic nature," he warned. "You'll never make it out of the
taiga. I chose these men specially; they know the territory and will be
good guides for you." Robert Indrikovich was acting out of good motives, knowing Bukharin's rash character and literally fearing for his life.
Even so, Nikolai Ivanovich did not discount the possibility that the
guards had been assigned in order to keep tabs on his contacts with the
people. It was Stalin's suspicious nature that forced Bukharin to think
this way. For example, I know that the young secretary for the Altai
Territory Party Committee, who came to see my husband a few times,
was later arrested. And I assume that our trip to Siberia and our stay in
Novosibirsk were used against Robert Indrikovich.

His chauffeur, whose chance appearance sparked all of these memories, had been quite at ease in the Eikhe household. He always sat with
us at the dinner table, took part in the conversation, enjoyed the hospitality of our host's wife (who later shared her husband's fate, a bullet in
the head), went out hunting with Nikolai Ivanovich, and met us whenever we came to town. My later encounter with precisely this chauffeur
compels me to believe that he must have been "working two jobs" while
he was taking care of Eikhe's automobile.

During our Siberian vacation, we were exactly one year away from
investigation. Later, when acquainting myself with the accusations
against Nikolai Ivanovich, I was astonished to read that this trip had
been taken for the purpose of fomenting peasant revolts and effecting
the separation of Siberia from the Soviet Union.

How pleasant it had been in my happy past to dip into my memories of our trip, but how awful it was to come again to Novosibirsk,
under guard, knowing that my husband was no more! Our trip together
had been joyful and happy, but my recent Siberian tribulations had been
horrible: how much water had flowed under the bridge in such a short
time! Nature alone had not changed. Somewhere, not so far away by
Siberian standards, the emerald waters of the Katun still flowed, proud
Belukha glistened in the sun, and at sunset Teletskoye sparkled golden
and lilac in silence. Drinking it in, Nikolai Ivanovich had exclaimed,
"It's a fantasy, a fable! Not nature!" And somewhere even farther away,
in a remote Altaic settlement, there still lived that collective farmer who
had come to "look at" Bukharin and had said in parting, "Be healthy,
my dear!"

But perhaps I am painting too rosy a portrait of the life of this Altaic farmer. It is not likely he was allowed to continue living in his settlement. More probably, he had occasion to be ruefully reminded of the day when he came "yours to see" and with an open heart treated Nikolai Ivanovich to flat cakes. And also, I wonder, did a similar fate befall the two ornithologists with whom we stayed on the shores of Teletskoye?

As for our two bodyguards, I do not know whether or not they were assigned as informers, but they certainly became personally attached to Nikolai Ivanovich during the month we spent together. Still, the service comes first! Yet one of them, during my most difficult days, would perform a very daring and noble deed, understandable only if his attitude toward my husband had not been changed by the trial. But more about that later.

Now I come back to the painful circumstances of my return to Novosibirsk.

[The Underground Cell]

May 1938.

Across from the Novosibirsk train station, Eikhe's former chauffeur and I stood by the car, looking each other straight in the eye. My face surely revealed my alarm and complete bewilderment; his showed cocky self-assurance. But I might have been mistaken about that. The downpour lashed us so furiously in the face that it was difficult to make out his expression clearly. Not speaking, he opened the front door of the car and gestured for me to sit next to him. We drove off down the road toward the most terrible "living quarters" of my life. After a short distance, he apparently decided he should say at least something, since we were, after all, old acquaintances. The best he could do was this:

"Did you get the owl to Moscow safely?"

Amazed as I was by such a question under our unusual circumstances, I had the presence of mind to reply, "We got the owl there, all right, but when we did, they arrested it."

He did not even smile. Since he had broken the ice, I decided to ask him a question: "Well, how is Robert Indrikovich? Is he still thriving, or is he no more?"

The driver kept his silence. At the time, I knew nothing of Eikhe's fate, but women who had been sent to the Tomsk camp from Novosibirsk said that harrowing interrogations had been conducted there to obtain testimony against him. Later, I would learn that Eikhe had been transferred from Novosibirsk to Moscow the year before and appointed people's commissar of agriculture following Yakov Yakovlev and Mikhail Chernov, who had each been arrested in turn. In other words, he was no longer in Novosibirsk. At the time, a transfer from one position to another served as prelude to arrest. So it would be with Robert Indrikovich.

Just as the thunderstorm ended and the sky cleared, we stopped at the building that housed the Investigative Department of the NKVD Siblag. The isolation prison for people under investigation was located in an underground chamber in a rather small courtyard. The chamber's flat roof, covered over with turf, rose only ten to fifteen centimeters above the ground. An elderly guard led me down an asphalt path to the base of this hillock and then down into the underground chamber. Rainwater had leaked into its corridor and pooled in the cells. The guard wore rubber boots; I, suede slippers. My feet were soaked.

There were six cells in the little chamber, three on each side of the corridor. All of the doors stood wide open. My cell, designed to hold four people, contained two sets of double bunks made of wood, with a little walkway between the planks. Yet I would be locked in alone. A tiny grated window, little more than a glass slit just under the ceiling, admitted no daylight. A dim electric lightbulb would burn around the clock. When we had first come below ground, I saw a rat running through the space between the window's double panes of glass, another one scampering over the planks of one of the lower bunks. Hearing our steps, it leapt down to the floor, then back up onto the planks, disappeared, then reappeared. I stood before the open cell door, hesitating to enter this pit. Even the jailer, it seemed, was taken aback by the necessity of throwing me into it. He brought me a pail and a rusty tin can and said, "Bail the water out, else ye can't get in."

I took off my soaked slippers, put them on an upper bunk, and set to work, standing ankle-deep in the water. Filling pail after pail and mounting the stairs again and again, I poured out the water in the prison courtyard until only little puddles remained in the indentations of the stone floor. From my things, I retrieved only a warm scarf; the guard carried my suitcase to the storeroom. This fine leather suitcase, the one Nikolai Ivanovich had brought back from London, remains in my possession today, faded and scratched all over, with the stains of crushed bedbugs inside, as a memento of what I have endured. It is, along with some of his paintings, Bukharin's sole surviving property.

Having bailed out the water, I entered the cell. The guard locked the door, the bolt clanked, the lock clicked, the keys jangled. For a moment I stood in a daze, unable to move, but quickly regained my senses. I had learned, by this time, not to be surprised by anything. Surveying the surroundings, I decided to make my home on the upper-left bed boards; higher up, it is always drier. Although a thick layer of green mold covered every wall, the cell was an end one, so the left wall, which adjoined the next cell, was not so wet as the right, which came up against the earth. Also, water continued to seep from pits and crannies on the right wall, formed little streams, ran down the side, and dripped onto the floor. At constant, unvarying intervals I heard: drip . . . drip . . . drip. There were no mattresses on the bed boards, not even poor ones stuffed with straw. I laid out my fur coat, folding it over so that half served as bedding, half as blanket. The scarf I rolled up and put under my head. All the comforts of home. The window slit, too, was on the left side. Through it, I could glimpse the bright green grass of spring growing on an untrampled patch of prison courtyard. When other prisoners were taken out for a walk, I could see just ankles and feet. Pulling myself up onto the bunk, I went to sleep. But the guard, observing through a peephole in the door, woke me immediately and warned that sleeping during the day was not permitted. Half-awake, I barked something back and instantly dropped off again. From then on, the guard left me alone.

I woke up covered with fleabites. My body itched all over. I had to get up, climb down, take off all my clothes, and shake the fleas out of them. The clothes themselves had managed to get damp and could be dried only with the heat of my own body.

I was called out for an interrogation that very first evening. The questioner was Chief Skvirsky himself, the head of the entire Third Department. In a rather small office, I saw a man about forty-five to forty-seven years old with the look of a wild beast that had just caught a long-awaited prey. I was never told his first name and do not remember his exact rank, but rumors circulated that he had been demoted from being a director of the NKVD in Odessa and sent to Novosibirsk. Perhaps in order to prevent further descent down the ladder, he exhibited exceptional ferocity. He reported that he was interrogating me on direct orders from Moscow. This assignment from high up obviously flattered him, as his self-satisfied, obnoxious expression revealed clearly.

"The investigation knows for a fact," he announced, "that Bukharin was connected, through you, with a counterrevolutionary youth organization. You were a member of this organization, the liaison between Bukharin and the organization. Name your fellow members. Until you do, you will sit and rot in the cellar."

I denied, first of all, that Bukharin could have any connection at all with a counterrevolutionary youth organization, even if one had existed, because he was a revolutionary, not a counterrevolutionary, and for the same reason I could not be a liaison between any such organization and him.

"Insolent bitch! Counterrevolutionary swine!" Skvirsky yelled. "Even now, after the trial, you dare state that Bukharin was not a counterrevolutionary?"

"Yes, I dare state it, but I consider it pointless to talk to you about it."

"Will you also say that you had no relationship with Bukharin at all?"

"No, I will not say that. I was his wife."

"His wife? We know for a fact that your marriage was a fiction to cover Bukharin's counterrevolutionary ties with young people."

I had thought I was ready for any accusation Skvirsky might make—wrecking, terrorism, or something of that sort—but I could never have imagined he would declare our marriage a counterrevolutionary sham. This absurd charge deeply unsettled me. I naively attempted to refute it by pointing out that we had a child.

"It has yet to be proved, yet to be demonstrated, by whom you had this child!"

This interrogator's ridiculous, senseless slander was more insulting than his vulgar abuse, but, since I now understood that I was dealing not only with a lowlife but also with a mentally limited clod, I became indifferent to his stupid, loudmouthed accusations.

"Such insolence!" Skvirsky bellowed. "She dares state that Bukharin was not a counterrevolutionary! There is no place for you on Soviet soil! Shoot her! Shoot her! Shoot her!"

I felt the hopelessness of my situation, but this made me bolder, more decisive. I was able to shout contemptuously at the top of my voice, "It's you who have no place on Soviet soil, not me! It's you who should sit behind bars, not me! Shoot me right now! I don't want to live!"

I expected this monster to beat me up at any moment or do who knows what to me, but nothing of the sort happened. In fact, surprised by my response, the chief only peered at me with his evil, hawklike eyes. I was satisfied. We had fought to a standoff. The interrogator fell silent, and I believe I detected a glimmer of respect for me. He lifted the telephone receiver and said indifferently, "Take away the prisoner."

Before the convoy guard appeared, Skvirsky had time to remind me, "Keep silent, and you'll rot in that cell!"

But I had time to retort, "I don't care."

It was now late at night. As it drizzled outside my cell, little streams of water again slowly wormed across the floor, and I realized that bailing water out of this place was the labor of Sisyphus.

Because of the interrogation, I had neither the strength nor the desire to pull myself up to the upper bunk, and I lay down on the lower one, directly on the bare boards. Yet it felt as if I were lying on a fluffy feather bed, simply because I could not see Skvirsky's raptor-like face in front of me and because I had walked out with dignity.

Happiness, I thought, is a remarkably relative concept. Even in great unhappiness there are flashes of happiness; life had more and more convinced me of that. At this moment, lying in the cell of my imaginary feather bed, satisfied with my conduct at the interrogation, with my emotional outburst and my revolt in defense of human dignity, I was happy.

The silence of this cell, broken only by the sound of water dripping regularly from the wall onto the floor and by the occasional swish of the guard's peephole, cast me suddenly into a state of unworldly, fabulous bliss. Like Alice in Wonderland, I kept falling and falling down a deep well, but unlike her I knew my longitude and latitude, and I knew that I was not in Australia and not in New Zealand but in a country with the name Soviet Union, in the country of "the dictatorship of the proletariat"—meaning, in those days, the country of the absolute Stalinist monarchy. Also unlike Alice, I did not have to be told that saying what you think and thinking what you say are not the same thing. Indeed, our whole nation had wonderfully mastered this lesson: to say what you thought was dangerous (even though it did not always turn out that way for me). In short, I was not exactly the Alice of Lewis Carroll's imagination.

I lay immobile on the planks and repeated Aleksandr Blok's poem "On Trial," under my breath. Several of its lines had become precious to me, because I related them to my own situation, and I often recalled them in my cell:

> *But what can we do when deceived*
> *By that fine dream, as by all other dreams,*
> *When life lashes us without mercy*
> *With the cruel braid of the whip?*

> *Life, so brief, spares us little time*
> *So the dream was right to tell us lies—*
> *After all, were there not the moments*
> *When you found your happiness with me?*

Alone with my thoughts, I tried to decide this question for myself: Was the dream that lied to Nikolai Ivanovich and me right or wrong? Neither he nor, even more so, I had foreseen such a terrible end. Consequently, the dream had indeed lied to us. And yet, of course, I decided that "the dream was right to tell us lies." Though for only a short time, we had lived happily together.

But by August of 1936, immediately after the trial of Zinoviev and Kamenev, Nikolai Ivanovich was suffering torments for what he called my ruined life and for the grim future of our newborn son. I was able to console him only with the assurance that it was immeasurably easier for me in those trying days to be next to him, and that I did not regret, never would regret, having linked my life with his. Even now, many years after his death, I affirm that still. Yet, quite possibly, my assurances then may have troubled his soul all the more, though he smiled in response, looking at me through tears.

I do not know where I would have wandered in my memories if a rat had not suddenly jumped on my leg. I shuddered and jerked my leg back; the rat flipped onto the floor and instantly vanished. Since Nikolai Ivanovich had taught me to like animals, I cannot say that I desperately feared the creature, but its abrupt leap onto my leg had caused a momentary fright and revulsion. It was not long, however, before I overcame squeamishness, and the rat began to brighten my solitude. Every day, to the surprise of the prison guard, I would feed it some bread. My daily bread ration, doled out each morning, was five hundred grams. Usually, a little extra slab of bread was stuck on with a wooden pin to make up the exact weight. Without fail, this slab went to the rat. The rest I consumed at once. It was more filling this way, and, besides, there was no place to keep any leftovers. As soon as the rat sniffed the aroma of bread, it ran right out of its corner, stood up on its hind legs, and begged for its share. I recognized it as the same rat every time. The second one, which still ran occasionally between the double panes of my window, could not get into my cell.

Aside from the rat, the night of my interrogation was memorable because I suddenly heard an unexpected rapid tapping on the wall. This form of communication had not been used by inmates in either the Astrakhan prison or the transit prisons I had experienced. Desperately, I looked at the wall, trying to understand what was being communicated and how I might answer, straining to recall what I had been told about this kind of signaling. Finally, the forgotten information floated up to the surface of my mind.

Long, long before, some ten years before I found myself in this solitary cell, I had been taught the alphabet of prison-wall tapping by

Nikolai Morozov, a famous populist and member of the People's Will Party. Before the revolution, Morozov had spent a total of more than twenty years in the Schliesselburg and in the Peter and Paul Fortress; in the final months of his stay in the latter, my father was also imprisoned there. Both were set free by the revolution in the fall of 1905.

Afterward, the two men were united by their mutual interests in astronomy and ancient history. Morozov's multivolume work *Khristos* [Christ] was published sometime in the latter half of the 1920s. During this period, he visited my father, Larin, rather often. Unfortunately, I cannot relay the content of their discussions; I was not always present, and they were too complex for my youthful mind. I can remember only that Morozov once demonstrated that Italians and Jews have common origins, that in his view they were one and the same nation. Also, he tended to explain various linguistic formations in a way of his own that Larin always contested. As a scholar, Morozov did not work solely in the fields of astronomy and history but also in those of physics and chemistry. Many of his scientific works were written in prison.

Because he had survived twenty years of confinement and also kept himself morally and physically fit, Morozov was a legendary personage to me. When I looked at him, something extraordinarily bright seemed to shine from his charming countenance. He was over seventy then, but he was in no way a decrepit old man. Though deep wrinkles did indeed line his wise face and magnificent forehead, through his glasses peered kind, expressive, and youthful eyes quite out of keeping with his chronological age. I grew shy whenever I saw him—in fact, lost my composure in his presence—but my desire to know how he could have endured more than two decades in prison ultimately gained the upper hand, and I decided to broach the subject. In reply, he explained to me his sensation of time during confinement:

"In prison, time passes much more swiftly than on the outside, because the brain nourishes itself on extremely monotonous impressions. The borders of the passing years are smoothed down. Everything blends together."

He also told me about a period in which he was permitted to work, on either a vegetable or a flower garden; I do not recall which. Finally, he was able to pass his time in scientific studies, so the necessary conditions must have been created for these activities. In any event, Morozov had communicated with inmates in cells adjoining his by tapping on the walls. I was especially intrigued by this and asked him to explain how it was done. Taking a piece of paper from Larin's desk, he drew a graph of six lines across with six columns down. He wrote out our thirty-three-character alphabet in sequence in the spaces, working across each line:

six letters each across the first five lines, then only three letters left on the sixth line.

"First," Morozov explained, "you tap the number of the line. Then, after an interval, you tap the number of the letter on that line. Got it?"

"Got it," I replied.

"Let's try it," he said. Balling his hand into a fist, he tapped a single short word on the desk. At first, I could not catch it, because while I was trying to understand the first letter, Morozov was already tapping the second, then the third, and I lost track. Only on the third or fourth try did I cry out joyfully, "Khristos! Khristos!"

Beside us on the desk lay a recently issued volume of Morozov's massive study. Evidently, Christ figured so prominently in his thoughts that he used precisely this name to test my ability: Khristos.

Following the test, Morozov observed, "It's interesting, of course, to note how convicts of tsarist times communicated with other inmates, and not only those in nearby cells, for a chain of tapping could be set up. But, practically speaking, you will never have occasion to use it."

While I was remembering this scene, the wall was still trying to establish contact with me. Then it fell silent. It was my turn to take the initiative. To revive the prison alphabet in my memory, I first solved the task Morozov had once set me and tapped out the word "Khristos" on the planks with my fist. For practice, I tapped it out several times.

Later that night, when the guard had begun to doze in the corridor, I risked tapping to the next cell. So it was that the populist Morozov's prediction did not prove true: his lesson offered not only historical interest but also practical application for my future. Soon, I had discovered that the next cell held four prisoners: three biologists and an NKVD officer from Yagoda's time, who was the wall tapper. All four men had received ten years in the camps as a first sentence and then been rearrested for a new investigation. Though my correspondent refused to reveal his name and former position, he told me he had already received his second sentence: "the supreme penalty." He had appealed but had no hope of reversal, because he had held a senior post under Yagoda. I gave no personal details about myself, either. I simply tapped out that I was in prison under the *chesir* article and was also undergoing a new investigation.

"Did you hear about the last trial?" the NKVD official suddenly asked.

"Very slightly. I do not know the details," I tapped back.

"The bastards murdered Bukharin."

Everything went dim before my eyes, and I felt my heart pounding. "Right, a snitch-informer," I decided, for it seemed suspicious that he had mentioned only Bukharin. Why not Yagoda first? He should have been closer to him. Also, he did not mention even one of the others brought to trial. I asked him to tap out his final sentence once again.

"The bastards murdered Bukharin," I heard again, and my doubts faded away. Every single letter of his sentence, like a metal weight, banged into my brain. The word "murdered" instead of "executed," it seemed to me, especially emphasized the banditlike character of the judicial farce, depriving it of all political coloration. Although it would be best to cut off the conversation, since I still feared this might be provocation, the temptation was too great. I had a passionate desire to find out as much as I could.

"Who are these bastards who murdered Bukharin?" I decided to ask my neighbor. "Why do you feel sorry only for him and not the other condemned men—Rykov, Rakovsky, Krestinsky, and others? Why not even mention your chief, Yagoda?"

Instead of answering, my interlocutor, understanding now that I knew more about the trial than he had supposed, asked for the surname of my husband. I replied only that my husband had also been sentenced at the trial and shot. This communication opened up my correspondent, who tapped, "Don't take offense. I mentioned only Bukharin because I have loved him since my Komsomol years and believe this loss is irreparable."

Obviously, it had not occurred to my neighbor that I was Bukharin's wife. He had decided that I was offended because he had not mentioned the name of my husband.

He continued, "This certainly does not mean that I do not care about the destruction of the others. Yagoda's fate is tragic. He tried to hold back the terror but gave in under pressure from the main criminal. Bastards, every one of us: Yagoda, and I, and those who have replaced us. We became criminals because we did not murder the one who forced us and forces our successors to commit crimes. I have three days left to live, and I am not afraid to say that this main criminal is Stalin!"

There was nothing new here, yet the conversation left me with a gloomy impression. I was unable to sleep for the rest of the night. Clearly, I had been wrong to suspect my neighbor behind the wall of being a stoolie.

During the following days, I grew attached to this condemned man who knew the true story of the trials and loved Nikolai Ivanovich still. In the evenings, listening to his distinct tapping on the wall, I could not reconcile the firm, even tap of his hand with the death sentence. When I heard his last words—"Farewell, the sentence has been confirmed!"—I was deeply shaken.

I got actual chills and shudders, as with fever. "And the same thing will happen to me," I thought in those minutes.

As the NKVD man went out to meet a bullet, I thought of Genrikh Yagoda. Back in the Tomsk camp, Sofiya Yevseyevna Prokofieva, wife of Yagoda's former assistant Georgy Yevgenevich Prokofiev, had told me a grim story she heard from her husband. Stalin, angered because Yagoda had not obtained confessions to the murder of Kirov from Kamenev and Zinoviev in the 1935 trial, called him in and said, "You work poorly, Genrikh Grigoriyevich. I already know for a fact ['know for a fact,' the expression used so often by investigators, was also a favorite of Stalin's] that Kirov was murdered on instructions from Zinoviev and Kamenev, but so far you have not been able to prove it! You have to torture them until they finally tell the truth and reveal all of their connections." In relating this incident to Prokofiev, Yagoda broke down and sobbed.

In the same vein, Sofiya Yevseyevna told me that Yagoda had tried to oppose the persecution of former Mensheviks. I would later find some confirmation of this in the stenographic record of his trial. Chief Prosecutor Vyshinsky showed Yagoda a document taken from NKVD files and attached to the dossier compiled by Stalin's investigators. It included a note (to whom, is not indicated) about the existence of a Menshevik center based abroad and its supposedly active work in the USSR. Yagoda's reaction was written on the document: "This has not been a party for a long time, and it's not worth fussing over." At his trial, Yagoda "confessed" that he made this decision in order to "protect the Mensheviks from disaster, diverting the blow from them because they were in contact with the Rightists."*

This version undoubtedly sprang from the creative imagination of the investigators, so we must believe that Yagoda actually did put up some opposition, however ineffective, to the persecution of former Mensheviks.

Other incidents connected with Yagoda lived still in my memory. In the mid-1920s, or perhaps closer to the late 1920s, specialists from the old intelligentsia who after the revolution had worked loyally for the Supreme Soviet of the National Economy and the State Planning Committee were being persecuted. My father, Larin, doubting the justice in

*Court Record in the Case of the Anti-Soviet "Bloc of Rightists and Trotskyists," p. 511.

these arrests, telephoned Yagoda to ask to see the dossiers of the investigation. He wanted to examine them for himself and then go over to the OGPU [the political police, successor to the Cheka and the GPU] and personally go over the matter with People's Commissar Yagoda. I can remember a courier appearing with packets with five wax seals. My father pored over them, then drove over to the OGPU to talk with Yagoda. The arrested were released.

But in the 1930s, such a thing could not have happened in your wildest dreams. For example, at the end of 1930 or the beginning of 1931, Sergei Groman turned to my father for help. He was the son of the former Menshevik Vladimir Groman, who had worked on the State Planning Committee and had just been arrested. (He would be tried that March along with the United Bureau of Mensheviks.) By this time, my father was powerless to help the younger Groman, who was eventually arrested. In fact, even Politburo members now had no access to the NKVD.

One biographical detail about Yagoda obliquely led to thoughts of my own investigation and sparked the recollection of a painful episode from the not so distant past. Commissar Yagoda was related to Yakov Sverdlov, a member of the original Bolshevik leadership who died in 1919, by having married his niece, the daughter of Sverdlov's sister. Nevertheless, in 1934, Stalin ordered Yagoda to arrest Sverdlov's son Andrei and his closest comrade, Dima, son of the famous Bolshevik revolutionary Valerian Osinsky. Yagoda could not have been the initiator in this case; he never took such a step on his own. Both of the young men, twenty-two to twenty-three years old at the time, studied in one of the military academies and were well known to me. I was terribly upset by their arrest, which was inexplicable to everyone in the social circles to which we belonged.

When I told Nikolai Ivanovich about these arrests, he was extremely surprised and decided to call Stalin for an explanation. He managed to reach the tyrant right away. "Let them sit in jail," Stalin answered; "they're freethinks." (I am not mistaken; he said *vol'nodumy* [freethinks], not *vol'nodumtsy* [freethinkers].) When Bukharin asked how their freethinking manifested itself, Stalin was not very coherent. "It's sort of," he said, "well, they have Trotskyist views."

The arrests of Andrei and Dima along with Stalin's conversation recall an incident from the reign of Emperor Paul I, as one document from that ancient time so eloquently illustrates:

Mister General from the Cavalry von der Palen:
Upon receipt of this message, place in the fortress the prosecutor

of the military collegium, Arseniev, who came to me with a request for the position of prosecutor in the senate and who is, one must assume, a freethinker.

Respectfully yours, Paul

Nikolai Ivanovich asked Stalin to release the young men. He saw no crime in their "freethinking" and laughed sadly at the remark that "they're freethinks." Although Bukharin mentioned Dima by name in this conversation, he assumed that Osinsky himself could petition the general secretary for his own son and concentrated on securing the release of young Sverdlov, because his father was dead.

"Koba, I am asking in memory of Yakov Mikhailovich. Take pity on these kids. Their arrest might only embitter them and bring them to a bad end. They are both promising, capable youngsters."

"I don't handle these matters. Call Yagoda," Stalin retorted irritably and slammed down the phone.

Nikolai Ivanovich considered it pointless to call the people's commissar.

Soon afterward, Andrei Sverdlov and Dima Osinsky were both set free. Unfortunately, although I did not learn it at the time, this story would have a tragic continuation. Meanwhile, thoughts of their arrest, which had once so distressed me, brought me to unsettling reflections upon my own case: Whom could the investigators have recruited in their imaginations for the alleged counterrevolutionary youth organization mentioned by Chief Skvirsky? Now I reasoned that it would be precisely those two, Andrei Sverdlov and Dima Osinsky, who would be assigned the leading roles.

And if the prisoners A. Sverdlov and D. Osinsky were set down as "freethinks" in 1934, what could they be made into in 1938, during the period of mass arrests? It was obvious: terrorists, wreckers, traitors to the motherland. Dima's father had already figured in the Bukharin trial—not as a defendant but instead, for some reason, as a witness for the prosecution. He had recounted dreadful, terrible crimes that both he and Bukharin had committed. His involvement in the trial strengthened my supposition that his son and Andrei had been arrested again.

Many others their age could have been arrested at the same time, the many children of persecuted parents. I was their peer in both age and biography. Thus, I imagined the so-called case against me was being constructed.

But mulling over my investigation kept bringing me back to Yagoda—and not because for many years I wore the Moser Brothers watch he had given my mother long before, in 1925, when they had traveled together to take the cure in Sukhumi, a fine present that had since disappeared in some prison dungeon.

Yagoda himself I knew only slightly and remembered but dimly. I believe I saw him only once in my childhood, when the triumphant chords of Beethoven's *Egmont* Overture resounded throughout our apartment. The pianist was his wife, Ida, skinny and frail, with a pointed little face that resembled, in the opinion of many who had known Sverdlov, her famous uncle's. As she played, Yagoda leaned his elbow on the spinet and rested his face in his palm, looking sad and pensive as he listened to the music.

In my cell, I had recalled Yagoda because of the NKVD man just taken off to be shot. I was less interested in the actual fate of the former people's commissar than in the extent to which he was responsible for it.

One memory rushed in upon another, no matter how hard I tried to drive them away in order to get some sleep. I knew I needed to conserve my meager strength; the next day would probably bring another contest with Skvirsky.

By now, chilled to the bone by the musty dampness of the lower bunk, I finally returned to horrible reality, no longer imagining that I was lying on some feather bed but feeling the hard bed boards. My thin, bony sides were aching. I had to rouse myself to climb back up to the upper bunk to my lifesaving fur coat and curl up in a ball in order to warm my frozen legs. But as soon as I closed my eyes, the image of a child appeared before me. It was Yagoda's son. Not only that night in the Novosibirsk isolation cell but more than once along my long, tormented path, the boy would come to mind. I did not think of him because I sympathized with his father, toward whom I felt nothing but ill will. No, it was for some other reason that this boy, eight-year-old Garik, lived in my imagination and troubled my soul.

Yagoda's entire family was cut out at the root, rooted out of life. His aged mother was arrested, his wife was shot, and two of his sisters lived in Astrakhan exile when I did and were arrested there. Finally, his mother-in-law (Sverdlov's sister), who crossed my path in the Tomsk camp, was transported away before I was taken to Novosibirsk, and although it was rumored that she went to the Kolyma camps, she may well have been shot. What stories her knowledgeable son-in-law could have told! In any event, the result of these persecutions was that Yagoda's son had no kin left in the world. True, on the Sverdlov side some relatives had been distinguished from "sinners" like the rest of us, if only because Sverdlov had not lived until 1937. If he had, he would have received the same reward as his closest friends, cohorts, and relatives. For one thing, the man who later became "Father of all the Peoples" well understood Sverdlov's true attitude toward him since the time of their exile together in Turukhansk.

For whatever reason, the surviving relatives on the Sverdlov side did not take care of Yagoda's son in the same way that, for instance, my mother's sister and her husband took in my son and gave him a home until 1946, when they themselves were arrested and Yura was returned to a children's home. But we should not be too severe in our judgment of the Sverdlov clan. Andrei Sverdlov was "now here, now there"—that is, in prison and out, and back again. The other relatives were also stuck in a quagmire. Besides, who could forget that when young Andrei had first fallen into Yagoda's clutches, he had been spared by "our Father-Tsar"? (Stalin loved to appear to be a kind savior.) What reason could these relatives have for worrying about the Yagoda kid?

Be that as it may, when Sofia Mikhailovna Sverdlova found herself in the Tomsk camp with me, she worried about her abandoned grandson. Making an exception to the rule, the authorities allowed her to inquire about him. They gave her his address and let her write him a letter. Before she disappeared from the camp, she succeeded in receiving two responses from him. I saw the envelopes with the address written in the uncertain hand of a child and read the short, heartrending lines:

> Dear Grandma, sweet little Grandma!
> Once again, I did not die! You are the only one left to me on earth, and I am the only one to you. If I do not die, when I grow up big, and you get real old, I will work and feed you.
>
> Your Garik

The second letter was even shorter:

> Dear Grandma, once again I did not die. I don't mean the time I already wrote you about. I die many times.
>
> Your grandson

Because the rest of us were not permitted to know anything about our orphaned children and because correspondence with relatives was prohibited, these letters from a child were a big event in camp. Alas, not a happy one. Every mother was moved to think of her own child. We also wondered what could have happened to Garik. Many, I among them, believed that only special measures could have driven him to this grim state of mind. Similarly, when my son, Yura, was retrieved from a children's home in his second year of life, he was nearly half-dead. So for me, Garik's words "Once again I did not die" became something of a symbol. In my confinement, against the background of day-to-day hopelessness, there were special, unbearably difficult moments when it seemed that survival was unthinkable . . . yet I remained among the living. On such occasions, I repeated the words of Yagoda's little boy: "Once again I did not die."

I never forgot the impression produced by the boy's short letters, expressing in childlike fashion but with striking accuracy the horror and tragedy of his situation. Twenty years later, when I returned to Moscow, I tried to find out what had happened to him, but all my efforts were in vain.

And Yagoda? He did not disappear without a trace; his end is known; his hands are forever washed in blood. Above all, he was guilty of carrying the secret of Stalin's crimes through all of his final years as people's commissar and for being coperpetrator. He was by no means, on the other hand, guilty of those crimes charged against him at his trial.

Three people's commissars headed the OGPU-NKVD under Stalin: Yagoda, then Yezhov, then Beria.

Nikolai Yezhov, a mentally limited fanatic, believed blindly in Stalin and gave him absolute obedience. He was not organically bound to the persecuted Bolsheviks of Lenin's generation; besides, when he took over, the terror was running on smooth tracks. Yet, by the end of his career, he did not survive his own "Yezhovshchina," the "time of Yezhov," as the terror of 1937–38 was sometimes called.

Lavrenty Beria was the perfect man for Stalin. He had a shady background and a deceitful mind.

Genrikh Yagoda differed from these two in that he was a professional revolutionary, a member of the Bolshevik Party since 1907. In other words, he had not entered the Party simply to further a career. When it fell to his lot to begin the extermination of his Party comrades, the task did not come easy, but the powerful Stalinist bureaucratic machine sucked him into its irresistible vortex. For this reason, it is Yagoda who provides a particularly telling example of personal corruption and spiritual degradation.

Even so, I had to agree with my neighbor behind the cell wall that Yagoda was a tragic personage who had gone through an emotional drama. Resisting internally, he fell more slowly than many, and he became superfluous to Stalin less because he had been witness and collaborator in crime (on that count, the tyrant could delay his destruction for a while) than because he proved unfit to realize Stalin's grandiose plans for additional crimes. From the standpoint of today, it is difficult to determine which crimes Stalin committed through Yagoda, which behind his back. But there can be no doubt that he found it easier to work with Yezhov and Beria.

In his last years, Bukharin came to regard Yagoda as a corrupt official and careerist who had forgotten his revolutionary past, but he also had a purely psychological reason to hate the man. He told me that Yagoda had once been on rather close terms with Rykov (as was confirmed at the trial); they both hailed from the Volga—Rykov from Saratov, Yagoda from Nizhny Novgorod. Rykov commanded great respect for the revolutionary work he did in Nizhny; it was there the two became fast friends. Later, when Rykov was at the peak of his fame, having replaced Lenin as chairman of the Council of People's Commissars, Yagoda especially valued his friendship. Alas, Yagoda belonged to the sort of friends portrayed by the poet Nekrasov: "I shared with them my last penny, and sweet was the friendship I won, but my pockets are now empty, and my dear friends are gone!"

When political differences arose in the Party in 1928, Yagoda, who understood better than most the overall situation in the countryside, was closer to the views of Bukharin and Rykov than to those of Stalin, and we have to assume that he already knew the latter's true character. But as soon as he felt the opposition's position in the Politburo grow shaky, he did not stand fast but traded his personal views for the sake of his career. From that moment on, Nikolai Ivanovich felt only hostility toward Yagoda and delighted in telling me the following story.

In the summer of 1935, Nikolai Ivanovich drove outside Moscow to see Maxim Gorky at his dacha. Everyone sat down to tea on the terrace: Gorky, his widowed daughter-in-law Nadezhda Alekseyevna (called Timosha by the family), Nikolai Ivanovich, and an old hanger-on, a palm reader, who had apparently come back with the great writer from his years in Italy. After a bit, Yagoda showed up. He used to drive out there rather often, because he was attracted to Timosha. He was also drawn to Gorky, who as a native of Nizhny Novgorod had been close to the Sverdlov family and had adopted Yakov's older brother. This man, Zinovy, had never accepted the revolution and lived outside the Soviet Union.

When Yagoda joined the group at the tea table, the palmist asked, "Show me your hand, Genrikh Grigoriyevich." Yagoda calmly extended his hand. After scanning the lines of his palm for a moment, the old fellow brusquely tossed the hand aside and said, "You know, Genrikh Grigoriyevich, you have the hand of a criminal!" Yagoda got flustered, turned red, and answered that palmistry was not science but a worthless occupation. Shortly afterward, he left.

As Nikolai Ivanovich saw it, the most remarkable thing about this

incident was that Gorky did not reprimand the old man for his tactless-
ness, either in Yagoda's presence or after his departure.

Yagoda a criminal? Yes, of course. A miserable coward? Absolutely. His moral ruin long preceded his physical destruction. But even
the most daring of heroes would hardly have wanted to take his place
and could not have changed anything. Consider Ivan Akulov. In late
1931, after the trial of the United Bureau of Mensheviks, Stalin apparently wanted to mix up the cards and appointed Akulov, a man of un-
bending will, crystal-clear honesty, and prodigious courage, to be
Yagoda's assistant. As such, he began to put the OGPU in order, so he
very quickly found himself out of place there. He was transferred to a
post in the USSR Procurator's Office for a short while, then was made a
secretary of the Central Executive Committee of the USSR. In 1938 he
was shot.

History has yet to give Stalin full credit for a principal part of his
criminal nature—that is, his subtle mastery of the executioner's art. Still
less can we really know exactly what refined methods he used to drive
each of his executioner-victims into a dungeon constructed by the victim himself. In this vein, Yagoda's dramatic history gave me food for
thought during my sleepless night in a solitary cell at Novosibirsk prison.

[Vision of Golgotha]

Morning sneaked up without having any effect on the amount of light in
the cell. The dim electric light bulb went on burning, as always; the cell
became no brighter. However, sounds could now be heard in the corridor; bolts clanked, prisoners were taken out on latrine call, and trusties
dished out breakfast, consisting of a bluish kasha made from barley with
some kind of sickening fat poured over it, the long-awaited bread ration,
and hot water. Immediately, the rat ran out, snatched its piece of bread,
and, once satisfied, scurried under the bed boards. The elderly guard,
after observing through the peephole, came into the cell and good-
naturedly grumbled:

"What'cha doing feeding it, little girl? You'll get so many rats in
here there'll be no room for you. Now, before you there was a woman in
here, and she screamed about the rat so loud nobody could get any rest.
That's the way you're supposed to be."

"There's no living with rats or without them; the rats don't change
anything."

The jailer shook his head and went out, locking the cell.

Thus passed my days, faceless and gray, equally closed off from natural light. I realized I had better think up some kind of activity to drive away the black thoughts. I tried to get permission to receive books, but without success. Once, noticing a rusty nail on the floor in a corner of the cell, I scratched out sixty-four squares on the bed boards and made checkers of two different shapes out of bread, one for my side, one for the opponent. But every night, while I was asleep, the small fry of the rats and mice, which I had not taken into account, gobbled up my checkers. Ultimately, I preferred to eat the bread myself.

In the mornings, like a prayer, I repeated from memory Bukharin's letter "To a Future Generation of Party Leaders." I could not allow myself to forget a single word, even though it seemed then that his letter would go with me to the grave.

That unusual spring, which had so beguiled us with its early warmth, took a sharp turn in reverse. Every day, I was taken out for a ten-minute walk, but more than once the little prison courtyard was covered with snow, or the green patch of grass by my window turned gray from the morning freezes, or else driving cold rains poured down.

But one day the jailer came into my cell, announcing, "Hey, the weather's fine today! The bosses are gone [it was Sunday]. You can take a longer walk."

In the yard, it was uncommonly warm and uncommonly quiet. I could not hear the incessant clatter of the typewriter from the window of the Siblag Investigative Section, as I normally would on weekdays. From somewhere, the wind wafted in the intoxicating aroma of a cherry tree in bloom, and alongside my grated window, in the grass, sunny dandelions poked up on thin little stalks. High in the cloudless sky, a flight of swallows spiraled down and then shot straight back up, again and again, with elegant thrusts of their bow-shaped wings.

"Look, look, Anyutka! Swallows!" Nikolai Ivanovich would have cried out, enchanted, but the familiar voice was not heard, and I, barely able to hold back my tears, asked the old guard to take me back to my cell. Gloom corresponded better to my mood at that moment than the bright day within the stone bowl of the prison courtyard. Back in the cell, I felt the need to break down and sob, to splash out the emotional hurt that had accumulated, but I could not.

To pass the time and distract myself, I mentally repeated verses. Vera Inber's line came to me: "When it's properly bad for us, that's when we write good verses." It was "properly bad" for me, unbearably oppressive and lonely, and though I did not entirely agree with the poetess that verses composed under such circumstances would necessarily turn out well, I decided to try my hand. Otherwise, in this dank cellar, without books, overwhelmed by terrible thoughts, I would go out of my mind.

I would have to compose and memorize in my head. I had no paper or pencil; we were not allowed to write. To express my mood after walking in the courtyard, I managed to compose five lines as a beginning:

> *Sorrow condensed in a cloud,*
> *Then fell on the heart like fog.*
> *Distance transparent and blue*
> *Seems like a haze, like a fraud*
> *Seems the tremor of blossoming spring. . . .*

Just as I was beginning to memorize these lines and to continue the poem, the door burst open and two men strode into the cell: Skvirsky, who had not summoned me since my first interrogation, and (as my jailer later informed me) the administrative chief of the Novosibirsk Region NKVD. Taking advantage of the warmth in the cell, I had been lying in my underwear, covered only with my scarf in order to save my skirt, which was beginning to come apart at the seams from the damp.

"Were you not taught in camp to rise before the commandant!" Skvirsky shouted. "Get up immediately!"

"They taught us, but I was a poor student," I answered, remaining in place.

"Going to keep mum a long time, Princess Tarakanova [Cockroachia]? I warned you: if you do not expose the counterrevolutionary youth organization, you will rot here in this cell."

"I will stay here as long as you keep me here, since unfortunately I have no way to get out."

"If you have chosen such conduct, to remain silent, keep in mind that a bullet awaits you."

"In that case, there's no reason to worry: I won't be rotting in this cell."

Looking at me with curiosity, the administrative chief did not let fall one word. My "guests" left the cell. And my first effort at poetry remained incomplete.

Time passed. I felt worse and worse. The dampness was taking its toll; I began coughing heavily, and I slept uneasily. At night, I was plagued by hallucinations, or perhaps it was simply a terribly insistent, recurrent dream. . . . In an upper corner of my cell, just beneath the ceiling, I would see a tortured Bukharin crucified on the cross, as on Golgotha. A black crow pecked at the martyr's bloody, lifeless body.

Perhaps I was tormented by this particular vision because I had been thinking of Morozov and his book *Khristos*. For whatever reason, the nightmare returned for several nights, and I let out such screams of horror that they could be heard in the corridor. The jailer, sure that I had been frightened by the rat, came into my cell.

"Why are you screaming? Did the rat bite you?"

"Oh, no. I dreamed a terrible dream."

I now understood perfectly well, after Skvirsky's visit, that my life could be snuffed out any day. But I wanted to forget myself, to look back into my happy past and recall that unforgettable evening in the Crimea that set the stage for my romance with Nikolai Ivanovich.

I tried to capture the memory in poetry, and though my verses were far from perfect, they remain dear to me even today as a reminiscence of bright hours. These lines were typical:

> *How cheerful and happy you were*
> *On the Crimean eve I remember*
> *That began the beginning of things*
> *As soft breezes whispered, barely audible. . . .*
>
> *The darkening heavens gazed down*
> *With millions of luminous eyes,*
> *As if they were determined*
> *To watch us even more closely.*
>
> *And the very waves of the sea roared aloud*
> *That you would be mine very soon.*
> *Pounding their surf upon the shore,*
> *They playfully made sounds like laughter.*
>
> *It was late when we parted that evening.*
> *You said not a single word,*
> *But your eyes could not stop smiling,*
> *And your hand lay firmly upon mine.*
>
> *I was no more than sixteen then—*
> *Sixteen exciting, full years.*
> *Alas, I am now more than twenty,*
> *But the light from our past is still clear.*

I had occasion to reread these verses rather recently, and the line "Alas, I am now more than twenty" made me consider how relative is our perception of age and time. Eight years is a long time for a young person, in any event, but of the eight years from ages sixteen to twenty-four, it was the last two, from August 1936 to August 1938, that seemed so very long, because they were filled with excruciating agonies. And yet today, when I am more years past seventy than I was then past twenty, how much I would like to have back my "more than twenty"—though, to be sure, without that horrible cell in Novosibirsk!

[The Rightist and Trotskyist Oppositions]

Not one of my experiences with Nikolai Ivanovich, even the kind that I treasure forever in memory—the first kiss, the birth of a child, the fleeting excitements of youth—was ever the embodiment of pure, light-hearted joy. Invariably, our life together was burdened in unseen ways with the complex social climate of those years, the political discussions, debates, and dissensions, and finally the terror.

I grew up among professional revolutionaries who, having made their revolution, stood at the head of their country. Not surprisingly, then, the internal life of the Party began to interest me very early on. My father fostered this development, but my interest in politics was especially strengthened by my closeness to Nikolai Ivanovich. It seemed that, in his most difficult days, fate drew me inexorably toward him.

During the Sixteenth Party Congress, in 1930, for example, I met with Nikolai Ivanovich by chance in the Crimea. At the time, there were conflicting opinions (as there still are today) about why he did not attend the congress. Some people charged that he boycotted out of pride; others, his "well-wishers," suggested that he suffered a failure of nerve and did not want to subject himself to a difficult test. Let me explain the truth. First, Bukharin was not chosen to be a delegate, an unprecedented event for someone who was a member of the Central Committee. Second, not long before the congress opened, Nikolai Ivanovich came down with a serious inflammation in both lungs, grew very weak, and was given doctor's orders to go to the Crimea. In other words, there was nothing premeditated about his departure from Moscow.

In fact, any split in the Party ran counter to Leninist precepts and could therefore, it was believed, only weaken the dictatorship of the proletariat. In February 1929, the so-called Right Opposition on the Politburo—Bukharin, Rykov, and Tomsky—had indeed been persistent in refusing to admit the error of their views and had demanded removal from their posts rather than share responsibility for Stalin's policies. But by November 25 of the same year, after their views had been declared incompatible with Party membership, they were forced to concede their mistake in a statement to the Politburo and to the Presidium of the Party's Central Control Commission.

By contrast, the earlier opposition group, the so-called United Trotskyist Opposition, had not renounced its views so quickly and had in fact defended them at the Fifteenth Party Congress, in 1927. But is it proper now, when reflecting on the past, to judge which group looks better in the eyes of history? In the final analysis, each side surrendered. A "magic word" exerted a sobering effect on both: threat of expulsion from the Party. As soon as the leaders of the United Trotskyist Opposition received the clear message that it was time to decide whether or not to remain in the Party, all 121 who had been expelled at the Fifteenth Party Congress, including Trotsky himself, immediately called for the dissolution of their faction and for total subordination to the decisions of the congress. When their collective statement did not produce the desired results, the oppositionists turned in individual statements at the earliest possible moment, renounced their views and conduct, and were reinstated. This gave Sergo Ordzhonikidze, chairman of the Central Control Commission, the right to declare at the Sixteenth Party Congress that the Trotskyist Opposition no longer existed. Indeed, aside from Trotsky and two or three diehards, no one else remained in the faction.

True, their collective statement at the time was not so humiliating as the one made later by the Rightists; there was, for example, no recantation of their views, only the promise to fight for them within the confines of Party rules. But this contrast is to be explained, if I may put it this way, not by the quality of the persons involved but by the quality of the time. The wheel of history began accelerating for Stalin.

Is it fair to say, as some do, that Stalin earlier crushed the "New" Opposition of 1925 as well as the "United" Opposition of 1927 with the hands of Bukharin, Rykov, and Tomsky? No, because for these three men the struggle for their views against the Trotskyist Opposition was not a struggle for power. For Stalin, however, it was a brilliantly played game of chess. By stirring up discord among the Bolsheviks and setting them against one another, he was able to remove from the political arena all of the major figures who had played prominent roles in Lenin's day. Unfortunately, the Bolsheviks did not figure out Stalin's game all at once, but individually, one after the other, and some of those who did catch on tried to use it to their own political advantage. With hindsight, we can now see that most of Stalin's victims failed to spot the hangman behind these political frays. He won, and victory brought him one-man rule.

Both the Trotskyists and the Rightists strove to stay in the Party despite Stalin, suffering humiliation and swallowing their dignity. But the Party lost its former face and became the party of Stalin. Remaining in *his* party, then, the former oppositionists in both groups turned their creative thought to preserving Party unity while submitting to Stalin's dictates. Herein, it seems to me, lies one of the essential causes of the tragic fate that would later befall the old Bolsheviks.

And the Sixteenth Party Congress would be unique. At preceding congresses, there had been talk of ideological differences and clashes between opponents, but at this one the Party took up arms against an "army" that had already capitulated. Thus began the "slaughter of the innocents." The Party demanded repentance and self-incrimination, self-incrimination and repentance. One of the targets, Tomsky, declared that it remained only for him to put on a hair shirt and go seek penance in the Gobi Desert, living on wild honey and locusts, but that "repentance" was a religious, not a Bolshevik, term.*

[With Bukharin in the Crimea, 1930]

But let us return to the summer of 1930.

I happened to come to the Crimea with my ailing father and was living with him in Mukhalatka, in a rest home for members of the Politburo and other leaders. Nikolai Ivanovich had intentionally chosen to live apart in a dacha in Gurzuf. Soon after we arrived, we paid him a visit. He made a dismal impression, looking sad and emaciated. There could be no talk of his attending the congress in such a condition. When we saw him again a few days later, he was a bit stronger physically but in the same, if not even more despondent, mental state. Both times we found him in bed.

Even in the Siberian prison, my Crimean meetings with Nikolai Ivanovich appeared before my mind's eye with remarkable clarity. It seemed that I inhaled the aromas of youth, not the musty stink of my cell. I could recall how strongly I felt drawn toward Gurzuf, knowing that I had promised to visit Nikolai Ivanovich and that he could be waiting for me. My mother had not been able to get leave to come with

*Stenographic Record, Fourteenth Congress of the VKP(b), pp. 259, 267.

my father, so I was caring for him alone. His health did not allow him to ride frequently to Gurzuf (indeed, I cannot say that I wanted him to come along), but it was too cruel to leave him by himself for an extended period of time, since he could not even dress and undress without help. Nevertheless, not wanting his helplessness to restrict my life, he readily encouraged me to go see Bukharin. Even so, I was never completely at ease when I left, which cast a bit of a shadow over my ardently awaited meetings with Nikolai Ivanovich.

There was no regularly scheduled transport, either by land or by sea, from Mukhalatka to Gurzuf. When I went with my father, I was entitled to ride in the rest-home car, but on my own I had to catch a ride. The first time I went alone, I found a light truck going to the Gurzuf repair shop. We set out from Mukhalatka at daybreak and arrived in Gurzuf in the early morning.

Nikolai Ivanovich was delighted to see me. "I had a premonition you would come today!" he exclaimed.

After a quick breakfast, Nikolai Ivanovich grabbed a book with a newspaper folded over it, and we went down the steep path that led to the sea. It was a quiet morning. A friendly little wave, frothing slightly as it turned over the sea pebbles, rolled up on shore and released a consoling sound, more sigh than rumble.

We sat down at the foot of a cliff that rose above our heads, providing pleasant shade. I wore a sky blue chintz dress edged with chamomile; my black locks fell down almost to that wide border. I can recall this now without fear of seeming immodest, for it was so long ago and I am so unlike that former self that I might as well be writing about another person.

In my childhood, someone had once joked that I had one eye like the sea and the other like the sky, and I had repeated, "One like the sea-ee and the other like the sky." This "sea-ee" had amused the grownups, including Nikolai Ivanovich, and suddenly he recalled it.

"You've grown up without our noticing it," he said. "You've become an adult, and your eyes are no longer different from each other—both are like the sea-ee."

I was amused by this reference, but shy. The conversation somehow did not catch on. Nikolai Ivanovich was noticeably nervous. Neither of us felt like talking about what was bothering us: the Party congress. Our feelings for each other were driven inside, and neither of us could resolve to bring them out into the open first, even though it was already obvious to both of us by this time that they had undergone a transformation. For me, it was childish respect, and for him, solicitude toward a child, that had turned into love.

He unfolded the newspaper in which he carried his book. It reported the addresses of the delegates to the congress, prompting him to comment irritably about Yemelyan Yaroslavsky's speech, "Yaroslavsky believes that the Trotskyists no longer exist and that we, whom they all call the Rightists, constitute the main danger now. What nonsense, what *erundistika!* [Nikolai Ivanovich loved verbal curlicues, as I called them, and frequently instead of the word *erunda,* 'absurdity,' used the word *erundistika,* "absurdistics.'] We have never had an opposition like the Trotskyist Opposition."

He was talking not so much about the ideological position of the Trotskyists as about their methods of fighting for their views to the detriment of Party discipline. Bukharin was, of course, a fierce opponent of their ideological position; he and Trotsky were diametrical opposites.

Tossing the paper with the speeches aside, Nikolai Ivanovich took up his book, Knut Hamsun's *Victoria.*

"Few," he said, "have been able to write such a delicate work about love. *Victoria* is a hymn to love!"

I presumed now that he had not brought this novel by chance. He began to read selected passages aloud:

What is love? It is the wind rustling through the rose bushes. No, it is a flame burning red in the blood. Love is an infernal music; to its strains even the hearts of old men must leap into dance. Like a marguerite, it opens up with the onset of night; like an anemone's, its petals curl up from a breath and die at a touch.

That is what love is.

Interrupting his reading, he gazed pensively over the waters into the distance. Then he turned his gaze on me, then again back at the sea. What was he thinking then?

At last he continued:

Love is the first word of the Creator, the first thought that dawned upon him. When he said, "Let there be light!," love was born. Everything that he made was good. Not one thing that he made did he want to return to nothingness. And love became the source of everything on earth and the ruler of everything on earth, but its path is strewn with blossoms and blood, blossoms and blood!

"Why blood?" I asked.

"You want there to be nothing but blossoms? It doesn't happen that way in life; there are always tests; love has to overcome, overpower them. And if it doesn't overcome the tests of life, doesn't overpower them, then it wasn't there in the first place, not the true love of which Knut Hamsun writes."

Nikolai Ivanovich next read to me the passage in which the old monk, Friar Vendt, talks about eternal love, love unto death, and tells how sickness had chained a man to his bed and caused his hair to fall out, so his beloved wife, in order to be like her husband, cut off all her tresses. Then the wife was stricken with paralysis, could no longer walk, and was forced to sit in a wheelchair, which her husband wheeled about, loving her all the more. To even the situation, he splashed sulfuric acid on his face, disfiguring himself with burns.

"Well, what do you think about a love like this?" Nikolai Ivanovich asked.

"Fairy tales is what your Knut Hamsun is telling you! Why make yourself ugly on purpose, turn yourself into a leper, throw sulfuric acid in your face? Is it true that love requires this? What nonsense!"

My answer amused Nikolai Ivanovich, and he explained to me that "his" Knut Hamsun was expressing the power of love with this story, its intrinsically sacrificial nature. Suddenly, looking right at me sorrowfully and anxiously, he asked, "Would you be able to love a leper?"

I lost my composure. Sensing the hidden purpose in his question, I was unable at first to answer.

"Why do you keep silent and not answer?" he asked again.

Disconcerted, I blurted out with childish naïveté, "Love who? You?"

"Yes, me, of course, me," he stated outright. He was smiling, happy and touched by the way I had guarded my feelings with childish hesitation.

But just as I was ready to say that I could love him (although there was no need for the future tense, since it was already true in the present), Nikolai Ivanovich stopped me: "No, no, you don't have to, don't answer! I fear your answer!"

He was not yet ready to dot the *i*. Because of the great disparity in our ages, he was afraid to let our emotions take their course. Still, one way or another, Knut Hamsun had helped us bare the feelings we had been trying to conceal.

Over the long years of my tribulations, I would recall Nikolai Ivanovich's fateful question more than once: "Would you be able to love a leper?"

That day, I remained in Gurzuf only a few hours. The truck driver, a big-hearted albino named Yegorov who had long white eyelashes growing out in clumps, hurried me along. Ah, how I did not want to part with Nikolai Ivanovich! But I had to return to my father in Mukhalatka.

A later trip to Gurzuf brought me many worries and much joy.

As soon as I arrived at the dacha where Nikolai Ivanovich was staying, I was told he had gone for a swim in the sea that morning and had disappeared. Alarmed, I ran down to the shore. A crowd had gathered; people were looking out to sea with binoculars. On the beach lay Nikolai Ivanovich's things: a pair of light-colored linen pants, a light blue satin cossack shirt hot from the sun, and, despite the heat, a pair of boots. These were the extent of his "riches." A heavy rock rested on top of them to keep the wind from blowing them away. By now, it was after lunchtime, and even I, who well knew how far Nikolai Ivanovich might swim out from shore, began to get seriously worried. Finally, someone decided to send out a motorboat to search. When it eventually came alongside a border patrol vessel, Nikolai Ivanovich was discovered aboard, detained as a suspicious character. He had swum into the forbidden zone and been forced to board the ship to identify himself. When he explained that he was Bukharin, the border guards refused to believe him. Someone asked to see his documents, a really ludicrous demand under the circumstances. Nikolai Ivanovich replied that if it would confirm his identity, he would happily drop his trunks, since he could do nothing more. This was met with friendly laughter, but some "vigilant" loudmouth piped up, "Give up this idea that you're Bukharin. Why pretend he would swim out so far? Better tell the truth, who you are and for what purpose you swam out here."

(If Prosecutor Vyshinsky had known about this incident, that purpose would have been instantly determined at the trial.)

Finally, the ship's captain wisely decided that if the detainee truly was Bukharin, people would eventually come looking for him, and they did.

By that evening, when Nikolai Ivanovich was safely deposited back ashore, the crowd had grown larger, having been swelled by Party workers from the nearby rest home Suuk-su and by delegates arriving after the conclusion of the congress. Someone in the throng shouted, "Nikolai Ivanovich, when will you stop playing pranks?"

Uplifted by his new athletic record and exhilarated by his "first arrest" under the Soviet regime, Bukharin could not restrain himself and shouted back for all to hear, "When you stop calling me a rightist opportunist!" Some people laughed heartily. Now that the congress was over, it was possible for Party members to laugh and joke and even sincerely rejoice that Nikolai Ivanovich had been found safe and sound. But at the same time, some people suspected even more strongly that his illness must have been diplomatic if he was able to perform such a feat of swimming.

We climbed the hill to the dacha. On the table in Bukharin's room lay an envelope addressed to "Nikolai Ivanovich" in Rykov's hand. Someone coming to the Crimea from Moscow had dropped it off. Excitedly, Nikolai Ivanovich opened it and found a postcard inside, the final lines of which I recall practically word for word: "Come back in good health. We [Rykov meant Tomsky and himself] conducted ourselves with dignity at the congress in respect to you. Know that I love you as not even a woman in love with you could. Your Aleksei."

He also wrote that he considered it a big success for all three of them that Nikolai Ivanovich had not attended the congress. His presence would only have complicated the situation. In the trying conditions of the meeting, Rykov explained, Bukharin could hardly have maintained the calm necessary, at least on the surface, while Tomsky and he had been able to do so without supreme effort. Rykov added that Bukharin's absence was good for another reason as well, which did not need to be stated.

He had in mind a situation that had arisen from a conversation between Bukharin and Kamenev in July 1928. Although the incident was then two years old, Stalin had not forgotten it. In fact, it had been precisely then, in 1928, that he began laying the foundation for the myth of the Bloc of Rightists and Trotskyists, working on it as the "painstaking builder" for the next decade, so that in 1938 it could rise up as the infamous edifice of the Bukharin trial. In that vein, the show trial was labeled "The Case of the Anti-Soviet Bloc of Rightists and Trotskyists."

[Bukharin's Conversation with Kamenev and Its Fateful Consequences, 1928–1929]

According to Nikolai Ivanovich, the famous conversation occurred when he and Sokolnikov, who both lived in the Kremlin then, were returning home from a session of the July 1928 plenum of the Central Committee. Along the way, they ran into Kamenev, stopped, and started talking. Bukharin, disturbed not only by the divergent views that had arisen in the Party but also by the general secretary's coarse and treacherous conduct in sessions of the Politburo and the plenum, talked about him in a tone of extreme irritation and disappointment, condemning his moral qualities as well as his political line. I recall also that Nikolai

Ivanovich, from what he told me, admitted to Kamenev and Sokolnikov that they had been absolutely right at the Fourteenth Party Congress, in 1925, when they advised delegates not to reelect Stalin as *gensek* [general secretary]. Bukharin went on to say that Stalin was an unprincipled intriguer who in his pursuit of power would change his politics at any given moment, depending only on whom he wanted to be free of. He purposely stirred up discord and did not bring the Party together; his politics led to civil war and famine. Nikolai Ivanovich added an unflattering opinion of Molotov: Stalin, he said, surrounded himself with faceless drones subordinate to him in everything, like the dull-witted Molotov, that "lead butt," who was still struggling to understand Marxism. (Actually, Nikolai Ivanovich used ruder expressions to describe Molotov, improper to repeat here. My husband was by nature excitable and outspoken.)

I believe that Nikolai Ivanovich told me no further details of this conversation, but perhaps I have forgotten. I do, however, definitely remember his saying that there had been not one word, not even a hint, about organizing a bloc including himself and other members of the opposition, on the one hand, and Kamenev, Zinoviev, and the Trotskyists, on the other. Indeed, at that stage, such talk would have had no chance of success, for the power had already been lost. Stalin was already the Party's *polnovlastnyi khozyain,* or all-powerful master. And so he was called Khozyain, the Boss.

Bukharin's conversation with Kamenev was purely emotional, not conspiratorial, a sincere and direct outpouring of concerns following the stormy debates in the Politburo and at the July plenum that very day.

But what compelled him to bare his soul to Kamenev, of all people, considering they were diametrically opposed on the question of the New Economic Policy? Because back in 1925, at the Fourteenth Party Congress, when Kamenev stood opposed to Stalin and Bukharin, he had stated that the general secretary was not the kind of person who could unite the Party leadership. Three years later, having gained his own experience of Stalin's character, Bukharin had come to the same conclusion. That conviction, coupled with his strong irritation, prompted him to speak frankly to Kamenev; psychologically, no other explanation is possible. After all, when Nikolai Ivanovich declared at the Fourteenth Congress that "an unprecedented campaign" had been directed against him personally, he was referring to Kamenev and Zinoviev. It was in following the latter's lead that Stalin later began to denigrate the Bukharin school with the term *shkolka.** Incidentally, Bukharin had been the

---

**Stenographic Record, Fourteenth Congress of the VKP(b),* pp. 109, 149.

main target of Kamenev and Zinoviev's attack in 1925 for the same ideas that Stalin assaulted in 1928.

Bukharin had supported Stalin's policies back in 1925 at the Fourteenth Congress, but not from any lust for power, as some interpreters claim; his later opposition to the general secretary demonstrates that completely. We can understand Bukharin's position by considering some of Stalin's remarks during the congress. "It's a strange business," he said. "People introduced the New Economic Policy, knowing that NEP was the revival of capitalism, the revival of the kulak [rich peasant], that without fail the kulak would rear his ugly head. And yet, when the kulak began to show himself, they started shouting 'Watch out!' and went crazy. And then their distraction reached the point where they forgot about the *serednyak* [middle-level peasant]."* And more: "If you were to ask Communists what the Party is more prepared to do, to strip the kulak or not to do so but instead make a union with the *serednyak,* I think that 99 out of 100 Communists would say that the Party is more prepared for the slogan: Beat the kulak. As for the suggestion not to dekulakize but to implement the more complex policy of isolating the kulak by means of a union with the *serednyak,* this is harder to swallow."†

Back to Bukharin's conversation with Kamenev, I happened to witness an incident when I was still a girl that proved Rykov and Tomsky did not know about the famous talk and could not therefore have been part of any "bloc." Already by 1928, I was frequently visiting Nikolai Ivanovich. Once, I found him lying on a couch in a little room next to his study, looking gaunt, haggard, and distressed.

"How good that you have come, Larochka. [Taking a first name, Lara, from my last name, Larina, he always called me Larochka in my childhood; later, Anyutka, from Anna.] I'm in a bad way. Cats are clawing at my soul and giving me no rest! Do you understand me?" But he answered himself, "No, you don't understand me; you're too little. How good that you can't comprehend everything!"

"I'm not so little," I objected, feeling hurt. "I understand a lot."

By that time, I had already read the stenographic records of the July plenum, secretly taking them from the drawer of my father's desk. These transcripts always had the words "Top Secret" written across a soft pink cover. Naturally, this inclined me to take a peek. So in general, as far as my youthful understanding allowed, I was up-to-date with events taking place at that time.

*Ibid., p. 47.
†Ibid., p. 48.

I peered into Nikolai Ivanovich's face. Not as I was accustomed to see it—joyful, with blue eyes radiant—his face looked gray, his gaze overcast. Instantly, I understood that black storms were hanging over his head. But I could not understand how great a storm was in the offing.

Unable to control my nervous tension, I broke down crying. Trying to explain, I blurted out, "I'm so sorry for you, but I can't help you in any way!"

(Later, Nikolai Ivanovich more than once recalled this painful moment and how I had reacted toward him.)

There was a short, gloomy pause; then Nikolai Ivanovich suddenly said, "Don't you feel sorry for me, Larochka. Feel sorry for the muzhik peasants."

These words he uttered very quietly, as if unsure whether to carry on such a conversation with a very young person, no matter how close to him.

I do not know what direction this conversation might have taken, a dialogue between the forty-five-year-old Bukharin, who treated me with such tenderness, and a girl in her fifteenth year of life, drawn to him as a plant to the sun. Before I even managed to grasp the meaning of his last sentence, Rykov ran into the room in great agitation. Stalin had just told him that Bukharin was negotiating with Kamenev to form an anti-Stalin bloc and had accused him to his face of giving prior consent to the move, along with Tomsky. Rykov had replied that such charges were incredible and were clearly meant as provocation. At that, Stalin divulged the details of Nikolai Ivanovich's conversation with Kamenev, including the digs at himself and the unflattering characterization of Molotov.

Nikolai Ivanovich turned pale; his hands and lips trembled. "That means Kamenev informed. The scoundrel, the traitor!" exclaimed the stunned Bukharin. "There's no other way this could have become known. The meeting was accidental, outdoors, in the Kremlin, when I was returning from the plenum with Sokolnikov. No one could have eavesdropped."

He basically confirmed Stalin's account of the substance of the conversation. Rykov became so enraged that he could not talk properly. He screamed, stuttering even more than usual.

"You're a silly woman, not a p-p-politician! Who did you decide to op-p-pen up to? Who did you find to b-b-bare your soul to? Haven't they tormented you enough? *M-malchik-bukharchik!* [Little tyke Bukharchik!]"

At that time, Rykov distrusted Kamenev and Sokolnikov alike. He suggested that the latter might be the informer and could even have arranged the "accidental" encounter, but Nikolai Ivanovich categorically rejected this view.

"I'll see," said Rykov, "how good you look in the Politburo when you tell Molotov that he's a blockhead and a 'lead butt.' "

Nikolai Ivanovich was completely aghast.

I do not remember the exact date of this confrontation, but I clearly recall that the weather was still warm. Rykov had run in wearing a gabardine coat and cap. Therefore, it must have been no later than the beginning of autumn in 1928 that Stalin knew about the content of Bukharin's conversation with Kamenev. Because of my extreme youth at the time, the reader may not have full confidence in my recollection and understanding of this incident, but there is documented confirmation.

For example, at the Sixteenth Party Congress, in 1930, responding to remarks about factionalism and Bukharin's "negotiations" with Kamenev, Rykov said, "You know perfectly well that when Bukharin's conversation with Kamenev was discussed [N.B., he says 'conversation,' not 'negotiations'], I regarded this matter, this conversation [again, the emphasis on the word] with the greatest censure and stated so immediately."*

At the same congress, Tomsky observed that the infamous conversation, though private, had assumed a political character because of the sharp personal attacks and characterizations.†

Finally, in his closing words at the 1938 trial, Rykov, forced to express himself in the language dictated by his interrogators, said, "From the very beginning of the organization of the bloc, all of the activity sprang from Bukharin, and in certain instances he confronted me with an accomplished fact."‡ Undoubtedly, the phrase "accomplished fact" referred to Bukharin's conversation with Kamenev.

As a further example of documentation, Trotsky's bulletin, published in Germany, printed a supposed "Transcript of Bukharin's Conversation with Kamenev" on January 20, 1929. It was presented as a letter written by Kamenev to Zinoviev but intercepted. Although I did not see this document until I returned to Moscow from exile, I believe it included everything Nikolai Ivanovich told me, plus a multitude of trifles and small details I had not previously known and do not feel myself competent to judge accurately. But there can be no doubt that the

*Stenographic Record, Sixteenth Congress of the VKP(b) (Moscow, 1935), p. 273.

†Ibid., p. 269.

‡Court Record in the Case of the Anti-Soviet "Bloc of Rightists and Trotskyists," p. 653.

"Transcript" truly reflects both Bukharin's political views and his attitude toward Stalin in 1928, as well as the climate in the Politburo at that time.

This document includes an incident that is firmly implanted in my memories of childhood because Bukharin and Larin recalled it so frequently in conversation as "the story of the Himalayas." It gives convincing proof of Stalin's coarseness and treachery. A tense situation had developed in the Politburo prior to the July 1928 plenum because, on the one hand, divergent views on domestic policies had arisen while, on the other, a statement was being prepared in which the Central Committee would declare to the Sixth Congress of the Comintern that no such disagreements existed. Stalin, not entirely sure that he would be successful in pushing through this statement, tried to sweet-talk Bukharin. He called him to his office and said, "You and me, Nikolai, are the Himalayas. The others [the rest of the Politburo] are nonentities." At one of the sessions of the Politburo, as the debates raged, Nikolai Ivanovich, becoming angry with Stalin, decided to reveal these words, which so clearly proved the general secretary's hypocrisy. Stalin, outraged, started shouting at him, "You lie, lie, lie! You want to turn the members of the Politburo against me."

"And whom did they believe?" my father remarked when Nikolai Ivanovich first told him this story. "Stalin, of course. Who wants to be a nonentity?"

"The Himalayas" were recalled fairly frequently. They held a special meaning: Don't make political gaffes or stupid mistakes.

"Don't make any more Himalayas," Larin would warn Nikolai Ivanovich.

"Do it without Himalayas," Nikolai Ivanovich would urge Larin before my father made a speech.

In the "Transcript" Bukharin is not quoted discussing any kind of bloc but instead asking Kamenev something quite different: "You will determine your own line, of course, but I would ask that you not help Stalin crush us with the aid of your approval of him." How brightly is Bukharin's nature manifest in those words! Such was his childlike forthrightness, his political naïveté, which often got him into trouble yet won him sincere and devoted friends!

Other things in the "Transcript" also strike me as completely realistic: for example, when Bukharin is quoted as asking, "What can you do when you are dealing with an opponent like this Genghis Khan?" And remarks about the "low culture of the Central Committee," and so on.

But other moments are obviously fabricated. In light of what I have said, Bukharin could not have made the following "communication" to

Kamenev: "Only Rykov and Tomsky know that I have spoken to you." (Nikolai Ivanovich is quoted using the familiar form of address, "thou," which he and Kamenev did not use with each other in real life.) In addition, the reported circumstances of the conversation are false; the two men are shown meeting in Kamenev's apartment.

Finally, the "Transcript" inadvertently exposes its own invention. "No one," Bukharin is supposed to have said, "should know about our meeting. Don't talk with me by telephone, for they are listening in on my line. The GPU [State Political Administration, or political police] is following me, and the GPU is watching you." We must assume that if Nikolai Ivanovich had suspected that the GPU was tapping his telephone and watching Kamenev, he would have been more cautious and would have found a better place to meet than the latter's apartment, no matter how ardent his desire to form a bloc.

Certainly, Nikolai Ivanovich knew that leading Party officials were being listened to in their apartments. I recall one example clearly. Stalin, usually so tight-lipped that he never let drop a superfluous word, would become expansive when drunk. In that condition (I do not recall exactly when, but I think it was in 1927), he showed Nikolai Ivanovich the transcript of a conversation between Zinoviev and his wife. Political topics were intermixed with private, even intimate matters that greatly entertained the Boss. Apparently, this was not wiretapping but some kind of recording that used the telephone somehow. I cannot say how it was accomplished, but everything said in Zinoviev's apartment was recorded. My husband could never shake the horrible impression left by this encounter with Stalin.

The "Transcript" was just one example of the basic methods—intrigues, fabricated documents, deceit—Stalin used to set the Bolsheviks against one another.* So that it could achieve his desired aim, a third character is brought into the supposed conversation. Grigory Sokolnikov was an extremely convenient figure for the necessary insinuations. On the one hand, he shared Kamenev's political orientation; on the other, he had been connected with Bukharin since their school days. In fact, Kolya Bukharin and Grisha Brilliant (Sokolnikov's real

*For example, in the summer of 1935, the plenum of the Central Committee was presented with a fat folder containing materials compromising to Avel Yenukidze. At the plenum, he was expelled from the Party for moral corruption, malfeasance in office, and so on. Other charges against him lay ahead. Nikolai Ivanovich returned from the plenum downcast; he believed in these documents and told me, "The bureaucracy is going to ruin!" Bukharin knew Yenukidze, an old revolutionary and good-hearted fellow; he bore his fall heavily. At that time, the possibility of a fabrication seemed out of the question.

name) became friends while young boys still living with their parents, a circumstance that always leaves a special stamp on the heart and fosters maximum trust in relations between comrades. Thus, Sokolnikov is shown not only accompanying Bukharin in the "Transcript" but also conducting preliminary negotiations about the bloc and organizing the meeting between Nikolai Ivanovich and Kamenev in the latter's apartment. With Sokolnikov included, the insinuation of conspiracy looks more true to life, more convincing; the document therefore creates the required illusion and confirms that Bukharin desired to organize a bloc against Stalin.

But the illusion is just that: it is completely obvious that Sokolnikov knew from attending the July 1928 plenum that a bloc between Bukharin, a man losing his position in the Party, and Kamenev, a man previously humbled into supporting Stalin's policies over Bukharin's, would be a fantasy.

Even so, I will not categorically assert that no meeting between Sokolnikov and Kamenev took place. What actually went on backstage in this affair, with the tragic consequences for Bukharin, is lost in oblivion. But I am absolutely certain that Bukharin did not entrust Sokolnikov with conducting negotiations with Kamenev, that he did not play the hypocrite in front of Rykov and me that autumn afternoon, and that there was no reason for him to tell me almost ten years later exactly what happened in the famous conversation, unless he was telling the truth.

From a meticulous study of the "Transcript," I have gained the impression that Kamenev did not write it, even though a phrase has been inserted to make the uninformed think that he is writing Zinoviev to ask him to delay his return to Moscow. The confusion in the supposed letter, the disconnected exposition, is striking and not at all characteristic of Kamenev, whose literary abilities are highly regarded.

But it is even more revealing that, when summoned to the Central Control Commission, he confessed that the "Transcript" was correct except for some "misstatements" (what misstatements could there be in one's own version?) and that Bukharin confessed to the truth of the document "on the whole."

Who actually wrote down this purported conversation between Bukharin and Kamenev? Today, one can only guess. Undoubtedly, the chance meeting and animated conversation in the Kremlin between Kamenev, Sokolnikov, and Bukharin did not pass unnoticed by the GPU. As we know, the walls have ears. Also, any one of the three participants might have let things slip "in an intimate circle." In that case, it would have been only a matter of technique for experienced hands to reconstruct the conversation.

Nor should the possibility be ruled out that Kamenev was called in to give an account directly to Stalin himself and was questioned prejudicially, after which a stenographic record of his testimony became the basis of the "Transcript." But I cannot with confidence support any one of these suppositions over the others.

On January 30, ten days after the publication of the "Transcript," Bukharin sent an explanation of his sharp pronouncements about Stalin to the Central Committee. This statement became known as Bukharin's platform. In it, he assailed the general secretary's policies as synonymous with a military and feudal exploitation of the peasantry, with the disintegration of the Comintern, and with the installation of bureaucratism in the Party.

A special commission to look into the question of Bukharin, in particular his conversation with Kamenev and his January 30 statement, was created by a joint session of the Politburo of the Central Committee and the Presidium of the Central Control Commission. The chairman of this special commission was Ordzhonikidze, who did everything possible to keep Bukharin, Rykov, and Tomsky in the Politburo, but on condition that Nikolai Ivanovich admit that his alleged negotiations with Kamenev were an ideological error. Furthermore, he was to explain that he had mentioned the notion of military-feudal exploitation polemically, in the heat of the moment. Making these conditions was the only way Ordzhonikidze could save the situation at that moment. He drafted the following resolution:

"The special commission proposes to the joint session of the Politburo and the Presidium of the Central Control Commission that all of the documents on hand (the stenographic record of speeches and so forth) be removed from circulation and that Comrade Bukharin be granted all of the necessary conditions for normally continuing his work as editor of *Pravda* and secretary of the Comintern Executive Committee."*

As a matter of fact, even before the July 1928 plenum, working conditions for Bukharin and Tomsky had become unbearable. A "political commissar," as Nikolai Ivanovich put it, was assigned to the editorial offices of *Pravda:* G. Krumin, formerly editor of *Economic Life.* At the All-Union Central Soviet of Trade Unions, Tomsky was saddled with Lazar Kaganovich. Both Tomsky and Bukharin, for the first time, asked to be relieved of their posts, in November 1928.

Now they, along with Rykov, rejected Ordzhonikidze's proposed conditions, explaining that they could not change views they considered

*Stenographic Record, Sixteenth Congress of the VKP(b), p. 579.

to be correct; instead, they would end the battle by turning in their resignations from their posts.

Finally, on February 9, 1929, at a joint session, the Politburo of the Central Committee and the Presidium of the Central Control Commission delivered themselves of a resolution, its first section bearing the momentous title "Behind-the-Scenes Attempts of Bukharin to Organize a Factional Bloc against the Central Committee." It read:

> 1. Comrade Bukharin and Comrade Sokolnikov, during the July plenum of the Central Committee (1928), without the knowledge of and against the will of the Central Committee and Central Control Commission, conducted behind-the-scenes factional negotiations with Comrade Kamenev on the question of changing the policies of the Central Committee and the composition of its Politburo.

> 2. Comrade Bukharin conducted these negotiations with the knowledge, if not the consent, of Comrades Rykov and Tomsky, who, knowing of these negotiations and understanding they were unacceptable, concealed this fact from the Central Committee and the Central Control Commission.*

As my account has made clear, this resolution in no way reflected the true state of affairs. Bukharin carried on no conversations about altering Central Committee policies or forming a bloc or changing the composition of the Politburo. This was not because he did not want these changes but because there was no sense in discussing them with the likes of Kamenev, who had just been reinstated in the Party and sent, like Zinoviev, to work in the Central Union of Consumers' Cooperatives. Also, Kamenev was not a member of the Politburo or Central Committee and was politically closer to Stalin than to Bukharin.

If Bukharin wanted to talk about changing the course of the Politburo and removing Stalin from the post of *gensek,* it would have been sensible to meet only with actual Politburo members, and only with those in whom he would have to sense the potential for support—that is, Kalinin and Ordzhonikidze—since his only visible adherents, openly opposing Stalin in the Politburo, were Rykov and Tomsky. And to take such a step, he would have to be certain that any negotiations would achieve the desired effects, would not inflame the Politburo even more, and would not hasten the rout of the opposition (I am conveying his

*Stenographic Record, Sixteenth Conference of the VKP(b) (Moscow, 1962), p. 745.

122 THIS I CANNOT FORGET

train of thought). Of course, my account has already refuted the resolution's claim that negotiations about a bloc were conducted "with the knowledge, if not the consent, of Comrades Rykov and Tomsky."

Along with the resolution, the Politburo and the Central Control Commission demanded that all the documents concerning Bukharin, Rykov, and Tomsky be circulated, thus rendering their position all the more hopeless, all the more catastrophic, even though they were not relieved of their posts. Indeed, why remove them? Stalin was not hurrying events along; as always, he pursued his perfidious tactics in good time, waiting it out. Besides, he could not yet decide the question of removal, even in "friendly collaboration" with the Politburo. The resolution had gone on to note that removing the three men would give ammunition to enemies of the Party, who would say, "We've got what we wanted."*

In that vein, the resolution inadvertently affirmed Bukharin's conviction that Stalin had leaked the "Transcript" through the GPU:

> The fact that the Trotskyists published Kamenev's "Transcript" is now known to the whole world. In the near future, most likely, this "Transcript" will be published in the foreign bourgeois press. Doubtless the Trotskyists, in publishing this "Transcript," acted like the White Guard, wishing to create a rift inside the Politburo.†

An incredibly "difficult" prediction, but it came to pass! What foresight! "Bourgeois press"? This referred to the *Socialist Herald,* published in Paris by émigré Mensheviks and therefore considered to reflect the interests of the bourgeoisie by Stalin and the other Bolsheviks.

Finally, the thunder clapped, and immediately afterward, the long-awaited rain poured down on the political crop cultivated by Stalin. . . .

On March 22, just before the April Central Committee plenum (in other words, at just the right moment), the prediction of the resolution came true: the "Kamenev Transcript" was indeed published in the *Socialist Herald,* ostensibly reprinted from the organ of the German Trotskyists. A stroke of luck for Stalin? Possibly, but he was always "lucky." And it would also seem to be more than luck that this was not a copy of the original document but a superbly edited text, convincingly seeming to be Kamenev's own, personal version.

The *Socialist Herald* "Transcript" was reproduced and distributed

*Ibid., p. 751.
†Ibid.

to members of the Central Committee prior to the April plenum. Thus was the groundwork laid for removing Bukharin from his senior positions. The delegates forgot the claim of two months before that the Party's enemies would exult at such action and crow, "We have got what we wanted." It was now clear that, with Bukharin's downfall, it was the "friends" who got what they wanted.

So low had Nikolai Ivanovich fallen that even the *Socialist Herald* had a victory celebration and printed fabricated slanders of Stalin attributed to him. "The *Socialist Herald!*" "The *Socialist Herald!*" was heard from all sides at the plenum. Yes, that is the way it was; you couldn't escape it! I well remember the details of my husband's account of these events. The very convening of this plenum prepared the way for the removal of Bukharin and Tomsky. Rykov, as chairman of the Council of People's Commissars, would last a bit longer.

How did the protagonists of this drama—Sokolnikov, Bukharin, and Kamenev—comport themselves afterward?

Sokolnikov fell silent. He did not speak up at all at the succeeding Party congresses, the sixteenth and the seventeenth, though he served as a delegate to them and remained a member of the Central Committee. Inclined by nature to play an active role and make full use of his outstanding oratorical gifts, he nevertheless did not publicly recant, did not stigmatize anyone, did not shout "hurrah" for anyone. As for Bukharin, he never mentioned this incident, this rout of the so-called Right Opposition, in any of his succeeding articles and speeches. It was Kamenev, now completely broken (and possibly acting on orders from above), who placed an article in *Pravda* decrying his "negotiations" with Bukharin. And into the text of his speech to the Seventeenth Party Congress, in 1934, he inserted terminology that would later prove useful in the trials. The "second wave of counterrevolution," he said (the first being Trotskyism), "passed through the breach opened by ourselves; this was the wave of kulak ideology." Then, without any logical connection, he recalled his "negotiations" for a bloc with Bukharin.★

That Seventeenth Party Congress, by the way, strikes us today as a totally depressing event. The delegates, apparent "victors" but actually future victims of Stalin, sang enraptured dithyrambs to the leader. Embodying the working class (or the proletariat, as it was then called) and the peasantry alike, they bore on their shoulders the whole weight of industrialization and collectivization. Deprivation lay behind; the shining future lay ahead. It would be free, egalitarian, plentiful, this society

★*Stenographic Record, Seventeenth Congress of the VKP(b)* (Moscow, 1934), p. 518.

with new productive forces at work, altered productive relationships, and a new, socialist man. What had been envisioned in their dreams, or imagined in tsarist prisons at hard labor, in emigration, and in the post-revolutionary collapse under fire in the civil war, would now, it seemed to them all, truly come to pass. Their belief was genuine and sincere. Anyone who does not grasp this fact has lost his feel for history. Bukharin expressed it clearly when he called Stalin "the field marshal of proletarian forces,"[*] although he was at the time speaking principally about the development of industry and the threat to the world evident in the rise of fascism.

In any event, the whole matter of the "negotiations" left Bukharin with a rancor against Kamenev that never waned from 1928 on. One summer Sunday in 1934, we drove outside Moscow to Ostafiyevo, a rest home for the Central Executive Committee that had formerly been the estate of the Vyazemsky princes. We had traveled several hours just to see the old park there and a monument to Pushkin. We were invited to stay for dinner at the rest home, which had a dining area situated on a large terrace. Just as the food was served, Kamenev, who was taking a rest there, sat down at our table. The two "friends" exchanged greetings: Kamenev quite amiably, I thought; Bukharin rather coldly. Suddenly, Nikolai Ivanovich got up from the table, "remembering" that he had a meeting back at the *Izvestia* editorial offices. We said our good-byes and abruptly drove off. "I beat it from Kamenev," he explained to me, "so as not to give him something to put in a 'transcript' and in a speech to the next congress."

In sum, the incident of 1928 was a milestone in the biography of Bukharin, not only because Stalin used it for his own purposes but because it radically changed the character of its victim. At age forty-five, Bukharin finally got a full dose of what politics in the Stalin manner was all about. He reckoned that he had been betrayed, and he was demoralized by the whole business. He became more circumspect ever afterward and less trusting, even in his relations with Party comrades; he began to suspect many of his fellow workers of being agents specially assigned to watch him. Now sorrow peeked out at times through his passionate love of life. He was easily wounded and fell sick from nervous strain.

The finale of this story was told at his trial. There, the last act of the scenario was played out. Today, we understand that long before the actual "performance" Stalin, like a mole, had been burrowing underground tunnels, leaving false paper trails in preparation for the trial of

[*]Ibid., p. 129.

the Anti-Soviet Bloc of Rightists and Trotskyists. As early as 1928, perhaps, the idea of future show trials had not yet taken clear shape in the Gensek's imagination (although I wouldn't rule out the possibility), but the likelihood that everything would come in handy someday, somehow—this Stalin did not lose sight of, I am certain, because this was the essence of his style.

At his trial, Bukharin stressed twice that his meeting with Kamenev had taken place at the latter's apartment, that same apartment where, according to the "Transcript," he had warned that the "GPU was stationed." He admitted in the courtroom, in other words, what previously he had categorically denied. Furthermore, in the dock he interpreted his conversation with Kamenev as libel against the Party leadership, did not mention the only conversation that had actually taken place, and instead confirmed the other, invented meetings with Kamenev listed in the evidence brought against him.

At the trial, in other words, the fictitious Bloc of Rightists and Trotskyists became the guiding star, the framework on which falsified crimes were hung like hornets' nests. The accused were fastened to the make-believe Bloc of Rightists and Trotskyists with heavy chains, like convicts in a galley.

[Bukharin's Character and Ideals]

I needed this long digression in order to explain clearly what Rykov meant when he wrote on his postcard that Bukharin's absence from the Sixteenth Party Congress had been a success for reasons he "well understood."

The postcard brought Nikolai Ivanovich great joy and relief. If he had regretted his absence at all, it was only because he was afraid that his like-minded comrades Rykov and Tomsky would resent having to face the music for him as well as for themselves. Or face the ridicule, as Nikolai Ivanovich put it, since the opposition had already, as I've noted, surrendered in advance of the congress. Even though both Rykov and Tomsky visited him and appreciated the seriousness of his illness, he had been tormented by the possibility they would be upset with him. And he fretted that he could not know, as he recuperated in the Crimea, whether he might be able to muster his strength enough to make an appearance, even toward the end of the congress, since that seemed to him to be his duty toward his comrades. Intuition told him not to try. Aleksei Ivanovich's postcard put an end to his worries. It convinced

Nikolai Ivanovich that he had acted properly with respect to his friends.

Rykov's concern that Bukharin's presence would complicate their position is explained not only by the results of the Kamenev conversation. He was also thinking of Nikolai Ivanovich's complex character, which he knew very well. He believed that it would not be easy for Bukharin to maintain the relative calm and restraint that he and Tomsky achieved only with difficulty. Indeed, if Nikolai Ivanovich had been forced to a painful submission to what was then considered "the will of the Party" and had found no sympathy among the delegates for either himself or his two comrades, he might well have "exploded." It was not rare for his emotions to get the better of his reason. Precisely such an explosion, which would have been disastrous then, was what Rykov feared. He was a man with a practical cast of mind; his judgment was more sober.

I knew that these two, Rykov and Bukharin, cared deeply for each other. Yet there were times when Nikolai Ivanovich really caught it from his older comrade, because Rykov never knew what to expect from someone like him, to whom political calculation was in the last analysis completely foreign. Nikolai Ivanovich might have flown off the handle at the congress because his statement on November 25 of the preceding year admitting the error of his views had been made under duress, in dread of remaining outside the Party and in deathly fear of its splitting. He could certainly retort sharply and viciously to unfounded attacks. And, in the furious energy of his political passion, he had been known to seize hold of an opponent with a death lock. At the same time, his nervous temperament was surprisingly delicate—pathologically taut, I would say. Even on ordinary days during that tempestuous epoch that called upon him to play a leading role, his nature, exceptionally sensitive and alive, could not bear nervous overloads, for its "tolerance" was unbelievably slight, and the emotional strings would snap.

This character trait brought on consequences undesirable for a man of politics. Despite his boldness in open polemics, he was not always able to pursue matters to a victorious conclusion, even when he was clearly right. For example, acting on Stalin's advice, he gave up at the February–March 1937 plenum and begged forgiveness for declaring a hunger strike to protest the outrageous charges of treason brought against him. (There is another possible explanation, which I give in detail later.) He could also capitulate simply to spare someone's feelings. For example, he apologized to the poets who felt stung by his criticism at the First Congress of Soviet Writers, in the summer of 1934, even though his remarks on the necessity of improving poetic craftsmanship had been fair and offered with the best of intentions.

Emotional tautness, acute sensitivity—these very traits would plunge him at times into a state of hysteria. He wept easily, although not at the drop of a hat; always, the reasons were serious. When he found out that the October uprising was not so bloodless in Moscow as in Petrograd, that in fact several hundred people had perished, he burst out in sobs. On the day of Lenin's death, I saw tears in the eyes of many of Vladimir Ilyich's comrades-in-arms, but no one wailed like Bukharin. At the time of the collectivization in 1930, when he was traveling through the Ukraine, he saw packs of children begging for alms at the little local stations, their stomachs swollen from hunger. Nikolai Ivanovich gave them all his money. When he got back to Moscow, he stopped by to see my father, told him about the trip, cried out, "If more than ten years after the revolution one can see such things as this, what was the point of doing it?," collapsed on the couch, and sobbed hysterically. My mother calmed him with valerian drops.

And intense experiences could physically incapacitate Nikolai Ivanovich. He was ill after the July 1928 plenum; he was again ill after signing his name to his own capitulation on November 25, 1929; finally, he fell ill in the days preceding the Sixteenth Congress, in 1930. This solid, surprisingly strong man, a sportsman with the musculature of a prizefighter, literally wilted under severe nervous strain.

But don't let me leave the impression that Nikolai Ivanovich was a crybaby. This was far from being the case. Emotional hypertension was only one facet of his multifaceted, complex character. Bukharin was a revolutionary of great passion and unbridled spirit, whose potential for revolutionary work required dynamics, action. He was obsessed with the idea of humanizing society by means of a revolutionary transformation. To him, in other words, authentic human socialism seemed unattainable without a change in human nature, without improvement in the culture of the lower ranks—that is, those people considered "of base descent" before the revolution, the working class and the peasantry. Perhaps this desire of his, because so many Bolsheviks shared it, may seem somewhat banal to some. But with Bukharin it developed into a passionate, ever shining, all-absorbing dream; brilliantly expressed in his fiery speeches, it became the one and only goal of his social and political life.

"Let us renounce the old world, shake its dust from our feet"— these lines from a revolutionary song that Nikolai Ivanovich knew and loved were the motto of his life right up to his final years, the catastrophe of 1936 through 1938, when his endeavors were paralyzed.

And so Ilya Ehrenburg was absolutely right when he wrote, "There are gloomy people with optimistic ideas; there are also merry pessimists. Bukharchik was by nature a surprisingly sound person; he wanted to remake life because he loved it."

In fact, Bukharin believed that the new world should be realized no matter what had to be done, although he definitely did not believe in the concept "No matter what the cost, at any price." Moral conflicts always troubled him; he saw a tragic side to the most humane ideas. It is true, of course, that in the early postrevolutionary years, the time of civil war when two worlds collided, Nikolai Ivanovich did not always find it possible to fight for his ideals with a "spiritual weapon" alone and even sanctioned "the word of Comrade Mauzer." But subsequently he became convinced that the goals of revolution could be attained at minimal expense. To this aim he turned all his thoughts, theoretical inquiries, and political activity.

[A Letter to Yezhov and a Poem for Yura]

Now let me return to the day Nikolai Ivanovich swam out of sight in Gurzuf.

Toward evening, when it was beginning to get late to return to Mukhalatka, he walked me to the repair shop. There, we learned that the repair work was nearly complete, so, rather than drive back and forth again, Yegorov had decided to spend the night. I was upset for my father's sake but managed to reach him by phone and let him know I would be home the following day.

And so, stuck in Gurzuf for a very prosaic reason, I experienced the thrillingly romantic Crimean evening I would try later to recapture in the verses I composed in that solitary cell in the miserable underground prison in Novosibirsk.

That stark contrast later is not unlike the very air of that Crimean interlude, warmth of summer intermingled with the political chill before the storm, that enveloped my happy hours with Nikolai Ivanovich, but they were indeed happy no matter what.

I find it awkward to talk about something so precious. Whoever does talk a lot about such a thing cannot really value it. Yet, as I descend into the past, into reminiscences of a distant life that few have been forced to experience, I recall certain moments (all too rare, unfortunately) when something joyful balances or at least alleviates the somber aspects of my past. There in Gurzuf, Nikolai Ivanovich discovered a source of joy in our love. And, since he was going through trying times, our love seemed all the more radiant and beautiful to us both.

Back in Mukhalatka the next day, Sergo Ordzhonikidze scolded me for leaving my father by himself. He had arrived after the conclusion of the congress, along with Molotov and Kaganovich, and happened to glance at the window of our apartment, which faced a common terrace, only to find Larin struggling to remove his shirt. Sergo rushed to his aid and learned that I was in Gurzuf with Nikolai Ivanovich. As soon as he saw me, he gave me a full blast of his Georgian temper.

"You have lost all conscience!" he shouted. "Have you no shame, to leave your sick father like this? Bukharchik wasn't at the congress; he was amusing himself with little girlies!"

Perhaps he was actually angered by the suspicion that Nikolai Ivanovich had not been ill but had apparently ignored the congress in order to enjoy a good time in the Crimea. Later, trading outrage for mercy, Sergo sat me down on a couch, took his place beside me, and began to question me in detail about how Bukharin had felt during the congress. I was distraught and distressed. I explained how I got stuck in Gurzuf. I described the condition in which my father and I had found Nikolai Ivanovich on our previous visits. I told about his swim out to sea.

"If he had swum to Turkey," Sergo remarked, "I wouldn't have been surprised."

I did not understand. Could he be facetiously suggesting that one should pack off to Turkey to get away from such a congress? Or was he simply alluding to Nikolai Ivanovich's desperate, imprudent character, coupled with his physical strength?

If you sit behind closed doors, alone with yourself, you will without fail wander through the labyrinths of your memories. And if, moreover, you are in your twenty-fourth year and a gaping abyss lies ahead, and you sum up your life and come to the conclusion that a catastrophe has occurred and nothing can be done about it, then the need for memories expands beyond bounds.

Novosibirsk, summer 1938.

Suddenly, the bolt clanked, the door to my cell swung open, and the guard uttered words all too familiar to a convict: "Get ready for an interrogation!" Since my first interrogation, at the beginning of May, and Skvirsky's visit to my cell later, I had not seen the chief. Meanwhile,

I had been slowly burning out, was melting like a candle, was coughing more and more, and had come to expect my end soon, one way or another.

Back in the chief's office, I saw again the same hawklike eyes and heard the same insinuating voice.

"Do you, as before, refuse to expose the counterrevolutionary youth organization, and do you still deny that you were the liaison between them and Bukharin?"

I had nothing new to say.

"Do you expect me to believe that you were in love with that old bald-headed devil?"

This remark had a certain "novelty," at least, and I concentrated in order to give Skvirsky's rudeness the appropriate rebuff. His own head was covered with thick, wavy hair, which thoroughly pleased him since he had nothing else to be proud of. So I thought of a way to needle him.

"Does your wife love you only because of your lush chevelure? Who knows what will happen down the road? You could yet go bald," I declared, mastering my agitation, "and then what will be left of you? In that case, your wife will certainly leave you!"

It seemed to me I had taken my full measure of revenge. Skvirsky turned scarlet and bellowed, "Ugh, you're a brazen hussy, aren't you? I'll show you, you Bukharinist wretch! This is insulting impudence!"

"No more insulting than yours! I did not want to remain in your debt!"

"Shoot her, shoot her, shoot her! There's no room for you on Soviet soil!"

But his threats could no longer have the same effect upon me as before. Enraged, he sent me back to my cell.

August came. There had been no rains for at least a month, so it was a bit drier in the cell; the drops fell less often from the left wall and formed only thin streams slowly creeping along the floor toward the door. During my walks, the guard allowed me to pick sagebrush growing by the fence; I bundled in three large armfuls and spread them over the bed planks. The sagebrush killed the musty smell, made my bed softer, and, best of all, freed me from the bedbugs.

Nonetheless, the uncertainty of my situation and the conditions in which I found myself became unendurable. I saw that my fate would not depend on Skvirsky if I decided not to succumb to rotting away in this cellar. I resolved to remind Moscow that I existed, to write to Yezhov, leaving Stalin in reserve for later. Usually, the prison authorities would cooperate in providing paper for such declarations. Millions of innocent prisoners wrote their declarations and received the standard reply:

"There is no basis for a review of your case." A mammoth bonfire could have been set ablaze with all our declarations. Yet, since my declaration would not be for a review, I might not get the standard reply. I knocked on the cell door and asked the guard for paper for writing a statement. He replied, "I'll tell them." Quite soon afterward, I was let out into the corridor; in the corner stood a little table with a schoolroom spill-proof inkwell containing dirty, half-dried lilac ink, along with a pen and a piece of paper.

I remember the text of my statement almost verbatim:

Nikolai Ivanovich Yezhov
People's Commissar of the NKVD USSR
From Anna Mikhailovna Larina (Bukharina)
Novosibirsk Prison Isolation Ward
City of Novosibirsk

DECLARATION

Four months have passed since I was put in solitary confinement, in a damp cell in the cellar of the Novosibirsk isolation prison, to which I was sent from the Tomsk camp. I was sentenced to eight years' confinement in a camp before the Bukharin trial as a "family member of a traitor to the motherland."

At the present time, I am accused of having been a member of a counterrevolutionary youth organization and a liaison between Bukharin and this organization, and I am ordered to reveal everything about this organization.

Insofar as I did not belong to any such organization and think it unnecessary for me to prove this to you, I am unable to reveal anything about any such organization. I have been repeatedly threatened with execution. In the conditions of a damp cell, I am doomed to a slow death. I request that you alleviate my sufferings; it is easier for one to experience perdition instantly than to perish gradually. Shoot me. I do not want to live!

A. M. Larina (Bukharina)
August 1938

I returned to my cell with mixed feelings, relief as well as a vague oppression. Usually, with the aim of self-preservation, I would try to drive away any bitter thoughts about my child. But on that day, mentally bidding farewell to life, I could not help remembering my son and especially bidding farewell to him.

I recalled again how he would often call for his father in a ringing child's voice: "Papa, Papa, come Lyulya [come to Yura]." I found it surprising that he had not forgotten his father in the three and a half months since Bukharin's arrest. Ivan Gavrilovich, Grandpa, could not hear this call for his own son without weeping, and the boy, seeing him, would also begin to cry. I could not stand it and would run into the next room so that the little fellow would not see my tears.

I also recalled the moment I parted from my son. It was the day in June 1937 when an NKVD officer came to send me into exile in Astrakhan. The boy was then a year and one month old; he could not yet walk, and "good uncle," my brother, was holding him in his arms. Yura was amusing himself with some shiny baubles, the medals on his uncle's chest. A little later, sitting in the arms of my old grandmother, then past seventy, he looked sadly at me, as if sensing that in the next instant he would lose his mother. How hard was that moment of parting! I would never see my son as a child again.

Now I should hurry to write him a letter, I thought, because my declaration to Yezhov might speed up the determination of my case. I must write that letter without fail, even though he might never receive it. He is already in his third year, my child. . . . Does he understand any of this already? No, he does not understand a thing! Besides, how can I write? They allow paper only for declarations. Perhaps I should again compose verse, rhymed lines? That would be better, because the time passes less noticeably. But what could I talk about, from this cell? Of course, I decided, I must write him about his father, write in such a way that my boy would understand everything, if I ever had the opportunity to read him my poetry. I wanted to reflect Nikolai Ivanovich's life-assertive character, and his love of nature, without touching upon any political matters that would be inaccessible to a child. (One such quatrain would wedge its way into the poem anyway, as was later brought to my attention during an interrogation.)

Unfortunately, my memory has not retained the entire poem. I relied too heavily on this faculty and failed to write down the poem when I had the chance later. A large part is gone: the beginning is lost, and the sequence of the quatrains is broken.

Your father loved wide, expansive fields,
The cataracts of the mountain streams,
And he loved to walk along paths
Where human beings can never be seen!

He knew the song of every bird,
He could soar with the swallow's flight,
In his own movements he was as quick
As the surge of thought on the wing. . . .

Though he won the love of multitudes,
He was hated by terrible foes
Because, no matter how great the cost,
He fought to keep thought free.

By now, my son, you are surely grown
And have to take your own path,
But, my child, you look the same as he,
This man you have never been allowed to know!

I was not finding it easy to accustom myself to a feeling of fore-doom, to the thought that my existence might end any day, yet I did not once regret that I had lived only a short life with Nikolai Ivanovich and had been able to share his most difficult days.

I was aggrieved only by a feeling of guilt for an absurd incident that once caused a temporary rift in our relationship.

[Our Romance, Stalin's Wife, and Premonitions]

After he returned from the Crimea, Nikolai Ivanovich drove out almost every day to see us at our dacha in Serebryany Bor [Silver Pine Forest]. Mother was too amused by our infatuation to take it seriously; Father, who said nothing, was not at all amused. He and Bukharin had frequent discussions, mostly about economic matters. I soaked up everything like a sponge and tried to keep abreast of the many subtle changes in the political climate during those years.

During that autumn of 1930 and into early 1931, Nikolai Ivanovich and I tried to spend all of our free time with each other, often going to the theater and to art exhibitions. I loved to visit his Kremlin study, where the walls were adorned with his paintings. My favorite watercolor, *The Elbrus at Sunset,* hung above the couch. There was also a menagerie of stuffed birds, his hunting trophies: huge eagles with outspread wings, a blue-tinted blackbird, a black and ruddy redstart, and a bluish gray merlin. His butterfly collection, also displayed there, was especially bountiful. And on his large writing desk, making its home in a knot of wood, was a splendid yellowish brown stuffed weasel with a tiny head and a bright tummy, looking really alive.

The window with its broad sill was covered by a screen, forming an enclosure where ivy Bukharin had planted himself grew lush and wild. Amid the greenery, two motley little love birds sported about and twittered.

Nikolai Ivanovich loved to read aloud to me. He delighted in the passionate, audacious heroes of Flaubert's *Salammbô*. He was charmed by Romain Rolland's *Colas Breugnon,* though amazed that this kind of work should spring from the pen of this particular author. Rolland himself, as he explains in the introduction, was surprised by the book. After being locked up in the armor of his *Jean-Christophe* for ten years, he suddenly felt an "irresistible need for unrestrained Gallic fun, yes, even to the point of irreverence." Nikolai Ivanovich felt so close to *Breugnon* and delighted in it so much because he, too, felt the need for unrestrained fun "even to the point of irreverence," albeit a Russian variety.

I remember clearly his infectious laughter as he read how the merry jester Breugnon and his friend, the notary public Paillard, who got "true pleasure from telling you a tall tale with a straight face," taught a caged thrush to sing a Protestant (Huguenot) song, then released it in the garden of the Roman Catholic curé of Brèves.

Nikolai Ivanovich was inclined to play pranks himself. Once, as he told me, when Lenin kept refusing his invitations to go hunting because of the demands of work, he had a package delivered to Vladimir Ilyich as he was chairing a meeting of the Council of People's Commissars. It was opened to reveal a dead quail shot the day before. The identity of the joker was guessed at once. Lenin sternly shook a finger at Bukharin but was unable to restrain a smile. But the point was made.

During our courtship, nothing seemed to cloud our life. On Sundays, we always tried to get out of the city. I loved being with Nikolai Ivanovich on a hunt, loved watching his excitement when he made a hit, yelled, "Got 'em!," and ran to find the prize. (He hunted without dogs.) But when he missed, he was sincerely downcast. Often we walked through the forest, and we went skiing together. It was all wonderful— yes, truly wonderful!

Still, as our friendship continued, the main thing was not yet decided: for one thing, Nikolai Ivanovich wanted to spare me his political misfortunes because he loved me so much; for another, he was troubled by the immense disparity in our ages.

One evening, we decided to take a long stroll and caught the streetcar to Sokolniki, then a suburb of Moscow. Nikolai Ivanovich often used public transportation, and sometimes the passengers would recognize him and begin talking: "Hey, look, it's Bukharin taking a ride!" Or you would hear, "Hello there, Nikolai Ivanovich!" Some people would come over to shake his hand and wish him well. Although he was always embarrassed by this kind of attention, he was obliged to nod constantly.

On our way back from Sokolniki, we somehow found ourselves on Tversky Boulevard. We sat down on a bench opposite the Pushkin monument, which stood then on the other side of the square. Nikolai had finally made up his mind to have a serious personal conversation with me. Our relationship, he said, had come to an impasse. He had two choices: either to join his life with mine or to go off and not see me for a long time so that I could build a life apart from his. "There is another possibility," he said, half jokingly. "I could go out of my mind." Failing that, he wanted to choose whichever of his first two options would be the more attractive to me. I couldn't see any point in talking further, because I felt the matter would resolve itself soon. But Bukharin, the theoretician, could not accept that! He needed a logical justification for making a choice, he said, or he really would go out of his mind! (Of course, I can now see why this situation was more complicated for Nikolai Ivanovich than the usual love affair. Aside from the huge difference in age, he still saw me as Larochka, a little girl, and the daughter of an old friend.)

The only answer he got from me was tears. At this distance, I'm not sure why. I suppose those tears must have betokened both joy and deep distress, both youthful indecisiveness and the realization that sitting beside me on a bench on Tversky Boulevard was not some callow youth my own age but the man Bukharin himself. As the tears streamed down my face, Bukharin looked on in consternation; he had not expected a reaction like this. On the contrary, he had been convinced that I had already made my choice; otherwise, he would not have dared broach the subject. We sat a rather long time in silence, the tears rolling down my cheeks. Nikolai Ivanovich vainly tried to get me to explain what caused them. I just shivered. He took my frozen hands in his and warmed them. It was time to go back home.

But Nikolai Ivanovich did not want me to appear before my parents in such a state, upset, eyes red from crying. He suggested we drop in on his former young protégé Dmitry Maretsky, who lived not far away from Tversky Boulevard on Herzen Street, next to the conservatory. When we got there, it turned out that Dmitry Petrovich was not home. He had already been transferred to work in the Academy of Sciences, then located in Leningrad. But his dear wife received us graciously, and I can picture their little boy sleeping snugly in a small bed. We warmed ourselves with tea, rested a bit, and then headed home to the Second

House of Soviets (formerly and later again the Metropol Hotel), where many high Party and state figures lived. I had cheered up to the point of considering myself the happiest person on earth. Seeing that my mood had obviously improved, Nikolai Ivanovich suggested that we go together the following evening to see Mussorgsky's *Khovanshchina* at the Bolshoi Theater, and I readily agreed as we continued homeward.

It was well past midnight when we reached the Metropol. Mother was asleep. Father sat at his desk, working on his latest article. When he noticed my swollen eyes and Nikolai Ivanovich's look of dismay, he suggested that his friend stay the night. Bukharin accepted and lay down on the couch in the study. I slept poorly and woke up late the next morning. Nikolai Ivanovich had already gone off to work.

As I have noted before, my father had never interfered in our affairs, but that morning he suddenly spoke up.

"You should consider very carefully how serious your feelings are," he said. "Nikolai Ivanovich loves you very much. He's a sensitive, emotional man, and if your feelings are not serious, you should leave him alone. Otherwise, it might end badly for him."

His words, meant to put me on guard, actually alarmed me.

"What do you mean, it might end badly for him? Not suicide?"

"Not necessarily suicide, but he certainly doesn't need any extra worries."

Later, Nikolai Ivanovich told me that earlier in the morning he and my father had discussed our conversation on Tversky Boulevard.

He was supposed to come by that evening to escort me to the theater. There was no reason to doubt that after *Khovanshchina* everything would be decided (the way it was actually decided three years later). The talk with my father had helped me understand a lot and made me more decisive. That one day was enough for me to realize that Nikolai Ivanovich needed me to make the decision. But we did not meet that night, and the fault was entirely mine.

One of my classmates at the workers' school called unexpectedly to tell me I was required to attend team studies that very evening in order to prepare for an examination on political economy. (My goal was to enter the economic planning institute.) One may laugh today at the team method of study, but then I took it quite seriously. On my team we were all Komsomol members who considered it obligatory to pass all examinations with a mark of "good" or "excellent." One of my teammates was Grigory Sokolnikov's son Zhenya, with whom I would also study later at the institute. He lived in the Metropol and often dropped by to see me. Although I was completely indifferent to the boy, Nikolai Ivanovich noticed that Zhenya was attracted to me, became irritated with his attentions to me, and told me so.

On this occasion, no matter how much I may have wanted to go to the theater with Nikolai Ivanovich and talk with him afterward, I decided I could not fail to do my Komsomol duty. When I tried to reach Nikolai Ivanovich, I could not find him at work or at home. My parents were going out for the evening, so I wrote him a note. I explained why I could not go to the theater that evening and asked him to come by the next day after my examination. I stuck the note in the door and went off to my studies. Nikolai Ivanovich did not come the next day, or the next. I decided to take the initiative and telephoned him myself.

He talked to me coldly, drily, not at all in his usual way. At first, he refused to believe my explanation for not going to the theater. When I managed to convince him, he put a sharp question to me: "Are you really able to think only with a collective brain? What good is that team? Indeed, I permit myself to suggest that I might prepare you for political economy no worse than Zhenya Sokolnikov and his team!"

Before I could reply that this was a matter of my personal obligation to the other kids, he hung up. Nikolai Ivanovich may have been forty-two years old then, but he was as jealous and impetuous as any youth.

On the basis of what has come down to us about our great national poet Pushkin, Nikolai Ivanovich's close friends observed that the two had much in common. I have to agree. Bukharin was just as much a desperate man bereft of good sense, just as hotheaded, as Pushkin, although it was Slavic blood without a drop of African that flowed in his veins. Also like the poet, he was lively and life loving and could give his whole heart over to childish delight. And, again like Pushkin, Nikolai Ivanovich could swear like a trooper and was no less jealous in personal relationships.

I was crushed. I could not understand why this incident, which seemed innocuous to me, should provoke such a sharp reaction and cause a break in our relations. Nikolai Ivanovich steadfastly failed to appear. I phoned him at his office, where he worked as chief of the Scientific Research Center. (This was then a division of the Supreme Soviet of the National Economy, later of the People's Commissariat of Heavy Industry.) His dear, kind secretary Avgusta Korotkova, so small and slight that Nikolai Ivanovich called her Penochka, after the little peewit bird, always answered me in a soft, tender voice, "Nikolai Ivanovich is busy," "Nikolai Ivanovich is not at work," and, finally, "Nikolai Ivanovich is ill." I telephoned his apartment and found that he actually was ill.

I told him I wanted to come over, but he asked me not to; he was sending me a letter. It came soon afterward. He wrote that, when he found my note left in the door, he realized that he should step aside. In spite of the sad message of the letter, he rained countless compliments on my head in elevated language, enough to give me a high opinion of myself. Yet the phrase "My dear, tender, pink marble, do not break," made me laugh through my tears. Nikolai Ivanovich explained that he had fallen ill because our separation was so difficult for him. He emphasized that he was nonetheless determined to make way for youth, for he did not want to find himself in the role of King Lear, not even with such a beautiful Cordelia.

Oh, that *Khovanshchina!* And that note! What had I done? Even today, when I see a poster announcing that the opera is playing at the Bolshoi, that little note, neatly folded over twice and placed in the door, appears before my mind's eye, and I recall its consequences.

In fact, up until our last days together, Nikolai Ivanovich remained convinced that I had committed a faux pas in respect to him, especially since I had postponed our meeting the very day after he had initiated his serious talk with me.

Even so, when he recalled this incident, he would joke like a man who is sure of himself: "I'm not your Zhenya Sokolnikov, or your Vanka Petrov [references to this imaginary Vanka Petrov made us both laugh], that you can leave me such notes in the door!"

Khovanshchina was, by the way, Nikolai Ivanovich's favorite opera, and three years after the incident of the note, we would finally go together. Immediately after our separation, however, I did not see him. And he no longer came by frequently to see my father, nor visited at all without making sure beforehand that I would not be present.

In January 1932, Father fell seriously ill. I sent telegrams to Nikolai Ivanovich in Nalchik, where he was taking a rest, explaining that his friend Larin was close to death. Bukharin cut short his vacation to return to Moscow but did not manage to arrive until the day after the funeral.

After that, he began to turn up at our place again, primarily because he felt an obligation to show attention to my mother and me during our days of mourning. I cannot say that his presence did not begin to stir me again, but these feelings were drowned by my grief. I loved my father beyond all measure and was severely affected by his death. And there were other reasons for reserve between Nikolai Ivanovich and me. I felt a grievance in my heart against him, and since I viewed our former relationship as a bright but never to be repeated period in my life, I sought escape from my deep longing for him. It was then, and only then, that I began a romance with young Sokolnikov. Previously, Nikolai

Ivanovich's jealousy had been the product of his overactive imagination; there was no basis for it. My fling with Zhenya began only after our separation and began to fall apart when Nikolai Ivanovich reappeared and continued to visit. Time proved that my love for him had taken firm root in my heart. The same was probably true with him, although matters in his case were more complicated. For, as I would soon learn, he was not alone.

In February, a month after Father died, Nikolai Ivanovich sent me to the Molodenovo rest home outside Moscow. He came out for visits himself, very gloomy visits. We were both weighed down with matters we did not care to discuss. Once he brought with him the Sophoclean tragedies *Antigone* and *Oedipus the King* to read aloud to me. I was irritated with myself because I could not concentrate but noticed that Nikolai Ivanovich, even as he read, was also lost in thought about something else, some concern of his own. He soon stopped trying to read. I began talking on and on about my father, remembering various things about him. No matter how hard Nikolai Ivanovich tried to distract me from dwelling on my loss, he would involuntarily be drawn into this conversation himself.

On another occasion, after seeing him off, I wandered in solitude down a wooded path through a park. In the distance, I spied Yan Sten, an independent-minded Party man who always looked down on Stalin from a position of superior intellect. (For this attitude, he paid earlier than most.) There was something majestic in the proud bearing of this Latvian with his expressive, intelligent face, Socratic brow, and shock of light hair. Yan Ernestovich came my way, along with his wife, Valeriya Lvovna. They were young, handsome, happy, in love. I envied them, and the thought flitted through my head that everything was so simple for them, so complicated for me. (But perhaps it only seemed that way to me; everyone has problems.) We met and stopped to talk. Sten directed my attention to a little dacha some way off in the woods.

"Do you recognize who that is sitting there?" he asked.

In a wicker chair beside the porch, surrounded by pillows, wearing a fur coat, and covered with a plaid blanket, sat what appeared to be an old woman. I did not know her.

"That's Nadezhda Mikhailovna Lukina, Bukharin's first wife," Sten explained.

Nikolai Ivanovich had married Nadezhda Mikhailovna, his somewhat older cousin, before the revolution, but their marriage fell apart in the early 1920s. Nadezhda Mikhailovna, who became very ill from a virus that produced a deteriorating spinal condition, had at first been forced to spend most of her time in a reclining position, then gradually

THIS I CANNOT FORGET

became confined to her bed. After Bukharin and I married, she came to live with us. In the days of our ordeal, she gave our family all the warmth of her heart; the love she showed my son was deeply touching.

Nor did she ever waver in her friendship for Nikolai Ivanovich. In the period of his investigation, before his arrest, she sent her Party card to Stalin along with a letter stating that the accusations against Bukharin made her prefer to stay outside the Party. She herself was arrested toward the end of April 1938. Fully expecting them to come for her, she told me that she would take poison as soon as it happened. She did but was discovered and taken posthaste to the prison hospital, where they succeeded in saving her life. It is incomprehensible that they did this. Afterward, she lay like a corpse in her cell until she was taken out and shot. Her bright image lives in my memory to the present day.

Nikolai Ivanovich, as I knew, had also been married a second time. He told me that he had parted from this wife, Esfir Isayevna Gurvich, in 1928 or 1929, I forget which, at her request.

"A holy place does not stay empty long," Yan Sten remarked in jest, quoting a folk proverb, and gave me the name of a woman who had recently become close to Nikolai Ivanovich. I immediately believed him, because he was not the kind of person to pass along idle gossip.

Of course, he could hardly guess the effect this news would have upon me. Neither feeling my feet beneath me nor really perceiving the wide world around, I barely managed to find my way back to my room, where I broke down crying. After all, I had just seen Nikolai Ivanovich off; I was unable to understand what could be going on.

There would be no point in touching upon this unpleasant story if it did not contain a matter of special interest. Here is what Nikolai Ivanovich explained to me later on. Whenever he took the "Arrow" express train to Leningrad to attend a meeting of the presidium of the Academy of Sciences, or on some other business, he invariably encountered "the unknown woman" [so named after Aleksandr Blok's famous poem] in his compartment of the sleeping coach. Distrustful as he was and convinced that special agents were assigned to follow him, he could not believe that a woman informer would be sent his way. Nor did it bother him that this individual always traveled on the same day as he and in the same compartment of the same coach.

Subsequently, it became unnecessary for her to continue taking these trips to Leningrad; she was spending quite enough time with Nikolai Ivanovich in Moscow. After a year and a half, "the unknown woman" gave him an explanation of her business trips. At this point, she had become all too well "known" to him, and he trusted her. Admitting that the NKVD had indeed set her on his trail, she claimed that she had eventually told them that she had fallen in love with him and could not carry out this ignoble mission. Furthermore, she said, she had reported that there was nothing to reveal, anyway, unless they wanted her to lie. Perhaps so, but we know now that any thought or inopportune word uttered by Bukharin could have displeased Stalin and could have been used by the NKVD. Obviously, their conversations were being recorded, and we must understand that it was not too easy to refuse assignments of this kind. She may have told Nikolai Ivanovich the truth about the whole affair, but we cannot rule out the possibility that she spoke up only because she feared he would learn about her mission from some other source. What a horrible story!

Despite Sten's revelation, my newly aroused hopes for a resumption of my relationship with Bukharin were not crushed.

Several days later, he came again to Molodenovo. As chance would have it, he appeared at the very moment I was taking a stroll alongside the rest home with the newly arrived Zhenya Sokolnikov—this time, without a pang of conscience. Catching sight of Bukharin, Zhenya panicked and fled. Nikolai Ivanovich accompanied me into my room, then stated in an imperious tone, "So he's here, too! It's a good thing the era of duels has passed into history."

I could not contain myself. "Does it really make any difference to you?"

He peered into my eyes, trying to determine whether I had found out what he did not want me to know. We spent rather a long time in my little room. Nikolai Ivanovich told me about the doings at the Scientific Research Center and talked about his successful hunt in the environs of Leningrad, where he had just traveled with Sergei Kirov. When evening approached, he left for Moscow.

Throughout 1932, Nikolai Ivanovich continued to visit us at home rather often. I sensed that he was expecting to have a serious talk, but, things being as they were, I held my tongue. In November, I came home from the institute one afternoon to find Nikolai Ivanovich waiting for me. Pale and disturbed, he had come straight from the funeral of Stalin's wife, Nadezhda Sergeyevna Alliluyeva. Bukharin and she had been close personal friends. She secretly shared his views on collectivization and had found an opportunity to tell him so.

Nadezhda Sergeyevna was a kind, modest person with an attractive appearance and fragile constitution. She continually suffered from Stalin's crude, despotic character. Not long before, Nikolai Ivanovich had seen her in the Kremlin at a banquet in honor of the October Revolution. According to him, Stalin, half-drunk, had thrown cigarette butts and orange peels in his wife's face. Unable to bear such humiliation, she had got up and left before the end of the dinner. The following morning, Nadezhda Sergeyevna was found dead. Supposedly, she had shot herself, although the state press would report to the public that she died from peritonitis. As Nikolai Ivanovich stood in formal mourning beside her coffin, Stalin considered it timely and appropriate to walk over and explain that he had gone to his dacha right after the banquet and only in the morning had been phoned and told what had happened. This account contradicts the published reminiscences of Svetlana, the daughter of Nadezhda Sergeyevna and Stalin. Many years after her mother's death, she writes, Molotov's wife told her that Stalin had been sleeping in the room adjoining Nadezhda Sergeyevna's bedroom in the Moscow apartment and had not heard a shot. Were not Stalin's remarks to Nikolai Ivanovich an attempt to ward off suspicion that he murdered his wife? Whether murder or suicide, I do not know, but Bukharin certainly did not discount the possibility of murder. As he told it, the first to see Stalin's wife dead, after Svetlana's nurse had tried to wake her that morning, was Avel Yenukidze; he had been called by the nurse, who was afraid to tell Stalin directly herself. Could this be the reason Yenukidze was purged earlier than other members of the Central Committee?

Bukharin also told me that before the coffin was closed Stalin motioned for them to delay lowering the lid. He lifted Nadezhda Sergeyevna's head up out of the coffin and began kissing it.

"What good are those kisses?" Nikolai Ivanovich bitterly asked, as he recalled the scene for me on the sad day of the funeral. "He killed her!"

He also told me how once, by chance, he had called at the dacha in Zubalovo when Stalin was not at home. Nadezhda Sergeyevna was there, however, and they took a walk around the grounds outside the dacha, discussing this and that. Unbeknownst to them, Stalin arrived and crept up stealthily behind them. When they turned in surprise, he looked Nikolai Ivanovich straight in the face and uttered a terrible threat: "I'll kill you."

Bukharin took this as a crude joke, but Nadezhda Sergeyevna shuddered and turned pale.

About a month after the funeral, sometime in December, Nikolai Ivanovich invited me to the Hall of Columns in the House of Trade Unions, where the fiftieth anniversary of Darwin's death was being commemorated. Bukharin and Anatoly Lunacharsky gave addresses. I sat in the first row next to the academicians, the luminaries of natural science, who seemed impressed by both speakers' breadth of knowledge, apparently sharing their views and applauding warmly. Afterward, Nikolai Ivanovich wiggled his finger for me to come up to him on the platform. I did, and we went to a room behind the stage and joined Lunacharsky. I had seen him once before, in Red Square in January, when he delivered a funeral speech before the urn with my father's ashes and then descended from the Lenin Mausoleum to press my mother's and my hands in sympathy.

As we met again backstage, it was, of course, impossible to imagine that he himself had only one year to live and that in December 1933 Bukharin would mount the same rostrum of the Mausoleum in Red Square to deliver the valediction.

We exchanged greetings, and Lunacharsky said to Bukharin, "Time flies, Nikolai Ivanovich. We're getting older, but Anna Mikhailovna is blossoming and getting prettier. Such is the law of nature. There's no escaping it!"

He was the first person to address me as an adult by my given name and patronymic. I was flattered and felt like a grown-up. Then he suddenly asked to see my hand: Lunacharsky took an interest in palmistry. He examined the lines of my palm briefly, but intently, and then I saw him darken and could just barely hear him mutter under his breath to Nikolai Ivanovich, "A terrible fate awaits Anna Mikhailovna!"

Lunacharsky noticed that I had heard and tried to smooth over his dire prophecy. "Possibly the lines of your hand deceive me," he said. "That can happen!"

Nikolai Ivanovich, not the least perturbed, said simply, "Your forecast is mistaken, Anatoly Vasiliyevich. Anyutka will certainly be happy. We shall make every effort!"

"You do that, Nikolai Ivanovich," Lunacharsky rejoined with a faint smile.

Although I may not have fully believed in his fortune-telling, I was upset for a while, if not for long. I told my mother about it the same day, and she never forgot. Many years later, after my release from the camp, she recalled it over and over.

The scientific addresses ended rather early, and Nikolai Ivanovich, hoping to curtail my reflections upon my sad fate, suggested I ride with him to Lenin Hills to meet with Lenin's sister, Mariya Ilyinichna Ulyanova. When they had worked together in the *Pravda* editorial offices in the 1920s, he had formed a close friendship with her, which he preserved.

We arrived in the evening. Lenin Hills was desolate and gloomy. Mariya Ilyinichna was not home; the road to her house was piled with snow. The guard, who had worked there under Lenin, was clearing a pathway with a big wooden shovel. He greeted Bukharin like an old acquaintance and took off his fur cap, earflaps and all, to say hello. Then he treated us to hot tea and preserves, and we stayed awhile to chat. On the way back to Moscow, Nikolai Ivanovich told me that once, in the summer of 1928 or 1929 (or perhaps even earlier, I forget), he had come to Lenin Hills and seen a cat playing around next to this same guard.

"At least the cat is still alive!" Nikolai Ivanovich said then.

"I guard the cat," the guard replied, "but you don't know how to guard yourself. Ilyich [Lenin] is gone, and all you can do is start arguments."

"That guard is a wise man," Nikolai Ivanovich observed to me.

The months passed. At times, when Nikolai Ivanovich came to see my mother, I was not around. But each time, before leaving, he would stick a little note in my desk drawer: "I was here, your N.B." "I was here, your Kola." "I was here, I was here, I was here, your Nikolasha."

Oh, how they disturbed me, those little notes! Even so, I decided neither to phone him and invite him over nor to go to see him at his place.

Only at the end of 1933, in December, did a sorrowful circumstance, Lunacharsky's death, force me to turn to Nikolai Ivanovich, because he could help me gain access to the Hall of Columns, where the body lay in state. We walked together to stand by the coffin of the great prophet of my fate, and neither of us doubted any longer that his predictions would come true.

The following day, I saw Nikolai Ivanovich at the funeral ceremonies in Red Square. After the interment, I made my way through the crowd surrounding the Lenin Mausoleum and went up to him. He was burdened with sorrow, worn out from his speech, and, or so it seemed to me then, suddenly much older.

As we left Red Square together, walking down past the Museum of History toward Aleksandrovsky Gardens, Nikolai Ivanovich told me dolefully, "I've never thought of my own death. It's as if I always sensed my immortality more than my death. Only now, during Lunacharsky's funeral, did I feel that the same thing is waiting for me. I imagined my own funeral so distinctly: the Hall of Columns in the House of Trade Unions, Red Square, the urn of my ashes wreathed with flowers, and you, crying first over my coffin and then beside my urn. I imagined someone else, I'm not sure who, making the speech. 'He was mistaken more than once,' this orator will say, 'but, but . . . Lenin loved him.' And then he'll go on to something else." Nikolai Ivanovich said these things with a mournful look, completely unimpressed by the honors and splendor of the funeral he envisioned. He spoke about it as something inevitable and therefore clear in his sight.

"I don't want to listen to such nonsense," I interjected, becoming upset.

"But that's definitely the way it will be, and you'll have to go through it!"

This is how Nikolai Ivanovich imagined his death, and consequently his life, as 1933 drew to a close. Naturally, he could not foresee the accusations of treason and betrayal of his motherland.

We parted. He turned to the left into Aleksandrovsky Gardens, toward the Troitsky Gates of the Kremlin; I to the right, toward the Metropol. The notes he had left for me so often gave me the right to change the subject, to talk about life, not death, but I did not think it feasible to do so at such a somber moment.

And so, by an uneasy path, overcoming obstacles we set in front of ourselves time and again, we continued to proceed toward our goal, which was to unite our two fates. This uncertain period went "from congress to congress," I once jokingly put it to Nikolai Ivanovich, when at last we were able to laugh freely together. That is to say, from the Sixteenth Party Congress, in 1930, to the Seventeenth, in 1934, which was the last one Bukharin and most of the Central Committee members would attend.

As 1934 began, the year that would end with the resounding, fateful shot at Kirov, I discovered yet another note in my desk drawer: "I was here, your N.B." This finally made up my mind.

But it was by chance that we met soon afterward on January 27, my twentieth birthday. Nikolai Ivanovich was returning home to his apartment in the Kremlin after a session of the Seventeenth Party Congress at the Bolshoi, and I was coming from a lecture at the university, "Stalin Is Lenin Today."

We met by the House of Trade Unions, by the building that still today pains my eyes and forces me to turn away, averting my gaze. Yet, willy-nilly, my gaze is always drawn back to that street where, after such a long period of indecision, we both understood in an instant that the path had closed off behind us and that there was no going back.

We stood by the same door where a decade before, on January 27, 1924, Bukharin and others, the closest friends and comrades-in-arms of Lenin, grief-stricken, had carried him out, bearing the scarlet coffin on their shoulders, and trod in a slow funeral procession through the fierce frost toward Red Square. On their shoulders, they also bore their own destruction—in the short term, their political death; in the long, physical extermination.

As we stood there, cheered by our unexpected encounter, anticipating where it would lead, we could not know that it would be this very House of Trade Unions where, four years in the future, in March of 1938, in October Hall, Nikolai Ivanovich would spend the last, tormenting days of his life embroiled in a horrifying trial no better than a medieval inquisition, from which he would emerge onto this street carrying the death sentence, breathing here for the last time, if he breathed at all, the outdoor, nonprison air.

How cleverly fate is interwoven! Beside this building, which looks so somber to me today, precisely here, our feelings finally burst into the open that January of 1934.

We did not waste words: "Are you going to keep leaving me those notes? Do you suppose they don't disturb me?"

Nikolai Ivanovich, wearing leather jacket and boots, became greatly agitated as he stood beside me. His face flushed; he ran his fingers nervously through this goatee, which was still a bright, sunny amber. This was the moment of decision.

"Do you want me to come to your place right now?" he asked.

"I do," I answered confidently.

"But in that case I will never leave you!"

"You don't have to."

It was but a stone's throw from the House of Trade Unions to the Metropol.

We never again parted until the day of his arrest, February 27, 1937 (again the twenty-seventh, a fateful number). On that date, before he left to attend the final, decisive meeting of the February–March plenum of the Central Committee, knowing that arrest awaited him, Nikolai Ivanovich fell down on his knees before me and begged me not to forget a single word of his letter "To a Future Generation of Party Leaders," begged forgiveness for ruining my life, begged that I raise our son, Yura, to be a Bolshevik. "A Bolshevik, without fail!" he said twice.

And so in the cellar in Novosibirsk, casting my gaze from the past to the gloomy present and into the impenetrable future, that black inevitability, I began to regret the years I had lost in indecision, not the comparatively calm ones I spent with Nikolai Ivanovich at last. Yet even so, forced to admit that our life together had been very short in actual years, I did not, and to the present day still do not, have the sensation that it really was all that short, because the feeling of a much longer intimacy, including the years "from congress to congress," lives within me.

Running my eyes over the cell, glancing into the dreadful upper corner of my nightmares, I wanted so desperately to see Nikolai Ivanovich that my eyes sought out even that crucified, pale blue apparition. But it did not reappear. Only gloom, silence, oppressive solitude.

[Deeper into the Gulag]

One day in the middle of August, I heard the familiar clank of the door bolt. The guard opened the door and led a woman into the cell. And so it was that a live person stood before me—my new cellmate, Nina Lebedeva. Well past forty, she had already served a five-year term in a camp under article KRD (counterrevolutionary activity), which was widely applied at that time. Then, like me, she was arrested a second time, but charged with "wrecking" because of a fire in camp. This was a routine charge.

From the start, Lebedeva was taken out frequently for interrogations with Skvirsky. She would always sob when she came back. As an older woman, she assumed a protective, even warm, attitude toward me. After my months of solitude, I longed for human speech and trusted her completely. What a mistake!

I opened up freely to her, told her about the charge against me, and shared my speculations about how the imaginary counterrevolutionary youth organization could have been created by my tormentors. Naming the sons of Sverdlov, Osinsky, Ganetsky, and Sokolnikov, I pointed out that all but young Sverdlov were offspring of persecuted Bolsheviks. In short, through this Lebedeva I myself suggested a scenario for Skvirsky. Also, I often repeated my verses aloud so that I would not forget them. She either jotted them down without my noticing or memorized them— one way or another, they would appear in my file.

I talked quite a bit about Bukharin's trial, attributing the confessions of the accused to torture. I recounted in detail Nikolai Ivanovich's trip to Paris in 1936. Ostensibly, Stalin had sent him there to purchase the Marx archive, but the Gensek had a hidden provocational purpose: to "connect" Bukharin with the Menshevik émigrés, the adherents of the Second International.

Although Lebedeva asked about Bukharin's foreign contacts, I was not suspicious; I took her interest as a woman's natural curiosity. I explained to her that Bukharin, as the director of the Comintern and a Soviet representative at diplomatic receptions and on foreign missions, would have inevitably met with foreigners. Foolishly, I told her about the time Nikolai Ivanovich, traveling to Leningrad, had found himself in the same compartment with William C. Bullitt, the first U.S. ambassador to the Soviet Union, and had carried on a conversation, the content of which I did not remember. This disclosure would also be used against me. In a word, my candid admissions were suicidal, and my "file" soon bulged!

Around the middle of September, Lebedeva was removed from the cell. Evidently, she had earned herself better conditions of confinement.

Soon, I too took leave of that terrible cellar. One of my guards was cold and nasty, but the other, who was more flexible, talkative, and considerate, told me I would be departing from Novosibirsk shortly. It was he who allowed me to pick sagebrush in the prison courtyard, did not hurry me back to my cell during a walk, and even allowed me to sleep during the day. Never did I hear him shout, "C'mon, c'mon, back in your cell. The time for your walk is over!"

"You know, girlie," he said in passing (he intended no offense by calling me "girlie"; on the contrary, the word emphasized his kindly disposition toward me), "soon we will all be leaving here and going to a different place. Both you and us, the whole Investigative Department is transferring."

"Where to?"

"To Mariinsk, closer to production," he answered gravely, for this is how it had been explained at a general meeting of employees of the Siblag Investigative Department.

At the time, a large number of camps were concentrated around Mariinsk, a town in southwestern Siberia not far from Kemerovo. These camps included Chistyunka, Orlovo-Rozovo, Yurga, Yaya, Antibes, Novo-Ivanovsky, as well as others. Eventually, I would have the pleasure of seeing some of them from the inside. As a whole, they formed the Mariinsk camp system, which had a center, or capital, called Marraspred [Mariinsk distribution], from which prisoners were dispatched to one or another camp, depending upon the need for manpower.

I found myself at Marraspred a number of times. Once, I ended up in the same barracks, on the same bed boards, where the future Soviet marshal Konstantin Rokossovsky had served time. The camp command, which had come over to peer at me as at some rare specimen, a virtual museum exhibit, recalled aloud, "Rokossovsky sat there, right on that very spot. And now look who's here, Bukharin's wife!" Evidently, from their point of view, I defiled those bed planks. "They don't imprison innocent people around here," one of them said, but added, "Sure, Rokossovsky got put in by mistake, but they figured it out and released him." It was obviously considered proper to recount this incident in my presence. I was only a criminal.

In September the decision was made to transfer the Siblag Investi-

gative Department to Mariinsk. As my guard had suggested, the aim
was to reduce the cost of a prisoner's daily confinement, which included
the rising expenses of transport. More and more prisoners had not been
killed off, had served their "insufficiently long" terms (that is, ten years
or less), and therefore had to be transported for reinvestigation. By
1938, the maximum sentence had been extended to twenty-five years,
ensuring a broad field of activity for the Investigative Department.
Thus, for example, my friend Sarra Yakir received a ten-year addition to
her eight-year sentence for remarking in camp that the Mediterranean
Sea was no less beautiful than the Black Sea and that the embroidered
blouses sewn in Italy were lovely. Such "seditious" comments were seen
as praise for a capitalist state. (I do not exaggerate; that's the way it was.)
Her investigation was conducted on the premises, in the Tomsk prison,
and she was sentenced under article KRA, counterrevolutionary agitation. By condemning her right there, the Siblag "wise men" were able to
give the wife of General Yakir an eighteen-year term of confinement
without saddling the state with "undue" transport expenses.

It was only a few days after Lebedeva vanished that the "great resettle-
ment of peoples" began. I was taken to the train station in the same car
as before, driven by the same man, Eikhe's former chauffeur. This time,
he did not dare breathe a single word to me. A gray throng of exhausted
prisoners waited at the station. Such a vast number, of course, could not
have been kept in the underground isolation cells; they had been
rounded up from other Novosibirsk prisons. Only after they were
marched in a convoy around the station and had disappeared from view
toward the train did a man come up to the car to convey me there as
well.

A special train had been provided for this transfer, consisting
mainly of dark red freight cars designed in a previous age for the transport of livestock. At the head of the train, however, were three or four
passenger cars for the administration of the Siblag Investigative Department, including Skvirsky. I was not permitted to travel in a car with
other women prisoners, and a compartment in one of the passenger cars
was out of the question, since a Novosibirsk prisoner was not conveyed
in such comfort. It was decided, therefore, to put me in a "calf" car with
the convoy guards and their families.

My escort led me to this car. The women, uprooted from their
well-feathered nests, bustled busily about; their babies bawled. In this
unbelievable commotion, pushing and shoving, everyone was trying to
get a berth on the hastily constructed bed boards, afraid of winding up

on the cold, dirty floor. The women lugged a jumbled mass of house-hold items in bundles, baskets, suitcases, trunks. They stuffed the calf car with saucepans, tongs, skillets, iron pots, and samovars. They brought along their cats, dogs, and house plants—geraniums, rubber plants, century plants. "Wath out, wath out! You'll break my thentury!" a woman's voice pierced the air. They loaded on their accordions. A Russian village cannot do without them. Even though the convoy guards had supposedly exchanged their native villages for a "better life" in the penal system, they could not leave their accordions behind.

The men valiantly helped their families load their possessions onto the calf car and climb aboard. Only the "orphaned" wife and two chil-dren of my escort lacked the support of the head of the household, for he alone remained on duty. As one of the guards, passing by us, tossed his family's things onto the train, my watchdog's wife, holding one child by the hand and the other in her arm, kept getting crowded back, so she could not get up into the car. Her husband and I stood to the side, a few paces from the loading place. Finally, at the end of her strength and patience, she called out, "Yegor! Why are you standing there like a block? Give me a hand, your little girlie won't run away!"

But her Yegor, a servitor of rare breed, refused to budge from the spot.

"Go help your wife," I prompted him. "There's nowhere for me to run to."

"Nowhere? If there had been, you would have run. We know your kind!"

Trying to be helpful, I had set Yegor on his guard even more.

"Vaska!" he shouted to someone. "Be a friend, help my old lady. I'm on duty."

But his voice was drowned out in the noisy hubbub. Only after everyone else had clambered onto the train and the crush was over did we—I, Yegor, his wife and kids—get up into the calf car last of all. As expected, there were not enough places on the bed boards, and many people were on the floor, sitting on their bags with their mattresses, pillows, and blankets. The senior officer in the car ordered people on the bed boards to squeeze together, and we were able to find room for ourselves on the upper planks: I next to the window, my escort beside me, his family directly across from us. Worn out by the mobbing and her irksome boarding, Yegor's wife could not stop grumbling at him:

"To hell with you! What the devil is driving you to this Mariinsk, huh? Why couldn't you stay here in Novosibirsk? There's work enough for you, but no, you have to go off who knows where, into a hole in the ground!"

"Pipe down, city lady. You won't be any worse off there. They'll give you a big yard, you can plant potatoes to your heart's content, you can fatten up two big hogs, and the next thing you know, you'll be in the money. That's what you really love, but you never get enough."

Eventually, everyone got more or less comfortable and quieted down a bit. Unexpectedly, I found myself in company that was free and easy. Workers who had been hired from the outside to work in the camp system were called freemen, and, though confined to the grounds, they really did feel themselves to be free. Freedom, after all, is a matter of conscious choice. Nothing weighed on them. The shining, red-cheeked faces of their wives in the Tomsk camp particularly impressed me, compared with the haggard, harrowed, and hungry faces of the imprisoned wives of "enemies of the people."

The staff of this convoy in that prewar time was youthful, but one man wise with years was smuggled among them in our car. He sat not far off, so I could hear him sharing his thoughts with his young companions:

"When I was a boy, the livestock were pastured in the village, bringing good to the peasants, but what do you see today? The people are pastured, and there's so many people needing to be pastured that soon there won't be enough pastors for them; there won't be anybody at all left to pasture the animals, and nobody to sow the wheat. Just think of it, and horror grabs you! It's the end of the world, not life!"

He alone, of everyone in the whole freight car, was disturbed by what was happening; the rest regarded his observations with no more than passing interest.

Finally, an ear-splitting whistle sounded; the locomotive huffed and puffed and set its wheels in motion; we lurched forward. This movement of the car cage somehow deepened my suffocating sense of lack of freedom, intensified the prospect of never getting out from behind bars, and struck me altogether as a start in the direction of death.

At the stations we passed, celebratory portraits of the NKVD chief Yezhov were displayed, along with posters singing hymns of praise to the so-called Yezhov mittens, which mercilessly threatened the "wasp's nests of the enemies of the people." [In one famous poster, Yezhov, wearing "steel mittens," squeezes a snake with the heads of Trotsky, Rykov, and Bukharin.]

All at once, the blood rushed to my head. My heart constricted. What had been the point of writing my plea to Yezhov, "Shoot me, I do not want to live"? That could be managed without my making a request. Perhaps, after all, it was not a case of "I do not want to." I did want to see my son again someday. But was he alive? I no longer knew. My

declaration to Yezhov had given voice to my desperation, to the hopelessness of my situation, and to the terrible conditions in which I lived in
Novosibirsk. It had also presented a challenge: you have destroyed everyone dear to me, you murdered the man I loved ardently, you smeared
him from head to toe with filth—now, murder me, too!

But life was bubbling on around me: the wives of the convoy
guards, chattering merrily, laughing heartily, got ready for supper. Over
their boxes one woman spread a towel, another a rag, another a newspaper. They cut off thick slices of bread and fatback, ladled boiled potatoes
and cooked eggs from saucepans. The children grabbed their milk; the
men, their vodka. But these guards drank just a bit, a shot or two, not
enough to get drunk: the train might stop at any moment and become
crawling with commanders. The women tried to feed me, but my Yegor
prevented them. "Not permitted," he said.

All the others had a few bites, took a few nips, and began to enjoy
themselves. Out came the accordions, and in rich harmony these "free"
people sang "A Reed Sounded," the mournful song about a tramp:

> *A tramp is walking from Sakhalin,*
> *Long, long is his path,*
> *"Cover me over, bleak taiga,"*
> *The tramp longs for his rest.*

And then, singing *chastushki* [rhyming ditties] as the accordions
played, they sprang into a dance:

> *See, in our garden, at the back,*
> *The grass is matted down,*
> *But it's not the wind, not a storm,*
> *It's love that smoothed the ground!*

The men, crouched down on their haunches, kicked their legs this
way and that. And the women, waving their kerchiefs and moving with
surprising lightness, seemed weightless, though they were by no means
distinguished by graceful figures. I saw now that our world behind bars,
the world of the insulted, humiliated, and executed, was but a drop in
the sea of all life, a mere microcosm! Despite the horrors prepared for us
prisoners by fate, life went on. Life! . . . it is all-powerful! It cuts a path
for itself, like the delicate fairy-ring mushroom pushing up through hard
thick asphalt. Watching this merriment, I was for a while distracted from
my brooding reflections upon the future. After we had traveled three to
four hours without a stop, and as there was no toilet, I asked my escort

what I was expected to do. Yegor could only advise that I follow the example of the others. In the floorboards, close to one side of the car, a hole had been broken through. This was the makeshift toilet. Some people had friends form a screen when they did their business, but others, abandoning shame, brazenly went ahead in front of us all. I refused to take my escort's advice. "Then wait till they stop the train," he snapped, "but if you can't hold out, do it in the bowl." He was talking about my soup bowl. Toward evening the train stopped, and we all, man and dog alike, made a dash for the bushes. My faithful companion remained at my side; I barely managed to persuade him to look the other way. Suddenly, this servitor felt the same necessity but would not absent himself until he found a stand-in. Clearly, Yegor was endowed by nature with more than his fair share of thickheadedness, but, in his favor, it must be noted that the order to keep me isolated and under guard was evidently most strict.

The next day we arrived in Mariinsk. The isolation prison was nearby. It was spanking new, its builders having just reported, as prescribed, the shock-work completion of the project. The cell, solitary again but drier than the one in Novosibirsk, smelled of brick dust and fresh paint. Filings were scattered about on the floor, mixed with sawdust. The steel bed had a mattress, a slipcase filled with straw. But the new facility was found unfit for the confinement of prisoners. As so often happens with shock-work projects, there was an unfinished "little trifle"; in this case, the kitchen had not been completed. All of us prisoners were famished to such a degree that soon the investigators would be forced to certify, under article 206 of the Russian Republic Criminal Code (in the numeration used then), that the preliminary investigation had ended for each of us, for the obvious reason. Infuriated, Skvirsky ran out down the corridor while the prisoners sent up a great roar. We went without food for the next twenty-four hours. Finally, the command decided to evacuate us.

We were all sent to penalty cells in the nearby camps. I was taken to the one closest by, which bore the amusing name Antibes [pronounced *anti-byes,* which can be understood as "Anti-Demon"]. We prisoners smiled ironically at this, for it looked as if the authorities sought with this appellation to exorcise our demon, the demon of our counterrevolutionary core.

My escort for this transfer was a freckled, redheaded lad of eighteen years; he was friendly, chatty, and uncommonly kindhearted. When I ventured to ask his name, he responded at once, like a child: "They call me Vanyok." Strange as it seems, he was not surprised that I had asked and treated me not like a prisoner but like a young lady he would like to get to know better. Vanyok was the complete opposite of Yegor. Even so, as we started off on foot, he warned me what circumstances would require him to use his weapon, according to his instructions.

Having just emerged from a sunless cellar into the translucent radiance of an autumn day, I mentally threw off, as it were, the shackles of my confinement. What a delicious illusion! I could even think about my appearance: "How do I look today?" This was a mystery, since we were not given mirrors. I imagined my complexion had become like that of Katyusha Maslova, the heroine of Lev Tolstoi's novel *Resurrection*. That is, my face was probably "of that special whiteness observed in the faces of people who have spent a long time locked up, recalling the sprouts of a cellar potato," as the novelist described his heroine going from prison to court. Quite unlike the full-bosomed Katyusha, however, I was wasted in the extreme.

As we walked past the sturdy village houses outside Mariinsk, passersby hardly noticed us. Their eyes had become accustomed to the submissive plodding of prisoners under guard. I heard a dog barking, hens clucking; in gardens behind little fences, I saw the tops of potatoes gathered neatly into piles; here and there, the yellowed but still firm stalks of sunflowers poked up, shorn of their heads. Not far from us, some woman shouted after her darting child, "Maruska, don't go too far, you'll get lost. Maruska-a-a, don't go too far-r-r!"

The road we took seemed remarkably picturesque to me. To the left stood copses of birches and little islands of aspens. Bedecked in the brilliant hues of autumn, the trees sighed in the wind, letting fall their leaves, which spiraled in the air before dropping to earth like a gold-and-violet rain, releasing the final warmth stored up in the short but hot Siberian summer. To the right spread endless vistas: scythed meadows, a wheat field not yet completely harvested. Heavy, ripe, bent-over ears of grain rustled nearby. Beyond, I could see enormous haystacks and the yellowed stubble of a cropped field.

If someone had been able to peek into my soul at that moment, I would have been ashamed that this enchanting beauty of nature could delight me so, only six months after Nikolai Ivanovich's death. But Ilya Ehrenburg had set it down accurately: "A person can be consoled by a trifle, the sound of leaves or a bright cloudburst in summer." I remember that day as an extraordinary exception, never to be repeated in all the days of my confinement. But my mood was uplifted not only by nature, which struck me as fabulously beautiful after the impenetrable murk of the cellar, but by the young convoy guard who gave me the opportunity to enjoy it, who helped me understand that there were still people on earth who remained sensitive and considerate despite their highly unpleasant duties.

Soon afterward, sitting alone in the Antibes isolation prison, I composed verses that, I think, reflect my mood at the time better than prose.

Convoy Guard

He was young, the lad who led me,
A good boy, that convoy guard.
He was simple, and simple to him
Seemed this complicated world.

So-called enemies he led
From first light to nighttime dark,
Glum, obedient, they trod
Without dogs, without shackles.

We paused. He broke up branches,
Smoke curled up from the little fire,
And I thought, Could life be better?
Could it? No, not in that hour!

But not long past, in a dark cellar,
I was rotting, though alive,
When in the corner a vision
Rose vividly before my eyes.

I saw a crucifixion there,
On the cross a man, not Christ!
His arms limp, his lips blood-red,
I yearned for his embrace.

A great crow, black and evil,
Pecked into his heart, his brain.
Blood oozed out in scarlet drops,
The bird triumphed in its disdain.

For this crow thrived on the dead,
Gorged itself, could not be sated.
Throughout Russia it had spread
Fear, oppression, shame, and slavery.

Yet was it autumn, the woods clothed
In a golden sarafan [peasant's blouse],
As the artist loved to paint them,
The celebrated Levitan.

Sighs and moans blew through the forest,
Nearly drunk the fresh air made me.
Sunlight shone down so brightly,
But spread no warmth for me.

And the wheat began to sway
In a broad and golden wave.
Why was it standing still there,
Waiting for the curved blade?

At last, the evening slipped away,
Lighting the forest in the west,
And then I saw the camp ahead:
Isolator "Antibes."

Since the isolation section at Antibes was located well inside the camp compound, it was itself encircled only by a somewhat unstable wattle fence. My new cell was larger and brighter than the one at Novosibirsk, furnished with a rather wide grated window. The facility was only halfway below ground, so the upper bed boards were at ground level. Through the window, I could clearly see a part of the prison courtyard and beyond the wattle fence into the camp compound, where prisoners were marching in convoy to work: Antibes was an agricultural camp.

This investigative prison had previously been used as a punishment block for the camp. In the cell across from me were the three biologists who had been behind the wall at Novosibirsk with the doomed NKVD officer. Behind the wall adjacent to me was Zhigan, a bandit. Only a month before the end of his ten-year sentence, he found the anticipation of approaching freedom so unbearable that he broke out of the camp. He was caught. While he was confined next to me, he managed to bore a peephole in the wall for spying on me, then ground away until he could literally poke his head right into my cell. I was horrified to see his face staring at me with burning black eyes. I had no choice but to tell the guard, and Zhigan was taken off to another cell.

By this time, I was an experienced *zek* [from *zaklyuchyonnyi*, "prisoner"], having already been detained in many prisons: Astrakhan, Saratov, Sverdlovsk, Tomsk, Novosibirsk. I had become accustomed to an isolated existence without books, paper, or pencil, unable to do anything but string together rhymes and memorize them by endless repetition, read from memory the verses of my favorite poets, and repeat Bukharin's letter-testament, as I did every morning without fail.

After the dampness of my former cellar cell, Antibes seemed not only tolerable but, strange to say, downright cozy. In the evenings, birch logs crackled pleasantly in the oven in the corridor. We were also fed much better than in the other prisons: you got your fill of vegetables, and they weren't frozen, either; there were even pieces of pork floating in the soup. Not bad for that terrible time. Also, Skvirsky was not bothering me. That September and October of 1938 passed easily enough. By November, winter held the Siberian land in its icy grip; dazzling white piles of snow could be seen through the window.

And the waiting was becoming unbearable. Then, to my delight, a new jailer appeared: Vanyok, the boy about whom I had written my poem. Once, on one of my daily walks, I noticed a starving kitten with a typically plush Siberian coat sitting in the snow, shivering. I asked Vanyok for permission to take it to my cell. He considered a moment. "Why not? Take it," he decided. I named the kitten Antibes. Then, suddenly, another happy surprise: for the first and last time in all my years in prison, money from my mother came. It had taken a whole year to reach me. By this time, she was already behind bars herself.

In the prison commissary, Vanyok bought me a jar of plum preserves, a roll of white bread, a bag of candy puffs, a package of tea, cookies, and a can of milk. Thus the kitty and I were able to honor the twenty-first anniversary of the October Revolution. I spread a clean rag over the bed boards, and "my table was weighed down with victuals": cookies, preserves, bread. Right beside me, the kitten noisily lapped up milk I had poured into the emptied conserve jar. I snatched him up in my arms and loudly declaimed, "Antibesik, let us drink (milk, that is), to Stalin and to our 'happy' life! Hurrah to him, hurrah! For without him you would have frozen in the snow!"

Then disaster occurred. The door to my cell flew open, and in walked the chief of the camp's investigative section. He was furious.

"What's going on here? This is a new one: you've turned the cell into a zoo! And you permit yourself the impertinence of drinking to Stalin with a cat! Are you making fun of the Leader? And who brought you this cat?"

I tried to protect Vanyok. "No one brought him, I picked him up myself during my walk. He was freezing. I didn't let the jailer see me."

"Ivan, take this cat out of here! If this sort of thing ever happens again, you're fired!"

And Vanyok tossed the kitten back out into the frost. I was in solitude again until the second half of November, when they brought Nina
Lebedeva to me again. How pleasant! What a joy! Here were two old
acquaintances, virtually friends, having a reunion. At the time, I still
trusted her. Lebedeva artfully explained our temporary separation: supposedly, the authorities had concluded her case and sent her to a camp,
but, because of new circumstances (additional testimonies against her),
she was placed under investigation again. She wondered whether I was
still composing verses, so at once I recited my poem about the convoy
guard.

"What a long, complete poem! It's remarkable you were able to
memorize it all. That part about the crow is excellent. Repeat it for me!"

And so I repeated it, more than once.

"Really, it's wonderful! And the crow . . . that's Stalin, isn't it?"

"You can understand it any way you like."

"Obviously, it's Stalin. Who else could it be?"

I did not answer, but suddenly a disturbing thought flitted through
my mind: Could Lebedeva be a "plant"? But the suspicion was momentary.

I recited some verses dedicated to the October Revolution, lines in
which I expressed the anguish and emotional pain I felt sitting behind
bars on the anniversary date. But I also affirmed that "I celebrate this
day together with my happy land," for I could not be false to the revolutionary ideal. That is why I felt it so tragic that people who had devoted
their life to the revolution should now perish, branded as its enemies. I
knew that their confessions were all coerced fabrications, and I hated
Stalin with a passion, but I could not look at the October Revolution
itself through the prism of my miseries. I was not like the slave Mankurt
in the legend I would read many years later in *The Day Lasts Longer
Than a Hundred Years,* a remarkable novel by the Soviet writer Chinghiz
Aitmatov. His owners took away Mankurt's memory; he could no longer
recognize even his mother. If I were ever stripped of memory, I would
cease to be myself, but only in legend can a person's memory be taken
away. And whoever tries to ignore his memory will live with an impure
conscience. My slave owners were unable to erase my recollections, my
identity. I had grown up among professional revolutionaries, the Bolsheviks who fought for the October Revolution, for its ideals. They had
formed my worldview. Only because of them was I able to compose
verses like these:

> *I peer in silence through the bars,*
> *Only a flimsy fence I see,*

And the snow, gleaming in beauty
On today's most happy day!

But the limpid northern dawn
Returns to me an austere gaze,
Glinting coldly, like mother-of-pearl,
On this frosty, frozen morn.

Today, the pain is especially hard,
My heart constricts into a ball,
Against my will the teardrops stream,
Running in lines down my cheeks!

Yet, though behind iron bars I stay,
Feeling the anguish of the damned,
Still I celebrate this day
Together with my happy land.

The poem ended with these words:

Today I have a new belief:
I will enter life again,
And stride again with my Komsomol
Side by side across Red Square!

These last lines, I now regard as the ravings of a lunatic, a momentary idea born of the emotional distress I felt on the anniversary of the revolution. The whole poem has no poetic value, only psychological interest, because it mirrors an epoch. When I recited it to the prisoner wives of the old Bolsheviks, they were moved to tears and applause, precisely because it reflected their state of mind as well as my own.

Years later, when I studied the record of Bukharin's trial, I discovered these same thoughts in the testimony of many of the accused. After confessing to monstrous crimes, Arkady Rozengolts uttered the following words at the very threshold of death: "I say, May the great, mighty, magnificent Union of Soviet Socialist Republics live long, flourish, and grow ever stronger, proceeding from one victory to the next! Long live the Bolshevik Party with the best possible traditions of enthusiasm, heroism, and self-sacrifice, which can exist in the modern world only under the leadership of Stalin!"*

*Court Record in the Case of the Anti-Soviet "Bloc of Rightists and Trotskyists," p. 677.

About one thing Rozengolts was not mistaken: in our modern world that "best possible self-sacrifice" whereby accused men confessed to crimes they had not committed could indeed occur only under the leadership of Stalin. Even fascist Germany, at the Leipzig trial in 1933, could not force the Bulgarian Communist Georgi Dimitrov to confess to the provocational charge that he had burned down the Reichstag.

Bukharin's last statement also sounded his codefendant's theme: "Everyone can see the wise leadership of the country, guaranteed by Stalin. Conscious of this, I await the verdict. What is important here is not the personal tribulation of a penitent enemy but the flowering of the USSR, its international significance."*

Nikolai Ivanovich had said much the same thing to me when parting, taking his leave of me forever: "See that you don't get angry, Anyutka. There are irritating misprints in history."

And as Nikita Khrushchev would report to the Twenty-second Party Congress, our celebrated Red Army commander Iona Yakir shouted out just before the bullets struck him, "Long live the Party, long live Stalin!"

My cellmate proved to be a bird of a different feather. Again and again, she listened intently as I memorized my anniversary verses by repeating them aloud. She was not enraptured, but she did not protest.

After about two weeks, Lebedeva was called out for an interrogation. When she returned to the cell, she looked at me in a new way, coldly and disdainfully, and suddenly hissed, "At least I know why I'm in jail. My father was a big merchant [or factory owner, I don't remember which], he was a counterrevolutionary, no revolutionary, and I hate your revolution as much as he did. I enjoyed seeing your leader kill all of the prominent Bolsheviks, because they're all the same. What Stalin is, that's what Bukharin was. I hate you all alike!" She lifted her hand to strike me, but changed her mind. Immediately, she was removed from the cell. It was a frightful moment. Before she disappeared, I managed to scream that Stalin and Bukharin were not the same, but I knew she would never agree.

Shaken by this encounter, I broke down and cried. Even before this, my soul overflowed with unendurable pain. I found relief only in the short-term oblivion of sleep, but waking up was like being hit in the head with a hammer.

This business with Lebedeva was hard to bear not only because I finally realized that she had informed on me but also because I had

*Ibid., p. 689.

opened up to a person who did not share my pain, who, on the contrary, hated everything I held dear.

The black days of solitude returned. Storm clouds gathered over my head. The three biologists, according to Vanyok, had been tried, sentenced to death, and shot right there in Antibes, by the side of a ravine used for executions.

It was not until early December that I was finally taken to Skvirsky over in Mariinsk. He spoke with a new confidence.

"If previously," he began, "the material against you was not substantial, I now have sufficient evidence to prove that you belonged to the counterrevolutionary youth organization. Now, who else belonged to it . . . in addition to Sverdlov, Osinsky, Sokolnikov, and Ganetsky?"

I instantly knew who had supplied those particular names. I refused to make the admissions Skvirsky wanted, of course, and he sent me back to Antibes, guarded by a man from the Investigative Department. When we reached the camp, my escort led me on past the isolation prison and down the road toward the execution ravine. He announced that I was about to be shot but could save myself by exposing my counterrevolutionary organization. This scare tactic was much too transparent. After we proceeded a short way in silence, he turned back, and I was returned to my cell.

Finally, a bit later that month, my "moment of glory" arrived. I was summoned to the Antibes camp Investigative Section to meet with a Siblag official from Mariinsk. "Well now," he said, "it couldn't have turned out better. Your desire coincides with Moscow's verdict. Counterrevolutionary scum must be swept from the face of the earth!" He duly presented me with an official decision. Who signed it, I cannot say, because everything went dark before my eyes, and I could make out only the words "supreme penalty."

I had been tried many times, always in absentia, and had never seen my judges. For example, it was after I was sent to Astrakhan that a special board of the NKVD made its decision sentencing me to five years of exile. Then, only three months later, the decision was changed and I was arrested and taken to the Astrakhan jail, until a new decision sentenced me to eight years in camp. Still later, after I served out this term, another decision would arrive: in accordance with directive 185, or some such number, I was to be attached to another camp, outside the compound. In other words, I would not be permitted to go beyond the borders of the territory. The next decision would confine me to administrative exile in Novosibirsk oblast for another five years, and yet another would add ten years of the same. I would not succeed in serving that last sentence, however; the tyrant passed away. Thus, more than twenty years were taken away from me by these decisions.

But this decision to execute me did not catch me unawares or crush me with its suddenness, because I had psychologically prepared myself. Besides, death itself is not frightening; it is the moment before death, that horrible last instant. That is true not just for the cowardly but also for the brave, even for those of whom it is commonly said, "He looks death square in the eye."

It seems to me that anyone going to his execution has a special awareness of the world, a sense of renunciation of everything earthly. This perception appears quite naturally on its own; the instinct of self-preservation takes over.

Two men with revolvers in holsters led me again down the road past my cell. The sun had already sunk three-quarters of the way down past the horizon. In the hazy distance, through the gathering dusk, I could just see the dreadful ravine with its sparse birches. Suddenly, in an instant, I completely cut myself off from life. I was at the end, the end of perceiving things around me. A numbness seized my body and paralyzed my thought. It was as if I were tumbling into an abyss, an insensate clod in a landslide down a mountain. Then, unexpectedly, I heard a sound that struck me at first like the irritating blast of a siren. A human voice became distinguishable and then, at last, distinctly pronounced words. We all three halted at the very edge of the ravine. I turned around: about thirty to forty yards behind us, Vanyok was walking in our direction, and behind him ran a man in a light-colored fur jacket. This stranger shouted, "Vanyok, turn them back, turn them back!"

"Back, back, back!" Vanyok shouted, gesturing us to return.

A miracle had occurred.

We turned back.

[Return to Life—And to Moscow]

Gradually, I came out of shock. My feet, leaden, seemingly not my own, became more obedient. I began to apprehend the variety of sounds reaching me: the crunch of snow, the burring of wires in the wind, remote human voices, the sound of trees. The earth was gripped by a fierce December frost and the evening was windy, so the sensation of cold was particularly cutting. I shivered in my threadbare fur coat. My eyelashes covered over with rime; I could hardly open my eyes. My feet were soaked as I walked in Nikolai Ivanovich's worn-out high felt boots,

their tops turned down. But my head was kept warm by a quilted cap
with ear flaps; it had once belonged to Iosif Stalin, a chance inheritance.
At the end of 1929, following a conference of Marxist agronomists, my
father (or possibly Stalin) picked the wrong cap from two hanging on a
rack. The caps were identical except for the color of the lining, so, by
mutual consent, the two men decided not to exchange them. Mother
had packed this very cap in the single package she had managed to send
me before her arrest. Thus, by the irony of fate, I wore Stalin's cap
throughout my term of confinement. When friends learned that I had
survived a trip to the ravine, they joked that the cap of Stalin had transformed me into Achilles, minus the vulnerable heel.

As my petrified brain came slowly back to life, I began to think
again and made an intense effort to become aware of what was going on.
Beforehand, on the way to the ravine, I had been seized only by a fear of
nonexistence, that instinct to live that is planted in us all at the moment
of birth, the very same instinct that has so often led to foul deeds. But
what did I have to lose? Only the secret hope to see my son again
someday, and the love I bore for Nikolai Ivanovich, a love that continued to live inside me though he no longer existed. In the ravine, that
feeling would be extinguished with me, along with his letter "To a Future Generation of Party Leaders."

Now I concentrated on my surroundings as we drew even with the
man who had called off my execution. Red in the face from running,
wiping the sweat from his brow with his fur sleeve, he gasped, "Convey
at once to the chief." As we walked back past the isolation cells, I saw
that the jailer had carried out my suitcase. We turned onto the road to
Mariinsk. Now the forest where Vanyok had lit a fire in autumn seemed
small and dreary, and the field with its fallen hayracks, covered all over
with a thick layer of snow, seemed dead.

I was taken again to Skvirsky, sitting in his new office. This time, he
seemed unusually even tempered, as if subdued. Gone was the evil passion with which he had once attacked his work. For a moment, he only
looked at me silently, with some curiosity: here I was again, still alive. He
had rushed the order of execution, and now he felt relieved that he
would not have to report his inability to carry out the latest directive
from Moscow. Indeed, he had acted with such dispatch that I had not
been given the opportunity to appeal my death sentence to the Supreme
Soviet, although actually I had not even thought of that option. Why this
senseless protraction? To what court could the condemned realistically
appeal? There was no such court, after all. And so, this formality, allowing the prisoner to make an appeal, had not been observed. What they
didn't do to get around the law!

Finally, Skvirsky spoke calmly, with forced indifference, "So then, you have kept silent with us and refused to reveal the counterrevolutionary youth organization, but *there* they'll use methods that will force you to talk. They won't stand on ceremony with you *there.*"

"Where is *there?*" I asked. "And what about the death sentence, has it been rescinded? One minute more, and I would not be among the living!"

"Where *there* is, you'll see for yourself, and don't worry about the death sentence. It won't run away from you."

"Take her to her cell!" he shouted to the convoy guard standing outside the door.

They had finally finished the kitchen in Mariinsk, so I managed to have supper and breakfast in that prison before they took me off to the train station the next day. I wanted to know where they were sending me this time, but I realized from bitter experience that the convoy guard would not answer a direct question. I resorted to a ruse. Suspecting that my path led back to Moscow, I asked whether I could take my suitcase on the train or whether they would send it in the baggage car to Moscow. (To the best of my knowledge, prisoners' belongings were never sent as baggage.) The guard took the bait; he replied that I would have to take my suitcase to Moscow myself.

My heart started pounding, for I knew that Moscow, meaning Moscow prison, boded nothing good. In all likelihood, the death sentence would indeed not "run away" from me.

The train we took had come from the Far East. A rail car for transporting prisoners, a Stolypin car, had been hooked on toward the back. The convoy guard turned me over to the man in charge of this car, along with my package of documents, and ordered him not to let me mingle with the other prisoners. This prescription proved hard to fill. I went up the steps but stopped in horror at the entrance to a narrow walkway down one side of the car. To the side was a series of three-tiered compartments, called coupes, behind a sturdy wire grid running from floor to ceiling; the outside windows along the walkway were fitted with gratings. In other words, the prisoners were caged like animals at the zoo. The car was unbelievably stifling and evil smelling. The corridor, trampled with dirt, never dry because of the puddles of melted snow from the felt boots of the convoy guards who got off at the stops; the suffocating reek from the dirty, sweaty underwear of the prisoners; the "aroma" of the revolting salted fish and black boiled wheat (our rations); the horrific stench seeping into the car from the never cleaned toilet—these created the special atmosphere of the Stolypin cars, which transformed yesterday's people into today's creatures only resembling human beings. The car was crawling with criminals, easily identifiable by their speech and manner: thieves, robbers, recidivist bandits. Not a minute passed without exquisite cursing, the women outdoing the men in vulgar fantasy. Yet, through this relentless foul-mouthed din, a woman could be heard singing. In a voice husky from smoking, she rasped in despair, "I know the spring blooms not for me, and not for me the Don does flow, still my poor heart beats with a glow of rapture, though not for me."

I stood next to the toilet, guarded by the officer on duty at the head of the corridor, waiting for other guards to free a "coupe" for me by doubling up the one next to it. One of the prisoners begged insistently to go to the bathroom, but the guards were too busy to comply. Several minutes later, as I walked with the convoy guard to the emptied "coupe," the aggravated crook took a cap he had filled with his urine and splashed it on the guard. Walking alongside, I shared this "pleasure." My clothes, half-rotted from the cellar, tattered, fetid with mildew, now took on the odor of urine. As I passed a pack of women with dirty blunt faces and half-naked bodies decorated all over with tattoos, now crammed even more tightly together behind the wire screen "on account of me," one cried out, "Look, look, they're bringing Lady Blyukher!"

"They're bringing Lady Blyukher!" the others joined in chorus. "Once they were given automobiles; now they're transported with all the comforts!"

The train, I repeat, was coming from the Far East, where for many years Marshal Vasily Blyukher had commanded the Red Army forces. He had been executed recently, so evidently they took me for his wife.

Slowly, we made our way west. At times, the car was uncoupled for a while, then coupled to a new line of cars. Eventually, we pulled into Novosibirsk, where an unlikely incident occurred that I will never forget.

Without warning, the door to my "coupe" was unlocked, and a man stepped before me whom I recognized immediately: one of the two bodyguards assigned to Nikolai Ivanovich during our Siberian vacation in 1935. He was called Mikhail Ivanovich, I believe, but I forget his surname; he had seemed about fifty when we traveled together. I don't know how he gained admittance to the car. Possibly, his NKVD uniform gave him the right, or perhaps he had obtained special permission on some pretext or another. I looked at the familiar face with alarm, confusion, and, I must say, considerable animosity, absolutely certain in these changed circumstances that I could expect nothing good from this man. But just as I started to ask why he had come to me, what mission had been entrusted to him, he put his fingers to his lips, signaling me to keep quiet. He placed a huge package wrapped in paper and tied with twine beside me and instantly withdrew. I opened the package as soon as the train started moving again. It contained sumptuous provisions, thoughtfully gathered together as if by a loving hand: cooked meat, butter, sausage, white bread—I cannot recall it all. But I was even more amazed when I saw candy, chocolate bars, and oranges! It seemed like a fairy tale, a magic spell. In such surroundings, these products could well have been taken for a mirage, but they were the real thing. I peeled off a piece of orange rind and held it up to my nose. The forgotten lovely fragrance overcame the revolting smells of the car. My ravenous eyes consumed the gifts, but with an anxiety bordering on paralysis, I could not bring myself to touch them until the following day.

Both the contents of the parcel and Mikhail Ivanovich's special caution showed that he had assembled this gift on his own initiative. Moscow's summons to me would have gone through the Novosibirsk administration of the NKVD, of course; obviously, either by accident or by special inquiry, he had heard about my transfer, found out when the train would pass through town, and resolved to perform an act that for that time must be regarded as heroic. I assume that only a man who had not changed his previous attitude toward Nikolai Ivanovich, who considered it his duty to Bukharin's memory to help me, could be capable of such an act. So I want to believe.

Strange as it may seem, I became more and more uncomfortable with the "unconfined" space of my chamber as we advanced westward. It was unconfined only compared with the others, where prisoners were forced to take turns sleeping, either sitting down or half reclining while those who were awake stood and leaned on one another. About nine people could have found room to lie down in my "coupe." This was awkward for me in front of the other prisoners; they were people, after all! Yet these dregs of human society enjoyed other privileges from the command in the camps. Both groups, criminals and camp administrators, referred contemptuously to us political prisoners as *kontriki* [counterrevolutionaries]. The extraordinary parcel, if any of the criminals had found out about it, would have inflamed even greater hatred toward me.

But nothing disturbed my isolation. My "coupe" was at the end of the row, next to the convoy guard's post. Only the duty guard, forever walking up and down, keeping watch on the prisoners, stopped longer in front of me and peered intently into my chamber. Clearly, he was amazed by my isolation in such a tightly packed transport, as well as by my unusual parcel, from a commander at that. Gazing back, I remember my father's favorite song, picked up during his imprisonment before the revolution:

Sun goes up and sun goes down,
In my cell there is no light,
Day and night the sentries frown,
And on my window train their sight.

Now the train moved through the European part of the Soviet Union. These winter days of late December were short, of course, but to me they seemed incredibly long. I waited for the dark with impatience, but evening persisted in not coming soon enough. At night, things grew quieter, and the disgusting cursing that sounded all throughout the day finally stopped, as if a machine-gun clip had run out. I wanted to withdraw into myself, to focus on calculating how to defend myself against any charges at future interrogations. This task was especially urgent now that Lebedeva's reports had placed additional weights on the scales of my fate. But I simply could not concentrate, for as we drew ever nearer to Moscow, I could not help remembering how I had left in June of 1937. Left, with Nikolai Ivanovich in a torture chamber, still not tried or sentenced but in fact condemned to death before his trial, as he had been even before his arrest . . . left, tearing myself away in agony from our infant son.

[Last Months in Moscow after Bukharin's Arrest]

It happened without warning. Naively, I did not expect to be persecuted. I was more afraid for my mother. My own worries had to do with finding a job and feeding my baby. But suddenly, in June 1937, came a ring at the door!

We were living then in the Government House by Kamenny Most [Stone Bridge], a huge building that, with its gloomy gray walls, looked like the Moscow crematorium and is today known as the House on the Embankment, as in the novel by Yury Trifonov. The building had already been half emptied by arrests. In fact, about two months after Bukharin's arrest in February, we had been moved there from the Kremlin into an apartment vacated in this manner.

When the first month's rent came due from the housing department of the Central Executive Committee, I had no money to pay it. Nikolai Ivanovich had never saved a kopeck. He gave the royalties from his literary work to the Party fund and refused wages as chief editor of *Izvestiya*. He accepted money only from the USSR Academy of

Sciences, of which he was a full member. So I wrote a little note to Kalinin, the CEC's chairman:

> Mikhail Ivanovich!
> The fascist intelligence service did not materially provide for its hireling, Nikolai Ivanovich Bukharin. Since I am unable therefore to pay for the apartment, I am sending you the unpaid bill.

No second notice arrived.

We lived together: Bukharin's first wife, Nadezhda Mikhailovna Lukina, his father, Ivan Gavrilovich, my son, and I. The aged Ivan Gavrilovich, stunned by Bukharin's arrest and worn out worrying about what would happen to him next, went around repeating the same words over and over: "Nikolai, my pride! How did it happen? I can't understand it. My Kolka, a traitor? What nonsense!" Then, to distract himself, this former mathematics teacher at a girls' school before the revolution would sit for hours on end at the table, solving algebraic problems, filling one sheet of paper after another with formulas. It was as if he were trying to extract "the square root of evil" and save his sinking son. Everything going on politically remained beyond the old man's ken. He intended to write to Stalin, and perhaps he did. From time to time, he felt glimmers of hope that his son would return; after all, had not Stalin himself praised Nikolai highly? "They'll sort it out," Ivan Gavrilovich would say, as much to console himself as to hearten me. "It can't be that he won't return."

During the trying months after the start of Bukharin's investigation, Praskoviya Ivanovna Ivanova, whom we called Nanny Pasha, also lived with us. She had known me since I was a child, having raised my nephew, the son of the aunt who would later take care of Yura for eight years. Nannie Pasha was for us a member of the family. She tended the baby while I remained almost inseparable from Nikolai Ivanovich. When the disaster of his arrest occurred, she left another job without hesitation, when I asked, and helped us without remuneration, since of course we had nothing to pay her. After I was sent into exile, she stayed on to take care of Yura. When Mother was arrested, in January 1938, my son was taken off to a special children's home over Nannie Pasha's protests and pleas to be allowed to keep the boy she loved. Later, she joined the search for him and was the first to find him, only half-alive, in a children's detention center. After showing the authorities a letter from Ivan Gavrilovich, she literally tore the sick boy away from the place.

But all this was in the future. On that terrible day in June, I was sitting beside Nadezhda Mikhailovna's bed and Ivan Gavrilovich was at the table solving his eternal math problems when the doorbell rang. "They've come for me," said Nadezhda Mikhailovna. She reached over to her nightstand drawer for her poison while I went to open the door. No one had paid us a social visit in a long time, except for my old grandmother, who always telephoned beforehand. By mutual agreement, because I was trying to safeguard her, Mother and I did not visit each other, though she was helping us out materially. Then, suddenly, this ring at the door. A man in an NKVD uniform entered, holding a leather bag.

"If you please, I need to see Anna Mikhailovna," he stated with pronounced civility. "Might you be she?"

I confimed that I was.

"Present your passport," he said, coming farther into the room.

"What for?" I asked, still not suspecting a thing. "Don't you believe me?"

"Of course, I believe you, but it's a formality: I must check it documentally."

I became alarmed, for some reason thinking that he was going to tell me terrible news about Nikolai Ivanovich, most likely that he could not endure his torments and had succumbed. My hands shook as I held out my Soviet internal passport. He put it in his bag (I would never lay eyes on it again) and took out a small piece of paper. It was the first decision concerning me, signed by Yezhov himself.

Thus was I presented with the opportunity of choosing among five cities for my place of exile: Aktyubinsk, Akmolinsk, Astrakhan, Semipalatinsk, and Orenburg. The term had not yet been set; the five-year sentence would be sent out later.

"Take a trip to Astrakhan," the NKVD official advised. "It has the Volga, and there are fish, fruits, melons. A marvelous city."

"I'm not going anywhere," I declared confidently, "not to Astrakhan, not to Semipalatinsk. The Bukharin case hasn't been decided yet, and you have no right to apply repressive measures against me."

I went on to justify my position by explaining that I had been so strained and enervated during my husband's investigation that I was in no condition to take my infant son with me. The NKVD man suggested I leave the boy behind in Moscow, but I said I did not want to part with him. Besides, I went on, who would take in a "leper" boy, the son of Bukharin!

"No, no, it's wrong for you to think that way. The boy is not responsible for anything."

On the contrary, the boy was found guilty forever.

I knew perfectly well, of course, that my refusal to go into exile was a struggle against overwhelming odds, and therefore futile, but I did not want to give in without a battle.

"The decision is signed by Yezhov," the official reminded me.

"I don't care who signed it. You can evict me from here only by force."

He suggested I sign a receipt to the effect that I had been apprised of the decision. I did so, writing on the back that I refused to go into exile and laying out my reasons.

For the next two days, no one bothered me, but I was already preparing to leave. This was only psychological preparation, to be sure, since I owned so few things that it would require no special effort to collect them on short notice. I could not take our enormous and priceless library into exile, or even into the Government House. Not only would it not fit into our new apartment; it had been sealed. By chance, we did have the furnishings from Nikolai Ivanovich's Kremlin study. This complete office suite had been sent to him out of the blue by an admiring furniture maker, but Bukharin had been so offended by the value of the gift that he went to the factory and paid for it in full. Still, there was nothing really valuable in the House on the Embankment, aside from Nikolai Ivanovich's paintings, which I had brought over from the Kremlin.

Two days after his first visit, at about ten at night, the same courteous official appeared and graciously invited me to Lubyanka, the NKVD headquarters. "Not for long, not for long," he repeated. As I got into his sleek black car, it never entered my head that I might not return.

I was taken to an office where two men were seated: Yakov Matusov, apparently serving as chief of some NKVD department, and Mikhail Frinovsky, Yezhov's deputy. Matusov spoke first: "Why are you putting up such a fuss, Anna Mikhailovna? Don't you know that we don't play games? In your exile, all of your needs, work, and apartment will be taken care of. This is a short-term measure in your case, and you'll be able to come back soon."

"On the other hand, if you really want to avoid exile," Frinovsky put in, "you have to 'burn your bridges behind you.' "

"What do you mean by that?" I asked warily.

"That means a renunciation of Bukharin as an enemy of the people, published in the press."

"That's a vile proposal!" I shrieked. "You've insulted me. Astrakhan is better!"

Frinovsky's proposal, which I found beneath contempt, was not brought up again. I asked to be granted a visit with Nikolai Ivanovich before my forced departure. I knew that henceforth I would never see him again, and I wanted to say good-bye. My interlocutors denied this request, explaining that Nikolai was still under investigation.

"But if he is under investigation," I observed, "then no one has the right to call him an enemy of the people until the investigation and the trial are complete."

Both held their tongues at that but promised that I would be called back from exile for a meeting with my husband after the investigation. I knew, of course, that they were lying.

A few days later, an NKVD official arrived at the Government House to carry out my removal to Astrakhan, bringing not only a passenger car but also a truck for the transport of my "property." My insignificant "property" could fit comfortably into the suitcase from London and two rucksacks, but I decided to take advantage of the truck. For a long time, first in the vestibule of his apartment at the Metropol and later in the Kremlin, Nikolai Ivanovich had kept a very large wooden trunk, into which he put copies of the issues of *Pravda* and *Izvestiya* he had edited. In a flash, I tossed the newspapers out of the trunk and started filling it with winter clothing, which the official had suggested I have sent to me by mail. I also put in things belonging to Nikolai Ivanovich: his easel, his oil paints and brushes, along with my favorite watercolor, *The Elbrus at Sunset*. The trunk was so roomy that I could have put in his other paintings, too, but I decided they belonged more to his father than to me. I did not want to cause any further grief to Ivan Gavrilovich, who dearly loved his son's paintings. I added my husband's old suit, one that Stalin had advised him against wearing on a trip to Paris in 1936, along with the felt boots he wore for hunting in winter, his sports clothes, an old leather jacket, and, finally, two pairs of badly worn boots. Anything that recalled him was precious to me, and I hoped that there would come a day when I could show these things to my son. The NKVD official had watched me without speaking, but the old boots exceeded the limits of his indulgence. Losing patience, he asked me why I was taking all this old junk and told me to throw it away.

I had the presence of mind to answer, "Would that he had more property, so that you could see and remember what the fascist hireling Bukharin owned, the man who 'sold himself for thirty pieces of silver.' "

I had heard this biblical phrase used as an accusation against Bukharin and his alleged ties with Germany in a speech on the radio; I do not recall the orator's name for certain.

Who knows whether the NKVD official understood me? Perhaps

his own life took a similarly abrupt turn soon thereafter. One way or another, however, the enormous trunk was loaded onto the truck and transported as baggage.

[Exile in Astrakhan, 1937]

And then, Astrakhan. How distinctly it appears before my eyes even now! I arrived there exactly one day after the Red Army High Command had been tried: Tukhachevsky, Yakir, Uborevich, Kork, and the others.

The city was at once surprised and excited, stunned and yet removed from everything going on in Moscow; it was stuffy, dusty, filled with the flowering of the white acacia. We exiled relatives were an immediate sensation; people openly pointed their fingers at us. Word that we had arrived in town—the families of Radek, Bukharin, and formerly glorified military leaders, all now branded as traitors to the homeland—was spread by local NKVD officials and their wives as well as by the townspeople in whose homes we found lodging. NKVD headquarters was located on the main street, which bore Lenin's name. Along its humpbacked uphill incline, gray loudspeakers had been rigged up to posts. You had to stop up your ears to avoid hearing the blaring message of the news of the day, repeated periodically, as crowds of people gathered round: "The spies, traitors, and turncoats have been swept from the face of the earth. They wanted to . . ." And so forth. The newspapers were snatched up early in the morning at lightning speed, because so many more of us interested readers had been brought to town. Bukharin was not yet the "star of the show," but I knew he would be soon. In the papers, the names of the military men condemned in one closed trial were run through all the grammatical declensions. Their wives and children, crushed in spirit, half-mad, walked along Lenin Street looking as if their homes had burned down, greedily listening to what the soulless loudspeakers were broadcasting while trying to keep their children away from the onrush of the people.

The work and apartments promised in Moscow did not materialize in Astrakhan. Newcomers to exile were thrown together under one roof in a makeshift "waiting room"—actually, two adjoining rooms compactly furnished with cots. There we spent our first days, until the Astrakhan NKVD suggested we go out and find lodgings for ourselves in private apartments. This was difficult not only because of the expense (I was able to exist in Astrakhan thanks solely to my mother's financial support) but also because the local citizens, even those who had extra space and needed money, were scared off by the notoriety surrounding us and our status as exiles. It took a special NKVD directive to force the locals to let us rent. As the steamship-line worker who rented me a room explained, "With the people up there at the top, everything is subject to change; today they decreed that I should give you shelter, but tomorrow they'll bring charges against me because Bukharin's wife lived in my apartment."

In the "waiting room," I had been particularly struck by one old exile, the semiliterate Latvian housekeeper of Yan Ernestovich Rudzutak. Yan Ernestovich had not married, and for many years she had cared for him as if he were her own son. Sobbing constantly, she would tell not only us but also passersby in the street that she remembered Rudzutak as a child going from house to house begging alms because his family was so poor, that she recalled his working as a hired hand on a farm. In other words, she argued, quite logically, "Once Yan Ernestovich pulled himself up out of poverty and became a member of the government thanks to the Soviet power, he simply could not commit any crimes against that power." In total despair, sitting on a cot in the "waiting room," her face streaming with tears, the poor woman clasped her head in her hands and cried out hysterically, "Monsters, monsters! Only monsters could arrest Rudzutak. Give them time, and they'll kill him!" She could not understand who these monsters could be.

Later, when returning to Moscow from Novosibirsk, I assumed (correctly, as it turned out) that Rudzutak was no longer among the living, since his name had been mentioned at the Bukharin trial as a "Rightist conspirator." In all likelihood, he was persecuted because he had served as assistant chairman of the Council of People's Commissars under Rykov as well as, at the time of his arrest, under Molotov. He was shot in July 1938.

Seeing the old woman sobbing was doubly painful to me, because she awakened memories of my own childhood, when Yan Ernestovich Rudzutak used to come to our home. I recalled his kind, generous face, with his tired, expressive eyes peering through glasses. Having spent ten years at hard labor in a tsarist camp, he had a barely detectable limp caused by shackles. To me, he seemed too businesslike and taciturn, but once, at the end of a government session, he suddenly cheered up and played blind man's bluff with me, wrapping a towel around his eyes and laughing infectiously while I squealed in anticipation of imminent capture. Yan Ernestovich was a great nature lover and enthusiast of color photography, which was just getting started in our country. He used to bring by a huge number of his photos of Russian and Caucasian landscapes, all exhibiting a fine artistic taste and outstanding technical skill. After being sent on an official trip to America, he loved to expound on the technological marvels there. Once, at his dacha, he showed me a Radiola, which was both a radio capable of picking up all the countries of the world and a record player. At that time, it was a marvel. He would smile modestly whenever my father called him "Comrade Rudzutak" (never simply "Rudzutak") instead of "Yan Ernestovich," but to me, in my childhood, he was simply "Uncle Yan."

In vain did I try to calm the old woman, who kept sobbing and sniffling even through the night. But there was nothing I could say to console her, especially since, whenever I looked at her, the tears started rolling down my own cheeks.

Also in our group, Iona Yakir's wife, Sarra Lazarevna, and their fourteen-year-old son were doubly traumatized. It was bad enough that the number of days between the general's arrest and his execution were so few that human reason could not yet comprehend what had happened, but a second disaster befell the family as well. Not long before they arrived in Astrakhan, *Pravda* printed a statement in which Sarra Lazarevna supposedly renounced her husband as an enemy of the people. She disclaimed the story, but it caused both mother and son unbearable pain. That kind of dirty trick was never played on me, but Frinovsky's proposal suggests that the tactic of having wives of prominent, formerly popular figures renounce their husbands was dreamed up in the bowels of the NKVD. I assume that this same Frinovsky had the power to print a faked renunciation, if not on his own initiative, then on orders from Stalin. It is also possible that, in order to save her son, Sarra Lazarevna really did make the statement, but at the time I witnessed her sufferings, I did not for a moment doubt that her printed "renunciation" was a fabrication.

Another incident humiliating to Sarra Lazarevna comes suddenly to mind, even as I write these lines. She was unable to get over it for a long time. During the war, in the winter of 1942, we were transported from the Yaisk camp to the Iskitim camp, where forced laborers manufactured lime, using methods so primitive and hazardous that the majority of the men died. One of our convoy guards, a Ukrainian, strolled over to Sarra Lazarevna and said, "Well, Yakir, looks like your renunciation didn't help you. You're still doing time. You're a bitch, not a wife!"

Perhaps this man's father, having fought under Yakir's command, had instilled in him a respect for the general; perhaps the guard simply believed that Yakir was innocent; then again, perhaps according to his moral code the renunciation of a husband in any circumstances was considered ignoble. We had no way of knowing.

I have digressed somewhat from my recollections of our first days in Astrakhan. In the "waiting room" there I saw Yakir's son, Petya, for whom I had much sympathy. He came in with his mother, holding her hand; Sarra Lazarevna was barely able to walk. The boy's face, deathly pale, seemed even paler in the frame of his thick, curly black hair. In the ten days or so since the arrest of his father, he had lost a lot of weight, so he had to keep tugging at his light-colored britches, which kept slipping down. Petya was a handsome lad. His dark and by no means childish eyes were full of suffering. He looked from side to side, trying to find children he knew of roughly the same age who shared the same fate. When he caught sight of the daughters of Uborevich, Gamarnik, and Tukhachevsky, he sat down on a free cot and said aloud for all to hear:

"My papa didn't do anything wrong. All of this is fibs; it's stuff and nonsense."

"Petya, stop! Be still!" his frightened mother cut him off, but he cast a challenging gaze around the room. We were all silent, except Nina Vladimirovna Uborevich, wife of the Red Army commander, who was sitting next to me. Her eyes lighting up, she declared, "Well done, stout fellow!" She had spared her twelve-year-old daughter, Mirochka, the knowledge that Iona Emmanuilovich had been shot, but Petya later told the girl. It was impossible to keep anything from him. Petya was the only child to state out loud that his father was innocent. I think he was the only one who understood the whole business and realized that not only the military men but also all of the others accused were innocent.

As I mentioned earlier, Yakir supposedly shouted, "Long live Stalin!"—just before the fatal shot. True or not, his fourteen-year-old son considered Stalin to be the chief assassin.

Although I kept pretty much to myself once I was settled in Astrakhan, I did drop in on Nina Vladimirovna Uborevich a couple of times. She had insistently invited me over, since I had known her husband and could share my recollections with her. Thanks to her indomitable energy, Nina Vladimirovna had succeeded in obtaining a state apartment for herself and Mirochka, two rooms in an old half-demolished house, and managed to renovate it. She had brought along some furniture from Moscow, so the place acquired a cozy, homelike feeling.

The other exiles I saw once every ten days when we had to register the document issued us in place of a passport. I had not previously known any of these exiled wives, except for Karl Radek's wife, Roza Mavrikieyevna. I ran into her once as I wandered through the town looking for work. She stopped to have a word with me, but I cut her dead. Shocked at my behavior, she shouted after me that I would find it interesting to talk with her since she had just met with Karl, but I did not even turn around. I had read Radek's testimony at his preliminary investigation and at his trial, and I could not then understand or forgive his incriminating statements against Nikolai Ivanovich. The encounter with Roza Mavrikieyevna occurred before Bukharin's trial, of course, the trial of the so-called Bloc of Rightists and Trotskyists. Yet another weighty circumstance explains my action, as I will explain later. All the same, as I look back on it now, I cannot justify my behavior toward my former acquaintance.

To keep up with events, I had to ride every day to the train station to buy a newspaper. There was no radio in my apartment, and the newspapers in the city sold out early in the morning. Once, I came face to face with Petya Yakir at the station's newspaper kiosk.

"You're Bukharin's wife, aren't you?" he asked. He probably wanted me to confirm what he already knew. I did, and he immediately switched to the familiar form of address.

"Are you a Komsomol member?"

"I *was,*" I answered, but he obviously didn't catch the past tense.

"Me, too. They admitted me to the Komsomol a little while ago," he said happily. "Where do you think we go to register here? If we don't, we'll be dropped from the Komsomol."

I had to give Petya the sad news that, as exiles, we had already been dropped automatically. Grasping the situation at once, he looked at me in consternation and never again said another word about the Komsomol.

The fifth of September 1937 was an awful date in the life of the Astrakhan exiles. When my landlord came home from work, he announced that all of the other exiled wives had been arrested and that I would have to look for another place to live. The possibility that the "en-ka-ve-deshniks," the NKVD, might burst into his home and make a search did not much appeal to him. His dreadful report alarmed me, and I ran over to Nina Vladimirovna's apartment to check out this rumor. A young man unfamiliar to me opened the door. He turned out to be her brother, Slava, who had come to town to help her. He confirmed the story; Nina Vladimirovna had indeed been arrested. In fact, of all of the wives in exile here, only Sarra Yakir and I remained at large. Slava bitterly told me that, despite his entreaties, he was not allowed custody of Mirochka. His niece, like the children of everyone else arrested that day, had been taken off to a children's detention center in the city. They were eventually placed in an orphanage, apparently somewhere in the Urals. Then, when they grew up, they too were arrested.

From then on, I visited the Yakirs' place every day. A large family had joined Petya and Sarra Lazarevna there, including her father and her sister Milya, who came from Sverdlovsk with her two adolescent offspring. After Milya's husband, Garkavy, commander of the Ural Military District, had been arrested and imprisoned in 1937, he committed suicide by bashing his head against the wall of his cell. Milya was not an exile but she would eventually find herself in prison. The sisters' father, Lazar Ortenberg, had come from Odessa. He was a wonderful, wise, kind violinist, then already past seventy. Later, when Sarra Lazarevna and I were transported to camp, he sought out our car in the train at the Astrakhan station. We caught sight of him through the window, an old man striding with effort, supporting himself with a cane, and looking at us with mournful eyes. When the train began to move, he tossed his cane aside and ran as hard as he could alongside us (where did he get the strength?). He removed his hat, despite the freezing temperature, and used it to wave farewell to us.

Before then, I had become a part of that family, for it was easier for us all to bear our great sorrow together. Both sisters tried to instill hope in me; they were convinced Nikolai Ivanovich would not be shot: "They won't raise a hand against him!" Only the wise, levelheaded Ortenberg believed that I should prepare myself for the worst.

During those days, I got to know Petya much better. Fearless and indomitable, resourceful and straightforward, the boy had inherited these traits from his father. Events that shake the soul for a lifetime had left their stamp on his rebellious, inexhaustible character. Stirred by these tragic times, Petya tried to channel all of his energy into action, into good deeds. He cleverly succeeded in preserving some cherished photographs of his father by climbing up to the attic, right under the roof of the house where the family was living, and hiding them in a safe place. He lingered constantly around the prison, standing outside the building for hours on end, trying to find a way of telling the arrested mothers what had happened to their children. The guards repeatedly chased him away from the fence beside the prison courtyard, where he could look through the chinks and catch a glimpse of the prisoners on their walks. Finally, he managed his way inside the residence right across from the prison and got the permission of the tenants of a particular apartment to use their window. It was a precise calculation; he knew the exact location of the cell of the arrested mothers. He stood for a long time at the open window (or possibly on a balcony, I do not remember exactly) with a piece of paper pinned to his chest. In large letters was written the message "Mamas, don't worry! Children all right. In Astrakhan children's detention center." The wooden shield over the prison window, called a "visor" or "muzzle," was not so high that the mothers could not look out and see Petya with his message. They were moved to tears and amazed by his ingenuity.

He ran to the detention center every day to visit with the daughters of Uborevich, Gamarnik, Tukhachevsky, and others and to bring them something good to eat, if he could. Sarra Lazarevna told me he'd eventually given away all the jam his grandfather had brought from Odessa. He was not allowed inside but could talk with the children through a window. The same age as he, they had all lost not only their fathers but also their mothers, and they were being kept behind locked doors, as in a jail. Petya saw injustice in both this cruel treatment and the fact that, while his friends had been deprived of freedom, he still had his mother and family and could run around Astrakhan as he liked. "It's so unfair, so unfair," he said to me once as we walked together to the detention center. "I live with my mother, but my comrades have had their mothers taken away!" The poor boy did not realize what awaited him in the very near future.

Petya had started school back on September 1 and had quickly won authority among his Astrakhan classmates, despite a background that was unfavorable for that time. Once, some of the boys from school went with him to the detention center. One overly clever fellow in the group, meaning to alert the children that Petya had arrived, tossed a stone or lump of dirt at the window. The pane broke, and the schoolboys took fright and scattered, leaving Petya by himself. When a governess came out and confronted him, he took the blame for the broken window, not wanting to involve his new friends. Recognizing his last name, she said, "I get it now. You're Yakir, and that means you're a terrorist. You saw me standing by the window and tried to kill me."

Thus was Petya sent to the NKVD.

Arriving to visit the Yakirs that evening, I found Sarra Lazarevna in great distress because her son had not yet come home from school. Petya's grandfather and aunt were no less worried but tried to calm her. Slava happened to be there, so the two of us went out to look for Petya together. We returned around midnight, having failed to find him anywhere in the city. Petya came in right after us. He explained that he had been held all this time at the police station, where they demanded he sign a trumped-up statement that he was against Soviet power. "I told them I was definitely not against Soviet power," Petya said. "I simply did not agree with some of its measures. For example, I was against taking children away from their mothers." He kept quiet about any other "measures" he didn't approve of, apparently, or perhaps he didn't want to trouble his mother by repeating everything he'd said. With boyish pride, he told us that he'd signed the record of his interrogation. He did not yet understand that this interrogation had laid the cornerstone for endless miseries in prison, indeed for the rest of his dramatic and painful life. Such was Petya Yakir at fourteen.

When the other wives had been arrested, I lived at first in tense expectation. Eventually, I had grown a bit calmer, deciding that it was not by chance that Sarra Lazarevna and I had been "overlooked." Perhaps she had paid for her freedom with the fictitious renunciation in *Pravda,* and perhaps I had not been arrested because of my youth (amazing, how I continued to think good of my tormentor). The deluge of daily concerns also distracted me from the vigil of waiting for possible arrest. I had to find work and a new apartment; my landlord kept prodding me to move out.

In this connection, an amusing incident occurred. An old crone living next door advised me to take the streetcar to an area outside of town bearing the odd name Cherepakha [Turtle], because there, supposedly, one could easily find a room. Get off at the "Fridrendis" stop, she said. On the streetcar, I asked one of the passengers when that stop would come up. He looked at me in astonishment and replied irritably, "What do you mean, Fridrendis? There once was someone called Friedrich Engels, but perhaps you've never heard of him. Well, he is your so-called Fridrendis. Some culture! And you look like a girl from the intelligentsia. At the third stop, get off at the street sign that has the name Friedrich Engels written on it." I was embarrassed, but there was no point in trying to explain.

In any event, my search for a room on Friedrich Engels Street was now crowned with success. The minute I gave my name, I was refused. I did not believe it would be fair to hide my identity; besides, the NKVD had made that impossible.

Finally, I decided to accept an offer from Slava to move in with him. He was alone in Nina Vladimirovna's two small rooms. I had turned down this suggestion several times, since it appeared to me that Slava was interested in something more than alleviating my difficulties. I wanted to avoid any territorial proximity to him, but in the end there was no other way out. There was also a ray of light, apparently, in regard to work: the director of a fish cannery, with the approval of the Astrakhan NKVD, hired me as a secretary. I prepared to begin work on September 21. The day before, Slava came over to my room to help me move or, more accurately, walk to his place. I intended to leave the wooden trunk behind until I could find transportation. Before leaving, and ignoring the dispiriting circumstances, we sat down at the table and made a splendid meal of a juicy sweet melon. No sooner had we got up to leave than a knock was heard at the door. Officials presented an order for search and arrest. The melon had delayed our departure, so my poor landlord, who was forced to remain during the search of my room, had his things rummaged through as well.

During the search, I succeeded in hiding a photo of Nikolai Ivanovich in my shoe, under the inner sole. Later, I carried it into prison. This ruse would hardly have occurred to me if Slava had not told me that Nina Vladimirovna had concealed Uborevich's photo in the same manner. A second photograph I'd brought with me into exile was found and confiscated. Like the first, it had accidentally survived a search of our apartment in the Kremlin. It showed my husband with his arm around Kirov; both men were happy and smiling. The Astrakhan official who found it was clearly surprised to see the two men together in a friendly pose; it would have made more sense to him if Bukharin had been snapped pointing a revolver at Kirov.

[The Astrakhan Prison, 1937—Moscow's Lubyanka Prison, 1938]

In the corridor of the Astrakhan prison, I again came face to face with Sarra Lazarevna Yakir, for we had been arrested at the same time and were headed for the same cell. There we joined all those arrested on September 5: the wives of Gamarnik, Tukhachevsky, and Uborevich, along with Rudzutak's old Latvian housekeeper, still weeping, and yet two more women, wives of NKVD officials who had worked under Yagoda. In tears, all greeted Sarra Lazarevna and me, related their experiences since we had last seen them, and told us how moved they had been to see Petya Yakir in the window across from the prison and to read his words: "Mamas, don't worry! Children all right."

Several days later, the aged Ortenberg approached the prison fence during our walk and told Sarra Lazarevna that Petya had been taken away immediately after her arrest. They took him first to the children's detention center (thus, the boy found the "justice" of receiving equal treatment), then transferred him after three or four days to the prison. The old man had glimpsed his grandson once through a chink in the fence. He said, "Petya imagined himself a major criminal. He was walking along slowly with his hands folded behind his back, swaying his rear end."

I recall the Astrakhan prison less as the first on my journey into hell than as one different from all of the rest. To say that it lacked a prison regimen would be putting it mildly. Before we were taken on a transport, the woman guard would wish us the best and even give me a kiss, as the youngest prisoner. Like the prisoners there, the guards were all women, and we called them politely by their first name and patronymic. That was the custom there, the tradition.

The middle-aged guard Yefimiya Ivanovna was thin, round-shouldered, flat-chested, and wrinkled. Her hair was cropped short like a man's, and she wore a camouflage military shirt bunched up in back and drawn tight by a big leather belt from which hung a knot of jangling jail keys. An inveterate smoker, she would frequently take a pinch of makhorka from her tobacco pouch, roll it tightly in a strip of newspaper, lick it, and light up, emitting clouds of smoke. This habit had turned her fingers and teeth yellow.

She burned with curiosity about us, for the prison had never seen such prisoners before, many with names even she had heard of. Yefimiya Ivanovna often came to our cell and stared at us with apparent malice, but one time she suddenly broke out in a smile and, shaking her head with an ironic expression, uttered one word: "Heh!"

She would get angry when we took a long time washing ourselves. We were never taken to real showers but to a dirty, rudimentary bathhouse with wooden basins, so we had to wash thoroughly whenever we got the chance. Besides, we enjoyed coming out of our stuffy, overcrowded cell and splashing water on ourselves. This irritated Yefimiya Ivanovna, who always hurried us along and shouted, "Don't wash every part, you don't have to wash every part, that's a bad habit you got, I'm waiting on you a whole hour!"

When the cell was opened to feed us, she would ladle up the watery soup and with each bowl report in a guilty tone of voice, "Peas again!" or "Noodles again!"

In this prison, I was usually called by my maiden name, Larina. Bukharina would appear and disappear, for no apparent reason. Both names would be used sometimes; on occasion, only the married name. Therefore, when an investigator was directed by Moscow to summon me (and the other women) to fill out a questionnaire, he did not know who I was. When he asked where my husband worked, I answered, "Editorial board of *Izvestiya*." "Name his exact position," the man said. "On that board he could be a messenger of Bukharin." I had to spell it out. "Jokes are not in order here," he retorted. "I can go ahead and write you up as Bukharina in the dossier, but it won't help you any." I was obliged to assure him I was not joking. The next time he summoned me was to deliver the sentence: eight years in corrective labor camps.

Yefimiya Ivanovna, on the other hand, found out rather quickly that I was Bukharin's wife. One evening, at the start of her night shift, she came to the cell and issued a command in an official tone: "Well, now Bukharkina, come out into the corridor." Titters were heard; her mispronunciation struck us as funny. Now it seems strange that we were able to laugh, but in fact there was quite a lot of laughter in that cell, even though it was surely laughter born of nervous strain and complete despair, for our husbands had been killed and our children taken away. Also, we had become equals in our troubles—Tukhachevskys and Yakirs, Bukharins and Radeks, Uboreviches and Gamarniks: "Misfortune shared is half misfortune!" And, on the bright side, we thought it possible that our children would now have a better chance of survival in the orphanages, as "wards of the state." So it was not so strange that this comic guard made us laugh with her ridiculous face, misplaced severity, and remarkable obtuseness.

"Bukharkina! I told you to come out into the corridor!" she repeated, because I held back. I was stumped. Why was she calling me out alone? A herd instinct had already developed, for we were all Muscovites and had all received the same five-year term; later, we would all be sent on a transport at the same time, and finally, some of the women sitting next to me, the wives of Gamarnik, Tukhachevsky, and Uborevich, would be shot.

When I went out, Yefimiya Ivanovna took me to her "station" and sat me down at her little desk. On it lay her tobacco pouch; she lit her makhorka and sent up clouds of smoke. "Let's have a little chat, Bukharkina!" she began. "Tell me, now, how did you live with your spy? And that silk blouse you're wearing [actually, it was a knit], what money did he buy it with? What, you say you don't know? You know, all right. That's why you're behind bars, my dear. But whoever would've thought that Bukharkin was a spy! My sister thought the world of him."

I was getting depressed by all this. I felt it pointless to contradict the guard and refused to engage in a little chat. Yefimiya Ivanovna returned me to the cell.

The guard on the next shift, the one who later kissed me on my departure from the prison, was also an unusual woman, but I do not remember her given name and patronymic. It was her responsibility to bar communication between the cells, but she vigorously facilitated it. Once, sometime in October, she brought me a parcel from Roza Mavrikieyevna, Radek's wife, who was in the very next cell. It was half a loaf of the delicious Astrakhan white bread. She was able to receive such packages from her daughter Sonya, who had not yet been arrested. The guard warned me there was a little note shoved inside the bread, so that I would not swallow it. It read, "Know that it will be the same thing with

Nikolai Ivanovich, a trial and false testimony." Five months later, I would recall that little note during Bukharin's trial.

Radek and Bukharin did not behave exactly the same in the dock, but to determine the differences one would have to make a detailed study of the trial, which I could not do in confinement. Yet, even now, with the stenographic record of the trial before me, I am convinced that Roza Mavrikieyevna was essentially right.

In December, after the special board's decision to give me a term of eight years in confinement, I was sent to the Tomsk camp by way of the transit cells in Saratov and Sverdlovsk, as I have described previously. This was a difficult journey, but it was a hundred times easier than the one leading from the Tomsk camp to Novosibirsk and Antibes and, finally, to the Moscow prison late in December of the following year.

For as the train drew nearer to Moscow, all of these things appeared again before my mind's eye: the insulting proposal of Yezhov's deputy Frinovsky; the huge wooden trunk with my so-called property; the marvelous doomed boy Petya Yakir; the old Latvian woman so shaken by the loss of Rudzutak; the woman guard Yefimiya Ivanovna; and much, much else besides. And they troubled my soul.

At the outskirts of the capital, I stood closer to the wire grid so that I could see the familiar places through the window. Bykovo, Tomilino, Lyubertsy flashed by. And we were in Moscow.

> *Moscow! To the heart of the Russian-born*
> *What depth there is in that sound!*
> *How deeply does the heart respond!*

My heart responded with incredible pain!

Moscow now seemed to me covered in the shame of unbridled terror, awash in the blood of the innocent. This was the city of my childhood and youth, where I had lived so many bright and sunny days, but so many tragic ones as well.

It was in Moscow that I had been forced to abandon my year-old child, who no longer remembered me, whom I could not hope to see and in fact did not see then; finally, I was approaching the city where only nine months before they had killed my husband. Even so, the closer Moscow came, the greater my excitement. Yes, my own dear city might well strike me as somber, cold, and foreign, but I knew I could not put my foot on Moscow ground without trembling.

The prisoner car was stopped on a dead-end track in Kazan station. A jailer came for me and led me into a dark closet inside a Black Maria; my eyes longed for a glimpse of Moscow, but it was impossible to see outside. I assumed I would be driven to the NKVD inner prison in Lubyanka. I was not mistaken. After a degrading body search, I was sent to the showers. How clean and spacious the shower room looked to me with its gleaming white tiles after the filthy, cramped prison bathhouses with their heavy wooden washbasins. In Lubyanka, the corridor floors were parquet; the cells, supplied with a bed, pillow, sheets, and blanket. Formerly the office of an insurance company, the building would have seemed a palace to me after the Astrakhan prison, Tomsk camp, transport holding cells, and Novosibirsk cellar if I had not perceived it as *a death factory*. In this prison, Nikolai Ivanovich spent the last, tormented year of his life. Behind these walls, my mind told me, I too would end my days.

Having washed, I threw aside my torn clothing, those rags saturated with damp and the smell of urine, but the selection of new things to wear was limited. In my suitcase, I still had an outfit I had brought back from Paris; it was sufficiently modest yet pretty. I had become so thin that the skirt fell from my waist. I had to tie it in place with a strip of my worn-out blouse and cover the top with my cardigan.

I was led to a cell on the underground level. Once again, I was in solitary. The electric light was so bright that it irritated my eyes. Exhausted from my long, arduous trip, I flopped on the bed as soon as I undressed, shielding my face under the blanket. The guard ordered me to uncover my face. I turned toward the wall, but he forbade this, too. The blinding light and my nervous fears prevented sleep. I would get up from the bed and pace around the cell, then lie back down again. Finally, I managed to convince myself that they would hardly interrogate me on the day of my arrival and fell, at long last, into a deep sleep. I awoke with the guard nudging my shoulder.

"Are you *na by* [in the *b*'s]?" he asked softly.

I had no idea what he was talking about. The words *na by* I heard as a single word, *naby*. Never having heard this word before, I asked for an explanation.

"Your last name, does it begin with the letter *b*, Bukharina?" he asked in a whisper, as if my name concealed something explosive.

This question seemed all the stranger since I was alone in the cell. When I answered in the affirmative, he announced, "Get ready to see the people's commissar."

I became agitated not only because a summons to see the people's commissar, the head of the NKVD, indicated the extreme gravity of my situation but also because I felt revulsion at the prospect of laying eyes on Yezhov. The extent of my nodding acquaintance with him flashed through my mind: a word with him on the telephone before my departure to Paris and two chance encounters while walking in the Kremlin with Bukharin.

How would my Nikolai Ivanovich's namesake, Nikolai Ivanovich Yezhov, look me in the face now? Suffering had tempered my will and, in the final analysis, stripped away my naïveté, yet naïveté still made itself felt on occasion. I got ready with deliberate slowness in order to mobilize the maximum inner strength and to suppress the agitation that gripped me. For an instant, I worried that I was dressed too well; this outfit was not in keeping with my previous wanderings through prisons. But after thinking it over, I decided that the act of throwing aside my filthy rags had also rid me of any feelings of humiliation. I drew sheer Parisian stockings up my legs and put on dress shoes (the felt boots had completely fallen apart); I lacked only French perfume. I announced that I was ready.

Proceeding through an inner courtyard, we went up to the top floor and walked down a corridor lined with strips of soft carpet. I could see investigators hard at work in their offices. Many of the prisoners who would soon join me in the basement cell would recount the horrors of their interrogation, but such methods were not used on me.

In the corridor, the guards would snap their fingers or tap a key on their belt buckle as a prearranged signal to keep people under investigation from meeting face to face. Whenever my escort heard the signal, he immediately ordered me to turn to the wall or directed me into a box, a little structure attached to the wall. Finally, I was taken into an office, where I saw a burly, oversized Caucasian with muddy-brown, bullish eyes, and not the little bright-eyed Yezhov.

As I was walking down the long, secretive, soundless corridor, preparing myself for interrogation and expecting momentarily to see Yezhov, I had set my mind so firmly on his image that it had not occurred to me that I might be meeting with someone else. That is, someone other than the people's commissar who had helped carry the repressions to an unprecedented height and helped destroy Nikolai Ivanovich, someone other than the people's commissar to whom I had written my declaration "Shoot me. I do not want to live!"

"Yezhov is not Skvirsky," I had thought, steeling myself for battle. And I felt the need to meet precisely with Yezhov, no one else. Not just to sweep away the charges brought against me, for I could do that with any investigator. No, I considered it my moral duty to refute the charges of Bukharin's complicity in any kind of counterrevolutionary practices whatever, to declare proudly that the trial was a fabrication, and to produce the appropriate proofs directly before Yezhov himself. To be sure, after the loss of Nikolai Ivanovich, my representations would no longer make any sense, and, alas, before that loss, they would have had no effect, but self-respect demanded that I speak out!

Yet there, instead of Yezhov, was this tired, indifferent, unfamiliar person looking at me. Later, I learned that this was Bogdan Kobulov, chief of the NKVD Special Department and deputy assistant to Lavrenty Beria. For a moment, his face registered inexplicable surprise. He even recoiled. I'm not sure what he found so astonishing: perhaps my Parisian dress, so out of place; perhaps my exhausted, drawn aspect, like a living mummy; possibly my youth. But the flare-up of amazement in his eyes quickly subsided, and they reassumed their previous sleepy, indifferent expression.

He put a question to me: "With whom have you spoken in the camp?"

"Since I am not yet a corpse, I have spoken with many people. I didn't keep count. Anyway, I was summoned here to speak with the people's commissar!" I burst out like this because I was impatient to see Yezhov right away.

"You want to speak with the people's commissar in particular? You have something to communicate to him?"

"Since he summoned me, he is obviously interested in speaking with me." After a moment's reflection, I added, "And, yes, I do have something to tell him."

Kobulov picked up the telephone.

"She is with me now. May we stop by?"

And so at once we went to the people's commissar.

In the spacious reception room outside his office, the typist, apparently a Georgian, and two men, also Georgians, broke off their conversation and trained their eyes on me. Kobulov opened the door, allowing me to enter first.

The commissar's office, carpeted from wall to wall, seemed enormous to me. At the far end of the room opposite the door stood a massive desk on which lay a fat portfolio, also remarkably large, and a mountain of folders, presumably containing the files of those under investigation. Behind the desk sat a man, but not the one I so urgently wanted to see. In my surprise and nervousness, I experienced double vision for an instant, just as in a camera before it comes into focus: superimposed on the eyes of Yezhov were the eyes of Beria, which then settled firmly into place alone, and I could see that they were staring intently at me. Reaching the desk, I clapped my hands and exclaimed:

"Lavrenty Pavlovich! Where has our 'glorious people's commissar' gone, the one who terrified 'the wasp's nests of the enemies of the people'? Has he slipped away along with his 'Yezhov mittens'?"

How brash is youth! Yet I could not conceal my astonishment and joy (indeed, I did not think it necessary) when I guessed that Yezhov had probably been arrested.

[Confrontation with Beria]

Though obscure to us, it is fate that blazes our pathway through life, fate that predestines our apparently chance meetings. That is why we sometimes say, "It must be fate!"

I knew Beria, even though he did not belong to the circle of people close to me, the society of old Bolsheviks. Our acquaintance, in fact, was pure coincidence, if there really is such a thing.

In August 1928, my father, who had taken part in the work of the budget commission of the USSR government, was invited by the aged Georgian Bolshevik Mikha Tskhakaya, chairman of the Transcaucasian Central Executive Committee, to come to Tiflis [now Tbilisi] to discuss the budget for Transcaucasia (or perhaps only Georgia, I'm not sure now). Mother and I went with him so that, once business had been taken care of, we could all spend our vacation in Likany, near Borzhomi. (Incidentally, I recalled Likany more than once in the years to come because it was there, sitting on a park bench, that the Bolshevik writer Silvester Todriya, famous then in Georgia, warned my father, "You Russians don't know Stalin the way we Georgians do. He'll show us all something beyond your wildest imagination!")

Beria, as chief then of the Georgian NKVD, did not merely take part in the budget discussion but hosted the meeting at his dacha in the picturesque environs of Tiflis, near Kadzhory. I recall the latter name now, I suppose, because it reminded my father of Pushkin's verses referring to a stream with a similar name, the Izhory:

> *Riding on toward Izhory,*
> *Up I gazed into the skies.*
> *They recalled for me your glances*
> *And the blueness of your eyes.*

It was my first visit to Georgia, and I was enchanted. Naturally, I could not foresee that the name of our host receiving us so graciously in Kadzhory would one day be synonymous with butchery.

After the men had a very long discussion of budget matters, we all sat down to a supper that included native Georgian dishes and an aromatic Georgian tea. At the table, Beria turned to my father: "I didn't know you had such a charming daughter."

Only fifteen at the time, I blushed and hung my head. So my father replied, "I don't see anything charming about her."

Beria turned to Tskhakaya. "Let us drink, Mikha, to the health of this little girl! May she live long and be happy!"

The second time I encountered Beria was in the summer of 1932, some months after my father's death. Aleksei Rykov, learning from Mother how hard I was taking our loss, invited me to join him on a vacation trip to the Crimea. We found Valerian Kuibyshev there with some of his relatives: his daughter, his son, his brother Nikolai (also a Bolshevik) with his wife, plus Mikhail Feldman, Kuibyshev's private secretary. (Nikolai and his wife were later shot.) Kuibyshev did not tarry long, since he wanted to take his large and jolly troupe by steamship to Batum and continue overland to Tiflis and Likany. To distract me from my grief, he urged me to come along.

Upon our arrival in Batum, Kuibyshev was met by Beria. By now, the Georgian NKVD chief and I were "old friends."

"Aha, who do we have here?" he exclaimed the moment he saw me. "The little girl has grown up!"

Beria accompanied our party from Batum to Tiflis, entertained us at his dacha, and then set off with us to Likany.

Consequently, I socialized on a daily basis with the future head of the NKVD for a week or more. He chatted with me a number of times, mainly about the natural beauty of Georgia. He also expressed his condolences for the death of my father.

Even looking back through the prism of his later atrocities, it is impossible to detect anything evil in the rather intelligent, businesslike man who, like all Georgians, was so unaffectedly hospitable. You can imagine how he received such an honored guest as a member of the Politburo in his own home. Of course, his talks with Kuibyshev, then the chairman of the State Planning Committee, dwelt principally on the economic problems of Transcaucasia. Fortunately, this honored guest would not in the future enjoy the very different hospitality of Beria's "luxury apartments" in Lubyanka, for he would eventually take leave of life by another route, the second major political figure after Kirov to be killed in mysterious circumstances. If he had survived to fall into Beria's clutches in the dread time of the terror, he would have undoubtedly felt "the turning of the screw."

In brief, then, these chance encounters were the prologue to my reunion with Beria in the dungeons of the NKVD.

The commissar offered me a seat in front of his desk. I sat down and asked again about Yezhov.

"Does it really interest you that much?" he asked, deflecting my question. Then, to distract me further, he tossed in a completely extraneous remark.

"Why are you limping, Anna Yuriyevna?"

This was odd. I was not limping at all, but I suggested to him that it might look as if I was, since the surprising replacement of the "glorious people's commissar" had made me weak in the knees.

"You're not limping? I'm glad that you're not limping, that it only seemed to me that you were," he said, as if a limp would be the greatest misfortune of my life!

"It's not Anna Yuriyevna but Anna Mikhailovna," Kobulov corrected the commissar. Beria stuck his nose in my "case," which was lying on the desk. The folder, so fat I could not imagine what it was stuffed with, was labeled "Bukharina-Larina Anna Mikhailovna." (Or possibly Larina-Bukharina, I don't recall for sure.)

"It's all right," Beria said. "She's Yuriyevna, too."

Indeed, my father had used Yury as his first name in the Party.

Kobulov, understanding nothing, shrugged his shoulders in confusion but kept quiet.

"I should tell you," Beria went on, "you look more beautiful than when I saw you last."

Peering through his pince-nez at my pale, haggard face, he was lying brazenly. Insincerity had evidently become a habit with him. This false compliment disgusted me, to say the least, and I answered venomously, "That's odd, Lavrenty Pavlovich, that I've become so beautiful! In that case, ten more years of prison, and you will be able to send me to Paris for a beauty contest."

Beria's face eased into a smile. "What have you been doing in camp, what work?"

"I cleaned latrines," I replied, without hesitation. I could have explained that there was no industry in the Tomsk camp, the only one I had been confined to so far, but I wanted to answer Beria exactly as I did, meaning to emphasize that there could be no talk about beauty here, that compliments were out of order. Besides, I was simply stating a fact: after Bukharin's trial, the head of the barracks ordered me to chip out the waste in the frozen toilet with a crowbar. It gave her genuine pleasure to assign this work to me in particular, Bukharin's wife, and it was to her dismay that the job proved beyond my strength and I had to be removed from my "present position" after only three or four days. Yet and still, taking into account the amount of effort I exerted to make that toilet usable, the true extent of my latrine-cleaning days is those few days multiplied a hundredfold.

"Cleaned latrines?" Beria responded in surprise. "What, they couldn't find other work for you?"

"Why should they? For the wife of a master spy, an arch traitor, they found the most appropriate work. And why should you be surprised, Lavrenty Pavlovich? If our entire life has been turned into a big pile of shit, it's not so bad to dig in a little pile!"

"What!" he exclaimed, and I repeated what I'd just said.

The epithet I bestowed on life is so coarse I nearly omitted this incident from my story, but I want my reminiscences to be entirely honest. Evidently, after all the indecent cursing of the prisoners in the Stolypin car, it no longer shocked me to say something vulgar myself or worried me in the least how Beria would react. Neither was I deterred by the possibility of being charged with counterrevolutionary slander against our wonderful reality. One thing did pique my interest, though: How would this new people's commissar take my ironic characterization of Bukharin as a master spy and arch traitor?

Beria, resting his elbows on the desk, looking through me as if with X-ray eyes, said nothing for a while. Then he tossed a few phrases in Georgian back and forth with Kobulov, who exclaimed, "My, my, what a filthy mouth you have. Aren't you ashamed of yourself?"

"I am no longer ashamed of anything," I shot back, although I cannot truthfully say now that I was not embarrassed.

Because of my prolonged isolation, I had no idea what was going on in the country. Specifically, I did not know how the new people's commissar was carrying out his duties or what connection he had with the trials. Beria did not make me wait long to learn the answers, although he did proceed cautiously now, step by step. After a short pause, he gently asked, apparently out of the blue, "Tell me, Anna Yuriyevna, what was it that made you love Nikolai Ivanovich?"

I was thrown off balance. His conciliatory tone and the courtesy of referring to Bukharin by his given name and patronymic seemed to be promising signs. Immediately, I assumed that the Boss had commissioned Beria to expose Yezhov, treacherously dumping on him the blame for all of the mass repressions, including Bukharin's death. If I was right, it was too late to save Bukharin, but the horrible charges against him would be retracted.

I evaded a direct reply, remarking only that love is an intensely personal affair and I had no intention of answering such a question, no matter who asked it.

"But even so, even so," Beria persisted, "we are aware that you loved Nikolai Ivanovich very much."

He did not employ the standard interrogator's phrase "We know for a fact," so I answered, "Indeed, you know it for a fact."

Beria smiled again. Suddenly, an idea dawned upon me, and I tossed his question back at him: "What about you? What was it that made you love Nikolai Ivanovich?"

Beria grimaced in alarm.

"I loved him? What do you mean by that? I couldn't stand him."

Apparently, he had missed the hidden catch in my trick question.

"But Lenin," I continued, "called Bukharin the legitimate favorite of the whole Party. If you didn't love him, it follows that you were an illegitimate exception in the Party ranks."

"What is this, something Bukharin told you?"

"No, not Bukharin. I read it in Lenin's 'Letter to the Congress.' "

I don't remember now whether I had actually read the document, but I was familiar with its contents.

"Lenin wrote that a long time ago," Beria observed. "It is inappropriate to refer to it now."

I still had hopes that the new people's commissar would at least not call Nikolai Ivanovich a traitor and had had nothing to do with his destruction. But Beria changed the subject now that the conversation had taken an unwanted turn for him.

He asked what I'd been fed that day, and I replied that meals were not specially prepared for me. He asked Kobulov to go get some sandwiches and fruit and turned his attention to some documents in a folder. I recognized my declaration to Yezhov.

"Anna Yuriyevna, do you really not want to live?" he asked. "This is hard to believe. You're so young; you have your whole life ahead of you!"

"When I wrote Yezhov, I was in a state of total desperation. I saw no prospect of anything but a slow wasting away. Because nothing remained to me but a monstrous nightmare, because I lived as if in a fog of blood, because they had killed Nikolai Ivanovich and all those I respected, took away my baby and doomed me to waste away in a damp cellar, and then repeatedly executed me [I was thinking of the several threats of execution and the walk to the ravine after the reading of my death sentence], nothing remained for me to do but plead for death."

Beria listened with head lowered, looking up at me from under his brows. Some sort of momentary disturbance flickered across his face. Perhaps for an instant something human awoke in his soul.

"It's not possible to execute someone repeatedly," he said. "Execution is one time only. And Yezhov would certainly have shot you."

I tried again to find out what had happened to Yezhov, but Beria let me know that he alone could ask questions.

"Well, are you too going to execute me?"

"That all depends on how you conduct yourself."

How many times and to how many prisoners had the interrogators repeated this rote phrase! It was already clear that my conduct was not to Beria's liking. Finally, he moved my "case" file closer to himself. Obviously, he was very familiar with it. Flipping cursorily through the pages, he stated:

"A counterrevolutionary youth organization connected with Bukharin through you. . . . This is nonsense. And this, that Bullitt wanted to send you to America after Bukharin's arrest? Also, fantasy. Do you have any idea who you were talking to in your cell? Before you bare your soul, you should find out who is listening to you! Especially, in your position."

The commissar seemed now to be showing a downright paternal interest in me. I had to confess that I had found out who my cellmate was only at the last minute, just before she was taken off. I also told Beria how she had nearly favored me with a slap in the face and stressed to him that she hated me not because she thought I was a counterrevolutionary, wife of an enemy of the people, but because she saw me as the wife of a Bolshevik revolutionary. It was for that reason she'd told such egregious lies about me.

"She didn't lie about everything," Beria interjected. "Sverdlov, Andrei Yakovlevich. . . . Did you know him?"

I knew that, on the basis of my cellmate's reports, Andrei Sverdlov had been named in my "case" as a member of the alleged counterrevolutionary youth organization.

"I did," I hastened to reply, "but it does not follow that Sverdlov was in a counterrevolutionary youth organization. You just said yourself that the story of this organization was nonsense."

"I was expressing my opinion only in respect to you. That doesn't mean we have no counterrevolutionary youth organizations at all. Why are you defending Sverdlov like this? Could it be he was in love with you?"

"I am defending him only because I am convinced he could not have had any connection with counterrevolution. As far as love is concerned, ask Sverdlov, if you're interested. He never professed any love to me."

From my "case" file, Beria pulled out pages of poetry written in an unfamiliar hand. Again, only my cellmate had ever heard my verses.

Yury Larin, Anna's father, with Anna's mother, Yelena Grigoroyevna, in exile abroad. Geneva, 1904.

Yury Larin with Anna's mother, Yelena Grigoroyevna. Berlin, 1922.

Anna Larina (age three) with her mother's sister, Mariya Grigoriyevna Milyutina.

Yury Larin,
Anna's father, 1925.

Anna Larina's father, Yury Larin, *second from left*; her mother, Yelena Larina, *to his left*. Standing next to Larin, *on his right*, is his secretary, Zinaida Kastekskaya. Sitting is Vladimir Smirnov, a leading Soviet economist of the time and a family friend. Outside Moscow, 1919.

Anna Larina (age fifteen), 1929.

МОСКОВСКОЕ ОХРАННОЕ ОТДѢЛЕНІЕ

Bukharin's police record upon his arrest in Moscow, 1909.

Members of the famous "Bukharin School" of the 1920s, in 1926. *Left to right, bottom row*: Ivan Kravel and Vasily Slepkov; *middle row*, Dmitry Maretsky, Aleksandr Zaitsev, Bukharin, Yan Sten, and Aleksandr Slepkov; *top row*, Grigory Maretsky, David Rosit, Aleksei Stetsky, and Aleksandr Troitsky.

Bukharin, *third from right, second row*, with a group of exiles in Onega, Arkhangelsk district, 1911.

Bukharin with his brother Vladimir and his father, Ivan, mid-1920s.

Bukharin and Mariya Ilyinichna Ulyanova, Lenin's sister, at the *Pravda* editorial office, mid-1920s.

The tenth anniversary of the newspaper *Pravda*, 1922. Bukharin, the chief editor, sits in the center of the second row, to the right of Mariya Ilyinichna (Lenin's sister).

Bukharin speaking in Petrograd (later Leningrad), 1920.

Lenin *second row, third from right*, Bukharin *second row, far right*, and Trotsky
with delegates to the First Congress of the Communist International.
Moscow, 1919.

Bukharin, 1925.

Anna Larina, 1931.

Bukharin between Stalin and Sergo Ordzhonikidze, atop the Lenin Mausoleum, October 1929, a month before he was expelled from the leadership.
Credit: David King.

Left to right: Bukharin, Lazar Kaganovich, Anastas Mikoyan, Aleksei Rykov, Valerian Kuibyshev, Joseph Stalin, Kliment Voroshilov, and Yan Rudzutak, atop the Lenin Mausoleum, 1926.

Lev Kamenev giving a
speech in Red Square,
early 1920s. Bukharin is
second to the right of
Kamenev.

Bukharin, Yan Sten, *center*,
and Vyacheslav Molotov, *to
the right*, at the Kremlin
wall in Red Square, 1925.

Bukharin, Rykov (in dark suit), and Stalin leading the funeral procession for Feliks Dzerzhinsky across Red Square, 1926.

Bukharin (hands clasped) and Lenin, *far right*, at the Presidium of the Ninth Communist Party Congress, in 1920. Mikhail Tomsky is seated to Bukharin's left, Lev Kamenev (with glasses) in the center, and Aleski Rykov in the forefront.

Bukharin, Sergei Kirov, *center*, and Vyacheslav Molotov at a Leningrad Party meeting, 1926.

Bukharin, Stalin, and Voroshilov among a group of delegates to the Fourth All-Union Congress of Soviets. Moscow, 1927.

Bukharin, 1929.

Meeting Maxim Gorky
in the train station, 1928.

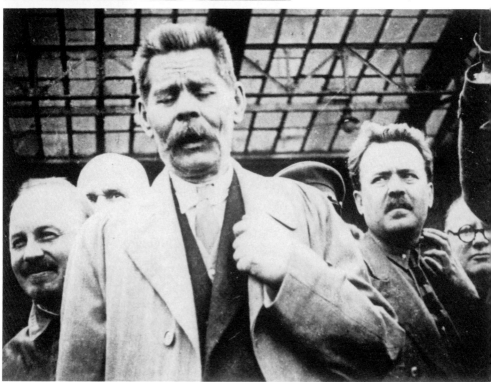

Bukharin in one of the despised Kremlin suits. London, early 1930s.

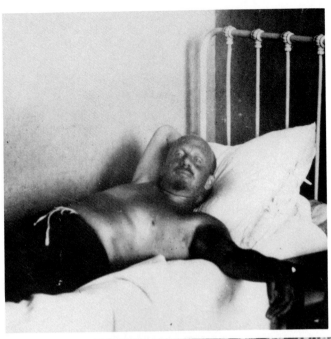

Bukharin during his
illness in the Crimea,
1930.

On vacation in
the Crimea, 1930.

Anna Larina (age seventeen) at the vacation retreat
in Serebryany Bor.

Hotel Lutetia in Paris, where Bukharin and Anna Larina stayed during his last trip abroad, in 1936.

Bukharin among his colleagues in the People's Commissariat of Heavy Industry, 1933.

At the Seventeenth Communist Party Congress, January 1934. *Center row, left to right*: Mikhail Tukhachevsky, Sergo Ordzhonikidze, Mikhail Kalinin, Stalin, Vyacheslav Molotov, Kliment Voroshilov, and Sergei Kirov.

Lavrenty Beria (in dark jacket), new head of the NKVD, 1938, and, *to his left*, Nikita Khrushchev and Stalin.

Prosecutor Andrei Vyshinsky summing up the case against Bukharin at his trial. Moscow, March 1938.

Stalin and then head of the NKVD Nikolai Yezhov, December 1937.

Bukharin and Trotsky as depicted in the Soviet press during the former's trial in 1938. The beast was captioned "The Right-Trotskyist Monstrosity," and the hand was labeled "Gestapo."

Anna Larina's son Yury, *center*, in the orphanage, about 1949.

Larina and her son Yury in her Siberian exile in 1958, two years after their first reunion in 1956, with her children by her second husband, Nadya *standing* and Misha.

Yury Larin, the son of Nikolai Bukharin and Anna Larina. Moscow, 1960.

Anna Larina with her son Yury in his Moscow apartment, 1980.

Left to right: grandson Nikolai, son Yury, Anna Larina, and Stephen Cohen, in Moscow shortly after Bukharin's rehabilitation in 1988.

Anna Larina and Valery Pisigin at the Bukharin Exhibit at the Central
Museum of the Revolution, honoring the 100th anniversary of
Bukharin's birth, in October 1988, the year of his rehabilitation.

"Well now, Anna Yuriyevna, it turns out that you write poems. Not bad, if I do say so myself. Who taught you this, Bukharin or Larin?" Not pausing for a reply, he recited:

> *Though he won the love of multitudes,*
> *He was hated by terrible foes*
> *Because, no matter how great the cost,*
> *He fought to keep thought free.*

"What did you mean by those lines?"

"Just what you see; they have no hidden meaning."

"We always put a stop to any of Bukharin's harmful thoughts."

I thought to myself, "He says only, 'Bukharin's harmful *thoughts.*' That's not so awful." I felt my spirits rising. Beria had not brought up wrecking, spying, and spreading terror, or any connection with fascist intelligence operations.

"And the crow, this crow of yours. Who is he?" the commissar asked in a raised voice and read the lines from my other prison poem:

> *A great crow, black and evil,*
> *Pecked into his heart, his brain.*
> *Blood oozed out in scarlet drops,*
> *The bird triumphed in its disdain.*

> *For this crow thrived on the dead,*
> *Gorged itself, could not be sated.*
> *Throughout Russia it had spread*
> *Fear, oppression, shame, and slavery.*

"Who is this crow?" Beria asked again.

"A crow is a crow!" I shouted, making up my mind not to engage in any explanations, despite my increasing anxiety. "It is a constantly recurring nightmarish vision that tormented me in the cell, as you can gather from the poem."

"That's not all one can gather," Beria noted.

My agitation grew, but Kobulov, who came back into the office at that moment with sandwiches and fruit, inadvertently spared me further explanations. Evidently, Beria was not interested in dotting the *i*, anyway, for he suddenly changed his tone. Perhaps Caucasian hospitality took precedence even in this situation, perhaps there were other considerations; I couldn't tell.

"Let's interrupt the conversation, Anna Yuriyevna," he said, pushing the sandwiches, tea, and a bowl of oranges and grapes toward me. I refused them.

"You won't eat? Why won't you? I wanted to have tea with you. If you don't want to eat, I won't talk with you."

Words cannot convey my surprise at this remark.

"That must mean," I countered, "that you have no particular need to talk with me. You were an excellent host to Kuibyshev, Lavrenty Pavlovich; on that visit, I sat at the same table with you and we had supper together, but now the circumstances have changed."

"Why only Kuibyshev? Was I a poor host to Larin? You have obviously forgotten some things."

"I have forgotten nothing, though it was ten years ago. I remember the toast you made at the dinner table: 'Let us drink to the health of this little girl. May she live long and be happy!' Nice sentiments, but alas, they did not come to pass!"

"Is she also the daughter of Larin?" Kobulov blurted out in disbelief, disgusted by this apparent connection to yet another discredited man.

"Not that Larin," Beria explained. "But Yury Larin, a most original, talented man, with a fantastic imagination."

After Lenin delivered his opinion of Larin's imagination at the Eleventh Party Congress, in 1922, people usually referred to this supposedly inordinate gift whenever his name came up.

"I had great respect for him," Beria went on. "We interred him with honors in Red Square."

(As if *he* had had anything to do with my father's interment!)

Perhaps Beria thought that his praise for Larin would make his hostile attitude toward Bukharin more persuasive to me.

"It's a good thing Larin died in time," I observed. "Otherwise, he would have perished in exactly the same way as his comrades, and then you wouldn't be able to recall him so fondly."

"Why do you have such a poor opinion of your father?" Comrade Larin was an unusually devoted member of the Party."

"And the other Bolsheviks who perished, and Nikolai Ivanovich, were they in fact less devoted members of the Party?"

The decisive moment had arrived.

"You can ask this now, after the trial?" Beria answered, getting louder. "You can continue to think that Bukharin was devoted to the Party? He was an enemy of the people! A traitor! The leader of the Bloc of Rightists and Trotskyists! And you know what that bloc was. In the camp, you had an opportunity to learn about the trial from newspapers."

So this is what had been hiding under the mask of phony courtesy: lies and hypocrisy! The floor swam beneath my feet, the room went dark before my eyes, and Beria's face became a gray, amorphous mass. From that instant on, I felt the same hatred for the "new people's commissar" as I had for the old. Beria studied me, evidently gauging the effect of his vile words.

I turned aside to evade that steady stare. To my left, I now saw a window with blinds. I imagined I could hear, or perhaps I actually did hear, the sounds of the city coming from there: automobiles honking, streetcars clanging. I conjured up Theater Square, today called Sverdlov Square. And on it the Metropol, with the mosaic by Mikhail Vrubel on its façade and the little mast turrets on its roof—the Metropol, like a giant ship forever docked at that square, where I had grown up and been happy. It was right nearby, but unreachable. If only I could go downstairs and walk past the Kitai Gorod [China City] wall and the monument to the first printer, Ivan Fyodorov, then continue down the narrow sidewalk where in the early 1920s one could see Chinamen with long jet-black pigtails wearing wide blue overcoats down over their bloomers, trading their homemade toys, round paper honeycombs and little balls bouncing on thin rubber bands. And catty-corner to the Metropol was that ill-fated building with columns where the trials were held, those shameful, unjust spectacles!

During the interrogation, if the term suits my exchange with Beria, the strain on my nerves kept rising, and finally I burst out crying.

"Have you always been such a crybaby?" Beria asked and pushed the glass of tea even closer toward me. I shoved it back.

"It's a superb tea. You are making a mistake to refuse it, Anna Yuriyevna. Comrade Larin exerted no small effort to organize the production of tea for us in the Caucasus. This is the very same tea."

Yet, because of Beria's terrible attack upon Nikolai Ivanovich, I was still unable to say a word. What could have cut me so deeply? You'd think that such epithets as "traitor," "enemy of the people," and "betrayer of the motherland," loudly broadcast over and over in regard to famous political figures, the champions in fact of the October Revolution, and somewhat less loudly voiced in regard to millions of less famous people placed under arrest, had become so firmly established as part of the national vocabulary that they had lost the power to shock. Yet, when Beria uttered them, I was seized by a powerful sense of indignation, perhaps because he had only moments before expressed views that seemed quite reasonable and humane. He had, for example, brushed aside many of the unfounded accusations made against me in Novosibirsk. I believed that his remark "Before you bare your soul, you should find out who is listening to you" indicated that he considered my statements in prison a natural reaction to events but felt I had been foolish to make them in front of the wrong person, thereby worsening my case. Finally, it's quite possible that our past socializing had given me reason to hope that he would at least spare me the indignity of calling Nikolai Ivanovich a traitor in my presence.

But at last I made myself say to him everything I had planned to say to Yezhov.

I declared that he should not expect me to believe something he himself did not believe. It was in fact completely incredible to me, I went on, that the overwhelming majority of Bolsheviks had betrayed their ideals by seeking to restore capitalism in the Soviet Union, the very system they had fought against all their conscious lives. *This was my chief point.*

I would have known this truth, I went on, even without being married to Bukharin. But since I did know the accused men and had been present with them at many events, I was able to detect the falsehoods and inventions in the trial testimony.

"Interesting, interesting. What did you manage to pick up?" the people's commissar asked.

I cited a number of examples I noticed during the reading of the newspaper accounts in camp. For example, Akmal Ikramov, formerly secretary of the Uzbek Central Committee, testified under questioning that he had met with Bukharin in 1935 for the purpose of holding counterrevolutionary discussions; furthermore, they had met in an apartment on Zubovsky Boulevard, along with their wives. But in fact the apartment described was completely unknown to me; I had certainly never been in it.

A second example had persuaded me even more strongly that the trial was nothing but a staged performance. Ikramov testified that during the Eighth Congress of Soviets, in December 1936, when the so-called Stalin constitution was passed, he had met with Bukharin *on the empty stairway* (the producers and directors of this extravaganza had prompted the poor man to give the exact location, so that the tale would be more convincing), where they held conversations of a conspiratorial nature. Supposedly, Bukharin had told Ikramov that if an intervention did not take place soon (an "intervention" by fascist Germany is the implication), they—that is, the wreckers and saboteurs—would be rounded up. I was citing all of this testimony to Beria from memory.

I did not waste time trying to prove to him that neither Ikramov nor Bukharin was capable of such conspiracies; *that was already my basic position.* Rather, I only wanted to make the point that my husband was not even present at that congress. He considered it impossible to attend, even though he was a member of the constitutional commission, because he was already under investigation. In fact, he was already an outcast, never left our apartment, and sat at home with me to listen to Stalin's report on the radio.

I brought up Paris, and Beria listened with rapt attention. I had accompanied Nikolai Ivanovich there on an official trip in 1936, and so I could explain that he and the other members of his commission had negotiated with the émigré Menshevik Boris Nicolaevsky to buy the Marx archive. I told Beria how horrible I felt when Bukharin at his trial lied that Nicolaevsky had been initiated into the underground conspiratorial activities of the Bloc of Rightists and Trotskyists and lied, too, that he had used the official trip as cover for talks about the conspiracy and had even asked for the support of the Second International in the event of a debacle. I knew firsthand that the negotiations with Nicolaevsky were concerned entirely with business, in keeping with the official purpose of the trip. There was a political connotation to only one chat, when Bukharin and Nicolaevsky disagreed, as would be expected, about ideology.

To take yet another example, Bukharin testified that a connection between the Bloc of Rightists and Trotskyists and the Menshevik center abroad was maintained by Rykov through Nicolaevsky. Rykov was forced to admit this, as Yagoda himself confirmed. Yet I knew, from Nicolaevsky's own lips, that he had had no contact whatsoever with Rykov. Nicolaevsky had brought up the subject himself during a conversation with Bukharin in Paris, as I listened, because he wondered whether we had any news of his brother Vladimir, who was married to Rykov's sister and lived in Moscow.

"I am convinced that Nicolaevsky has already refuted these false statements of Bukharin and Rykov in the press," I declared to Beria. Many years after my release, I learned that I had been right.

"Representatives of the Second International might want to refute that testimony for conspiratorial reasons," Beria remarked.

In these words, I recognized the familiar mark of Stalin.

"Perhaps I have said enough to prove my point?" I asked.

"No, no, go on. It's interesting to see how everything has been fractured in your mind."

"I understand everything perfectly, as would anyone in my shoes."

Next, I referred to the testimony of Vasily Yakovenko. A Siberian of peasant stock, he had won glory as the leader of the partisan movement against the White Army of Admiral Kolchak. After Yakovenko was arrested, a copy of his testimony was sent to Bukharin, who would be picked up soon afterward. It seems that Yakovenko claimed that he had met Bukharin at Larin's dacha in Serebryany Bor and had been commissioned by him to go to Siberia to organize a kulak uprising for the purpose of splitting the territory off from the Soviet Union.

Only one part of this story was true: Bukharin had indeed happened to run into Yakovenko at Larin's dacha. Here's what happened. Nikolai Ivanovich, my father, and I were sitting together on a bench near the yard fence, when we noticed Yakovenko walking down the path alongside, bent over and thinner than normal, not at all like himself. He had always been a hardy, truly powerful lad, a tall, strong, and handsome Siberian, but now he was sick, feeble, supporting himself with a cane. Nikolai Ivanovich knew him only slightly, but Father was a close friend, so he asked Yakovenko to stop and sit awhile. Joining us, he explained that the doctors had discovered he had a stomach ulcer at an advanced stage of development and he would have to go rest in the hospital (not foment kulak uprisings). He was in such pain that he could not sit long. We spoke of nothing but his health and the prospects for the harvest.

"Well, how were the prospects?" Beria asked ironically, implying that he did not much believe my story.

"I don't know; that is irrelevant here."

Not only Yakovenko's incriminating testimony but also Bukharin's reported reaction to it had shaken me. Before Nikolai Ivanovich was arrested, he had been outraged by the tale; he read it aloud to me and asked whether I recalled the incident. but at his trial he confirmed both the incident and the place of meeting, Serebryany Bor (though without mentioning Larin's dacha, evidently not wanting to drag in my father's name).

I was deeply worried, for I recognized that my eyewitness observations placed the noose around my own neck; still, once Beria had called Nikolai Ivanovich a traitor, I was unable to hold my tongue. I did keep quiet about one specific item in Bukharin's trial testimony that had stunned me, however, his statement that among his so-called fellow conspirators he had called Mikhail Tukhachevsky a potential "Napoleonchik" [little Napoleon]. In fact, as my husband had told me himself, it was Stalin who called Tukhachevsky "Napoleonchik" in a conversation with Bukharin, who then tried to persuade him that the general by no means yearned for such power. Therefore, the insertion of this specific epithet in the false testimony indicates that Stalin participated directly in the composition of the trial scenario. No one else could have known to put his words into Bukharin's mouth.

Nor did I tell Beria how surprised I had been by Bukharin's forced admission that he had sent his former protégé Aleksandr Slepkov to the North Caucasus to organize a kulak uprising there. On the contrary, I knew very well that Nikolai Ivanovich's protégés, Slepkov among them, had been sent by Stalin to the provinces in order to isolate him, which made him very sad.

But I did cite one more weighty fact that gave the lie to the trials. Not long before Radek's arrest, I heard him talking with Bukharin; it was meant to be a private conversation, but I was in the next room and the door was open. I heard Radek assuring Bukharin that he had not been involved in any conspiracy against Stalin or in any other crimes. Yet, after his arrest, both at his preliminary investigation and at his trial, Radek confessed to horrific crimes and impeached Bukharin.

"From Radek's conversation with Bukharin," I asserted to Beria, "one can conclude only one of two things: either Radek himself took part in counterrevolutionary activity and gave false testimony against Bukharin [of course, I categorically rejected this possibility, but I was trying to prove logically that my husband was not involved in crimes] or both men were innocent. Two accomplices could not have had the conversation I overheard."

I assumed that I had slain Beria with my list of inconsistencies, particularly with this last story. But he regarded me with unperturbed calm and declared, "Your argumentation is not convincing, Anna Yuriyevna. These considerations you bring forward, based on facts you allege to be true, require the confirmation of witnesses. On what basis should I believe your story that Radek in private with Bukharin denied his involvement in crimes, when both of them, and other defendants as well, confessed at the trials to having committed evil deeds against the Soviet state? Where is the guarantee that everything you have just told me is not your own invention?"

He had listened to me with undivided attention, and he knew perfectly well that nothing I had said was the fruit of my imagination. Yet his scholastic objection threw me for a loss. It would be impossible to find witnesses. But I quickly came up with a pertinent rebuttal.

"I don't need any witnesses," I retorted. "You expressed surprise, even indignation, that after the trial I was unable to believe that Nikolai Ivanovich had participated in crimes. I have demonstrated why it is impossible to believe that; from my point of view, the reasons I have cited are sufficiently convincing. If you do not believe what I say, there is no point in talking to me."

"If I am talking to you, there's a point," Beria said with emphasis.

"Now, how do you account for the confessions of the accused, since you don't believe in them? Bukharin, evidently, suggested to you that the testimonies were obtained through torture."

"When we talked before his arrest, he dismissed the testimonies as outright libel; consequently, he said they must have been forced, coerced by pain, for mankind has not yet spawned such a quantity of scoundrels willing to lie of their own volition. Nikolai Ivanovich came up with various suppositions about the methods used to obtain such testimony, and he did not exclude torture. Which methods are effective in extorting lying accusations from someone, you would know better than I."

"We treat enemies as enemies; that's the way you have to treat them!"

"To my mind, it makes sense to find out the truth, even from your enemies. If the methods of your investigation produce false testimony, they make no sense, not even in regard to your enemies."

I cannot recall Beria's answer to this.

His aim in conversing with me was not clear. Impulsively, I started to ask him, but since his face happened to look severe at that moment (his expression changed frequently), I held back, partly because I assumed he would not tell me the truth in any event, partly because I probably feared his answer.

Toward the end of our conversation, he asked me several questions that are not without interest. I will recall as much as I can. He asked how close Maksim Maksimovich Litvinov, then people's commissar of foreign affairs, had been to Bukharin; had he ever come to visit? I gathered that Litvinov was being undermined and did not rule out the possibility that he had already been arrested. I replied that they were not at all close and that Litvinov had never visited Bukharin.

"What now, are you saying that they did not know each other, that they were not even acquainted?" Beria asked with a smirk.

With the best intentions in the world, I could not say they were not acquainted.

"Your answer is very indefinite, quite nebulous. Evidently, you are guided by a desire to wall Litvinov off from Bukharin."

"My answer reflects the actual state of affairs: they were acquainted, but not close. I cannot put it any other way."

The next question surprised me greatly: "What character assessments did Bukharin make of Soviet political figures?"

It seemed more than strange that Beria should interest himself in this point several months after Bukharin's death. I had to answer that Nikolai Ivanovich never discussed this particular topic with me. Besides,

since he, Beria, had just observed, "You cannot execute someone repeatedly, execution is one time only," the question lost meaning with
Bukharin's death. The people's commissar did not yield on this point
right away, but he got no other answer from me.

The next question concerned me personally. Had I met with anyone in Moscow before going into exile? I did not immediately come out
with the truth. At first, I said I hadn't met with anyone at all, but, unable
to bear my lie, I changed my answer, or "confessed":

"I saw one person, but I will not say who. I will not give his name."

"Why not?"

"You would start persecuting him for this, but in my most difficult
days he did not act like a miserable coward, as so many others did. He
showed me the utmost solicitude and warmth, and I do not want him to
suffer because of it."

At that, Beria and Kobulov burst out laughing.

"It was Sozykin, Nikolai Stepanovich, wasn't it? He's the one who
showed you consideration," Beria said sarcastically, shaking his head.
"What naïveté! You met him at the Moskva Hotel, didn't you?"

I could literally hear my own heart beating. In an instant, I was
compelled to change my attitude toward a man who had seemed a bright
spot in my disastrous life. I had so often reflected that there were few
people like Kolya Sozykin.

Here is his story. Kolya Sozykin, a former classmate of mine at the
institute and the Komosomol organizer in our group, telephoned me not
long before Bukharin's arrest. A native of Stalingrad, he had returned
home after graduation to work, but now, as he explained, he had been
transferred back to Moscow to the planning department of the newly
organized People's Commissariat of the Defense Industry. He was living in the Moskva Hotel until an apartment could be found for him. I
took all of this at face value, but Nikolai Ivanovich had his doubts: "Who
in the People's Commissariat of the Defense Industry could have
needed a recent graduate, a specialist in a different field, so badly as to
drag him to Moscow from Stalingrad and then present him with a room
in the Moskva Hotel? It looks as if your Sozykin is a plant." I refused to
believe this. Nikolai Ivanovich did not go so far as to object to our
meeting; he simply warned me to be extra careful and not say anything
unnecessary. Besides, we had been secluded together from August 1936
to February 27, 1937, virtually isolated from the outside world. Just
once I had gone out to pay a visit to my mother. Bukharin always stayed
at home, and he wanted to know what people were saying about current
events.

I saw Sozykin only one time before Nikolai Ivanovich's arrest. It seemed natural to me that he expressed an interest in my husband when we met at the Moskva Hotel, and how could I possibly keep from telling him that Nikolai Ivanovich absolutely denied his guilt? Yet this was precisely the "unnecessary" thing it was dangerous to talk about. After the arrest, I saw Sozykin once more at his hotel, but I was unable to think or speak about anything but the horrible February–March plenum. My former schoolmate tried to calm me: They would sort it all out, you see. He bought toys for my baby, and candy.

"You felt sorry for him and wanted to protect him, Anna Yuriyevna, but he didn't spare you. No, no, he didn't feel a bit sorry for you! He gave a very bad report of you."

"I don't care what kind of report he gave about me. What is important to me is that he is not the Sozykin I thought he was, and that hurts. Besides, he could not have said anything bad about me unless he lied. I told him about the events of the February–March plenum and about Bukharin's conduct there. That's all he could pass along from me. Evidently, there is more than one such testimony against me in your files. One more, one less, does that change anything? You think I was wrong to tell Sozykin about the plenum; I think I did the right thing, because I told him the truth about Nikolai Ivanovich."

"So then, you feel sorry for everyone," the people's commissar concluded. "And so Litvinov's ties with Bukharin, you don't want to reveal them, either."

"I know nothing about any 'ties' between Litvinov and Bukharin. As far as I understand it, you are interested in counterrevolutionary ties, but no such ties could have existed between them. What sense would it make for me to shield Litvinov? He's much too large a figure for me to have any influence on his fate."

"You will tell the investigator about Litvinov," Beria said. Then he abruptly asked, "Did you know Valentin Astrov? He helped us a lot, and we spared his life."

I was not acquainted with the man, but I knew he had been one of Bukharin's protégés in the 1920s.

"Evidently, this Astrov told lies about Bukharin and about his own comrades, Bukharin's protégés. What methods brought him to this point I do not know, but I'm not Astrov and I'm not your accessory. Even if I wanted to, I couldn't help you. As you put it so well, they execute you only one time; it's impossible to be executed more than once."

"Yes, yes," said Beria, not in the least deterred. "It's not enough that Larin's daughter married Bukharin; she has to defend him as well."

I could barely restrain myself from using foul language in reply.

Beria saw that mentioning my father drove me to near frenzy. As a sadist, he may have derived pleasure from this.

"What has Larin got to do with it? Don't mention his name! If I were not Larin's daughter, I would not be Bukharin's wife. You know this as well as I! They were friends!"

Beria gazed at me searchingly, knitting his brows, and kept silent for a while. I was shaking with nervous agitation, while he seemed to be mulling over something and making a decision of some sort. Finally, he spoke:

"Whom are you trying to save, Anna Yuriyevna? After all, Nikolai Ivanovich [once again, he used Bukharin's given name and patronymic] is no longer with us. *Now save yourself!*"

"I'm saving my clean conscience, Lavrenty Pavlovich!"

"Forget your conscience!" Beria yelled back. "You blab too much! If you want to live, then shut up about Bukharin! If you don't shut up, here's what you'll get." Beria aimed his right forefinger at his temple. "So will you promise me to shut up?" It was not a question but a categorical, commanding statement, made as he peered straight into my eyes, as if he had already given the promise for me. I felt as if my life were being decided in that instant, whether I would still breathe, whether my heart would still beat. I promised to shut up. Besides, I suddenly suspected that it was Beria, not the Boss, who for some reason wanted to save my life. This suspicion influenced my decision to a degree.

I had conducted myself with dignity throughout this conversation, and yet just before the end I could no longer hold out and had given up. My soul felt dirtied by the degrading promise.

Jumping ahead, I have to say that I broke my vow the very next day. I wrote Stalin a little note, not a declaration but just a few words. At first, I could not decide how to address him. It was impossible for me to write the words "Comrade Stalin," and using just "Stalin" seemed too crude (as if he did not deserve such crudity!). So I called him by his given name and patronymic:

Iosif Vissarionovich!
    Through the thick walls of this prison I am looking you straight in the eyes. I do not believe in this monstrous judicial process. What you had to gain by putting Nikolai Ivanovich to death I cannot understand.

That is all I was able to write. I signed with both my surnames and left the note in a box on the little table in the corridor, and they led me back to my cell. I do not think Stalin ever saw my message, but Beria surely would have. Why did I write it? Obviously, to recover some spiritual peace after my degrading promise to the people's commissar.

"Well, it's time to conclude our conversation," Beria said. "I hope we can have tea now. Would you like some fruit? The grapes are wonderful. You haven't eaten grapes for a long time."

But again I turned down his hospitality.

"You won't get away from this fruit," he said and handed them in a paper package to the convoy guard assigned to take me back to my cell.

As soon as we got out into the hall and the door of the commissar's office closed behind me, I gave a great sigh of relief. One more trying episode in the swirl of those dramatic years now lay behind me.

To me the newly installed people's commissar of the NKVD had not acted like the man I remembered from my trips to Georgia or yet like the brute he actually was, according to the numerous stories and reminiscences I would hear later from people who were interrogated by him. But it was clear that he was an unprincipled careerist serving only Stalin, so long as Stalin was dictator. Had the tyrant's power wavered, Beria would not have hesitated to dig a knife into his back. The people's commissar of the NKVD was not corrupted by Stalin; he was a criminal from the start. And eventually, retribution would be paid!

[Portrait of Father]

Solitude yet again, severance from the outside world.

It is difficult to convey the spiritual turmoil that consumed me after my conversation/interrogation with Beria. No special courage had dictated my independent conduct. In fact, though it may seem strange, what really helped me endure with dignity was the feeling that there was no way out. Even so, my conscience was tormented by the promise not to talk about Bukharin. Not to talk about the subject that was rending my heart! But then, I had purchased my life with this promise, and forcing them to make me keep silent forever might have been too drastic a measure. As I've said, only the short note to Stalin freed me from self-contempt.

Beria's hostile attacks against Bukharin were obviously playacting, as was his fooling around with the name Larin, trying to contrast the honest and devoted Party man Larin with the "traitor" Bukharin. This was all the more maladroit since, from the Bolsheviks' point of view, Bukharin's biography was politically purer than Larin's.

Father occupied a special place in my heart, and I am much indebted to him. Not only our relatives but also his comrades knew about my exceptional attachment to him.

I once read somewhere in Romain Rolland's work that he had chosen for his motto Beethoven's phrase "Durch Leiden Freude" [joy through suffering]. I can't really say that these words became my motto, but at times I, too, was seized, quite against my will, with a joy in my suffering. So it was when I sparred with Skvirsky, and when I suddenly found myself in the lap of nature after the gloom of the cellar, and especially whenever I thought about my father. And, recalling him, I would always wonder, Who would have been arrested first, Bukharin or Larin, if death had not helped my father leave life in time? Which one would have given incriminating testimony against the other? These thoughts are not shocking, when you consider all that I had seen. Rykov impeached Bukharin; then Bukharin impeached Rykov during investigation, after arrest, and in the dock. Studying the trial, I discovered that Bukharin testified first against Akmal Ikramov, who also impeached him. This was more than enough to prove to me that the juridical proceedings were an abominable show and that it lay beyond human powers for the defendants to behave otherwise. The recognition that my father had not been forced to drink this bitter cup was my moment of shining grace. At least in this I was lucky, I said to myself with bitter irony more than once.

Larin's colleagues, his closest comrades, all of those who wanted to hand down the story of this extraordinary man to succeeding generations, perished during the terror. One of them, Georgy Lomov, told me not long before his arrest that he was finishing a book to be called *Larin and the Supreme Soviet of the National Economy.* But he left life tragically, and the book perished along with its author. Bukharin was also preparing to write about Larin someday, so yet another potential contribution to my father's memory was killed along with him.

But if forgotten now, Larin was very popular among the workers, the students, and the intelligentsia in the first years after the revolution. Once I heard this ditty sung at the May Day demonstration:

> *We're taught to read books*
> *For the wisdom of Bukharin*
> *And from morn till night*
> *To gather round Larin.*

Mikhail Aleksandrovich Lurye became Yury Mikhailovich Larin in his prerevolutionary conspiratorial correspondence while in exile in Yakutsk. The patronymic came from his own first name, the surname from Pushkin's *Eugene Onegin*, but wanting to distinguish himself from the character of Tatyana's father, Dmitry Larin, "a humble sinner and a slave of God," he added the first name Yury. For some reason, the first letter of this name, *Yu,* would get attached to his new surname, and occasionally his friends would facetiously call him Comrade Yularin. He was the son of Aleksandr Lurye, an important engineer and specialist in railway transport who lived in St. Petersburg, hobnobbed with the upper crust, and, according to rumors Larin heard, was admitted to the court of Nikolai II as a valued technical expert.

Larin's mother was the sister of Ignaty Granat, compiler and publisher of a famous encyclopedic dictionary. Her marriage to Lurye fell apart under tragic circumstances. An attack of scarlet fever when she was pregnant with my father led to terrible complications: progressive atrophy of the muscles and an in utero infection of the fetus. Aleksandr Lurye abandoned his ailing wife before the birth of their son and soon thereafter made the divorce legal.

She went to stay with her sister in Simferopol, in the Crimea, where my father was born. He grew up in the family of this aunt, Friderika Granat (married name, Rabinovich), who had many children of her own. His uncle Ignaty, the lexicographer, became his guardian and financial support, and later would help him during the repressions of the tsarist government and during his emigration. After the revolution, uncle and nephew developed a strong intellectual friendship.

Larin never knew his father, and in fact laid eyes on him only once. After becoming famous as a revolutionary, he decided to go meet the man. He went to his father's place of work and asked to be announced as Mikhail Aleksandrovich Lurye. When he entered a large office, he saw a man sitting behind a desk with horror written across his face. Immediately guessing why, Larin looked at his father with revulsion and was able to utter only a few words: "I am mistaken. You apparently have the same name as the Lurye I wished to see." With that, he turned on his heel and left the office. The father, who had said nothing, did not try to call back his son, who bore the disfiguring effects of the disease contracted in his mother's womb.

This terrible illness began to advance noticeably when my father was nine or ten years old. His uncle Ignaty arranged for him to travel to Berlin to be examined by specialists, but even the medical lights of Germany could not stay the progress of the disease. Nevertheless, beginning in 1900, Mikhail Lurye plunged into the revolutionary movement, at first in Simferopol, then in Odessa, where he directed a student Social Democratic organization until he was sent back home under the

open surveillance of the police. There, exposing himself to extraordinary danger, he organized the Simferopol Union and then the Crimean
Union of the RSDRP [Russian Social Democratic Workers' Party].
These efforts earned him eight years' exile in Yakutiya on orders from
above, but he escaped in 1904 and emigrated to Geneva, where he
joined with the Mensheviks. In the 1905 revolution, influenced by the
events of January 9, Bloody Sunday, he returned to St. Petersburg and
became involved in hectic revolutionary activity, but in May he was
arrested and imprisoned in the Peter and Paul Fortress. He was liberated
from the prison hospital by the October strike. Since he had illegal status, he moved to the Ukraine and directed Spilka, a Marxist organization uniting Bolsheviks and Mensheviks. Representing Spilka, he attended the Fourth Congress of the RSDRP, in Stockholm in 1906, and
the London congress in 1907. Back in the Ukraine, in Skvir, he was
arrested twice but escaped and began working in Baku.

In 1912, he emigrated again, barely eluding a guard's bullet as he
crossed the border. There he joined a coalition of radical socialists that
included Trotsky's group, the Bundists, and others. Soon after his return to Russia in 1913, he was arrested in the midst of giving a lecture at
a workers' club in Tiflis and taken to the Metekh prison. He was transferred to the St. Petersburg prison but after a year was pronounced
terminally ill by a medical commission and sent abroad.

World War I found Larin in Germany, where he was arrested once
again, but since he was not subject to mobilization in Russia, because of
his illness, he was released and sent to Switzerland. Before the war, back
in 1912, Larin's disagreements with the Mensheviks had become more
severe; he broke openly with the "liquidators" faction at the beginning
of the war. Larin took an internationalist stand; he used every possible
aspect of the legal press for agitation against the war and in support of
socialist revolution.

Immediately after the February 1917 revolution, he returned to
Russia, began publishing the journal *International* and affirmed his adherence to the Bolsheviks at the Sixth Congress of the RSDRP. About a
thousand workers from Vasilevsky Island, the largest territory of Petrograd, declared themselves in solidarity with Larin and also joined the
Bolsheviks. At this congress, he delivered a speech calling for the creation of the Third International. He was frequently interrupted by
stormy applause, and when he concluded, the audience shouted, "Long
live the Third International!"

Larin took an active part in the October Revolution as a member of
the Executive Committee of the Petrograd Soviet. Because of his articles
about German economics, later collected into the book *State Capitalism*

in Wartime Germany, Lenin chose him to undertake the organization of the economy in revolution- torn Russia. "Fate sent me the good fortune," Larin recalled later, "to stand beside the cradle of Soviet economics and politics in general, and the Supreme Soviet of the National Economy in particular. On October 25, 1917, Comrade Lenin said to me, 'You have been concerned with the organization of Germany's economy, its syndicates, trusts, and banks; now concern yourself with ours.' And I did."*

It is hard to imagine how a man physically handicapped from birth could lead such an active, courageous life. Easily recognized by the tsarist police because of his impaired condition, he was somehow able to put up with endless pursuits, and even to escape from prison. How could he make his getaway, when it cost him great physical effort to move from place to place? His comrades helped him, of course. Father told me how he was carried out of his Yakutsk exile in a big wicker basket, then hidden, and how, for a pittance, some adolescents helped him clamber over the prison wall in Skvir so that he could jump into the arms of his friends waiting on the other side, who passed him physically from one to the next. He also told me what happened when the steamship he was taking to the Stockholm congress ran aground on a sandbank: a comrade hoisted Larin on his back and climbed down a rope to the lifeboat.

And how did my father become so prolific a writer, since his hands were so feeble that he was able to lift the telephone receiver only by supporting his right hand with his left? Yet, because he did not like to dictate to a typist or stenographer, he wrote every word himself by placing his whole hand and wrist on the paper and scraping out the letters with a peculiar back-and-forth movement. Nevertheless, the sum of his writings—his books, brochures, and articles for newspapers and journals—would make a substantial edition of collected works. Because of his affliction, everything was difficult for Larin and could be achieved only by persistent practice. But since I may not be the most dispassionate of observers, let me quote Valerian Osinsky, the famous Bolshevik, who wrote an article dedicated to my father's memory:

> This was one of the most important, exceptional, and original workers among us, one of the major figures of the October and post-October periods, a person of rare devotion to the working class and the socialist revolution.

*Yu. Larin, *U kolybeli: narodnoye khozyaistvo* [At the cradle: the national economy], no. 11 (1918), p. 16.

From 1917 to 1931, he invariably comes to mind in one and the same way: a tall man in whom a strange disease has paralyzed one side of his distinctive, original, and attractive face. Only with difficulty can he move his facial muscles and mouth, yet his speech is always lively, witty, engaging, so almost every meeting gave him extended time to speak. With good-natured cunning, he was always able to obtain this, and the meeting never had cause to complain.

He was unable to put on his coat by himself, one of his hands did not function at all, and it was with a strange, angular, and peculiarly deft motion that he wrapped his scarf around the bad side of his neck, shuffled through papers in front of him, or raised a glass of water to his mouth. Likewise, he moved from place to place in an original fashion, throwing out his legs and his helper cane in geometric patterns. He was an intelligent, exceptionally vivacious person who knew how to make the best of the external shackles that nature had clamped on him, and who was never willing to give up and capitulate to them.

Every year of living in the world was for him a victory and a conquest: his bold mind and lively revolutionary will overcame his physical debilities, as if personifying the great vital force of that movement of which he was a part.

Of Yury Larin, of Mikhail Aleksandrovich, there remains only a handful of ashes. But, all the same, the man who was able to etch his own profile, a lively and unforgettable profile, so brightly on the background of this grand epoch will never die in our memory.*

The origins of our lives, mine and Larin's, were amazingly similar. The mother who gave me life died from rapid consumption when I was about a year old. My father had abandoned us eight months earlier. Larin had married my mother's sister, Lena, and the pair became my parents, which is what I have always called them. In fact, these matters were family secrets, and I might never have known the truth, if my relatives had not told me in order to spare me the fear of inheriting Larin's terrible disease.

I was born in 1914. After my mother died, war and emigration separated me from my adoptive parents, so I lived until March 1918 with my mother's father, a lawyer, in Byelorussia. Life was exceptionally hard on him. Before I was born, he lost his thirty-five-year-old wife, my grand-

*Izvestiya, January 18, 1932.

mother, who left behind six children; then he buried my real mother when she was only twenty-two; next, his only son died just past his twentieth birthday; and at one point he nearly had to bury another daughter, my adoptive mother, Lena.

We lived in the little town of Gory-Gorki. Then as now, the famous Goretskaya Agricultural Academy stood there, located in a large, picturesque park with enormous centuries-old lindens, birch groves, motley patches of flowers in the center, and a little gurgling brook at the edge. In my childhood, this park seemed fabulous and wonderful to me. Not far off, on the slope of a hill, a tiny church rose up, always glinting in the sunshine, as I recall it now.

I remember myself at a surprisingly early age. I was about four when I began to take an interest in my absent parents. "Where is Papa, where is Mama?" I would ask Grandpa and Grandma. (Grandpa's second wife was an exceptionally kindhearted person who loved me very much.) Once, my grandfather gave me an answer I remember all too well: "Your parents are Social Democrats. They prefer to sit in jail, to escape arrest by running abroad, to sitting here beside you and cooking you kasha." I had no idea what Social Democrats were, but there was a jail not far from our house; Grandpa called it a stockade and had told me once that thieves and bandits were "sitting"—or doing time—there. I was crushed by this information about my parents and did not have the nerve to ask about them again.

Once, I happened to discover that the lilacs, jasmine, and roses in our garden had been cut down. It was winter and there was no firewood, so Grandpa suspected that the soldiers in a military unit quartered next door had hacked down the bushes for fuel. But when I became very upset and asked who could have done such a thing, he answered, "It's your Bolshevik Social Democrats who have torn up the flowers." I was horrified that my parents could be such people. Today, I can see that my grandfather probably did not much welcome the revolution and held a grudge against his daughter. When I grew older and came back from Moscow to visit him one time, he uttered words that stung me badly: "Lena went from one jail to the next. A beauty like that, and she married a cripple." It is a good thing he did not live to see Lena go from one jail to the next for long years under Soviet power.

When Mother and Father returned to Petrograd after the February Revolution, she came to see me in Gorki. Mama pleased me; she was beautiful and elegant and had large, gray, kind eyes with long, fluffy eyelashes. I decided that Social Democrats were not so bad, after all. She cried and kissed me on parting but nonetheless stopped short of taking me back with her. People were frightened and hungry in Petrograd. Mother, bearing pies baked by Grandma, went immediately to the Astoria Hotel, where the revolutionaries who had returned from emigration were living. Trotsky was visiting Larin, and no sooner did she enter her room than the police arrived, to arrest him. So Trotsky was taken off to prison with Grandma's pies.

I came to know my father first through letters. From Petrograd, I would receive epistolary fairy tales, in both prose and verse, always signed, "Your Papa Mika." A lisping nanny had called him Mika in childhood, and the name stuck. I have forgotten the content of these tales, but years later I did find one surviving letter, telling a story about a mouse society. A few of its members were overstuffed sluggards lying on their sides; they were the mice exploiters (evidently, he wanted me to become accustomed to Marxist terminology). But most of the mice were skinny toilers, the mice exploited, who had to bring the fat mice clean straw for bedding and food. Thus my father gave me my first lesson in Marxism.

In March, when the Soviet government moved from Petrograd to the new capital of Moscow, my parents came for me, and I was introduced to my father. And something terrible happened as soon as I looked at him: I was frightened by his appearance. I saw how he walked, jerking his legs out ahead of him, I saw how he used his hands, and, considering Grandpa's story about Bolshevik Social Democrats tearing up flowers, I thought he looked extremely scary. I crawled under the sofa in terror, crying and sobbing, "I want to go to Grandpa!" Nothing could persuade me to crawl out. Finally, Mother resorted to driving me out with a stick, and there stood Father before me, flustered and red in the face. By evening, however, he had won me over, and we became friends.

Even though my shameful act was committed when I was only five, it tormented me for all the years that followed. I believed I had caused my father the kind of pain he could never forget, despite my unusually great love and solicitude for him, which was perhaps comparable to the love of a mother for her ailing child. I helped him in every way I could: dressed him, undressed him, went with him to meetings. As I gradually became accustomed to his looks, his face began to look even handsome to me. I caught myself thinking that perhaps my love beautified his face. But when Lunacharsky bade Larin farewell in his funeral oration, recalling that "those magnificent Larin eyes seemed to shine even in the dark," I knew that his face really was magnificent.

When I grew up, I began to understand that my father was a brilliantly original individual, a richly endowed, boldly thoughtful person who could make bold decisions. Accepting the restraints of Bolshevik Party discipline did not come easily to him.

With my own eyes, I saw the extreme intensity of his activities during the civil war years, 1918–21. We were living then in room 305 of the Metropol, and although Father often went out to the Supreme Soviet of the National Economy, to the All-Union Central Executive Committee, or to the Council of People's Commissars, he maintained his office in our apartment, with his secretariat installed in the next room, in order to facilitate his work. He was a member of the State Planning Commission and the Presidium of the Supreme Soviet of the National Economy, managed the Department of Legislative Proposals under the Commissariat of Labor, and ran the Economics Department of the All-Union Central Executive Committee. In the spring of 1918, he was included in the delegation that drew up economic and legal provisions to the Brest-Litovsk peace treaty. Often, meetings of the Presidium of the Supreme Soviet of the National Economy were held in his office, between walls crowded with bookcases. Working intensely, the economists mapped out a plan to put the country's economic life in order. The coat rack in the entranceway could not hold the outer garments of all who attended, so a pile of clothes would be lying on the floor.

Later, Georgy Lomov recalled, "Larin's office consisted of a room packed with people and delegations, mostly of workers, who showed up from everywhere. Together, they and we decided the better part of their questions, and quite frequently in the first days the comrades who awaited a decision took part in making it."*

At the time, I noticed only the external setting in which I lived, but I later learned from Father's stories that a number of bodies held meetings in his office: the Committee of Political Economy, of which he was chairman and later vice-chairman; the commission concerned with the planning and distribution of the country's material resources; the Council on Transport, which was specifically responsible for ferrying troops to the front; and the commission for monitoring the number of men in the army, so as to furnish them with weapons and supplies. Tukhachevsky was involved in the latter two groups, which worked without letup, and sometimes he stayed overnight at our place. The country was so impoverished, according to my father, that Tukhachevsky and his fellow commissioners included the number of *lapti* [bast sandals] pro-

*Cited from V. Drobizhev and A. Medvedev, *Iz istorii sovnarkhozov* [From the history of the Councils of the National Economy] (Moscow, 1964), pp. 126–27.

duced in the villages among footwear assigned to the army, since there were not enough shoes.

In addition to the numerous workers' delegations from the provinces and the members of the Presidium of the Supreme Soviet of the National Economy, all of the luminaries of economic thought in the country appeared in Larin's office either separately or in groups.

Lenin used to come. For me at that time, he was an equal among equals, and my recollection of him is dim. I am not going to relate how he burred his *r*'s, screwed up his eye, and spoke in a grave manner, or "extra-importantly," as many have reported in their memoirs. But I do recall one amusing incident. Once, after Bukharin had just left the office, Lenin and Larin began to talk about him. I couldn't understand what Lenin was saying about Bukharin, but I did catch one phrase: "Bukharin is the golden boy of the revolution." This comment became widely known in Party circles and was often repeated in conversations between comrades, obviously as a figure of speech. But since I took everything with childish literalness, I was thrown into complete confusion. "That's not true," I interjected. "Bukharin is not made of gold, he's alive!" "Of course, he's alive," Lenin said. "I was just talking about his hair."

I cannot possibly remember everyone who came to see my father. David Ryazanov and Yan Sten come to mind, as does the exceptionally modest and for some reason continually morose Daniil Sulimov, chairman of the Russian Republic, who complained that he could not manage to get an audience with Stalin. Nikolai Sukhanov and Nikolai Morozov, I have already mentioned. Then there was the diplomat Christian Rakovsky, and the poet Demyan Bedny, and the stage director Vsevolod Meyerhold, who once remarked to Larin, "I love you, Mikhail Aleksandrovich, because you show the same character in politics as I do in art." He was referring to my father's penchant for innovation. Akmal Ikramov, the masterful and much loved ruler of the Uzbek Republic, used to come often to Larin's office in the middle or late 1920s. His sweet, intelligent wife, Zhenya Zelkina, assistant people's commissar of agriculture in Uzbekistan, used to come by even more frequently, because Larin sat on a commission that was working on land and water reform for the province.

One habitual visitor, who also lived in the Metropol, was Yelena Usiyevich, daughter of the well-known revolutionary Feliks Kon. Along with her husband, Grigory Usiyevich, she had returned from emigration at the same time as Lenin, whom she knew rather well. She was remarkably energetic, exuberant, quick-witted, and talented. I recall that shortly after Lenin's death she went to see some theater piece in which he was portrayed in pantomime. Her grief was so strong that watching an actor mime a silent Lenin depressed her. Coming to us straight from the theater, she exclaimed, "Just you wait and see, Mikhail Aleksandrovich, they'll soon be putting on an opera with Lenin singing, 'It's like a delayed death!' [i.e., his comment about the Provisional Government on the eve of the October coup] And then he'll dance in a ballet." And she started dancing herself, picking up her feet and throwing her right hand, squeezed into a fist, toward the left, toward the right.

A passionate bibliophile, she dropped by frequently, not only to chat but also to "go a-hunting" for books. Unfortunately, she was not in the habit of conscientiously returning them, which angered my father. But she was so adept at changing his mood with a witty anecdote or a funny song that peace would be restored, laughter would ring out, and Yelena Usiyevich would carry off another book.

In sum, a great number of bright, talented people were concentrated around Larin because he was himself a remarkably sociable man and an interesting conversationalist.

The library that so tempted Yelena Usiyevich was quite large, for my father regularly purchased works of literature and economics from the used-book dealers. Crumbling mounds of used books were set out on display on the street beside the Kitai Gorod wall, directly across from the Polytechnic Museum. There, I recall, Larin acquired the classics of Russian and foreign literature in the magnificent editions of Brockhaus and Efron, along with books by many other authors: Fyodor Sologub, Dmitry Merezhkovsky, Nikolai Leskov.

He also bought several works by Yuly Aikhenvald, the famous literary critic, including a collection of articles called *Silhouettes of Russian Writers*. In fact, Larin had a high opinion of Aikhenvald and was saddened by his expulsion abroad. (The critic belonged to the outlawed party of Constitutional Democrats.) Father told me that during his official trip to Germany in 1924 he met with Aikhenvald and tried in vain to persuade him to return to Russia, promising to help him. At that time, Aikhenvald had two sons living in Moscow: Aleksandr, a Bolshevik and adherent of Bukharin's economic school, and Boris, who taught literature at the school I attended. Father had sent me there precisely because he hoped the son had inherited at least a portion of his father's abilities, and indeed he proved to be an outstanding teacher of literature, whose classes were extremely interesting. Both of these young men would perish in Stalin's reign of terror.

But aside from Larin's love of books and sociability, his character was essentially formed in the contradiction between his potential energy, which was inherent in his gifted and animated nature, and his kinetic energy, "kinetic" in the strict sense of the word (that is, limited as to possibility of movement). His physical impairment led to an overproduction, if I may put it that way, of creative energy. Larin's case is a graphic proof of the law of conservation of energy.

Larin's cast of mind made him, as Osinsky accurately noted, an economist inventor. Osinsky believed this must have been extremely difficult, for political economics is a field of knowledge that involves human relations. Consequently, in the flood of Larin's proposals and projects, there were some that could not be realized and failed to prove themselves. He was a visionary inspired by the revolution (and who among the Bolsheviks was not!), a designer in the best sense of the word. Lenin's comment about Larin's fantastic imagination, though hyperbolic, had more than a little basis in fact:

> Larin is a very capable person, possessed of a fantastic imagination. Fantasy is a quality of the greatest value, but Comrade Larin has a bit of an excess. For example, I would say that if the supply of Larin's fantasy were spread out evenly over the entire membership of the Russian Communist Party, that would be about right.*

Lenin, in the heat of debate, recommended that my father not be brought into governmental work, because of this characteristic, but instead be used as a lecturer and journalist, but it was this same Lenin who made use of what he called Larin's "enormous knowledge" for government planning. Nonetheless, once the famous statement had been made, Larin was forever after branded a fantasizer, even as many of his "fantasies" enriched the economic life of the country: the system of central boards, centers, councils of national economy, workers' control, housing cooperatives, state farms, the State Planning Commission, the uninterrupted workweek as a reserve provision in the First Five-Year Plan, and much else besides were introduced on the basis of Larin's proposals and economic calculations.

In the first years of the Soviet regime, Larin wrote countless decrees, including the decree on the eight-hour work day. He told me that he and Vladimir Milyutin wrote the first draft of the Decree on the Land. Many decrees signed by Lenin were actually written by my father. His intellectual productivity was unusual even for a healthy man and astonished everyone who worked with him; comrades often called him "Maestro" or "Our Unicum" [one of a kind]. He could calculate large sums in his head. Occasionally when I dropped by the office, I would

*V. I. Lenin, *Poln. sobr. soch.* [Complete works], vol. 45, p. 125.

hear Lomov saying, "Maestro, flick up your eyes!" This meant that Larin was being asked to do an economic calculation in his head, and he would indeed flick up his eyes, concentrate a short spell, and come out with the answer. (When Larin died, the Brain Institute took his brain for study.)

Although his creative drive was volcanic, the physically challenged Larin would say of himself, "God gives no horns to a cow that butts," even as he continued to "butt" with considerable energy. It was in fact not easy to work with him, although Aleksei Rykov, chairman of the Supreme Soviet of the National Economy, was able to do so with tact and precision, and their relationship remained warm right up to Larin's demise. On the other hand, the special character of my father's mind, what I have called creative overproduction, led frequently to conflicts with Lenin, which dismayed Larin. Perhaps the problem stemmed not only from the peculiarities of his character but also from the fact that nature had laid shackles far too heavy upon him, prompting him to compensate for his impotence with a free stream of thought. In other words, if he did not agree with Lenin on some point, he would boldly confront him. Usually, however, the "argument" ended with Lenin telephoning him soon afterward and making peace, probably because he didn't want to undermine Larin's continuing creative output. For Lenin would put him on yet another commission, enlist him to write more articles and brochures, ask him to give more speeches to groups of students or workers.

For example, I recall two speeches that Lenin, who was already feeling ill, asked Larin to give in Petrograd factories in 1922. For the one at the Baltic shipbuilding factory there, the topic was not assigned, so Larin chose it himself: the construction of socialist cities, the organization of everyday life under socialism, and the corresponding new architecture. I went along with him and saw Petrograd for the first time. (It was on this trip that Father showed me the cell he had occupied in the Peter and Paul Fortress.) At one factory, where the workers' club was on the top floor, the staircase was so steep that Father was afraid he couldn't make it to the top. He turned red in frustration. The workers immediately came up with a solution: they sat him down in a chair and straightaway whisked him upstairs and into the packed hall of the club.

Both of his speeches in Petrograd stimulated an unusually spirited response. The workers listened to his dreams with unswerving interest: under socialism all housing would have dining rooms, washrooms, and kindergartens, thus completely emancipating women from the hardships of daily life and ensuring their spiritual growth. When Larin said that every worker's family would have not only a separate apartment but also separate rooms for each family member, there was good-natured laughter. I don't think this was because his dream seemed too fantastic to them but, more likely, because at their cultural level they didn't feel any such need. They regarded separate rooms for spouses as an unnatural condition of life. "What are you laughing about, comrades?" Larin asked. "The door from one room to the next won't be locked." There was another burst of laughter. I laughed along with the rest, although I did not get the joke.

It is my impression that Larin's significance in the first years after the revolution went far beyond the posts he held. He was not a member of the Party's Central Committee, only of government executive bodies; he was not a people's commissar. But he recognized his own value and was, I believe, ambitious. His illness helped push him in this direction. It is significant that he signed one of his articles in imitation of Pushkin's "My Genealogy," which ends with these lines:

> *I am a reading man and poet,*
> *I'm simply Pushkin, not Musin [Musin-Pushkin,*
> *a noble relative],*
> *I'm not rich, and not at court,*
> *I'm just myself: a philistine.*

Larin probably used a whole quatrain as well, but I remember only his last two lines:

> *I'm not* narkom *[people's commissar] and not*
> tsekist *[Central Committee member],*
> *I'm simply Larin, Communist.*

Larin published a facetious article, this time truly fantastic, in *Pravda* on November 7, 1920, wryly signed "L. A. Rin." One passage concerned Bukharin. Larin's tongue-in-cheek thesis was that science would reach such a degree of development that every man could change into a woman, and vice versa, whatever one wished. For example, he went on, Nikolai Bukharin had decided to try the experiment and had become Nina Bukharina, a young lady with a long flaxen pigtail. As far as I recall, Nina found that she could not turn back into Nikolai.*

*In 1921, Nikolai Ivanovich recalled the fantastic Nina Bukharina in his speech to the Tenth Party Congress. In his rejoinder to Aleksandra Kollontai's article on love and morality, "The Cross of Motherhood," published in the journal *Kommunistka*, nos. 8–9, January–February 1921, in which she declared that women

Larin's range of interests was uncommonly broad. He took a serious interest in astronomy and kept up with the literature in the field; learned astronomers were astounded by his knowledge. Every time he was in the Crimea, he visited the Simeiz Observatory and in Leningrad, the Pulkovo. He also had an excellent knowledge of history and a passionate interest in archaeology.

His indefatigable nature shone through in everything. When a nationwide quiz was announced, he took part and won first prize. He was always drawn to innovators like Ivan Kazakov, who later stood accused at the trial with Bukharin and was shot. When he first met Larin, however, he was an obscure doctor considered a charlatan for his method of treating a wide variety of illnesses with a preparation (called lizaty or gravidian) derived from the urine of pregnant women. In order to prove the efficacy of this method, he paraded his patients into Larin's office when they could hardly stand on their feet and then brought them back later to show how dramatically they had recovered. Larin subsequently began to help him organize an institute of experimental medicine. Similarly, my father helped the veterinarian Tobolkin set up a monkey farm, again in the interest of experimental medicine. Also, he got involved with the soybean expert Bragin in the cultivation of soybeans, and so on.

Even little things caught his attention, like the name of the village *Kobyliya luzha* [Mare's Puddle]. When we were riding by this place one time, Larin decided to go talk to the chairman of the local soviet about changing the name. "Your village has inherited a name from its prerevolutionary past that is not very pretty," he said. "You ought to think up a new one." The chairman readily agreed. The next time we were in the vicinity, we could see from afar a new sign on the hut of the village soviet: *Derevnya Sovetskaya luzha, sovetskoluzhinsky selsky sovet* [Soviet Puddle Village, the Sovietpuddlian Village Soviet].

I cannot describe the dumbfounded expression on Larin's face.

Because unemployment still existed in the first years after the revolution, there were unemployment agencies. But so many people appealed to Larin for help in finding work that his involvement reached

---

shared her views more than men did, Bukharin said, "Even if the dream of Com. Larin were realized and I were transformed into Nina Bukharina, I would not go into raptures over this article." See *Stenographic Record, Tenth Congress of the RKP(b)* (Moscow, 1963), p. 325. The most amusing thing about this is that the name index of the Tenth Congress RKP(b) mistakenly lists the fantastic Nina Bukharina as the first wife of Nikolai Ivanovich (who was Nadezhda Mikhailovna Bukharina-Lukina).

such proportions that his office was jokingly called Larin's Employment Agency.

He also helped people unjustly accused of bureaucratism, people expelled from the Party unjustly, and, when possible, people persecuted unlawfully.

I want to tell one more story that clearly illustrates my father's character. A woman he didn't know came to his office and said that her husband had perished at the front; she needed help because she and her three small children were starving. At that moment, my father had little money on hand, although he gave her some small sum. But he immediately found a solution: he reached into a suitcase and pulled out an Arctic-fox fur that Mother had bought to stitch around the neck of her coat. He gave it to the woman, who went away completely satisfied. Mother was steamed: "Are you sure she wasn't a crook?" "Really!" exclaimed Father, at that moment beginning to suspect the possibility. The woman *was* rather well dressed.

Larin would not help people, however, if it ran against his moral principles. Once he received a call from the People's Commissariat of Foreign Affairs advising that a package addressed to him had arrived from Berlin through diplomatic channels. Usually, he was sent economics books this way, but this time he received a large and weighty parcel filled with women's underwear, blouses, children's things, toys, and the like. Father was perplexed, until an unknown woman phoned the next day and politely asked him to turn over to her the things her relatives had sent through the Berlin embassy in order to avoid customs duty.

"You won't get a thing," he angrily replied. "I do not permit the use of my name for such purposes."

"What then, are you going to keep another person's things for yourself?" the woman asked in alarm.

"No doubt about it," he snapped and hung up.

Everything was distributed to the cleaning women at the Metropol with an explanation of the source.

Perhaps the incidents I have recalled here will seem trifling, superfluous details unworthy of time and attention, but I think that these very trifles fill out and possibly even constitute the most essential elements in the complex portrait of my father.

[Childhood Friendship with Bukharin]

In the basement cell in Lubyanka, as I thought over my conversation/ interrogation with Beria again and again, mulling over each phrase, I absolutely understood how truly I had spoken when I said that had I not been Larin's daughter I would not have become Bukharin's wife.

Larin and Bukharin, friends since the time of emigration, first met in 1913 in Italy, where Nikolai Ivanovich had gone from Austria. Later, they were neighbors in Switzerland for a whole year, from the summer of 1915 to the summer of 1916. They were united by their opposition to the Menshevik policy of "defensism" and Russia's participation in World War I. From 1918 to the middle of 1927, our families lived in the Metropol. Father and Nikolai Ivanovich hardly saw eye to eye on everything, but their friendship was never jeopardized. They were completely candid with each other and tried to remain calm as they argued their differing views on various economic problems. Nikolai Ivanovich treated my father with great tenderness. Often when he arrived and found Larin alone, he would kiss him on the forehead, and he thought up all sorts of affectionate nicknames or called him simply Mika, like Larin's relatives. When there was occasion to use the given name and patronymic, as when the conversation acquired an elevated tone, Nikolai Ivanovich always used Yury Mikhailovich, not Mikhail Aleksandrovich. For this reason our son was named Yury, Nikolai Ivanovich's way of honoring the memory of my father.

It is no secret that of all my father's many friends who came to our home my favorite was Bukharin. In childhood, I was captivated by his irrepressible joie de vivre, his mischievousness, and his passionate love of nature, as well as his enthusiasm for landscape painting. Yet, absurd and laughable as it may seem, I do not believe I truly considered him a fully grown adult. I addressed all of Father's other close comrades by given name and patronymic and used *vy* [the formal "you"], but I addressed Nikolai Ivanovich as *ty* [the familiar "you"] and called him Nikolasha, which amused him and my parents alike. Even so, Mother and Father tried in vain to correct my familiarity, until they got used to it.

I remember clearly the circumstances of my first encounter with Nikolai Ivanovich. Mother took me one day to the Art Theater to see Maurice Maeterlinck's *The Bluebird*, and for the rest of the day I remained under the influence of the play, even dreaming when I went to bed about Bread and Milk and the world beyond, so calm and clear and by no means terrible. I could hear again the melodic song of Ilya Sats: "We go in a long line the bird of blue to find." The Cat appeared in my dream, big and man-sized as on the stage, and pulled my nose. I took fright and screamed, "Go away, Cat!" In my sleep I could hear Mother saying, "Nikolai Ivanovich, what are you doing? Why wake the child?" But I woke up now, and within the cat's face the features of Bukharin became more and more discernible. At that moment, I caught my own "bluebird," not in fantasy or fairy tale but on earth, for which I would pay dearly. Nikolai Ivanovich laughed merrily and then surprised me by repeating something I used to say when I lived in Byelorussia and saw a great many woodpeckers in the forest: "Woodpeck with its nose go tap-tap, go tap-tap." I had a particular fondness for woodpeckers because of their colorful feathers, red heads, and constant busyness, as Mother had told Nikolai Ivanovich, himself a great lover of birds. He thought it was hilarious that I had said "with its nose," not "beak."

Usually, Bukharin would drop in on Father for just a moment. It was not his nature to sit still long, and besides, time was always pressing. Yet, on occasion, he would visit for quite a while. He would sometimes arrive with his young political protégés in tow; in the later days, I well recall Yefim Tsetlin, Dmitry Maretsky, and Aleksandr Slepkov. They were a noisy group. On the door to Larin's office, there hung a merry notice written in my hand at my father's dictation: "You can argue as much as you like, but no smoking." And indeed they did argue as much as they liked.

Whenever Nikolai Ivanovich left us in those days, I always felt unhappy, and I began to drop in on him more and more often. He lived one floor below, in the corresponding three-room apartment, 205, located at the end of the hall. A fountain there, surrounded by a glass wall, had stopped running after the revolution, so Nikolai Ivanovich turned it into a menagerie. At various times, it housed huge eagles, a bear cub, and a little marmoset, all trophies from his hunts except the marmoset. At that time, 1925 to 1927, I frequently found Stalin visiting the apartment. Once, I heard him compliment Nikolai Ivanovich's father, but with sardonic humor: "Say, Ivan Gavrilovich, how did you make your son? I want to adopt your method. Oh, what a son, what a son!"

Once, Stalin took a tube of zinc white from Bukharin's box of oil paints and painted a slogan on a red rag, "Away with Trotskyism!" He tied the rag around the bear's paw and let the creature out on the balcony. Trying to free its paw, the bear waved the "banner" for all to see. Stalin considered Trotsky his chief threat at that time; it was not yet the turn of the Bukharinist "Right" danger.

It delighted Father whenever I went to see Nikolai Ivanovich. He'd say, "She's off to the salt mines." Assuming that his illness cast a shadow over my life and I was not getting my fair share of happiness, he even tried to "push" me onto his exuberant friend, in a sense. In the summer of 1925 we took our vacation in Sochi at the same time as Nikolai Ivanovich, and in 1927 we all went to Yevpatoriya. On each trip, following Father's wishes and with Bukharin's permission, I lived more at his place than at my parents'. With him I traveled to the mountains, went hunting, painted outdoors, caught butterflies and praying mantises, learned how to swim. What wonderful times we had!

My attachment to Nikolai Ivanovich grew proportionally stronger as I grew up. I was no longer satisfied by his visits to our place, though they were frequent. Moreover, it became clear to me that I was regarded merely as an accessory to Larin: Nikolai Ivanovich was not coming to see me. That was the case up until 1930, and I despaired.

Five years before, I wrote Nikolai Ivanovich the following verses when we got back home from Sochi. I was eleven years old.

> *Nikolasha-prostokvasha [sour milk],*
> *Our song starts in this fashion.*
> *Nikolai has lots to do,*
> *He's got skinny from it, too.*
>
> *Papers in his pocket stuffed*
> *Make them seem like pillows puffed.*
> *Off to Sochi to get well*
> *At the sea to gaze a spell.*

And so it continued, I do not recall it all. But it ended like this:

> *Seeing you I want to do.*
> *Without you I'm always blue.*

I showed the rhymes to Father. "Excellent!" he said. "Since you've written them, go take them to your Nikolasha." But I was too bashful to show Bukharin such verses. Father suggested I put them in an envelope and write on the outside, "From Yury Larin." I came to a decision: to ring his doorbell, hand him the envelope, and run away. But it did not turn out this way. Just as I came down the stairs, I ran into Stalin, who was obviously going to see Bukharin. After a moment's reflection, I asked him to give Nikolai Ivanovich this letter from Larin. Thus, through Stalin, I conveyed to Bukharin my childish confession of love. As soon as I got back home, Nikolai Ivanovich was on the telephone, asking me to come down. I was too embarrassed to bring myself to go.

Then came the sad year of 1927, when Stalin insisted that Bukharin move to the Kremlin. Without a pass, I could not enter freely, so Nikolai Ivanovich had to call the Troitsky Gates entrance in advance. Later, he did obtain a permanent pass for me, but it was always difficult to find him at home during that period. I intentionally changed my way to school, taking a longer route, so as to walk past the Comintern building, which stood across from the Manège next to the Troitsky Gates, in hopes of meeting Nikolai Ivanovich, who had an office there. Luck was with me more than once, and I would rush joyfully to meet him.

It was a tense period, with intra-Party debate reaching a fever pitch at the Fifteenth Party Congress. What time did Bukharin have for me! He even came less often to see Father, but stayed longer, always talking about current Party matters. At that time, their views coincided. And there was nothing to bother me in their discussions; my worries began only later, when I had grown older and Nikolai Ivanovich had come under fire.

I have already told "the story of the Himalayas." Nothing can better illustrate the climate of those years. After the Politburo session at which Bukharin had quoted Stalin's comment ("You and me, Nikolai, are the Himalayas. The others are nonentities.") and the general secretary had shouted back, "You lie, lie, lie!," Nikolai Ivanovich visited us and told the whole story. Mother was so incautious as to pass it along to an acquaintance who apparently informed "the right place." One way or another, within a few days, Stalin knew all about it. He summoned Bukharin and yelled at him that he was spreading slanderous rumors, as was undeniably clear from Larina's remarks: "And Larina is an honest woman and would not lie." (Later, when this incident lay far behind us, Nikolai Ivanovich would facetiously call my mother "Yelenka, the honest woman.") I cannot do justice to Nikolai Ivanovich's chagrin when he rushed back to our place or to the consternation of my parents. Mother admitted that she had committed a blunder.

But it was Father who took the affair most seriously. He was disturbed not only because Mother's indiscretion had caused our friend major difficulties but also because his family might be used in a disgusting political intrigue; the very possibility caused him to feel moral revulsion. He wrote a long letter to Stalin, then tore it up and contented himself with one sentence:

> We do not engage in informing.
> Yu. Larin

[Lenin's Death, Father's Death, and New Cellmates]

The fruit Beria ordered the convoy guard to carry to my cell softened the prison regime for me. The duty guard was so impressed that the people's commissar would give me such a present that he permitted me to turn toward the wall and cover my face with the blanket. But the eight months of solitary confinement (save the brief interval with the stoolie) without books, without any diverting occupation, was weighing more and more heavily upon me. The only way to distract myself was the old recourse of composing verses. Today, I cannot fathom how I was able to take up "poetic creation" immediately after my confrontation with Beria that night. But writing poetry, however talentless, was my salvation. I tried to capture in verse the death of Lenin, or more accurately, my childhood impressions of what had happened, but the words would not come. I managed only a few awkward lines:

> In those days, not much could I surmise,
> Still a little child was I.
> The extent of grief I realized
> Only from my father's eyes.

Yes, the eyes of my father had indeed disturbed me.

Late the night of January 21, 1924, Bukharin telephoned from Lenin's residence in Gorki to report that the life of Vladimir Ilyich had come to an end. I was still awake and saw with fascination that two tears, only two, rolled out of my father's mournful eyes and down his deathly pale cheeks. He did not sleep that night and wrote an article in memoriam. One of the first published in *Pravda*, it concluded as follows:

> Our proletariat shall be eternally proud, our country shall be eternally proud, that here in our midst there lived and fought, instructed and labored, a man whose name became a legend in his own lifetime and the hope of the oppressed of all countries. And it shall remain a beacon and banner in the struggle of the proletariat up to the complete victory of socialism everywhere.

As a young girl, I was of course moved not by the gravity of the loss, which had changed the course of history, but by its unusual effects in my own life: my father's eyes, seeming pained and dimmed, Bukharin's effusive sobbing, Lenin's funeral.

The funeral coincided with my birthday, January 27, spoiling my celebration. Father said, "Your birthday, the twenty-seventh of January, is canceled. [As if this were the latest decree of the Soviet regime.] From now on, it will always be a day of mourning, and we will commemorate your birthday on the twenty-seventh of May, when nature awakens and everything is in flower."

In fact, Father took me to the state registry on Petrovka Street to change my birth certificate. The clerk, amazed, stood his ground for a long time, advising us to celebrate on May 27 but leave the document unchanged. He finally gave in. Ten years after my birth, I was registered for a second time. This second birth certificate was used for my passport, which to this day lists my date of birth as May 27, 1914.

Because cars were not allowed there, I helped Father go by foot to the Hall of Columns of the House of Trade Unions, where Lenin lay in his casket. High-ranking Party officials had been alerted by telephone to appear at a certain hour. When we entered a room at the back of the Hall of Columns, we saw Nadezhda Konstantinovna [Krupskaya, the widow], Mariya Ilyinichna [Ulyanova, the younger sister], Zinoviev, Tomsky, Kalinin, Bukharin—the rest, I do not remember. The eyes of Zinoviev and Bukharin were red from weeping. With great emotion, I led my father up to the casket, then found a place for myself somewhere off to the side. I noticed Lenin's elder sister, Anna Ilyinichna, standing near the head of the coffin, stationary, like a sculpted figure, gazing into her brother's face as if not wanting to lose a moment of their final parting. I would learn from Nikolai Ivanovich that all of Lenin's relatives were against embalming his body and never went to the Mausoleum where later he was put on public display.

It is impossible to forget the funeral ceremony. Much has been written in prose and in verse about the occasion, but I witnessed it all: the fierce frost, the roaring bonfires, and the Red Army soldiers in long gray overcoats with peaked Budyonny caps pushed down on their brows, jumping up and down by the fires to keep warm . . . the trudging peasants, a multitude of them, wearing their bast sandals, their beards frosted over, frozen tears at their eyes . . . all of the people stricken with grief. From our window in the Metropol, we could see the round-the-clock procession through the Hall of Columns. I would get up from my bed at night and watch the unending stream of people moving in the glow of bright bonfires, an impressive and unforgettable scene.

Lenin's closest companions were incredibly shaken by his death. To my recollection, they were like nervous animals before an earthquake, instinctively sensing the approach of something unknown but terrible. They could not have foreseen, of course, that in the not-so-distant future Stalin would throw the majority of them on the scrap heap of history.

Many years later, Ilya Ehrenburg analyzed the situation accurately in a conversation with me: "Lenin's closest comrades made a colossal mistake. After his death, they made him into a god. Stalin took advantage of this deification, ingeniously charging everyone else with heresy to the cult of Lenin."

Later, it flattered Stalin to be called "the Lenin of today," but that does not mean that Lenin was "Stalin yesterday." To equate the two is indeed blasphemous.

The gift of fruit notwithstanding, my mood back in my cell is hard to describe. I brooded over the way I had acted in Beria's office. Before whom was I casting pearls! I began to recall remarks of his that had slipped past me in the heat of our exchange but now seemed especially offensive. How dared he say to me, "It's not enough that Larin's daughter married Bukharin; she has to defend him as well"? Not only his frequent references to Larin reminded me now of my father; so did the very cluster of grapes spilling out of his gift package. For Larin dearly loved his homeland: the Crimean coast, where the sea seemed brighter to him than the Mediterranean; the Crimean steppes, turning scarlet each spring when the poppies bloomed; the exceptionally fragrant Crimean roses, and the exceptionally tasty Crimean grapes, cultivated so skillfully by the Tatars, and precisely of the type before me, Alexandrian muscat. Pushkin wrote, "A wondrous land, delighting the eyes," and Larin frequently repeated his lines.

Imagination now transported me back to the Black Sea, and I decided to try composing some verses about it. These creative moments were the brightest in my joyless life: thinking about nothing else, losing myself in the writing. The memorization as well as the composition demanded concentration, giving me further respite from my sufferings. Undoubtedly, I had found a method of survival.

The poem I composed attempted to capture the sea in its different moods: flashing, changing colors, raging in a storm. I kept this poem in my memory, but when I was returned from the Moscow prison to a camp in the winter of 1941, I had a chance to write it down on a blank invoice of the NKVD Siblag Administration. And so, I still have it.

The poem also related a personal experience. Late one night in August 1931, while we were in the Crimea, Larin and I happened to go out to the seashore. A chauffeur drove us, since my father could not have made it on his own down the steep road. The moon was full; its silver track lay over the sea with remarkable clarity. Leaving Father to sit on a rock right beside the surf, I swam rather far out in the water. Suddenly, I was seized with a sense of approaching death. I turned back sharply and swam toward shore as fast as I could. I was already laughing at my unaccountable fear as I touched bottom and stood up, but just as I started to tell my father about it, a wave crashed over him and washed him into the water. I tried to hold him back, but I was not strong enough. We were pulled into the sea together, and we would both have perished if the chauffeur had not heard my desperate cry. As I recalled this accident in prison, it took on the character of an omen: Father did not live another six months.

And though we had long been accustomed to his delicate condition, no one would have predicted such an early demise. On December 31, he insisted that I go out and greet the new year with friends my own age. I usually spent New Year's Eve at home, but this time I went to a gathering at the apartment of Stakh Ganetsky, the son of a famous revolutionary. No sooner had I crossed the threshold than the telephone rang. "Return home immediately, I'm dying!" my father shouted. I rushed home in great distress. The scene there was hard to believe: my father, who usually moved from place to place with difficulty, was running at a furious pace from room to room. What caused his condition remains a mystery to me to the present day. My mother and I suspected a mental disturbance, so we called Professor Vasily Kramer, a famous neuropathologist. He canceled his holiday plans and appeared at midnight, but he was unable to discover any mental disorder. Internists would later diagnose inflammation of both lungs. For the next two weeks, Father died a painful death, sitting up in his armchair because he could not breathe at all lying down. He was in torment.

In my cell, it was perhaps more difficult to remember my father's last day than it had been to endure it, for I now looked on everything with a different perspective.

On the morning of January 14, Larin's condition took a sharp turn for the worse, and Mother informed his closest comrades. Aleksei Rykov soon appeared with his wife, Nina Semyonovna, and then Vladimir Milyutin and Lev Kritsman. At this juncture, Stalin phoned unexpectedly, but Father was unable to hold the receiver. "Too bad, too bad," said Stalin. "I want to appoint him people's commissar of agriculture. But since he's sick, I'll send over Poskryobyshev [Stalin's private secretary] right away to organize his treatment, and after the Politburo meeting I'll come tell him the news myself."

Let me digress a moment to recall two other remarkable telephone calls from Stalin. In 1925, he called to ask Larin to speak against Bukharin at the Party conference on the subject of Nikolai Ivanovich's slogan for the peasants, "Get rich!" In a private conversation with Bukharin, Father had already strongly expressed his opinion that the phrase "get rich" missed the mark; "enrich yourselves" would be preferable because "get rich" was the terminology of the bourgeoisie. As far as I recall, Nikolai Ivanovich agreed with him. It is very interesting that Stalin had turned to Larin in this fashion prior to the Fourteenth Party Congress, which convened shortly after the conference. At the conference, Stalin teamed up with Bukharin against Zinoviev and Kamenev's "New Opposition." Then, addressing the congress, he deemed his ally's slogan an error of little consequence: "I know," he said, "about errors made by certain comrades, for example in October 1917 [namely, Kamenev and Zinoviev's opposition to the armed uprising], beside which Comrade Bukharin's error does not even deserve mention."

If Stalin really felt this way, what was the point of his request to Larin? I do not doubt for a moment that Stalin was laying the foundation for Bukharin's political destruction even as he was standing together with him against Zinoviev and Kamenev.

The second telephone call I find remarkable came three to four months before Larin's death. "Comrade Larin," Stalin said, "in the very near future you will be elected a full member of the USSR Academy of Sciences." And indeed he was. When he told Nikolai Ivanovich about the call, his friend remarked, "From Stalin's point of view, to 'elect' educated Marxist-Bolsheviks to the Academy of Sciences is to place them on the historical scrap heap; that is, to assign them political death."

Indeed, Larin was removed from his government posts, where he did most of his work, and left with literally nothing to do, for he had exchanged not only woolen caps with Stalin at the 1929 conference of Marxist agronomists but also polemics. He had dared venture the opinion that the collective farms were not enterprises of a thoroughly socialist type, because they were established not from state property but on a generalized private property; consequently, only the state farms really should be considered true socialist enterprises.

But to return to my dying father. Larin was fully conscious up to the last minute, and Mother told him what Stalin had just said on the telephone. Everyone in the room was extremely surprised. Larin's character as well as his health should have disqualified him from being people's commissar of agriculture. Moreover, the two men did not at all share the kind of intimacy that would lead one to suppose that Stalin would pay a visit to the ailing Larin. Perhaps Vladimir Milyutin was the most astonished, since he had seen the general secretary some days before and had told him that my father was very ill, possibly dying. "Could he really have forgotten?" Milyutin asked, shrugging his shoulders.

Soon Aleksandr Poskryobyshev showed up, bringing along the future "physician poisoners," the Kremlin doctor Lev Levin and the famous cardiologist Professor Dmitry Pletnyov, who would both be tried alongside Bukharin. They diagnosed my father's condition as hopeless and made a quick exit. For some reason, Stalin's secretary remained and stood with my mother beside Father's bed to the very end. Sitting by the open door leading from the office to the bedroom, I could see my father's reflection in the mirror, but I was too distraught to go to him until he himself called me. I heard him ask Mother to have Poskryobyshev take the folder with his latest economic project to Stalin. Then he turned in my direction. My dying father's question both startled and bewildered me.

"Do you still love Nikolai Ivanovich?" he asked, fully aware we had not seen each other since March of the preceding year. I was flustered both by the necessity of answering in front of Poskryobyshev and by the concern that my answer satisfy my father's last wish, which I did not know. But I could not lie, so I answered in the affirmative, chancing the possibility that Father might be displeased and demand, "You must forget him!" Actually, he responded in a hollow, barely audible voice:

"It would be more interesting to live ten years with Nikolai Ivanovich than your whole lifetime with another."

In their own way, these words were my father's blessing.

Then he gestured for me to draw nearer, since his voice was getting weaker and weaker, and beginning to break.

"It's not enough to love Soviet power just because you live rather well as a result of its victory! You have to be ready to give up your life for it, or shed blood, if that is required!"

I took him to mean sacrificing one's life in the event of a foreign intervention against the Soviet Union. With a great effort, he raised his right hand slightly and curled it into a fist, but it immediately dropped back lifelessly on his knee.

"Swear that you can do it!"

I swore.

In the last moment before death, Father turned his head toward Stalin's secretary but was no longer able to focus on him: his head bobbed helplessly. Trying to say something, he could do little more than mouth words pitiably, indistinctly. We succeeded in understanding him

say, "Scatter my ashes from an airplane," and "We shall be victorious!"
A final breath, and his heart stopped beating.

My father's last words made me thrill with pride. What a great,
fervent faith in a more perfect society it was that enlivened and spiritu-
ally inflamed the Bolsheviks!

Recollecting my father's dying words in my cell in Lubyanka, I
shuddered. What was there left to believe in? Who was there left to
believe in? Everything important to me had been killed, trampled in the
dirt. Instead, we had millions of prisoners, endless transports, overcrowded prison cells, staged courtroom trials of men who not long
before had been praised as Bolshevik leaders, and a dictator sitting on a
throne.

And I was far from believing that things would change for the
better. One moment, it seemed my life would be cut short in an instant;
the next, I felt doomed to lifelong seclusion. So industriously did they
hide me that the latter alternative seemed more than plausible. At times,
after what I had lived through at the ravine behind the Antibes prison,
when I had inexplicably escaped being shot, I would fantasize that I was
not subject to death but rather, like Ahasuerus the Wandering Jew, condemned to eternal life and eternal wandering for striking Christ on his
way to Golgotha, I was condemned by the "Father of the Peoples" to
eternal wandering from one solitary cell to another for not cursing Bukharin.

But suddenly, a change brought my isolation to an end.

"Collect your things and let's go," said the jailer. I had no "things,"
except the clothes on my back and Beria's gift. I did not have the heart to
eat the fruit, but I could not throw it away. This time I carried the
package myself. We walked down the hallway of the second floor, which
was framed with a balcony. This setting did not look at all like a prison,
yet they led me to a cell. Judging by the light breaking through a barred
window, it was now morning. On one bed sat a scrawny middle-aged
woman with small, bright, expressive eyes and a mannish haircut. She
looked at my "baggage" with surprise (we soon made a feast of it) and
turned a penetrating eye on me. Schooled by bitter experience, I decided
to heed Beria's advice and avoid babbling.

My cellmate spoke first:

"I've seen you somewhere. Could it have been at Larin's?"

"Possibly."

"If I'm not mistaken, you're his daughter?"

I nodded.

"I remember you when you were a little girl, and I know whose wife
you are."

So I was "exposed" right away.

"What a mind Stalin destroyed! How could he raise his hand against him?" the woman said with unrestrained emotion and at once began to tell me her story.

Valentina Petrovna Ostroumova, a stenographer for government meetings, had recorded the speeches at Party conferences, Party congresses, and congresses of the soviets. She used to come to Father's office to correct the stenographic record of his speeches; she knew many of the Bolsheviks who were now deceased. Most recently, Valentina Petrovna had worked in the north for the Igarka Party Committee. On her summer vacation in 1938, she had flown back to Moscow and stopped by the apartment of her friend Yekaterina Kalinina, wife of Mikhail Kalinin, the titular Soviet head of state. The two women unburdened their souls, justly appraising Stalin as "tyrant, sadist, destroyer of the Leninist guard and millions of innocent people." (I cite her exact words.) I don't remember now whether a third person was present or the "walls were listening"; either way, both were arrested. Ostroumova was picked up at the airport as she was about to fly back to Igarka; Kalinin's wife was presented with the order for arrest at the entrance to the Kremlin, right at the pass point of the Troitsky Gates.

Since we were put together, I was able to witness the dramatic development of the investigation of Ostroumova's case. In her hatred for Stalin, she was ready to admit everything she had said about him but worried about the consequences for Kalinin's wife. In addition, her confession might have unpleasant results for Kalinin himself. Only because of these considerations did Ostroumova deny the conversation for a time. Later, it became clear that the investigator and Beria, both of whom interrogated her, were familiar with the contents of the conversation down to the smallest details. The people's commissar claimed that Kalinin's wife had told all; Ostroumova believed him and finally confirmed the conversation. Subsequently, Yekaterina Kalinina was brought in for a confrontation with her friend. In the cross-interrogation, Ostroumova realized that Beria had duped her, for Kalinin's wife denied everything. Such, at least, was Ostroumova's version of the story. We were not together long; she was taken off to places unknown. Judging from accounts I read in the 1960s, she never returned from the camp system.

I managed to see Kalinin's wife in the Butyrka prison after her sentencing, but we were not able to talk. I was transferred to this prison at the beginning of 1941 on my way to a camp. In the first cell they gave me, there was no free space, and I sat down by chance at the feet of Yekaterina Ivanovna, who was sleeping. I was not acquainted personally with her but recognized her face. She looked worn out and aged. Her cellmates told me that she had been given a long term for something close to espionage. (And why not? You're allowed to accuse innocent people of anything you please.) According to the gossip, she had been given an opportunity to write to the Supreme Soviet for a pardon but had proudly replied, "I demand vindication, not an act of mercy!" I cannot vouch for the reliability of these reports. Before Yekaterina Ivanovna woke up, I was taken to another cell. She was released shortly before her husband's death in the summer of 1946.

Several days after Ostroumova was taken off, I had a new cellmate, the wife of the military commander Ivan Belov. She sobbed continually for days on end and hysterically beat her head on the wall. After this, I was taken to a group cell.

When I sat down on the only free bunk there, the women told me right away that its previous occupant had been nursemaid to Lev Trotsky's grandson by his youngest son, Sergei.* They told me she had been very attached to the boy and tearfully repeated again and again, "There, there, Lyovushka [the boy was named Lev in honor of his grandfather], Grandpa will come and send his troops against them, those monsters, and he'll set us free."

Yezhov's secretary, Ryzhova, was in this cell, so the question I had asked Beria a number of times was finally settled. She told me that in her interrogation Beria had declared to her, "Your boss is an enemy of the people, a spy," to which she replied that she never would have thought it, since he only carried out the directives of Stalin. Beria shouted at her, "You didn't think right, you don't know how to recognize an enemy!" Ryzhova naively took his statement at face value, as was clear from her efforts to console me:

"If my Nikolai Ivanovich [meaning Yezhov] turned out to be a spy, then your Nikolai Ivanovich will be vindicated, if only posthumously."

I could not "enlighten" Ryzhova. I could only keep silent.

Sitting across from me was an old woman, the wife of a military man. She was bruised all over from beatings and plagued by hallucinations. "Vanya, Vanya!" she shouted. "Comrades, look out the window; they're taking him away to be shot!" Although we all tried to convince the poor woman that she was only imagining things, her shout was periodically repeated.

---

*Sergei Lvovich Bronshtein, an engineer who worked in the People's Commissariat of Heavy Industry under Sergo Ordzhonikidze, was not active in politics. He was shot, his wife arrested, and his son put in a children's home. The further fate of mother and child are not known to me.

Beside me sat Nataliya Sats, another "wife of a traitor to the motherland" who had been brought here for reinvestigation. Having contracted typhus in the camp, exhausted to the final degree, she resembled a puny little girl, though her head was gray. She was tormented most by her separation from a children's theater she had founded; she had poured much energy and talent into it. Her love for this theater was not only passionate but jealous; it was painful for her to realize that someone else, an outsider, had invaded her theater, as if abducting a child of her own flesh. Her longing to return to the theater was so strong that it seemed she needed only to step inside it once more, even if under guard, to derive satisfaction and lose her sense of confinement. In addition, of course, she worried about the fate of her mother and children, like the rest of us. With great ardor and tenderness she recalled her husband, Izrail Veitser, the people's commissar of domestic trade, who was eventually shot: "Where is my Veitser? Can it be that my Veitser has perished?" How often when talking with me would she sigh heavily and reiterate these words! Yet in spite of the oppressive conditions of our situation, Nataliya (Natasha to me) retained her creative energies and her sense of humor. She loved to tease me by calling me Larkina-Bukharkina. She would recite verses she had composed just before being transported back to Moscow from camp:

> *Farewell, Siberia, now comes the end*
> *To blizzards and to cloudless turquoise skies!*
> *Farewell, Zhigan!* You were my truest friend.*
> *For one last time I gaze into your eyes.*

From Natasha, I once again heard a French ditty that Nikolai Ivanovich loved to sing when we were in Paris: "Comme ils étaient forts tes bras qui m'embrassaient" (How strong were your arms that embraced me).

Also in this cell, fate threw me together with Sofya Kavtaradze, wife of Sergo Kavtaradze.† Though in her declining years, she retained the

---

*Zhigan, a favorite moniker of thieves and bandits.

†Sergo (Sergei Ivanovich) Kavtaradze, a leading figure in the struggle for Soviet power in the Caucasus. From 1922 to 1923, he was chairman of the Council of People's Commissars of Georgia; from 1924 to 1928, first assistant prosecutor of the Supreme Court. A participant in the Trotsky opposition, he was famous as one of the best-educated Bolsheviks in Georgia. Arrested in the years of terror, he was subsequently freed on Stalin's orders—an unprecedented event for a person with his biography. After his release in 1941, he became assistant minister of foreign affairs, and then ambassador to Romania.

beautiful, sensitive face of one of the intelligentsia, and her expressive eyes shone with nobility. I drew close to her. She taught me French; we got books from the prison library and read the French portions of *War and Peace* as our text. But our lessons came to an end when one fine day she returned from her interrogator brimming with joy. Gathering up her things, she explained that she was being released. We were all thunderstruck: this inexplicable event ran counter to the tenor of the times. Indeed, it remained unique in all the many years of my confinement.

The wife of the corps commander, Ugryumov, sat opposite me. (When I say "sat," I do not mean that literally; I have in mind the Russian expression "to sit in prison," to do time. We did not so much sit as sprawl out on the bunks.) Ugryumova was the only one in the cell whom I had known previously; we had begun our journey together through the camps in Tomsk. She looked about seventy. When I was first brought to the cell, she was sleeping, and I did not notice her. Suddenly, I heard, "My dear girl, so you are here, too! We kept trying to guess where they had taken you."

Ugryumova rushed over, picking her way through the narrow spaces between the beds, and embraced me with sobs and kisses. In camp, she had always been warmly affectionate toward me and had given me something extra to eat when she received packages of goods from relatives. She had been taken from the Tomsk camp long after me but was sent straight to Moscow, so she arrived in the NKVD inner prison well before me. Not having seen each other for almost nine months, we had much to talk about.

Ugryumova had been a good friend of War Commissar Mikhail Frunze's mother, who had told her that Stalin had murdered her son in 1925 by ordering him to undergo an unnecessary operation for a stomach ulcer. At the time, Frunze had been feeling quite well; in fact, an autopsy later would reveal that the ulcer had healed over, leaving a scar. Frunze failed to revive from the anesthetic used in the operation; his heart gave out, and he died at forty. Ugryumova repeated this story in the camp, where the practice of informing flourished, and was at once dispatched to the Moscow investigative prison and accused of malicious slander against Stalin.

This account of Frunze's death struck me as improbable, although Boris Pilnyak's *The Tale of the Unextinguished Moon* seconds it, in a sense. In 1926, when this novella was published but immediately taken out of circulation, I was still quite young and did not read it. Possibly Frunze's mother or some other relative had been Pilnyak's source of information, or, the reverse, his novella had influenced them. I have no idea on what basis she would make such an accusation against Stalin.

Yet, even though I had no illusions in 1938 about Stalin's bloodthirstiness, I had my doubts about his involvement in Frunze's death. It seemed unlikely that he had such evil designs as early as 1925.

"But why would he start with Frunze?" I asked Ugryumova.

"He wanted to get rid of him," she explained, "because Frunze, according to his mother, acknowledged Trotsky's authority and continued to hold him in great respect to the end."

Frunze's mother, she went on, was seething with hatred for Stalin and wanted to strangle him with her bare hands. The war commissar's mother and wife both died shortly after his death. Ugryumova told me all of this in a whisper, so that no one else could hear.

[Memories of Trotsky, and a Disturbing Interrogation in the Lubyanka]

Ugryumova's story reminded me of an incident in my distant childhood.

On November 7, 1924, the first October Revolution celebration after Lenin's death, my father stood on the rostrum of the Mausoleum in Red Square. At that time, not only the Politburo but also a wider group of Party workers were so honored. As in other instances, I helped Larin make his way to his assigned place and found myself in the top row, where stood Trotsky, Frunze, and Stalin. I forget who else was there, for a reason that was very painful for me then. Trotsky came over to me and asked, "What have you fastened on yourself?" He reached out and tugged at the colorful scarf, red with light blue blotches, which Mother, with my willing consent, had tied around my neck outside my coat to make me look spiffy. "Where is your Pioneer tie? Obviously, you don't know why the Pioneer tie is colored red! Red symbolizes the blood shed by the rebelling working class!" He delivered these words in a harsh, threatening tone, as if I were a Red Army soldier found derelict in his duty and subject to punishment. I was very ashamed and upset. The celebration was spoiled for me, and I wanted only to get back home as soon as possible.

To justify myself I blurted out, "It was Mama who tied a scarf around my neck instead of a tie!"

"You have a good mama," Trotsky countered, "but what a bad thing she did!"

That was exactly how he put it, "bad thing." Accusing Mama of a "bad thing" upset me even more, and the tears gushed from my eyes.

Noticing my pitiable appearance, Father turned to Trotsky and interceded: "Look, Lev Davydovich, what huge red ribbons my daughter is wearing in her hair! There's more than enough 'blood' there." They both laughed, and it seemed to me that Trotsky's eyes became a little more kind. Still, I was too distressed to take note of anyone but him and, involuntarily, those immediately at his side, Stalin to the right and Frunze to the left.

I did not know Trotsky. He did not visit Father or Nikolai Ivanovich, but I occasionally saw him outside the Revolutionary Military Council's building on Znamenka (now Frunze) Street. My school was just across the way, and our Pioneer squad held meetings on the lower floor of that building. One May Day, when we had boarded a truck to be driven around festive Moscow, Trotsky came over and ordered, "Children! It is obligatory that you sing this song: 'May the Red Army clench its bayonet in triumph with a calloused hand!' " He enunciated the words with such revolutionary fervor that we were inspired to sing the song in chorus the whole way without stopping.

On that occasion, Trotsky had seemed young and majestic. But now, in 1924, I detected a radical change in him. Only forty-five, he looked like an old man, at least to a ten-year-old girl. He was pale, and graying hairs poked out from under his budyonovka cap.

Trotsky and Frunze began to talk animatedly, but Stalin stood by silent. He would wave to demonstrators for a while, then go to the back of the rostrum and pace back and forth with his hands clasped behind his back, keeping his gaze fixed on these two. I had no idea, of course, that Trotsky's political career was in decline. Frunze would replace him as chairman of the Revolutionary Military Council in January 1925 (and then die after his operation that very October).

Clearly, Ugryumova's story had dredged up from the depths of my memory that incident at the Mausoleum, which I now viewed from a different perspective.

Perhaps my childhood recollections of Trotsky do not seem very significant. Although he harshly attacked my "bloodless" little scarf, I saw only that Mother might have made a slight error of judgment; certainly she had not done a "bad thing." On the other hand, I had not seen anything out of the ordinary in the way he imperiously commanded us Pioneers to sing about the Red Army. Yet now, looking back at these trifles, I see manifestations of the man's essential character.

I would spend more than two years in the Lubyanka inner prison. I would see people brought there from freedom and sent out to the camps, or to isolation prisons, or to be shot. But in my recollections the first impression remains the strongest, for after my months of total isolation, the several prisoners in the group cell seemed like an entire regiment to me; submerging myself in this sea of human suffering, I was distracted from my own troubles for a spell.

Etched in my memory is the first prisoner brought directly from freedom after I had been transferred to this cell. An uncomplicated but not unintelligent woman from a peasant family, she was a forester in Bryansk, was arrested there, and was sent immediately afterward to Lubyanka. She was interrogated by an "investigator" the day she arrived, then put in with us. Rosy, fresh, she differed markedly from the rest of us who had sat in prisons and camps for months and years and were pale, exhausted, and gray. She looked like a berry just picked in the forest, so I nicknamed her Little Strawberry. The name caught on, but the berry quickly faded. Of course, the investigator derided her as a "forest spy."

The first time she entered the cell, she was obviously fearful and glanced around suspiciously at everyone. Before opening up, she asked what we had been arrested for. Some kept silent; the others answered, "For nothing."

"Me, too. For nothing," she said and let out a heavy sigh, adding, "Apparently, it has now become the fashion to put people in prison for nothing."

She began to describe her interrogation, the rude and crude conduct of the investigator.

"The trouble is, they gave me an idiot for an investigator. I'll have to ask for an intelligent one. [As if this would change the situation!] He said to me, 'You don't have a head, just a suitcase full of bedbugs.' That's the clever thing he managed to think up, and also that I was a forest spy!"

She laughed through her tears. "No matter how much I explained to him, the boob, that our forest is out in the boondocks, we never see anybody, and I have no information of any kind—so how could I be a spy?—still he says, 'You knew how many trees stood on your section of land; that's information, so you are a forest spy!' "

The investigator neglected only to name what country she had provided with this "priceless information." When she argued that no country needed any such information and said he was speaking nonsense, he shouted, "I'll show you nonsense! I'll make you talk! Did you know Bukharin?"

"How in the world could I know him? He didn't make a habit of driving out to us in the forest."

"Why are you playing the fool, as if you never heard that Bukharin was an enemy of the people?"

"Heard it? Yes, I heard it. Both about the enemy of the people and about before that."

"And about before that" is exactly how she puts it. Perhaps this unfortunate woman had talked too freely back at home on the assumption that "nothing can be heard" in the woods, but someone was "listening," and this was the real cause of her arrest.

"What does 'before that' mean? I'll fix you with 'before that'! What Bukharin was 'before that' you'd better forget. Bukharin didn't confess for three months; he kept saying, 'I don't know anything. I'm not aware of anything.' He sat there like a little graven god! But when they put him in the special cell, that's when he started giving testimony. No one has yet held out in that cell. We'll put you in there; then you'll confess, too."

The forester's story was filled with details of incredibly crude acts demeaning to a woman, showing what kind of man could become an investigator in the NKVD main prison at that time. Certainly, not all of the investigators were like this; some were the sensitive sort, but that did not change the results of their "investigations" one whit. If they made the bed soft, the sleeping was still hard.

When Little Strawberry mentioned Nikolai Ivanovich, all eyes turned on me. The forester's story cost me sleepless nights. Who knows whether the investigator was simply browbeating a hapless woman or whether his words about a special cell had a factual basis. I do not rule out the latter possibility; in fact, I am inclined to believe it. And to believe that the stupid investigator revealed a secret that had been carefully guarded.

All value is comparative. It would seem I had nothing to grumble about in my new situation: there were people, and books, and a cot with bedding; the food was much better than in the camp, and the cellars were behind me. Yet there was a worm gnawing at my soul. Every day was spent in tense anticipation of my summons to the investigator. The doors of the cell opened often, and the guard on duty called out, "Who's in the *m*'s?" or "Who's in the *s*'s?" They never called me. Only once, in the first days of January 1939, several days after my meeting with Beria, was I summoned to an investigator, who presented me with a New Year's present.

"Sign the record of interrogation," he said.

I was extremely surprised, for no record of "interrogation" had been made in Novosibirsk or in Beria's office. I was even more amazed when the investigator pushed a clean sheet of paper toward me.

"I do not sign blank sheets of paper," I stated indignantly.

It was face down. He turned it over, and I saw a record of my interrogation already typed out, with his questions and my answers:

QUESTION: Were you in the counterrevolutionary youth organization?

ANSWER: I was not.

QUESTION: Did you practice counterrevolutionary activity?

ANSWER: I did not.

And so on. I do not recall the whole thing. Obviously, the "record" had been dictated from above. I signed it.

"Maybe you will see Moscow soon," the investigator said with a smile, assuming that I had been asked to sign such a document only for the purpose of my release. "Have you gotten homesick for Moscow?"

I shrugged my shoulders in confusion. A sensation of the greatest alarm and terror seized hold of me. To be released into the *freedom* of that time, and as a leper besides . . . better to stay here as an equal among equals. Even in the camp and the prison, there were people, though few in number, who tried to keep their distance from me, so what would it be like outside? In the event, such misgivings were pointless. The document produced no results and remained a mystery to me.

Time passed. Finally, toward the end of September, about ten months after my arrival, I was called to an interrogation. Once again, however, "interrogation" is not the correct term, for my exchange with the investigator was not an objective inquiry into a matter with the aim of discovering the truth. Nor was it the typical interrogation of the time characterized by prejudice and the use of physical torture or psychological control in order to obtain a prescribed false testimony. Rather, it was a refrain of the themes sounded in my conversation with Beria. Even so, this first summons after my extended "rest" hit me hard.

The office was familiar. Behind the desk still sat Matusov, who had joined Yezhov's deputy, Frinovsky (now arrested and perhaps already dead), in trying to convince me I had to go voluntarily into Astrakhan exile in order to avoid coercive measures. A tender little cherub in appearance, Matusov had outlived almost all of the high-ranking NKVD officers from Yezhov's time; he may even have gone back as far as Yagoda. I would learn later that he eventually died a natural death. I do not know his rank, but he was no minor investigator.

"Hello, Anna Mikhailovna! Glad to see you!" He hailed me in an inexplicable tone of delight, as if we were old-time acquaintances and I had dropped in for a visit.

"I am by no means glad to see you," I replied to his stupid greeting. "You did not make good on the promises you gave me before my exile. My 'needs, work, and apartment' were not provided. Besides, you did not make good on the main thing: you did not let me meet with Nikolai Ivanovich at the conclusion of his investigation. You did not give me the opportunity to take my leave of him."

At that moment, the office door opened and Andrei Sverdlov walked in. "For what purpose?" flashed through my mind. I immediately assumed that he had been arrested and brought in for a confrontation with me, since he had been mentioned in the report made by my treacherous cellmate in Novosibirsk and woven into the false story of a counterrevolutionary organization. Even though I had denied his involvement in any such group to Beria himself, I feared that Andrei had been made to confirm the tale, to impugn both himself and me. That would have been typical for the time. But peering more closely at him, I concluded that Andrei did not look like a prisoner. He wore an elegant gray suit with crisply ironed pants, and his carefully groomed, self-satisifed face bespoke total prosperity.

Sitting down in the chair next to Matusov, Andre gazed at me attentively, and not entirely without anxiety.

"Get acquainted, Anna Mikhailovna, this is your investigator," Matusov said.

"What do you mean, investigator! This is Andrei Sverdlov!" I exclaimed in complete bewilderment.

"Yes, Andrei Yakovlevich Sverdlov," Matusov repeated with satisfaction, as if to say, See what fine investigators we have! "The son of Yakov Mikhailovich Sverdlov. You will deal with him."

Matusov's announcement was so horrifying to me that I lost my composure altogether. It would undoubtedly have been easier for me to undergo the confrontation I had initially anticipated.

"What, don't you like your investigator?" Matusov asked, noticing the confusion and distress on my face.

"I do not know him as an investigator, but there is no need for an introduction. We have long been acquainted."

"Was he your friend, then?" Matusov asked curiously.

"Let Andrei Yakovlevich answer that question himself."

No, I wouldn't have called him a friend, but we had known each other since early childhood, when we played together, running through the Kremlin. (The Sverdlov family continued to live there even after the death of Yakov Mikhailovich in 1919.) Once Adka, as we called him then, tore the knitted cap off my head and ran away; I dashed after him but could not catch him. When I followed him to his house for my cap, Andrei took some scissors, cut off the top part, and threw it in my face. He was about sixteen at the time; I was ten. Perhaps this was his first cruel deed, and cruelty became instilled in his nature.

In our teens, before either of us was married, we happened to vacation in the Crimea at the same time. Sometimes he would come over from nearby Foros to see me in Mukhalatka. We took walks together, hiked in the mountains, swam in the sea.

I shared none of these details with Matusov but briefly answered, "I know Andrei Yakovlevich quite well. In such a case, so far as I know, he cannot act as my investigator. I have the right to refuse him."

But Matusov was adamant. Despite the circumstances, it was Sverdlov exactly who would be my NKVD investigator.

It was painful to see him in this role because most of his famous father's comrades-in-arms had fallen victim to the terror by this time. And many of his peers, also children of prominent Party men, were being persecuted, including his close friend Dima Osinsky, who got his first taste of prison grub along with Andrei in 1934. (Osinsky was arrested a second time in 1937, right after his father.) Finally, my meeting with investigator Andrei Sverdlov in the inner recesses of the NKVD was even more dramatic because it was none other than Nikolai Ivanovich who had pleaded to Stalin for Andrei's release after his 1934 arrest. If only Nikolai Ivanovich knew how Andrei had fallen, this "promising youngster," as he had characterized him to Stalin. Ah, if only he knew!

Andrei decided to speak.

"What are you [*ty*] babbling about me there?" he asked in a confident and familiar tone, letting it be known right away that my "babbling" would not affect the firmness of his position or cause any harm to his career. There was no doubt he was a man endowed by nature with careerist proclivities.

I explained that I was only expressing my concern that his first arrest might incur a second, and that this time they would fabricate a counterrevolutionary youth organization involved in terror, wrecking, and so forth and make me a member. I supposed that our acquaintance would facilitate this scheme and would help neither his position nor mine.

"How you express yourself," Andrei observed (now switching to the formal *vy*). " 'They would fabricate a counterrevolutionary youth organization.' We don't fabricate anything here."

In horror, I went silent and, strange as it may seem, only in that moment finally understood that a gulf lay between us. We stood on opposite sides of the barricade. I glared at Andrei with contempt, and at this point our first meeting concluded.

Two or three days later, we met again. The first shock had passed; you get used to anything. But something else bothered me now. Meeting him eye to eye, I was unable to tell him straight to his face what I thought of him. In fact, I was totally outraged and had an impulse, which I overcame, to slap him across the cheek. (I wanted to do so because he was one of our own, and for the same reason could not.) At the same time, I realized fully that Andrei's fall was not the result of some regrettable misapprehension of reality. It was engendered by an immoral, unprincipled mentality.

I was not caught unawares, as I had been with Beria, when I strove to prove things that did not require proof and that were, in fact, axiomatic for the people's commissar himself. Unfortunately, it became clear to me how much my conversation had made an impression on Beria: I was the only person who could possibly tell him much of what I said. By contrast, I prepared in advance for my second meeting with Andrei and determined to be more restrained. But I was not able to do so.

In fact, the interrogation did not turn out at all the way I had imagined. Andrei was softer this time; he looked at me more warmly; as he walked by, he shoved an apple in my hand. Still, as he sat down behind a desk in a narrow little office, he did not lose sight of his responsibilities as an investigator. For a moment, we looked at each other without speaking. My eyes filled with tears, and it seemed to me that Andrei was moved as well. Or perhaps I just wanted to detect at least this much humanity in him.

Our biographies were so similar. We were both children of professional revolutionaries who had managed to die a natural death; both of us had been true in equal measure to the Soviet order; both of us had been delighted to be friends with Nikolai Ivanovich, as we had discussed before my marriage. Finally, both of us had suffered a catastrophe—to different degrees, to be sure, but catstrophe all the same.

Andrei Sverdlov's new occupation could not be regarded as anything but betrayal. The eyes of Cain were looking at me. Even so, the guilty party behind his catastrophe as well as mine was one and the same person: Stalin.

Andrei's silence was unbearable, but I lost the gift of speech for a while myself. Finally, I burst out:

"What are you going to interrogate me about, Andrei Yakovlevich? Nikolai Ivanovich is no more; it makes no sense to obtain false testimony against him. The fight is over, so why brandish your fists? Besides, you know my life like the palm of your hand; you don't have to inquire about a thing. And yours was sufficiently clear to me up to a certain point. That is exactly why I defended you by declaring to Beria that you could not be part of a counterrevolutionary organization."

Hunched over, resting his elbows on the desk, Andrei looked at me enigmatically, apparently letting my words slide past his ears. Suddenly, he made a remark completely unrelated to the investigation or, more accurately, to the subject of our conversation.

"What a beautiful blouse you have on, Nyuska!"

(That's what my parents and all the kids my age used to call me.)

At that moment, I truly felt pity for the traitor, for he too was caught in a trap, though he had entered it from the opposite side.

"So you [*ty*] like my blouse?" (Like Andrei, I used either *vy* or *ty*, depending on what emotions had the upper hand.) "Then what don't you like?"

Andrei immediately pulled himself together, and the investigator showed through. He delivered himself of the familiar official phrases that I had heard so many times from other lips: "You are spreading harmful anti-Soviet inventions, saying that the trials are staged court-room plays and your Bukharin did not commit any state crimes."

The same old theme. But to hear it sung by Andrei Sverdlov was incomparably more painful than to hear it from Skvirsky or Beria.

"Do you really think," I exclaimed, "that the Bolsheviks betrayed the cause of their whole lives? Think so, if that is convenient for you and makes it easier to live. But can you sincerely believe that your close friend Dima is a counterrevolutionary and you are not? That Stakh Ganetsky is an enemy of the people, when you are his friend? You've probably interrogated them, too! You wouldn't do just me and not them!"

"It's none of your business whom I interrogate!" Andrei screamed.

Then, just like Beria, he fixed his attentions on my conversations with Lebedeva in our cell. He put it this way: "You babbled too much, both in poetry and in prose, and out of this babble you piled up a mountain of lies."

Yes, I had obviously lied, if it could be proved that Andrei Sverdlov, NKVD investigator, had belonged to a counterrevolutionary youth or-ganization. Of course, my real crime had been to compromise the trials in front of my cellmate, but I told Sverdlov now that I was completely confident that on the matter of the trials in general and Nikolai Ivano-vich in particular our opinions coincided. I could not resist stating this conviction, since the son of Yakov Mikhailovich Sverdlov was sitting behind the investigator's desk. (Of course, I had also considered it necessary to make the same declaration to Beria.) Andrei would undoubtedly have flown into a fury and tried to repudiate my words, but I cut him off, telling him that the "enemy of the people" Bukharin had telephoned Stalin after his, Andrei's, arrest to plead for his release.

My investigator's face dropped; he turned red in his distress.

"Really?" he asked, although he knew perfectly well this was the truth. I confirmed it, which put an end to all talk about interrogation; Andrei switched to family matters. He mentioned that his wife, Nina (the daughter of the Bolshevik revolutionary Nikolai Podvoisky), whom I knew, was doing well in a senior position in the Komsomol and "by the way," as he put it, sent me her greetings. This "by the way" greetings did nothing but irritate me; presumably, Andrei's wife did not know about the fireworks of our previous meeting in Matusov's office.

But I did not long remain in Andrei's debt and returned several greetings for his one. I conveyed greetings from his aunt Sofya Mikhailovna (his father's sister), with whom I had spent time in the Tomsk camp, and greetings from his first cousin, Yagoda's wife (and Sofya Mikhailovna's daughter). I hadn't really seen her in the camp but conveyed her greetings anyway. The camp grapevine reported that she had been in a camp in Kolyma before her husband's trial, then sent back to Moscow afterward and shot. Finally, I conveyed greetings from Andrei's nephew Garik, his first cousin's son. I quoted from the tragic letters the boy had written to his grandmother from the children's home: "Dear Grandma, sweet little Grandma! Once again, I did not die!"

My "greetings," except for the excerpt from his nephew's pathetic letter, did not reveal anything new to Andrei, but I assumed that receiving such "greetings" through me could not afford him great pleasure. Yet did his soul feel a chill, as mine did in moments of especially intense tribulations? Did Andrei understand that he was sitting in the wrong place? I doubt it.

I could see that our conversation was coming to an end, so I found an appropriate moment to ask my investigator to telephone my grandmother to find out whether she knew whether my son was alive and with whom he was staying. Andrei honored this request and made the call right away, as I waited. Thus I found out that Yura, then in his fourth year, was living there in Moscow with my aunt, my mother's sister. So, despite the burden of my interrogation, I left Andrei Sverdlov's office on soaring wings.

We would have three more sessions. But if I had managed to divine flashes of humanity in him before, they vanished altogether in these later meetings.

A year and a half passed before the first of these interrogations: February 1941. Andrei met me with a stern scowl and an incomprehensible scream.

"Are you going to give testimony soon?"

There was no logic or sense to this outburst. Sverdlov had never demanded any testimony from me eighteen months before.

"We have not yet interrogated you as we should! We'll put you in Lefortovo prison; then you'll talk! That's a military prison. You'll learn there what an interrogation is!" he shouted.

I had heard about the horrifying tortures in Lefortovo from the wives of NKVD men serving time with me in the Tomsk camp. Before I could manage to ask Sverdlov what purpose he could have for subjecting me to torture, I suddenly sensed, apparently because of the powerful shock that he of all people should talk to me that way, that I was losing my sight. At first everything went dim and began to swim around; then I could see nothing but a bright spot from the lamp burning on the investigator's desk.

"You've already inflicted the worst torture, Andrei Yakovlevich. I've gone blind!"

"What are you faking?" Andrei shouted.

"I'm not faking. I can't see you," I replied in a trembling voice.

I heard him calling the doctor. Someone, evidently the jailer, led me by the hand to the doctor's office. They turned a lamp on directly in front of my eyes, and lit matches, but still I could see nothing but a bright spot. This condition lasted for two days; on the third, my vision gradually returned. During that time, the prison guard looked after me most earnestly, his peephole swishing almost constantly, and my comrades in the cell helped me with everything. As soon as the guard was convinced I had completely recovered, I was summoned the next day to an interrogation.

This time, Andrei was disposed to be considerate and polite. He asked after my health, especially my eyesight. I made no complaints. But what, I asked, did they actually want from me?

"Anna Mikhailovna," the investigator replied, for the first time addressing me by my given name and patronymic, "you have to write about the last six months of Bukharin's life prior to his arrest."

I was completely baffled.

"What purpose can that serve now? Nikolai Ivanovich is no longer with us, you know. Besides, before his arrest he emphatically repudiated any involvement in counterrevolutionary activity. That's all I can write down, and that isn't what you want."

"Write how it was. If he repudiated it, then write, 'He repudiated it.' "

He moved some sheets of paper closer to me, but I refused to write at that very moment, in the presence of an investigator, and asked that I be given time to recollect and think over everything. And I wanted to write in private. Two days later, they led me to a chamber where, in a relatively short period of time, I indeed wrote about Nikolai Ivanovich's last months. I purposely left out many things, for example, his letter "To a Future Generation of Party Leaders," and many others escaped my memory because of my great distress. And I was further hindered by my inability to comprehend the point of procuring such a document after Nikolai Ivanovich's execution.

"Who needs this?" I asked Andrei at our final meeting, when I handed over what I had written.

"The Boss," he answered curtly.

I'm not sure about that. The curiosity to be satisfied might have been Beria's.

[Bukharin's Last Months of Freedom: The Paris Trip]

Now, so many decades after those dramas, I want to recall the very months I wrote about for Andrei, the last of Bukharin's life. Only now, after the passing of so much time, am I able to take up my pen to re-create the picture of my husband's tragic downfall, trying not to let the slightest detail slip by in the process.

It is not easy to mobilize my memory, to direct it down the channel of events dominated by the treachery of Stalin and the sufferings of Bukharin in disgrace. Human language is too poor a thing to transmit the force of this catastrophe. Besides, I am forced to live again those tragic days when the chiming of the hours at the Kremlin's Spassky Tower sounded in our ears as an implacable reminder of the approaching end. They tolled a funeral march.

I plunge back into that gloomy time only because I alone can produce eyewitness testimony. This is my duty to history and to Bukharin.

In August 1936, the names of Bukharin, Rykov, and Tomsky were mentioned at the trial of Zinoviev and Kamenev. Nikolai Ivanovich realized instantly that his head had thus been put on the block.

What came out in open court had certainly been prepared in secret. Stalin's last major secret tactic for multiplying the accusations against Bukharin and Rykov (at least, of those tactics known to me) was to set Nikolai Ivanovich up by sending him abroad.

Ostensibly, however, Bukharin was commissioned by the Politburo to travel to Paris in late February 1936 to purchase the Marx and Engels archive. It belonged to the German Social Democratic Party but had been transported out of Germany to other European countries after Hitler rose to power. Since even this expedient did not guarantee its safety in the event of a European war with Germany, and possibly also because there were financial considerations, the German Social Democrats decided to sell the archive to the Soviet Union. The three-member commission dispatched to purchase it included Bukharin, Vladimir Adoratsky, director of the Marx-Engels-Lenin Institute, and Aleksandr Arosev, then chairman of the All-Union Society for Cultural Relations with Foreign Countries.

When Stalin summoned Nikolai Ivanovich to inform him about the impending appointment, he expressed the desire to procure not only those documents of Marx and Engels we did not have but also those which we had only as copies. He named a price limit.

"Arosov certainly knows how to bargain," Stalin said, "but I have my doubts about Adoratsky's know-how. They might stick anything but Marx under his nose. You are the only one who can verify the manuscripts."

Nikolai Ivanovich could not have suspected that his trip abroad had been conceived for the purpose of provocation. Stalin was in a friendly mood and had even remarked, "Your suit, Nikolai, is threadbare. You can't travel like that; get a new one made up right away. Things are different with us now; you have to be well dressed."

That very day, a tailor telephoned from the wardrobe shop of the People's Commissariat of Foreign Affairs.

"Comrade Bukharin," he said with a heavy Jewish accent. "I have to take your measurements as soon as possible if I am going to sew you a suit in time."

Nikolai Ivanovich explained how busy he was and asked the tailor to make a suit without taking measurements: "At three o'clock this afternoon, we have a 'quickie meeting' at *Izvestiya,* and there's a load of things to do before departure."

"How can I do it without measuring you?" the tailor expostulated. "Trust my experience, Comrade Bukharin. No tailor has ever sewn a suit without having measurements."

"Then sew it from an old suit," Nikolai Ivanovich suggested.

This stratagem failed because the only old suit Bukharin owned was the one he was wearing. I had managed to toss out its predecessor. If he had turned his old suit over to the tailor, Nikolai Ivanovich would have had to appear in the editorial offices in his underwear.

"An old suit? The new one will turn out bad if it's done from an old one. Besides, I've always dreamed of seeing Bukharin at least once in the flesh, and not just in a portrait. Now I have the chance, and what a chance! Please grant me the pleasure, Comrade Bukharin!"

Thus the comic intertwines with the tragic. Nikolai Ivanovich granted the tailor the "pleasure" and therefore traveled to Paris in the new suit, was arrested in the new suit, and was shot in the new suit, unless Stalin ordered yet a newer one made up for the last occasion.

The commission seemed like the real thing. In a second meeting about the subject, Stalin handed Bukharin the Politburo's decision stating the purpose of the mission, naming its members, and, if I recall correctly, listing the people with whom the members should negotiate. In any event, I positively remember that Nikolai Ivanovich came home afterward and told me that he would be obliged to meet with the Austrian Social Democrat Otto Bauer, with whom he had crossed polemical swords more than once. Bauer was the ideologist of Austro-Marxism, one of the leaders of the anti-Bolshevik Second International and the Austrian Social Democratic Party. He would also have to meet with the prominent Austrian Social Democrat Friedrich Adler, secretary of the Second International, as well as the Russian Menshevik émigrés Fyodor Ilyich Dan and Boris Ivanovich Nicolaevsky, who published the émigré journal *Socialist Herald* in Paris (later in America) and would act as intermediaries. Referring to Stalin, Nikolai Ivanovich said, "That Koba, he's come up with a good one! Something out of a fairy tale: me and Dan together!"

Fyodor Dan had been one of the leaders of the Russian Menshevik Party, a member of its central committee. After the February Revolution, he became a member of the Executive Committee of the Petrograd Soviet, as well as the Presidium of the Central Executive Committee, and supported the 1917 Provisional Government. He was the champion of "defensism." At the end of 1921, he was expelled from the country as a counterrevolutionary and participated in the organization of the Second International. Dan actually edited the *Socialist Herald;* Nicolaevsky, a historian who was his close friend, was a far lesser figure in the Menshevik Party but was curator of the Marx Lenin archive in Paris.

"With these types I must be doubly careful," Nikolai Ivanovich said to me, meaning that it was the *Socialist Herald* that had published the so-called transcript. "They're capable of any provocation and could cause me more difficulties. I will deal with them only in the presence of Arosev and Adoratsky as witnesses."

On his way to Paris, Nikolai Ivanovich stayed for two or three days in Berlin. He was warmly received by our ambassador to Germany, Jakob Suritz, lived in the embassy, and rode around the capital with Dmitry Bukhartsev, an *Izvestiya* correspondent. He bought a lot of books written by various fascist ideologists.

One of the fascist newspapers or journals, taking note of his arrival in town, commented that although Bukharin looked like a pharmacist's bubble-shaped vial turned upside down, it had to be admitted that he was one of the most learned men in the world. Nikolai Ivanovich was greatly amused by the upside-down "bubble" but was fearful of any compliments in the press. "Koba is very jealous and vengeful," he said.

Since the Marx and Engels archive was scattered throughout western Europe, the commission headed first for Vienna and then for Copenhagen and Amsterdam, where a great many of the documents Nikolai Ivanovich had to examine personally were kept.

The commission then went on to Paris sometime in the second half of March. Bukharin was the only one of the three members to carry a diplomatic passport. As a rule, anyone with such a passport would stay in the embassy, but our ambassador to France, Vladimir Potyomkin, did not receive Nikolai Ivanovich in quite the same manner as Suritz had in Berlin. Potyomkin sent word that he should stay with his comrades in the Hotel Lutetia, ostensibly because the negotiations were to take place there, and also because it would be awkward to invite émigré Mensheviks to the Soviet embassy. Why Nikolai Ivanovich could not simply go from the embassy to the hotel for the negotiations was not made clear, but there was no point in objecting.

I had not joined my husband on this trip, because he thought it inappropriate to spend state currency on me. Besides, I was in my last months of pregnancy. Time passed; the trip dragged on. Unexpectedly, toward the end of April, Bukharin's personal secretary, Semyon Lyandres, invited me over to the editorial offices of *Izvestiya* late one night and I was connected by telephone with Paris. Nikolai Ivanovich said he was preparing a speech that would be issued as a pamphlet and therefore earn royalties. So he had called Yezhov, who was then director of the Party's organization department, and asked him to allow me to travel to Paris without an additional outlay of currency. Yezhov agreed. In fact, he telephoned me later and said, "Come to the People's Commissariat of Foreign Affairs and get your travel visa to Paris. Your beloved husband misses you: he can't live without his young wife!" The vulgarity in his tone surprised me, but I got the impression he wished me well on my trip.

I arrived in Paris on April 6, 1936, three days after Bukharin delivered his speech at the Sorbonne on the chief problems of contemporary culture.

Nikolai Ivanovich was accompanied by Aleksandr Arosev when he met me at the train station. He introduced us: "This is my friend Arosev. In Moscow, in 1917, we won the Soviet power together, and now in Paris we are trying to 'win over' the Marx archive."

"Flowers from Nikolai Ivanovich," said Arosev, presenting me with a bouquet. "This 'beardless youth,' being timid, does not himself give flowers to ladies, and so entrusted me to do it."

Nikolai Ivanovich blushed. I loved this adolescent shyness of his.

We drove through springtime Paris. The chestnut trees were already covered with a thick verdure of carved palmate leaves and upthrust, proud candles. I was enchanted by the beauty of the city. Driving past the Boulevard Saint-Germain and the Boulevard Raspail, where artists sat sketching, we came to a stop at the Hotel Lutetia, across from Boucicaut Square.

The commission members were staying in adjoining rooms. Adoratsky, who was dry and dogmatic, came to see Bukharin only when business required, but Arosev, who loved to talk over business with Nikolai Ivanovich or simply have a jolly chat, dropped by frequently. A bright and talented man with varied interests, he had studied at Liège as an émigré before the revolution, then continued his studies in the Petrograd Psychoneurological Institute. He wrote stories and novellas. He and Nikolai Ivanovich had spent a lot of time together before my arrival, roaming Paris, walking through the Louvre. Both loved life and joked a lot.

Unfortunately, I was unable to enjoy my three weeks in Paris as much as I would have liked. We made our way through the Louvre, but alas, at the Mona Lisa I fainted. Nikolai Ivanovich was so upset that he would not take me anywhere afterward without Arosev along. The three of us rode out to see Versailles. All of a sudden it got cold, the sky darkened, and snow began to fall on the blossoming trees. Besides, the palaces were closed, the fountains were turned off, and the wind swept you off your feet. Add my sickness, and Versailles struck me as less beautiful than our own Peterhof. To this observation, Nikolai Ivanovich replied that I was a great patriot. On the way back to our hotel, he tried his best to lift my spirits; he joked and sang and emitted piercing whistles by sticking two fingers in his mouth, just like a little kid, ignoring Arosev's reproaches.

Again with Arosev, we took a ride late one evening to Montmartre. The vast panorama of the city, twinkling with myriad lights, spread out before us, and lovers strolled along, kissing each other quite openly. Nikolai Ivanovich shook his head and even took offense: "Oh, what morals! The most sacred thing, right in public!"

Then he abruptly turned to me and said, "But am I not as good as the other men?"

Arosev was startled and didn't know where to look. In a flash, Nikolai Ivanovich turned upside down and began walking on his hands, drawing the attention of the romancing strollers. This was his tomfoolery at its height.

The very day I arrived, Nikolai Ivanovich told me how he felt about his speech at the Sorbonne, remarking, "I could have spoken considerably better."

He knew French quite well, expressed himself freely, and could read without a dictionary. Nevertheless, when it came to a speech, he decided not to go on without a prepared text. He had written this one in Russian; then André Malraux translated it into French. The text created an artificial framework that confined him. Typically, Bukharin was a passionate orator, developing his thoughts so that one seemed naturally to give birth to the next. Inspired himself, he inspired the audience. But at the Sorbonne, because of the language barrier, his oratorical potential was not fully realized. Even so, he said, he was warmly received before his speech and even more warmly afterward. His listeners included workers, intellectuals, and many French Communists. There were so many people wanting to talk to him that he had trouble getting out of the hall.

But the most sensational detail, in his view, was that the venerable Austrian Marxist Rudolf Hilferding had traveled from his home province to Paris especially to hear Nikolai Ivanovich speak. In the view of the Bolsheviks, Hilferding's *Finance Capital,* published in 1910 and later in the Soviet Union, contained a valuable theoretical analysis of imperialism. The book was recommended for study in the advanced economic institutes, though with reservations, to be sure, since his theory of organized capitalism had always been scored as fallacious. Bukharin had been accused of "creeping" toward this position, but he did not consider his views on the subject identical with Hilferding's.

When the Austrian came up after the speech, the two men did not say one word about the sale of the archive; their conversation was devoted entirely to theoretical matters. Yet, since this encounter had not been planned, Nikolai Ivanovich was frightened about Moscow's reaction if it was reported. "But it wasn't my place, after all, to chase him away," he said to me. "And besides, it was exceptionally interesting to talk with him."

None of the German Social Democrats participated in the negotiations for the sale of the archive. It was the Austrians Otto Bauer and Friedrich Adler who gave Bukharin and Adoratsky an opportunity to examine the documents; Adler had come to Copenhagen and to Amsterdam. Nikolai Ivanovich did not tell me whether or not Nicolaevsky had been present. There was no viewing of documents in Paris when I was there; if some were kept there, they were only a small part of the total and had been dealt with before my arrival. The negotiations dealt only with the price of the material: the "conditions of sale," as Nicolaevsky put it, or the "shameful business," in Bukharin's phrase.

As soon as the commission arrived in Paris, its members met with Dan and Nicolaevsky at the Lutetia, and all subsequent negotiations took place there. Since Bukharin's first meeting with Dan had occurred before my arrival, I write about it on the basis of what Nikolai Ivanovich told me.

Looking at Bukharin with evident coldness and intentional indifference, Dan did not notice Arosev and Adoratsky at all. To defuse the situation, Nikolai Ivanovich exclaimed, "How thin you have become, Fyodor Ilyich!"

"That's because the Bolsheviks have drunk all my blood," Dan returned. "For the same reason, you have grown stout."

"But you've had a good drink of mine!" Nikolai Ivanovich countered. "And not only in 1917 but also in 1929. [He was referring to the Kamenev "transcript."] Still, as you see, I am in good shape."

After this "amicable" exchange, they briefly discussed the documents and the price. Dan announced that thenceforward Nicolaevsky would conduct the negotiations alone, since he would take no further part in them.

Bukharin had not personally known either of the Mensheviks previously. He had seen Dan in 1917 but not talked with him; he saw Nicolaevsky for the first time in Paris.

As the negotiations continued, Nicolaevsky would usually call to schedule the next discussion, which had to be agreeable to all three members of the commission. Once, when he could not locate Arosev and Adoratsky, Nikolai Ivanovich canceled a meeting. In all cases but one, as I shall explain, the talk concerned nothing but the price of the archive.

Because the commission had arrived about the middle of March and I came at the beginning of April, I was not present for all of Bukharin's encounters with Nicolaevsky, but I did witness *all* negotiations taking place after my arrival. Therefore, I was able to sense the mood, learn what was being discussed, and come to know whether Nikolai Ivanovich could have talked with Nicolaevsky in private about political subjects or whether he avoided them, strictly adhering to the course of action he had set himself back in Moscow—that is, to have no conversations with the Menshevik without witnesses.

The German Social Democrats had set a very high price on the archive. Perhaps there was merit to the suspicions of some, especially Arosev, that the Russian Mensheviks wanted a cut of the deal.

When Dan and Nicolaevsky announced their asking price, every member of the commission dismissed it as "highway robbery" and pressured Nicolaevsky to make the German Social Democrats reduce it. He wouldn't respond, evidently stalling in the hope that Moscow would agree. Bukharin went to the embassy to telephone Stalin, who declared that the Soviet Union would never pay such a sum.

"You don't know how to bargain. You're not cut out for it, Nikolai. Let Arosev apply the pressure."

And truly, in my presence, the debates about the price of the archive became heated. Arosev argued with all his might.

The second time Nicolaevsky came to bargain, Nikolai Ivanovich reported, with the other two commissioners present and participating, that Stalin did not deem it possible to pay more than the price Moscow had offered in the beginning. Arosev urged Nicolaevsky to reconsider and lower his asking price; otherwise, he said, the commission would have to return to Moscow and forget the deal.

Meanwhile, I had caught a cold in Versailles and took to bed with a high fever. Arosev forthwith called the daughter of the late Georgy Plekhanov, founder of the Russian Social Democratic Party; she and her husband, a Frenchman, were both doctors. Lidiya Georgiyevna, if I recall her name correctly, determined that I had pleurisy and offered to take me to her husband's sanatorium outside the city. We drove there at once. Nikolai Ivanovich stayed, too, becoming inseparable from me. My temperature rose to forty degrees centigrade, which was so dangerous in my pregnant condition that Lidiya Georgiyevna came to see me even at night. I am indebted solely to her for my swift recovery. Refusing payment for my stay in the sanatorium, she limited herself to one small request, which Nikolai Ivanovich fulfilled with alacrity; she wanted a package of medicines sent to Leningrad for her mother, Rozaliya Markovna. Arosev showed up at the sanatorium once and reported that Nicolaevsky was lying low and had not shown himself at all. Apparently, the commission would have to go back to Moscow without the archive. I felt better after a week, and we returned to Paris.

When we got back to the hotel, Nicolaevsky did put in an appearance, having phoned in advance. As always, the negotiations took place in our room; all three commissioners were present. This time Nicolaevsky made a sizable cut in the asking price. Everyone took heart, especially Nikolai Ivanovich, who became convinced that the archive would be purchased. The difference between Stalin's bid and the Second International's last offer became negligible, and it was agreed that Adoratsky or Bukharin would contact the general secretary to conclude the deal.

Bukharin phoned Stalin, Adoratsky phoned Stalin, but he would not take the calls. Nikolai Ivanovich asked Poskryobyshev, Stalin's secretary, to pass along the Mensheviks' lowered price to the Boss; Poskryobyshev promised to report Stalin's decision to the embassy in Paris. The commission waited and waited, but no answer came. Nikolai Ivanovich grew irritable. "This whole story is beginning to disgust me!" he once shouted in anger, banging his fist on the table. When Adoratsky phoned, Poskryobyshev explained that Stalin was insisting on his original bid.

All three members of the commission were now in a foul mood; no one wanted to return home with empty hands. When Nikolai Ivanovich and I were left alone, he said, "That Koba! Will he ever give ground on anything? To haggle over such a sum, this is senseless for a state!" The only hope now was Nicolaevsky.

Subsequently, he just appeared without advance notice, explaining that he just happened to be passing by. Nikolai Ivanovich went for his comrades, but neither was in. It was obvious that he did not want to speak with the Menshevik while I was the only one present.

"It's a shame," he said, "that you have come without giving advance notice. The comrades are not in the hotel, and I'm not authorized to talk in their absence. I was sent only as an expert. [Adoratsky headed the commission.] I am not authorized to talk about the price of the archive."

"But you have probably agreed on the price with Stalin, and we can finalize the agreement when all of you are gathered."

Nikolai Ivanovich was forced to say that Stalin was sticking to the original bid. He could have withheld this information and postponed this discussion until the others arrived, but that was not in his nature.

"You put a low price on Marx," said Nicolaevsky unexpectedly.

These words threw Nikolai Ivanovich into a fury; put in such a defensive position, he went on the attack.

"So we're the ones who put a low price on Marx!" he exclaimed in an offended tone. "We're buying the archive, but you're trying to sell it. So who does not really value it?"

He began pacing the room nervously, as he always did when on edge.

"But you know what circumstances compel us to sell the archive," Nicolaevsky answered defensively.

"Well, if I were you, I would find a place to keep the archive and never sell it."

Nicolaevsky asked where that could be.

"Well, let's say in America. Keep, but not sell; no one there will pay you any money for it. America doesn't need these documents, but they can be kept there. But if you don't agree, Boris Ivanovich, and think that the archive is in such danger it is impossible to secure its safekeeping, why are you haggling over this pittance? This is a shameful business, shameful!"

"But Stalin, too, is clinging to this pittance," Nicolaevsky countered. "You represent a state, and for it your 'pittance' is no great loss, but for the German Social Democratic Party this 'pittance' of yours is no pittance; it very much needs the money."

"But if the archive is in danger, and the most valuable documents of Marx may perish, then in the name of saving them I would hand them over gratis. I would make a gift of them to the Soviet Union, but you, on the other hand, are being offered no small sum."

"Gratis, you say?" asked Nicolaevsky with an ironical smile.

"Were it within my power, I myself would pay you twice as much as you ask, if only to save the archive and stop this haggling."

"Of that I have not the slightest doubt," Nicolaevsky said emphatically, subtly referring to Bukharin's dependence on Stalin.

Nikolai Ivanovich went on, "I certainly do not rule out an attack by Hitler on the Soviet Union. I think a military conflict with Germany is unavoidable, and we must prepare for it not only in the military area but also in the creation of the necessary psychology in the rear. But the hardships in the countryside are behind us already. Therefore, I think that even though the war will be arduous, the victory will be ours, and we will use the great expanses of our country to preserve the archive."

Nicolaevsky had the last word: "We will not go down one more franc" (an exact quote).

From this ultimatum, there is no reason to conclude, as Nicolaevsky would later claim in his memoirs, that the German Social Democrats had changed their minds about offering the archive for sale. Rather, it would seem more likely that he was holding out for a higher price because he and the other Mensheviks wanted to make a commis-

258

sion on the deal, just as the members of our commission suspected.

In fact, when Nikolai Ivanovich told his two colleagues about Nicolaevsky's final statement, he mused, "Just who is this 'we' exactly? 'We' the representatives of the Second International? 'We' the Russian Mensheviks? Or 'we' the German Social Democrats?"

Nicolaevsky's demand effectively brought negotiations to an end, so he turned the conversation to another subject. Since this was obviously to be his last meeting with Bukharin, he took the opportunity to ask about his brother, Vladimir, who was married to Rykov's sister and lived in Moscow. Naturally, he assumed that Nikolai Ivanovich had run into this brother at Rykov's place, but he was mistaken. In recent times, Bukharin had seen Rykov only on occasion; at a Central Committee plenum, say, or at the Party Congress. He had not visited Rykov's apartment or even seen him before leaving with the commission; because the trip was organized on the spur of the moment, Rykov may not have even known about it. But even if the two men had met, Rykov would not have sent along his regards to Nicolaevsky, because they did not have that kind of relationship, nor did Nikolai Ivanovich think it proper for him to do so in Rykov's name.

Nicolaevsky then asked, "Well, how is life there now in the Soviet Union?"

"Life is wonderful," Nikolai Ivanovich answered.

As I listened, he spoke about our society with heartfelt enthusiasm. What he said differed from his writing at the time only in that he did not repeatedly mention Stalin, as he had to do within the Soviet Union. He praised the tremendous growth of industry and the development of electrification; he shared his impression of the Dnepr Hydroelectric Station, which he had visited with Sergo Ordzhonikidze. Citing statistics from memory, he described the largest metallurgical combines, which had been built in the north, and told about the rapid progress in science.

He concluded, "You wouldn't recognize Russia now."

I sensed that Nicolaevsky had expected a very different response and was unprepared for this kind of enthusiasm.

"And what about collectivization, Nikolai Ivanovich?" he asked.

"Collectivization is a stage that is now complete; a difficult stage, but complete. In time, differences of opinion are outlived; it makes no sense to argue about what kind of legs should be made for a table when the table is already made. At home, they write that I was against collectivization, but this is a ploy of propagandists, a cheap shot. I had indeed proposed another path, more complex and not so pell-mell, that would have led in the final analysis to production cooperatives, a path that did not involve the same kind of sacrifices but would have ensured that collectivization was voluntary. But now, in the face of approaching fascism, I can say, 'Stalin triumphed!' Come to the Soviet Union, Boris Ivanovich, and take a look yourself with your own eyes at what Russia has become. Would you like me to help you organize a trip with Stalin's permission?"

"Spare me, spare me!" Nicolaevsky exclaimed, waving his hands. "I shall never visit you. I just want to make one innocent request. Please take this package to Rykov."

He held out a parcel wrapped in yellow paper.

"Rykov?" Nikolai Ivanovich asked in surprise. "What could it be?"

"Don't worry, Nikolai Ivanovich; it's not conspiratorial documents. We have no contact with Rykov at all; he doesn't acknowledge my existence. There are only Dutch tulip bulbs in here. Your former chairman of the Council of People's Commissars is a great flower fancier, so I decided, despite everything, to send him some bulbs. Of course, it's entirely possible he will refuse to plant 'Menshevik' bulbs," Nicolaevsky joked, "but try to give them to him all the same. I'm sure that if Aleksei Ivanovich plants them with his own hands, they will produce nothing but 'Bolshevik' sprouts."

And thus the conversation came to an end. As Nicolaevsky departed, Bukharin said he would try again to reach Stalin by telephone, and if nothing came of it, he would definitely talk with him when we got back to Moscow.

Once we were left alone, Nikolai Ivanovich told me he was certain that Nicolaevsky had known that the other two members of the commission were not to be found (evidently, he would have telephoned them in advance) and had intended to have a private tête-à-tête. He must have assumed that Bukharin, in that situation, would be less constrained and would expound his thoughts about the Soviet Union more openly; also, he probably thought he could learn more about his brother.

"And these tulips!" Nikolai Ivanovich shrugged his shoulders in bewilderment. "In any event, I blabbed too much to him; I mean, that part about the propagandists and their cheap shots at me."

What I have set down was the sole content of Bukharin's meeting with Nicolaevsky when the other two members of the commission were not present. Before my arrival to Paris, Nikolai Ivanovich told me, there had not been any such private meetings. I remember this encounter very well and have transmitted it here with maximum fidelity. The very substance of the conversation demonstrates sufficiently that it was unique, for it is inconceivable that, had the two men repeatedly seen each other "in private," Nicolaevsky would not have found an earlier chance to solicit Bukharin's view of life in the Soviet Union, to ask about the collectivization, and to find out about his brother. Would he hold all of these questions back until their last meeting, and with me listening, just as Nikolai Ivanovich's stay in Paris was coming to end?

Several days before our return home, Bukharin was phoned by the chancellery of the president of France and then by the Soviet embassy, both warning him not to leave the hotel under any circumstances. German fascists were said to be plotting an attempt on his life, perhaps because his speech at the Sorbonne had been strongly antifascist. The French government put the hotel under guard; I recall seeing the police arriving to surround the Lutetia. For three or four days, Nikolai Ivanovich did not go out into the city, but no danger could ultimately restrain him. It was amusing to see the gendarmes standing guard over the hotel while the guarded one dashed around Paris.

Once he tried to drag the terrified Adoratsky out for a walk in the city: "Vladimir Vladimirovich! Let's go for a stroll. If something happens, you can shield me with your powerful chest," he joked.

When the French authorities found out that no warnings had any effect on Bukharin, they obliged him to move into the Soviet embassy. After we had been there a few days, a directive came from the Central Committee: the members of the commission must return home immediately. Germany gave Bukharin permission for a transit pass only, allowing no stop in Berlin. He was unhappy about this development, because he had planned to write a book about fascism.

On the train from Paris to Berlin, we were accompanied by German agents, who traveled in the adjoining coupe. At the Berlin railway station, we heard a radio dispatch that on such and such a train in such and such a coach, en route now to Moscow, the former director of the Comintern, Nikolai Bukharin, was returning from France, where he had been sent to organize a revolution.

[The "Letter of an Old Bolshevik" and Other Supposed "Recollections" of Bukharin in Paris]

We got to Moscow just before May Day. Nikolai Ivanovich immediately phoned Stalin to tell him that the documents were extremely interesting and had enormous value for the Soviet Union. He advised him to stop bargaining and buy the archive.

"Don't worry, Nikolai, no need to hurry," Stalin replied. "They'll give in."

Although Bukharin returned from Paris without the archive, it would turn out that he had not made this trip in vain. Like a cancerous tumor, it would send out extensive metastases. At Bukharin's trial, Stalin would reap the fruits of this trip in Moscow; Dan and Nicolaevsky, in Paris.

In the issues of December 22, 1936, and January 17, 1937—that is, some months after Bukharin's return from Paris—the *Socialist Herald* printed the long, anonymous "Letter of an Old Bolshevik." An editorial note in the December issue explained that the letter had been received just before the journal went to press.

"Unfortunately, the size of the letter and its late receipt," the note continued, "make it impossible for us to print it in its entirety in the current issue. We are compelled to withhold its conclusion until the first issue of 1937."

Whoever was the author of this fraud (and signed it "Y.Z.," using Latin instead of Cyrillic letters) did all he could to make it appear that Bukharin wrote the "Letter" when he returned home after his "private" meeting with Nicolaevsky.

The central theme of the piece, naturally, was the unprecedented and ever mounting terror within the Bolshevik Party, but it also included a discussion of the collectivization campaign of 1929–33 from a dissenting point of view. This topic, no longer being actively debated at the time, had to be inserted or the document would not have achieved its goal:

> The horrors attending the campaigns against the village, of these horrors you have only a feeble conception, but they, the top men in the Party, they were all well aware of everything going on; many of them took the horrors very hard. This was at the end of 1932, when the situation in the village was similar to the situation during the 1921 Kronstadt rebellion. In the broadest strata of the Party, they talked about nothing else but the fact that Stalin had driven the country into a blind alley with his policies, that he had "caused the country to argue with the muzhik," and that the country could be saved only by getting rid of Stalin.

Set off by quotation marks, the phrase "caused the country to argue with the muzhik" was indeed Bukharin's. So, too, was "had driven the country into a blind alley," which should also have been put in quotation marks. But these phrases, which dated from 1928, were widely known.

To verify Bukharin's supposed authorship, the "Letter" included the following meticulously contrived statement about rights in the Soviet Union: "It is no accident that a joke is now making the rounds that of all the rights won by the revolution the only one that Stalin does not dare to take away from government and Party officials is the right to hunt in summer."

Brilliant! Who did not know that Bukharin was an avid hunter? The implication was that only someone enthusiastic about the sport would make such a joke about this "right."

So, it all seemed perfectly clear: Bukharin must have written the "Letter" (I repeat) upon returning from his official trip and the negotiations in Paris with Nicolaevsky. At the same time, the suspicion was planted that Rykov was coauthor, for it also reflected the objections he raised during the collectivization. In the subsequent investigation, the NKVD would play up his family relationship to Nicolaevsky, as would Vyshinsky at the trial.

The "Letter of an Old Bolshevik" appeared in the *Socialist Herald* not long after a vigorous investigation into the case of Bukharin and Rykov had been mounted. The aim of their political opponents in printing such a document is completely clear. Weighing the situation that had developed after the trial of Zinoviev and Kamenev in 1936, and taking into account the trial being prepared against Radek, Pyatakov, Sokolnikov, and others, which started in January 1937, these adversaries knew that the fraudulent "Letter" would be sufficient to ensure both the expulsion of Bukharin and Rykov from the Party and their arrest.

Indeed, the *Socialist Herald* editor Dan and historian Nicolaevsky, "a major expert on the history of the Soviet Union," as he is considered in the West, understood this perfectly. How very different Bukharin was from such men: no matter how sharply he polemicized against these and other representatives of the Second International, no matter how strenuously he strove to smash them politically, he never put their lives on the line.

Of course, even without the help of the *Socialist Herald,* Stalin undoubtedly would have been able to destroy Bukharin and Rykov. Nevertheless, because Bukharin still retained his popularity in the Soviet Union both within the Party and throughout the country, among members of Communist parties in the West, and with the European intelligentsia, it was necessary to use every means to undermine trust in him. The judicial proceedings, added to the growing number of arrests of senior as well as rank-and-file Party members in both Moscow and the provinces, no doubt inspired anxiety and trepidation in many of those not arrested, including members of the Central Committee and Politburo—certainly Ordzhonikidze and Kalinin, at any rate. Also, distrust of the NKVD was mounting; therefore, materials produced in some other quarter, like the *Socialist Herald,* seemed to confirm the confessions tortured out of prisoners under investigation, making it easier for Stalin to realize his criminal plans, which were becoming increasingly complex. Previously, neither for the arrest of Zinoviev, Kamenev, and Radek nor for the arrest of the Central Committee member Pyatakov and the Central Committee candidate Sokolnikov had it been necessary to convene two plenums of the Central Committee and to create a special commission, but these actions were taken to decide the question of expelling and arresting Bukharin and Rykov.

The very act of passing information along to the *Socialist Herald* has to be regarded as criminal. Considering that the journal had exacerbated differences within the Politburo back in 1929 by publishing the "Transcript of Bukharin's Conversation with Kamenev," it becomes obvious that this new stunt was the logical next link in a chain leading to Bukharin's downfall. When I examine the basic positions of the "Letter," I am forced to conclude that Dan and Nicolaevsky consciously helped Stalin tighten the noose already drawn around the necks of Bukharin and Rykov.

Rather than focus on all of the arguments made in the document they printed, I will focus only on those I think were most damaging to both Bukharin and Rykov.

1. The Ryutin Platform

The "Letter" contains a rather detailed exposition of the anti-Stalinist platform of the Bolshevik oppositionist Mikhail Ryutin:

> The Ryutin Platform stood out from a number of others by its sharp personal attack on Stalin. Copied on a typewriter, it comprised in all slightly less than two hundred pages. Of these, more than fifty were devoted to a personal characterization of Stalin and an evaluation of his role in the Party and country. These pages were written with great force and acuity and made a real impact on the reader. Stalin was depicted as the evil genius of the Russian revolution who with his thirst for power and revenge had brought the revolution to the brink of disaster.

Bukharin knew no more about the Ryutin Platform than had been reported in the newspapers or in speeches delivered at Party meetings; he had not seen, much less read, the Ryutin Platform. In the letter he had asked me before his arrest to memorize, "To a Future Generation of Party Leaders," he deemed it necessary to address this issue: "I knew nothing about the secret organizations of Ryutin and Uglanov. Along with Rykov and Tomsky, I always expounded my views out in the open."

The "old Bolshevik" provides a detailed account of the secret Politburo meeting that discussed the Ryutin affair in 1932, but Nikolai Ivanovich had not been a member since 1929. He was isolated and had lost personal contact with Politburo members. To be sure, in his work as head of the scientific research section for the People's Commissariat of Heavy Industry, he was in contact with the Politburo member Sergo Ordzhonikidze. They were the best of friends, but it was not the custom to divulge what went on at Politburo meetings, especially such top-secret discussions. Finally, the author of the "Letter" was fully aware that people who simply read the Ryutin Platform but did not "inform the Party" (that was the formula) were linked with it and punished severely. Obviously, he knew that by a decision of the Party's Central Control Commission passed on October 9, 1932, and published in *Pravda,* nineteen people had been expelled from the Party for a greater or lesser degree of involvement in the Ryutin Platform, so implying that Bukharin somehow knew about its content was serious, indeed.

I do not dissociate Nikolai Ivanovich from that platform because I consider it to have been criminal. On the contrary, to have written such an anti-Stalinist statement in 1932 can only be deemed a heroic act. But from Bukharin's point of view, a conspiratorial speech at that time could, alas, bring the country nothing but repressions. Back in 1928–29, an open declaration against Stalin's policies by three influential members of the Politburo—Bukharin, Rykov, and Tomsky, men commanding more authority and popularity in the country than Ryutin—had not been crowned with success. Nikolai Ivanovich considered it necessary to curtail any further struggle. Dominated by Stalin, the Party had started down a different path, disposing of Bukharin's economic politics. Under such circumstances, he could find no more useful action than to close the ranks. In his view, focusing only on the gloomy pictures of the times of collectivization and not simultaneously noting the people's great enthusiasm for construction was to see and understand nothing in our history.

Inevitably, the content of the "Letter" from the anonymous "old Bolshevik" caused the question of Bukharin and Rykov's involvement in the Ryutin Platform to be raised at the February–March 1937 plenum. I remember Nikolai Ivanovich's account of the accusations against him:

"You're lying! You're lying!" voices resounded at the plenum. "You knew, but you didn't inform the Party!"

Nikolai Ivanovich objected, trying to argue that if he had actually advocated a platform like this he would have composed it himself, not entrusted the writing to Ryutin.

"But you did write it, and Ryutin approved it," Stalin shot back. "Ryutin was credited for conspiratorial reasons."

Nikolai Ivanovich demanded that the text of the platform be presented to the plenum, so that all could examine the writing style and see for themselves that he was not the author. But his was a voice crying in the wilderness.

Then Rykov, greatly agitated, stood up and tried to deflect the accusation by declaring that he had heard from someone (I cannot recall whom he named) that the platform said something like this: "Bukharin, Rykov, and Tomsky are exhaust steam and are not to be counted on in the struggle against Stalin." How, then, could the document be imputed to them?

Apparently the document really did include that observation.* Neither Stalin, Molotov, nor Yezhov denied it, and they were surely familiar with the text. But the familiar counterargument was instantly brought to bear:

"For the sake of conspiracy!" Stalin declared.

"In the aim of conspiracy!" shouted Yezhov and Kaganovich.

Rykov countered, "It's impossible to prove anything to you! Maybe we all exist purely for the sake of conspiracy." He sat down in his place.

But at the trial he would testify, "And in order to do this more easily [to conspire together], there was this phrase in the program itself that gave the feeling of a certain distance between it and me, Bukharin, and Tomsky; it said something of the sort that these three were like exhaust steam. This was done in the interest of double-dealing."†

Thus the unfortunate Rykov parroted his memorized lesson. And Nikolai Ivanovich would give similar testimony: "It [the platform] was called Ryutin's for conspiratorial purposes, as insurance against failure, in order to cover up the right center and its most prominent figures."‡

These two forced confessions, when juxtaposed with the proceedings of the February–March 1937 plenum, enable us to understand how the trial scenario was put together. I have drawn special attention to the Ryutin Platform simply because it constituted an essential part of the

---

*The clandestine document was not published until 1990. See *Izvestiya TsK KPSS*, nos. 8–12. [Trans.]

†*Court Record in the Case of the Anti-Soviet "Bloc of Rightists and Trotskyists,"* p. 151.

‡Ibid., p. 348.

charges "deliberated" by the court during the trial.

After Nikolai Ivanovich's arrest, new inflammatory material was inserted into the Ryutin Platform: the projected overthrow of Soviet power, plans for a bloc with the Trotskyists, the fomenting of a "palace revolution." These additions, so useful to Stalin, certainly did not reflect the true content of the document; otherwise, Ryutin would no longer have been among the living in 1932. (He was not shot until five years later.) I am sure these additions were not made before Bukharin's arrest, because the incriminating material sent to him at home while he was still under investigation contained, as best I recall, no mention of Ryutin, although there were allusions to terror, "palace revolution," and the like.

Few people were familiar with the actual contents of the Ryutin Platform. Members of the Central Committee who did not belong to the Politburo knew about the Ryutin "counterrevolutionary" group and its anti-Stalinist platform only from speeches and newspapers. Anyone who had actually read the platform in a conspiratorial way had already paid with his head by 1937. As a consequence, the content of the document could be deformed any way one chose; in this case, counterfeit material was used to suggest that Bukharin and Rykov had been involved in an actual political platform for change, thus making the criminal accusations against them look all the more plausible.

2. The Kirov Murder

No less damaging to Bukharin was the section of the "Letter" dealing with the murder of Sergei Kirov.

The anonymous work provides detailed information about Kirov, who was chief of the Leningrad Party. Noting that he had previously been in favor of Stalin's policies, the "Letter" reports that he had begun to manifest a conciliatory attitude toward former Party oppositionists. Supposedly, at a Politburo meeting in 1932, he had spoken against the death penalty for Ryutin. The "old Bolshevik" puts special emphasis on Kirov's prestige in Leningrad and the Party overall; for example, the story is told of the rapturous reception he was accorded at the Seventeenth Party Congress, in January 1934, replete with "a standing ovation at both the start and the end." At this congress, he was elected to the Secretariat of the Central Committee, entailing his transfer to Moscow. Kirov returned to Leningrad to turn over his work to a successor, and there he was killed on December 1, 1934.

In the "Letter," this sequence of events is presented in such a way as to implicate Stalin: Kirov's murder is connected with his election and the projected move to Moscow. Logically grounded conclusions are drawn from this connection. "It was important to determine," writes the anonymous "Bolshevik," "whether in the present instance there was no dereliction on the part of those whose duty it is to guard against an attempt. Who had an interest in the removal of Kirov on the eve of his transfer to Moscow? These questions were not raised by the investigation."

To imagine that Kirov would be elevated to his new elective post without the sanction of the Boss—or, in fact, without his initiative—is impossible. But precisely here one can recognize Stalin's familiar scrawl: he knew that Kirov would not be returning from Leningrad to Moscow. The Bolsheviks at that time, however, were not psychologically prepared to draw such conclusions about Stalin. Bukharin, by virtue of his character, was even less prepared than others. Endowed with the highest nobility, political honesty, and a considerable quotient of naïveté, he could not then plumb Stalin's intentions, even though he recognized the man's love of political intrigue, pathological suspicion, and thirst for revenge. Although Bukharin was therefore confident that the Gensek could remove any opponent, any potential candidate for his post, by political means, he never imagined that Stalin might eliminate him physically.

The biography of Kirov's murderer, Leonid Nikolayev, as given in the "Letter," impresses one with its scope, for the chief landmarks of his life from beginning to end are recorded. We learn that as a member of Komsomol he volunteered for the civil war front against Yudenich and played an insignificant role in the Zinoviev opposition, for which he was not punished. The writer stresses that Nikolayev worked for the GPU and that this aspect of his career was kept strictly secret. *At the beginning of 1934,* the account goes on, he was found with a diary that revealed his terroristic intentions and critical attitude toward the existing regime; the discovery caused his expulsion from the Party, but he was reinstated soon afterward. His excuse for writing down such thoughts was that he was ill from overwork. The "Letter" also reports that, despite these revelations, Nikolayev worked for security at the Smolny Institute, headquarters of the Party in Leningrad.

"Given these conditions," the author logically concludes, "it becomes completely incomprehensible how he could have been allowed to come into direct contact with Kirov while our leaders are furnished such tight protection." It is noteworthy that the "Letter," speaking on behalf of the Bolsheviks, draws an analogy between the murders of Kirov and the tsarist minister of the interior Pyotr Stolypin, killed on orders of the tsarist secret police: "In the December days of 1934, we suddenly took an interest in the assassination of Stolypin."

Perhaps someone will suggest that the "old Bolshevik" actually had good intentions, that he disclosed the secret of Kirov's murder in order to rehabilitate Zinoviev, Kamenev, and their codefendants in the eyes of Western public opinion. The "Letter" was published only a few months after the execution of these unfortunates, on the eve of the trial of Radek and Pyatakov, and during the investigations of Bukharin and Rykov; was it written in order to preclude further accusations of involvement in the murder? I know only one thing for certain: under Stalin's absolute rule, any publication that clearly implicated him in the most serious crime, a publication revealing the true circumstances in the investigation of Kirov's murder, could have only a disastrous effect on Bukharin and Rykov and rain miseries down on many other Bolsheviks.

Furthermore, it cannot be ruled out that Stalin intentionally promoted the spread of such information. In my view, this would be likely, however, only if it had become apparent to the Boss that information about the true motives behind the murder would leak out in one way or another. Then it would be expedient, from his point of view, to characterize the story as the invention of his political opponents. Bukharin, the presumed author of the "Letter," would therefore be branded as a virulent slanderer of Stalin.

3. About the Peasantry

Speaking for the Bolsheviks, the "Letter" states that during the time of collectivization, "many said that it would be better on the whole to have to deal with revolts." To be sure, I cannot vouch for the mood of every Bolshevik, but the reference here is to the *typical* mood. I did not observe Party workers in the middle and lower echelons, but I would suggest that none of them even dreamed of revolts—neither those who favored Stalin's policies without realizing how severely the peasants were oppressed, or the extent of the economic consequences, nor those who opposed the policies. After all, it was mainly the middle and lower echelons that were assigned the tragic mission of subjugating the peasantry. Death awaited those who refused orders.

But the author of the "Letter" does not have these strata of the Party in mind. He is referring to those in the upper crust who were inclined to oppose collectivization. Again, let me repeat that the "Letter" was calculated to imply that Bukharin and Rykov were the authors. Such a conclusion would easily be drawn by anyone who knew about Bukharin's meetings with Nicolaevsky during the official trip to Paris and about Rykov's family relationship to the Menshevik.

During collectivization, I was familiar with the moods of the leading oppositionists of the Party. When disturbances broke out in the country-side, Bukharin and Rykov, who did not give support to Stalin's policies in the Politburo, came to see my father. On a number of occasions, I heard them say (Bukharin especially, since he came more often) how much they feared for the welfare of the peasant, worried that the alliance with the middle peasant would be broken, and were concerned about the ultimate fate of the revolution. Also present for these conversations, on different occasions, were major Bolshevik economists: Osinsky, Lomov, Milyutin, Kritsman. They did not oppose Stalin's policy of collectivization but did regard reports on the situation in the countryside as tragic.

4. The Characterization of Kaganovich and Yezhov

The purpose behind the sensational "Letter" becomes crystal clear when one reads the characterization of Lazar Kaganovich and Nikolai Yezhov. This section is of no small interest, for it ensured Stalin the solid support of these two men in the destruction of Bukharin and Rykov.

On Kaganovich:

> He began to make his grand career in the Party at a time when there was a great demand for treachery, yet, on the other hand, was he not one of those who went on increasing this demand longer than others?

On Yezhov:

> If in respect to Kaganovich you are sometimes surprised that he took the path he did when he might have made his career by taking an honest path, in regard to Yezhov you feel no such surprise. He could have made his career only by means such as this.
>
> In all of my now long life, I have met few people so inherently repulsive as Yezhov.

The "Letter" might to some degree reflect Bukharin's attitude toward Kaganovich at the time of the Paris trip, but certainly not his attitude toward Yezhov. It was only later, after Kaganovich and Yezhov had betrayed him and Rykov at the December 1936 and February–March 1937 plenums, that he felt this way toward Yezhov.

Nikolai Ivanovich did value Kaganovich as a worker and considered him a capable, important organizer. I cannot deny that he also considered him treacherous, but not to the extent he later proved to be.

Bukharin's attitude toward Yezhov, however, was quite good. Although he recognized that Yezhov had attached himself to the apparatus of the Central Committee and groveled before Stalin, he also knew that he was by no means unique in this respect. In fact, Nikolai Ivanovich considered Yezhov to be an honest man sincerely devoted to the Party. This virtue, "devotion to the Party," was the quintessential attribute of a Bolshevik. It may seem paradoxical now, but Bukharin then judged Yezhov to be a man, though perhaps of little culture, who had a good heart and a clean conscience.

He was not alone in this opinion. I happened to hear the same evaluation of Yezhov's moral qualities from many who knew him. In particular, I remember clearly an exiled Kazakh teacher named Azhgireyev, who crossed my life's path in my Siberian exile. He had been close to Yezhov when the latter worked in Kazakhstan and was completely dumbfounded by his dreadful later career.

When the sunshine of Siberian spring finally began to radiate warmth, Azhgireyev and I could go outside the dilapidated hut in which we lived and froze through the long winter, and, without having to fear the frost, could sit side by side for a while on the mound of earth circling the hut. At such times, Azhgireyev would often strike up a conversation about Yezhov: "What happened to him, Anna Mikhailovna? They say he is not a human being any more, but a beast! I wrote him twice about my innocence. No answer. But he used to respond to the most trivial request; he always helped in any way he could. Now he's not the same Yezhov!" Indeed, no one could understand this metamorphosis.

I myself saw Nikolai Ivanovich Yezhov only twice, a total of several minutes in all. Both times, I was walking in the Kremlin with Bukharin, and Yezhov, catching sight of him from afar, hurried up each time with quick steps. His gray-blue eyes looked genuinely kind, and his face broke out in a wide grin, revealing a row of decayed teeth. "Hi there, namesake, how're you doing?" he greeted Bukharin, clasping his hand firmly. Then, after exchanging a few remarks, the two Nikolai Ivanoviches, executioner and victim, went their respective ways.

Bukharin was sincerely happy when Yezhov was appointed to replace Yagoda. "He won't stoop to falsification," he naively believed until the December 1936 plenum.

When you think of Yezhov, you have to wonder: in those days, could every innocent victim have become an executioner and every executioner a victim? Was it simply a game of chance? I do not want to believe so, but, alas, I am convinced that the choice was probably just that extreme. Given Stalin's absolute rule, his criminal plans for the extermination of the old Bolsheviks, his iron will in pursuing those plans, his monstrous repressions in all strata of society, his supernatural hypnotic power (as I would call it), and, let us not forget, a preeminence in the country so colossal that it had been raised to the level of adoration—given all this, the victim-executioner could free himself from his criminal function only by doing away with himself. (And in fact, among officials of the NKVD apparatus there were cases of suicide and flight abroad; the latter was possible because intelligence officers, unlike people's commissars, were given foreign assignments.) In such circumstances, even the assassination of Stalin would only have confirmed the existence of a conspiracy and led to the continuance of the same unfounded repressions, plus the shooting of the victim-executioner.

For his chief henchmen, Stalin knew how to pick precisely those men who preferred to live as executioners rather than to leave life with a clear conscience. They all lived in Moscow, performed their "labor" on Lubyanka Square, and entered the same mousetrap as the victims, only by a different entrance.

To return to the "Letter," the actual author consciously contrived to help the executioners. Surely, I do not have to prove that his characterization of Yezhov and Kaganovich did not originate with Bukharin. Since the *Socialist Herald* supposedly received the "Letter of an Old Bolshevik" in December 1936, it became known in the Politburo at the moment when Yezhov stood in the full flower of his "creative" powers as head of the NKVD, the very moment when Bukharin and Rykov found themselves in his investigative clutches.

It is not difficult to imagine what effect this "Letter" had on Yezhov and Kaganovich.

I have chosen to discuss above only four of the more telling passages in this extended hoax. Why "hoax"? To explain what I mean with perfect clarity and conclude my reflections on the subject, I am obliged now to bring up later events.

I did not get a chance to take a close look at the court record in the case of the Anti-Soviet Bloc of Rightists and Trotskyists until I returned to Moscow from my last exile, in 1959. Even today, those events of fifty years ago cannot leave me indifferent toward the revolting show trial. I read and reread the court record until I had learned this encyclopedia of lies practically by heart. The justness of the court's deliberations is perhaps succinctly exemplified by a little slip of paper pasted into the volume:

Erratum: On p. 528, line 23 from the bottom, the printed "we" should read "you."*

The staged episode involving "the criminal connection of the counterrevolutionary Bloc of Rightists and Trotskyists" with the Second International, supposedly established by Bukharin and Rykov through the Menshevik émigré Boris Nicolaevsky, especially caught my eye, of course, since I had been present at the meetings with my husband and Nicolaevsky. There is no point in refuting Bukharin's forced statement at the trial about "the conspiracy," but it is extremely important, I think, to bring maximum clarity to the *Socialist Herald* articles.

I first learned about the "Letter of an Old Bolshevik" in 1965 from Ilya Ehrenburg, who had read it in Paris. I then acquainted myself with these materials.

Back in 1959, in the period we are accustomed to calling Khrushchev's "thaw," Boris Nicolaevsky admitted for the first time that he had written the "Letter of an Old Bolshevik" that had caused such a stir in its day. Evidently, rumors of his authorship had begun to leak out, and he could do nothing but announce that he himself, a Menshevik not an old Bolshevik, had written it. But he claimed that it reflected the substance of long conversations with Bukharin in Paris, discussions of matters not connected with the official trip to purchase the Marx archive.

Nicolaevsky's explanation for admitting his reprehensible act— "reprehensible," since his "Letter," as I hope I have been able to show, had a blatantly provocative aim—was that after Stalin's death a whole sheaf of letters had been written to the editors of the *Socialist Herald,* including one from the British Museum, asking whether it was not now time to reveal the identity of the "old Bolshevik."

I think it improbable there was actually such a rash of inquiries; if so, they were most likely organized by Nicolaevsky in order to facilitate still more inventions.

Certainly, it is unlikely that any Bolshevik would have written to the editors of the *Socialist Herald* at that time, except anonymously, even if he did consider it advantageous to himself (which is very doubtful) to send a letter to the press organ of the émigré Mensheviks and ask that the identity of the so-called old Bolshevik be revealed at last. After all, the Bolsheviks' attitude toward the *Socialist Herald* was by no means friendly.

After making his admission in 1959, Nicolaevsky promised the editors of the journal that he would write detailed recollections of his talks

*Ibid., p. 529.

with Bukharin, but he did not do so for another six years.

In December 1965, as introductory material to the republication of the "Letter of an Old Bolshevik" in the *Socialist Herald,* Nicolaevsky printed his version of his conversations with Nikolai Ivanovich in Paris in 1936. These recollections appeared in the form of an interview in which Nicolaevsky answers questions about the "Letter" posed by interviewers.

I cannot accurately surmise what source Nicolaevsky used to glean information that had not previously appeared in the Soviet press. Possibly, it was slipped to him specially in the expectation that he would publish it. In any event, Nicolaevsky skillfully reworked this information and filled it out with reflections attributed to the old Bolshevik, reflections that he as a Menshevik, with his splendid knowledge of Bolshevik Party history, could reconstruct with no great effort. Sad to say, not everyone in politics is decent.

At his trial, in March 1938, Bukharin was forced to testify that he had entered into an agreement with Nicolaevsky in Paris, had initiated him into conspiratorial plans, and had asked that the leaders of the Second International start a press campaign in defense of the Soviet conspirators if they failed. But Nicolaevsky responded that same month by printing a refutation of this forced testimony:

> Without exception, all of my meetings with Bukharin, as well as with the other members of the commission, proceeded within the confines of precisely these negotiations [i.e., for the purchase of the archive]. Nothing even remotely resembling conversations of a political nature took place during the course of these meetings.

One could assume that Nicolaevsky might be concealing the truth in order to shield Bukharin, except for one fact: the provocational "Letter" had already been published.

When, almost three decades later, Nicolaevsky suddenly produced his version of his conversations with Bukharin, these "recollections" were so extensive that if such talks had really taken place there would have been no time left over for business negotiations.

The basic foundation for this ex post facto creation was provided by facts well known to Nicolaevsky the historian, but in order to give them greater verisimilitude, Nicolaevsky the writer touches them up with colorful details. I cannot deny that he shows a truly creative imagination, but it is inappropriate here, for only truthful recollections of Bukharin can sustain interest. False accounts lead researchers astray, especially foreigners who use Nicolaevsky's publications. This happened, for example, to the American Sovietologist Stephen F. Cohen when he was elucidating several matters in his superb book *Bukharin and the Bolshevik Revolution*, and to others as well.

For one thing, Nicolaevsky tries to portray himself falsely as Bukharin's trusted confidant rather than as his political opponent.

I have already explained what actually happened when Nicolaevsky asked after his brother in my presence, but what does he write in his "recollections," the so-called interview?

> The first evening, when he [Bukharin] came to see me, his first words were "Greetings from Vladimir." Later, when Bukharin and I found an opportunity to talk alone, he added, "Aleksei [Rykov] sends you his greetings." This set the tone for our subsequent talks.

Thus, Nicolaevsky exploits his family relationship with Rykov in order to characterize his conversations with Bukharin as talks based upon mutual trust.

To attempt to show that he was close to Bukharin, Nicolaevsky reported in this 1965 "interview" that in Amsterdam and Copenhagen, where he worked on the documents of Marx and Engels, Bukharin took him in his free time through the museums. Certainly, Nikolai Ivanovich had enthusiastically told me about his visit to the museum of natural history in Amsterdam, about its priceless collections of butterflies. Since the bulk of the archive was located in Copenhagen, he was kept very busy there; I recall nothing about visits to museums in Denmark, but I could have forgotten. But when Nicolaevsky claims that Nikolai Ivanovich filled his briefcase with photographs of paintings by the old masters in a Copenhagen museum, I begin to doubt that the Menshevik ever was in Denmark. Nikolai Ivanovich owned no briefcase, nor did he bring any photographs with him from Copenhagen to Paris. He told me that Friedrich Adler had accompanied him from Vienna to Denmark and Holland; there was no mention of Nicolaevsky in that regard.

When you know for certain that someone lies in big things, you do not trust him in small ones. Even if we suppose that Nicolaevsky was actually in Denmark and Holland, why should Bukharin spend any free time with him and not with the other two members of the commission? In Paris, as I've noted, every encounter I saw between Bukharin and Nicolaevsky was official.

Rather than touch upon all of the questions raised by Nicolaevsky's inventive improvisation, I will focus only on those that particularly struck me.

For example, even though Nicolaevsky speaks fairly about Bukharin's humanitarian motives—about what Nikolai Ivanovich called socialist or proletarian humanism set in opposition to fascism (as illustrated so vividly in his appearance at the Sorbonne, his last public speech)—he also invents a plethora of incidents and opinions that are alien to Bukharin. And when an interviewer asks, "Were Bukharin's views known to Stalin?," Nicolaevsky gives himself away entirely, declaring, "Stalin could not have failed to know the essence of Bukharin's views. Bukharin not only propagandized his views widely in the ranks of the Communists but also wrote openly about proletarian humanism in the press."

Nicolaevsky's reference to Bukharin's supposed remarks about Lenin's political testament is frankly ludicrous, in the full sense of the word. Bukharin is quoted as asserting that the testament had two parts— the shorter, about the leaders; the longer, about the tasks of the Party— and then explaining what principles Lenin deemed necessary to lay at the foundation of politics. Supposedly, also, Bukharin brought up two of his own pamphlets: "The Path to Socialism and the Worker-Peasant Alliance" (1925) and "Lenin's Political Testament" (1929). The first was written at a time when Stalin did not contest Bukharin's views and when his position seemed secure. Consequently, when expounding Lenin's views, he did not give citations from the original materials. The second was a speech delivered at a somber meeting to commemorate the fifth anniversary of Lenin's death, after Bukharin had come under fire from Stalin. For this reason, he gives citations from the last works of Lenin. This was the chief difference between the two pamphlets.

Nicolaevsky claims in his interview that he had not read the first work. This ploy allows him to create a conversation in which Bukharin maintains that the pamphlet was based on personal talks with Lenin, who (again, according to this "interview") felt that Nikolai Ivanovich was the ablest person to expound his thoughts if he were not able to do so. But, in fact, Lenin did manage to explain himself in his last articles: "Pages from a Diary," "About Our Revolution," "On Cooperation," "How Can We Reorganize the Rabkrin [Workers and Peasants Inspection]," "Better Less, But Better." And really, did Bukharin need to waste his time in Paris explaining to this "poorly educated" historian that Lenin's testament included the thought that it might be possible to arrive at socialism without resorting to coercion against the peasantry? Can we really believe that Nicolaevsky, with his firm knowledge of the history of the Social Democratic movement in general and the Bolshevik

Party in particular, however hostile his attitude toward Lenin, never actually read him?

And it is certainly beyond belief that the ailing Lenin (as suggested in the "interview") would summon Bukharin and, over the protests of his wife and physicians, lead him out into the garden. This little scene in no way corresponds to the character of Bukharin or to his actual relations with Vladimir Ilyich and Nadezhda Konstantinovna. Bukharin was indeed one of the few who visited and talked with Lenin during his serious illness, but only when the doctors gave permission. Nikolai Ivanovich told me that one time he rode to Gorki with Zinoviev and saw the ailing Lenin through a fence.

But the author of this "interview," citing Bukharin as his source, reports not only these unimaginable talks with Lenin but also their content. Supposedly, the two men spoke mostly about "leaderology," the problem of succession. (Whom Lenin supposedly named as his successor, Nicolaevsky does not say.) Such a conversation would not at all have been in the Bolshevik tradition. The outstanding figures in the Party were thrust forward by history, and in those times they were called Party leaders, not the "Great Leader," as later became the rule.

In conclusion, I want to mention some of Nicolaevsky's invented incidents that are not so important in the political sense.

A conversation he creates about the writing of the Soviet constitution, enacted in December 1936, is simply mind-boggling. Supposedly, Bukharin said to him, "Look carefully, the whole new constitution was written with this pen, from first to last." And here he pulled a fountain pen out of his pocket and showed it to the Menshevik. "I performed this work alone, only Karlusha helped me a little. [Nicolaevsky must have known that many people called Radek "Karlusha."] I was able to come to Paris only because the work was completed."

This scene is entirely the fruit of Nicolaevsky's imagination. Far from writing the entire constitution, Nikolai Ivanovich wrote only the legal part. He wrote at home with a standard-tip school pen; he did not like the "fountain" pen type. He did not take this school pen to Paris; consequently, he could not have shown it to Nicolaevsky. Furthermore, Bukharin needed no help from Radek, just as Radek, a member of the constitutional commission, needed no help from Bukharin.

I was amazed to see myself introduced as a personage in Nicolaevsky's imaginative play:

> Bukharin was obviously tired; he longed for many months of vacation, wanted to take a trip to the sea. At that moment his young wife came up to us. She was expecting her first child, also

needed rest, and showed obvious satisfaction when her husband began to speak of the sea.

Here the improviser's creativity knows no limits. One was permitted to take a leave of many months only when ill; moreover, Nikolai Ivanovich was looking forward to taking his vacation in the Pamir Mountains. There was no talk of going to the sea; neither Bukharin nor I could have cherished such daydreams. I expected the baby any day and in fact gave birth several days after coming home from Paris.

Nicolaevsky even permits himself this fiction:

> When we were in Copenhagen, Bukharin recalled that Trotsky lived not too far off, in Oslo, and said, "Why not take a trip for a day or two to Norway to visit with Lev Davydovich?" And then he added, "Of course, there were great conflicts between us, but this does not prevent me from holding him in great respect."

Although I was not in Copenhagen, I see perfectly well that this is another of Nicolaevsky's concoctions. I don't even mean the fact that Bukharin could not have traveled to and from Oslo without a visa, so the trip would have had to be clandestine, something he would never have agreed to do. More to the point, Nikolai Ivanovich told me that in his polemical skirmishes with Trotsky he had lost respect for him. I expect the same could be said for Trotsky, so he would hardly have welcomed Bukharin with open arms.

Nicolaevsky's story about Bukharin's meeting with Fanny Yezerskaya produces no less astonishment. Formerly Rosa Luxemburg's secretary and a member of the German Communist Party, she had worked in the Comintern and been part of the opposition. When Hitler came to power, she emigrated to France. She was never close to Nikolai Ivanovich but had made friends with my parents. In fact, Fanya Natanovna, as she was called in our family, had known me since I was a little girl. Nicolaevsky claims that she urged Bukharin to become head of a foreign oppositional newspaper; he alone, in her opinion, could handle the job of editor and ensure that the journal was well informed about events in Russia. In other words, she supposedly proposed to Bukharin that he become a nonreturnee and remain in Paris. According to this account, Bukharin turned down the offer only because he had become accustomed to the setup in the Soviet Union and the accelerated pace of life there.

In actual fact, the only time Yezerskaya met with Bukharin during our trip was in the Hotel Lutetia. I was there at her arrival and departure and heard the entire conversation. They spoke about the Seventh Co-mintern Congress and the united front in the battle against fascism. Yezerskaya said that life was hard for her in France; she was working in a factory. She had many questions about life in the Soviet Union, and Nikolai Ivanovich told her approximately the same things he had said to Nicolaevsky in the conversation I've already described. Nothing in Yezerskaya's talk with Bukharin even remotely resembled Nicolaevsky's crude fabrications in the "interview." How is it possible to lie so blatantly? Evidently, by the time of publication, Yezerskaya was either no longer living or no longer able to read Nicolaevsky's "works."

Had Bukharin's official trip coincided with the trial of Zinoviev and Kamenev (August 1936), his mood might have corresponded to Nicola-evsky's assessment. Even then he would have rushed back to Moscow to refute the accusations, but it is conceivable, under such circumstances, that someone might have naively decided to ask him to remain abroad, assuming that in France or another western European country, or perhaps in America, he would escape harm—all the more so since life had not yet proved the opposite to be true for others.

But the Paris trip ended in April, and I don't have to prove that, up until August, Nikolai Ivanovich did not foresee his downfall. His articles and speeches, including the Sorbonne speech, prove this. The very fact that not long before the catastrophe he, a middle-aged man, not only joined his life with me, a young person, but also wished to have a child speaks volumes. Can one suspect Nikolai Ivanovich of passionately wanting a child who would, like himself, be doomed to excruciating agony?

The subjects of the conversations Nicolaevsky invented between himself and Bukharin were truly seditious for those times. To stress this point, he reports that Arosev, supposedly present at one of them, became frightened and remarked, "Look, we're leaving, but you'll be able to write up sensational memoirs." Nicolaevsky has himself replying, "Let's make an agreement: the last one living will write openly about our meetings." He failed, of course, to take me into account. Indeed, could it ever have entered his mind that I would read his compositions? Nicola-evsky miscalculated: the last one turned out to be me.

I trust that I have revealed the true value of B. I. Nicolaevsky's "recollections." I consider both the "Letter of an Old Bolshevik" and the "interview" with Nicolaevsky to be spurious documents, the latter composed almost thirty years after the first.*

---

*A fuller account of the Nicolaevsky question is given in the Russian edition of this book.

There is another strange document connected with Bukharin's visit to Paris: the memoir of Lidiya Osipovna Dan, wife of Fyodor Dan and sister of his fellow Menshevik leader Yuly Martov. Twenty-eight years after Bukharin's departure from Paris and twenty-six years after his death, it was published in *Novyi zhurnal* [The new review (New York)], no. 75, 1964, after the death of its author.

What interests me is her account of Bukharin's meeting with her husband.

I have already described the one time they met, which Nikolai Ivanovich had anticipated as "something out of a fairy tale," and Dan's refusal to participate further in the negotiations for the sale of the archive.

But Dan's wife writes that Nikolai Ivanovich was feeling absolutely doomed that April and came on his own to Dan because "his soul simply craved it." She asserts that Bukharin said, "Stalin is not a man but a devil." And also: "Stalin will gobble them all up [the Bolsheviks]." By her account, he returned to Moscow only because he did not want to become an émigré.

The very title of this memoir, "Bukharin on Stalin," points to the supposed purpose of Bukharin's visit, but could he have actually gone to Dan in April 1936 in order to compromise Stalin, when he had no reason to? He could not have gone to see him any later!

The story is sprinkled with inane details, like this: "But look here, Fyodor Ilyich," Bukharin supposedly says to Dan, "if fascism flares up here, you go straight to our embassy and they'll give you refuge there." Or this: "He [Bukharin] obviously regretted that such a mighty force as Dan was going to waste." Actually, Bukharin thought Dan's work was valueless. On the other hand, he did not wish him ill at the hands of the fascists and did want him to join a united front against them.

This fabricated memoir attempts to prove that Bukharin was Dan's welcome, if not invited, guest. And historians abroad found this easy to believe, operating on the principle that what the pen has writ the ax cannot split.

According to Lidiya Osipovna, the visit occurred after the Marx and Engels documents had all been examined and the haggling over the price had begun, but I was in Paris then and can attest that Nikolai Ivanovich never went to see Dan. Yet and still, Dan's wife (or perhaps someone acting in her stead) writes that Bukharin was so carried away by his attacks on Stalin that he stayed from two o'clock in the afternoon until eight at night. This simply could not be. I was so close to giving birth, as I have noted before, that Nikolai Ivanovich would never have left me alone for such an extended period.

Even if I were not an eyewitness to the truth, I would be unable to believe that Bukharin would have met unofficially with Dan because "his soul simply craved it." But, since I cannot assume that everyone will accept my testimony, I will try to disprove this falsehood by means of Lidiya Osipovna's article itself. After this ultra-sensational secret meeting with Bukharin, she reports, in which he was far more candid than even in his supposed meetings with Nicolaevsky, her husband told no one about the incident, "not even Nicolaevsky, the most natural person to tell, for he considered that this might become dangerous to Bukharin in some way." Therefore, we are asked to believe that Dan did not impart his "dangerous" information to Nicolaevsky and then further demonstrated his "protection" of Bukharin by publishing the "Letter of an Old Bolshevik" in the *Socialist Herald.*

Fyodor Dan passed away in 1947, nine years after Bukharin's execution. At that point, there was no need to fear unpleasant consequences for Nikolai Ivanovich. Yet Dan took the secret of their meeting and the inflammatory quotation "Stalin will gobble them all up" to the grave. Surely, the best time to reveal this accurate prophecy would have been right after Bukharin was shot. Why, then, did Dan keep silent? Evidently, because what could not have taken place did not in fact take place.

Other inexplicable "reminiscences" by Dan's wife also arouse one's suspicions. For example, she writes, "Although the authorities undoubtedly knew at least about the meeting and the negotiations in the Lutetia, the meetings there and the others with Nicolaevsky and Dan, not one word was said about them at the trial." This contradicts the actual accusations made against Bukharin and Rykov during the trial, where interventionist intentions against the Soviet Union were ascribed to Dan himself. In fact, he was called a German spy and an agent of German intelligence in the fantastic testimony of the accused Mikhail Chernov, former people's commissar of land—and a former Menshevik, a detail that the prosecutor Vyshinsky [himself a former Menshevik] accentuated. ("Rather than strain to make out someone else, wouldn't it be better, cousin, to take a look at yourself?" as Ivan Krylov wrote in "Monkey and Mirror.") Chernov further testified that, in their criminal designs, Bukharin and Rykov were connected with representatives of the Second International through Nicolaevsky.

I haven't been able to find out whether the manuscript of Lidiya Dan's reminiscences is actually kept in the British Museum, as stated in the preface to the posthumous publication. If such a script exists and is in her own hand, I can only voice regret that this sister of Yuly Martov, whose moral qualities were deservedly prized by political friend and foe alike, resorted to such a falsification. I myself doubt it.

[The Storm Descends: Stalin and Bukharin]

Bukharin's regret over his unproductive Paris trip did not last long. In fact, he put it behind him after Stalin said, "Don't worry, Nikolai, we'll acquire the archive; they'll give in yet." Nikolai Ivanovich resumed his normal life, absorbed in his work for *Izvestiya,* for the Academy of Sciences, and for the commission to draft a new constitution. Nothing clouded his sunny disposition. Several days after our return, a son was born to us, and the forty-seven-year-old father was cast into a state of pure joy. He was happy; he truly exulted! He could not have suspected what a heavy fate awaited his son, but something else did worry him. "Yurochka!" he once exclaimed to the infant, half joking. "I fear when you grow up, I'll be old and moldy and won't be able to walk with you in the forest to go hunting! No, no," he dispelled his own misgiving, "I'll be hardy for a long time yet. We'll roam the woods together, and I'll tell you lots of interesting things." His knowledge of the Russian forest could perhaps be compared only to that of the nature writer Mikhail Prishvin.

Soon after Yura's birth, we left the city and lived nearby the station Skhodnya, where dachas belonging to *Izvestiya* editors were located. Karl Radek's was not far from ours. This was the only summer when, because of the baby, Nikolai Ivanovich made it back to the dacha every night for two months running, often after working at the newspaper until quite late. He had never before had a dacha where he could stay on a permanent basis. Instead, he had stayed for short periods at dachas in Lenin Hills, with Stalin in Zubalovo (mid-1920s to 1928), and with Rykov in Valuyevo, right beside an aspen forest into which he would dash to go hunting for hazel grouse. Later, he stayed at my father's dacha in Serebryany Bor. After all, Bukharin was always in motion, and the settled dacha way of life was not in his character.

Nikolai Ivanovich's vacation came in early August, and he decided to fulfill his cherished dream, a visit to the Pamir Mountains. Briefly, we had considered postponing his trip to the following year, since the baby and I could not travel, but we came to the conclusion that there was no point in putting it off. The past year of intensive work demanded intensive rest. Relaxation, reunion with nature—these were indispensable to him. We assumed there would be time enough for us to travel together in the future.

Nikolai Ivanovich left straight from the dacha for the Pamirs. The day before, he had brought his luggage from Moscow, filled with the requisite accoutrements for his vacation: a sketchbook, paints, and canvases for landscapes; cartridges, small shot, and a rifle for hunting. The car stood ready beside the porch, fussed over by the chauffeur Nikolai Klykov, or Klychini, as my husband called him. He had become such a close personal attendant that Nikolai Ivanovich never sat down to table without inviting him to join in. Usually, they would get to talking. In plain language, Bukharin would explain both the national and the international political events of the day to Klykov, who was keenly interested. Nikolai Ivanovich never spoke down to him, for they conversed as equals—and on more than one occasion the editor borrowed money from his chauffeur. On the road, they often sang Russian folk songs, a special passion for Bukharin. You would hear a duet like this one: "Pretty me, ah pretty me, and yet so poorly dressed; / No one wants me for a bride although I am the best." Or like this: "By the silver river, on the pure white beach; / Long I sought the footprints from a maiden's feet."

Bukharin did not look like a refined intellectual, though few could compare with him in intellect. He wore Russian boots, but not because they had become the fashion among the Bolsheviks during the civil war and after; he had begun wearing them in his youth, long before the revolution, because they suited his way of life. Instead of a hat, he wore a cap, because, as he put it, a hat on his head looked like a skullcap on a pig. In fact, he never wore a hat except when traveling abroad. The first time he was invited to a diplomatic reception in Moscow, the Commission of Foreign Affairs warned him over the phone to dress accordingly, but he replied, "The Russian proletariat knows me in a leather jacket and cap, boots and a cossack shirt, and that's how I will appear at the reception."

His behavior was in harmony with his appearance. He could spit like a muzhik through his teeth or whistle like a street urchin, and he permitted himself impish pranks. At the same time, he was a person of remarkably fine sensitivity, almost maidenly shyness, and, as I have already noted, an emotionality so intense that it verged on the pathological.

He could look completely different, from one moment to the next. Sometimes, he looked like a simple Russian muzhik with merry, clever, darting eyes; at other times, a thinker with a deep, pensive, sorrowful gaze fixed on some distant point.

Similarly, his eloquent manifestos and pamphlets, painstakingly written in a minuscule hand, and his complex theoretical investigations, overflowing with foreign words and phrases accessible only to a limited circle of readers, alternated with speeches, articles, brochures, and books written in a popular style for a wide public audience. (My father gave me Bukharin's exceedingly popular *The ABCs of Communism* to study when I was thirteen years old.)

On the other hand, he never posed as one of the people, never played up to the people—rather, he was the living flesh of the people, a simple man and intellectual at one and the same time, an uncorrupted, pure spirit to the end of his life. This is what Klykov found appealing in him, and this is why Bukharin in turn felt so naturally at ease with his chauffeur.

And so, the last happy minutes—everything is ready for departure. "We're off, Klychini!"

Nikolai Ivanovich said farewell to me and Yura, kissed the boy, and added, "You'll grow like the tsarevich in *The Tale of Tsar Saltan,* not by the day but by the hour. When I come home, you'll shoot the kite out of the sky. Then we can go running with you!" [In Pushkin's tale, the tsarevich shoots an arrow through a kite that is attacking a swan.]

The little tyke looked up at his father with bright, shining eyes and smiled, obviously without understanding but with incredible happiness.

"Let's sit a moment before leaving," Nikolai Ivanovich proposed, in keeping with Russian custom.

The day was hot. An immense ravine cut through the tract of dachas; in memory, its outline now reminds me of that Siberian gorge where I was once taken to be shot. We sat down on the overhang in the shade of spruces and burst into song: "Sasha, five years I have lived with you, angel without flaw, / Perhaps the hour of reckoning has struck, and I have broke my vow!" We sang loudly and merrily. The neighborhood kids ran up to listen. Finally, we stood up and went to the car. Nikolai Ivanovich got in next to Klykov and, radiant with anticipation of the pleasure of the trip ahead, peered out the car window. I would never again see Bukharin like this.

But just as the travelers were about to start off, Nikolai Ivanovich's thirteen-year-old nephew, who lived with us in the dacha and was also named Nikolai and called Kolya, started bawling. (He was the son of Nikolai Ivanovich's younger brother, Vladimir.) Through his tears, sobbing, the boy cried out hysterically, "Uncle Kolya, don't go! Uncle Kolya, don't go!" There was something eerie and mystical in that sobbing, as if the boy had a presentiment that he was seeing his uncle for the last time.

"Don't be so quick to bury me, Kolya!" Nikolai Ivanovich said to calm his nephew. "I'll come back soon, you'll grow up, and we'll ride in the mountains together. I have common sense enough not to break my neck."

At last, the car drove through the gates, disappeared from view, and headed for the airport. At that moment, I could never have guessed that in the days immediately ahead the joy of life would desert us. The summer day was so hot and sunny, and the baby was smiling. (Still, young Kolya went on sobbing for a while.)

Nikolai Ivanovich was accompanied on his trek by his secretary, Semyon Lyandres, father of the writer Julian Semyonov, whose work became extremely popular in the 1970s and 1980s. Because Semyon was not blessed with good health, Bukharin tried to talk him out of a trip that demanded physical strength and training, but in vain.

Semyon had revered Nikolai Ivanovich ever since they had worked together in the Supreme Soviet of the National Economy; he had served under him as a secretary and then transferred with him to *Izvestiya*. I know well that Nikolai Ivanovich in turn was attached to Lyandres.

After Nikolai Ivanovich's departure, two weeks passed without any real cause for concern, even though I received no word from him. He was venturing into wild areas where no post office, let alone telegraph, would be found. I easily calmed myself with the thought that he was not alone in the mountains. In addition to Semyon, I supposed, there would be a guide who would to some degree guarantee the safety of the trek.

Shortly before his departure, as I remember now, Nikolai Ivanovich had come home with the grave news of Grigory Sokolnikov's arrest. Significantly, Bukharin failed to such a degree to foresee the impending mass terror and the imminent trials, mere days away, that he absolutely ruled out political motives in this arrest. He assumed that Sokolnikov had overspent government funds when he was Soviet ambassador to London; in a word, Nikolai Ivanovich put the whole thing down to financial impropriety and hoped for Sokolnikov's speedy release.

But soon the last day of tranquillity drew near. Disaster fell upon us all at once, like a squall. The trial of Zinoviev, Kamenev, and the others, the so-called trial of the Trotskyist United Center, began on August 19, 1936. There was the horrendous accusation that they were involved in the murder of Kirov; there were the terrible, incomprehensible confessions of the accused. I recall Zinoviev declaring in the dock that individual terror might contradict Marx but that in the final analysis all means are acceptable in times of war. This particular choice of phrasing put me on guard. Allegedly, Zinoviev and Kamenev had ordered Kirov's assassination, but their motives were left unexplained. Even so, I have to admit frankly that I came to the conclusion that the defendants must be guilty of something or other, perhaps a secret conspiracy against Stalin. But when they began to point their fingers at Bukharin, Rykov, and Tomsky, I went crazy. The shock was so great that by that evening I had lost my milk.

On August 21, the State Prosecutor's Office announced an investigation in the case of Bukharin, Rykov, Tomsky, Radek, and others mentioned in the trial who were presumed to be involved with the defendants in counterrevolutionary activity. Angry resolutions had been passed at Party meetings: "Put the accused in the dock!" and the like. The following day, Mikhail Tomsky's suicide was reported. Since I had heard nothing from Nikolai Ivanovich, I suspected he had already been arrested. I tried to find out something from *Izvestiya*, but no one there knew anything either. Finally, on August 25 or the day after, Bukharin's secretary at the paper, Korotkova, called to tell me that he had flown out of Tashkent, would arrive in Moscow in the afternoon, and had asked me to come meet him. She had already alerted Klykov to come pick me up in Skhodnya; he showed up soon afterward, his face grim and sallow.

"Well," he said, "we parted so joyfully, and now what a sad meeting!"

We took the baby to my mother's apartment in the Metropol and my old grandmother to a communal apartment on Novo-Basmannaya Street. On the way, I managed to whisper to her, "Nikolai will not live; they'll shoot him for sure!" Granny looked at me with delirious eyes. Later, I would remember my statement time and time again. It meant that I already understood a lot at that moment.

I want very much to look honestly inside my former self, to perceive Nikolai Ivanovich as he actually was in those days, and to avoid any aberrations. This is not so simple as it may seem. The perspective of viewing things from the present can add a lot, it can make you wiser than you were, and then it can seem that you also saw things earlier that way.

"When face to face, the person cannot be seen. You must survey the big things from a distance." Applied to the infamous events of 1936, these words of the poet Sergei Yesenin were right twice over.

We were a bit late getting to the airport. Nikolai Ivanovich, keeping out of sight, was sitting on a bench in a corner. He looked ill and distraught. He had wanted me to come to the airport because he feared he would be arrested there. At his request, Semyon Lyandres had stayed around to shield him from curious, possibly hostile glances. Bukharin was often recognized in public, and it was very painful for him at the moment. He did not have the heart to look people in the eye, so abominable did he consider the accusations brought against him. His things, the suitcase and the rest, he had left in Frunze perhaps, or possibly in Tashkent. They would show up much later. The only thing he had grabbed to bring along with him was a little bell, the kind they tie to domestic animals in the mountains so that they won't get lost. He held it in his hand. Over his shoulder hung a pair of decorative wool socks. These and the bell were a gift for Yura, although the boy was not yet four full months old and could have slipped completely into one of the socks. At the moment, however, I was not thinking of the comically eccentric aspect of this gesture. Nikolai Ivanovich spoke first:

"If I could have foreseen such a thing, I would have run a mile away from you!"

I tried to mollify him. "They'll sort it out, you know. It'll get cleared up." But I was also pessimistic about the whole thing. Catching sight of Klykov, Nikolai Ivanovich felt ashamed and burst out, "It's all a lie, a lie, Nikolai Nikolayevich, and I will prove it!"

Klykov reacted to Bukharin's cry from the heart with a look of anguish and kept silent.

At last, the forlorn chauffeur asked, "Where to, Nikolai Ivanovich?"

Bukharin hesitated, constantly looking around to see whether they had come with an order for his arrest. He expressed his doubt that the Kremlin guard would let him in to our apartment. Of course, he could go to the dacha instead, but there was no *vertushka* [special dial] telephone there with a direct line to Stalin.

"What will be will be!" he finally replied to his chauffeur. "Let's go to the apartment."

We stopped by the Metropol for the baby and then headed to the Kremlin through the Borovitskiye Gates. As usual, the guard on duty stopped the car to check documents. Nikolai Ivanovich presented his official card; the guard honored it as if nothing were amiss.

"Maybe he doesn't read the papers?" Nikolai Ivanovich remarked, and we drove up safely to the entrance.

In our apartment, Bukharin's aged father, all agitated, met his son with these words: "What are you doing, Kolka, traveling all the time, while God knows what's going on here!"

But Nikolai Ivanovich did not seem even to hear his father. He ran swiftly into his study and started dialing Stalin. An unfamiliar voice answered:

"Iosif Vissarionovich is in Sochi."

"In Sochi at such a time!"

How painful it is to recall this now. Here was Nikolai Ivanovich seeking salvation from his own executioner! Obvious as this may seem now, it was not so then, at that tragic moment. Perhaps it seems impossible that Bukharin could not understand, could not even imagine that the shameful show trial of Zinoviev and Kamenev could have occurred only if Stalin had wished it. The instinct for self-preservation kept this thought from him, although it should indeed have been obvious to him that it was Stalin who had already succeeded not only in crucifying Zinoviev, Kamenev, and other Bolsheviks but also in putting into their mouths the words that incriminated them and implicated their comrades. On the contrary, Bukharin felt unbelievable rancor toward "the slanderers" Zinoviev and Kamenev, but definitely not toward Stalin. His hatred of these two, especially Kamenev, had deep roots, as should be obvious from what I have recounted about them earlier.

Toward Genghis Khan, as Nikolai Ivanovich had dubbed Stalin at the time of their sharpest disagreements in 1928, he had changed his attitude and saw now little but morbid suspiciousness. He thought that salvation lay in dispelling that suspiciousness. At least, that was his view in the beginning; I have to report that truth, galling as it is to recall it. Possibly, if Bukharin had thought differently, he would have lost the impetus to oppose the incriminating testimony.

Many others, at that time, were unable to separate truth from falsehood and also remained in a state of unending consternation. In *Catastrophe and Rebirth,* prison memoirs that are remarkably subtle in the psychological sense, Yevgeny Gnedin wrote, "I have noticed, by the way, that remarks encountered in the memoirs of Ilya Ehrenburg about the naïveté of seemingly level-headed people provoke needless incredulity in modern readers."

This naïveté led many to believe in the trials for the simple reason that they would have otherwise been at a loss to explain what was happening. Similarly, those who did not believe in toto nevertheless believed that a plot against Stalin had been uncovered. So long as they themselves were not accused of a nonexistent plot, the people who knew him best and appreciated his moral qualities could readily believe that others would plot against the leader. Finally, naïveté was manifest when the accused continued to seek salvation from the tyrant himself. There was a certain logic in this, to be sure, for indeed the only one who could save them from the terror was the very one who had inspired and organized it. Still, it was naive to assume that their "dear father" would spare them, would not have them put to death.

It is difficult to believe that Bukharin became one among the many in this regard; in the beginning, that was indeed the case. He saw salvation only in Stalin.

I remember numerous examples of this widespread naïveté, but I will mention only the most glaring.

Twenty years later, after my release and return to Moscow, I got to know an old Bolshevik named Nikanorov who had also suffered in the years of the terror. He had served his term of confinement in the same camp as Ivan Makhanov, the chief designer at the artillery design office of the Kirov (Putilov) factory. According to Nikanorov, Makhanov told the following story, which greatly upset me and left an ineradicable impression.

During the trial of Zinoviev and Kamenev, the chief designer, Makhanov, and the director of the factory, K. I. Ots (later shot), had an appointment with Stalin to discuss problems of production. As they sat in the waiting room beforehand, they saw Lenin's sister, Mariya Ilyinichna Ulyanova, and his widow, Nadezhda Konstantinovna Krupskaya, go into the Gensek's office. Makhanov and Ots could not hear everything in the conversation that followed, but through the shouting and swearing one sentence reached them distinctly. Stalin screamed, "Who are you defending? You are defending murderers!" Then Mariya Ilyinichna and Nadezhda Konstantinovna were conducted out of the office by two men who had to brace them by the arms. Pale and shaking with emotion, the women were unable to walk by themselves. Had they, too, the Ulyanovs, failed to understand that the show trial was Stalin's doing? It is well known that relations between Nadezhda Konstantinovna and Stalin were strained by the rudeness he allowed himself to show her during Lenin's illness. Yet to whom did the women turn for help in the battle against despotism? And before whom did they defend the honor of the Party and plead, as a bare minimum, for the lives of Zinoviev and Kamenev? The criminal dictator himself.

And, similarly, the celebrated Red Army commander Iona Yakir, who had demonstrated his courage not only during the civil war but also in the period of unbridled terror, tried to save arrested military men by appealing directly to Stalin. For example, Yakir's wife, Sarra Lazarevna, told me that he turned to the Gensek after the arrest of Dmitry Shmidt, tank commander of the Kiev Military District, who was charged with intending to organize a terrorist act against Voroshilov. Yakir was able to meet with Shmidt in prison. According to the usual version, Voroshilov arranged the visit, during which Shmidt repudiated his testimony and found an opportunity to give Yakir a note for Voroshilov denying the charge. But Yakir's wife told me that the prison meeting was actually arranged through Stalin. Aloud, Shmidt confirmed his incriminating testimony to Yakir but on parting did surreptitiously slip into his hand a note to Voroshilov denying any involvement in terror and explaining that his testimony had been wrenched out of him by torture. Yakir sent the note to Voroshilov, but Shmidt's situation did not change: he remained in prison. Yakir also turned to Stalin after the arrest of Ilya Garkavy, commander of the Ural Military District, and in many other instances.

I mentioned earlier the letter Robert Eikhe sent from his prison cell to Stalin, discovered in the tyrant's archive when he died. How many such letters were addressed to the "Father of the Peoples" is beyond reckoning.

And so Nikolai Ivanovich, too, placed his hopes in Stalin, continued to be amazed that the Gensek could have gone to Sochi at such a time, and waited impatiently for him to return. To judge from Makhanov's story, however, Stalin was right there in Moscow for the Zinoviev-Kamenev show trial and did not leave for Sochi until afterward. There, the bloodthirsty leader did not simply rest: he combined relaxation with energetic efforts to escalate his tyranny. Or, more precisely, he rested twice over, for tyranny is gratification for a sadist.

Nikolai Ivanovich did consider it pointless to telephone Yagoda, although of course he could not foresee that the head of the NKVD was living out his last days in office and would join Bukharin as a fellow defendant in the dock.

Meanwhile, there was nothing to do but wait and see which would come first: Koba returning from Sochi, or the prison doors slamming shut.

We were sitting by the telephone on the desk in Nikolai Ivanovich's study. Little birds twittered in the animal enclosure there; in the stroller, a hungry child kicked his feet and howled till he was red in the face. I picked him up and pushed a dry breast into his little mouth. Grandpa Ivan Gavrilovich had bought some milk in a store, not "from one cow only," as experts in Skhodnya had recommended. He took up his grandson and fed him himself. Now an oppressive silence reigned in the study. While we still had some time left, Nikolai Ivanovich told me how he had found out about the Zinoviev-Kamenev trial.

Because Semyon Lyandres had fallen ill, they came down from the mountains to Frunze earlier than planned. Once they got there, Nikolai Ivanovich lay down to rest and fell asleep. He was awakened by Semyon, who held out a newspaper to him and exclaimed, "Nikolai Ivanovich, can you really and truly be a traitor?"

"Semyon! You must have lost your mind," Bukharin replied, shaken. But when he glanced at the paper, he was horrified.

Semyon himself confirmed this account when I saw him in March 1937, after Nikolai Ivanovich's arrest.

They got to Frunze on August 25, or perhaps August 24, I'm not sure now; at any rate, it was the day when the sentence of the supreme penalty had been announced for Zinoviev, Kamenev, and the others but, apparently, not yet carried out. Immediately, Nikolai Ivanovich sent Stalin a telegram requesting a delay in executing the sentence and asking for a direct confrontation with Zinoviev in order to find out the truth. Today, such an act may be regarded as a total misapprehension of what was going on; the truth was not at all what was needed. Naturally, the telegram produced no result. To think, as Aleksandr Solzhenitsyn does, that Bukharin could have somehow altered the course of events—"Did he spring into action and hold back all this repression?"—is to understand nothing of the situation that had developed. Considering the actual circumstances and Bukharin's position while under investigation, such an approach would have been quixotic.

As we sat, Ivan Gavrilovich neatly laid the newspapers reporting the trial down on the desk. Nikolai Ivanovich spied the report of Tomsky's suicide that, as best I recall now, explained that he had killed himself after getting mixed up with counterrevolutionary Zinoviev-Kamenev terrorists. "Nonsense!" Bukharin exclaimed, adding some vulgar expressions. I noticed that he was more disturbed by this interpretation of Tomsky's suicide than by the loss of a dear friend—a morally pure comrade, as he had once characterized him. Most probably, it was at this instant that he realized that the situation of many, including himself and Rykov, was hopeless. By now, my husband's disposition changed not only daily but hourly.

He had first heard about Tomsky's suicide back in Tashkent, with a singularly striking effect. I learned about this incident from a later account by the writer Kamil Ikramov, son of the first secretary of the Uzbek Central Committee, Akmal Ikramov. When Bukharin and Lyandres went from Frunze to Tashkent on their way back to Moscow, it was decided to put Nikolai Ivanovich up in a governmental dacha. The Uzbek Central Committee's second secretary, Tsekher, asked the dacha superintendent, Shamshanov, to meet the guest and take him to the dacha. From the newspapers, it was already well known that Bukharin was under investigation on charges of the most serious crimes against the Soviet state. Shamshanov, very apprehensive, refused to go alone, without witnesses, and asked Tsekher to accompany him. At the dacha, these two showed Nikolai Ivanovich the latest newspapers. He blurted out, "The dirty will not stick to the clean!" Undoubtedly, at that moment he considered the dirty to be the accused, the "slanderers," and by no means the great initiator and organizer of the unprecedented slander. If he had thought otherwise, he would not have allowed himself to talk this way in front of outsiders. Tsekher asked, "Do you know that the other day Mikhail Pavlovich Tomsky committed suicide?" Bukharin had not known, of course; in Frunze, he had seen only the recent accounts of the trial. And so, according to Shamshanov, who told the story to Kamil Ikramov toward the end of the 1950s, something terrible happened: blood spurted from Nikolai Ivanovich's eyes.

That is how tragically he suffered the suicide of his comrade. In addition, Tomsky's suicide indicated to a still greater degree the gravity of the new situation.

Tomsky settled accounts with life in an instant. He understood that the terroristic orgy instigated by Stalin presaged an excruciating end. Obviously, his was an act of courage, although suicide is not easy to judge in any case. In the first days, Bukharin and Rykov hoped to prove that they had not been involved in any crimes. But if Bukharin senselessly put his money on Stalin alone, Rykov banked all of his hopes—also in vain, alas—on certain members of the Politburo and on members of the Party Central Committee. So Nikolai Ivanovich told me after his brief conversation with Rykov during the December 1936 plenum of the Central Committee.

A rather interesting detail: When a reexamination of the trials took place under Khrushchev in the early 1950s and I was summoned to the Party Control Committee to participate, an official informed me that several of Bukharin's letters repudiating the slanderous testimonies against him had been discovered in Stalin's archive, but not one letter from Rykov. I assume that he did not bother writing the Boss.

But Nikolai Ivanovich was gullible. Stalin, exploiting this trait, feigned love toward him, all the while secretly preparing his downfall.

There was more than one reason for Stalin to make a display of exceptionally warm feelings toward Bukharin until he was ready to strike. For one thing, it was well known that Lenin sincerely loved my husband. Stalin had to imitate his predecessor for the time being, but recognized that the relationship between Lenin and Bukharin was a huge obstacle to his ambitions. For precisely this reason, he could not hope to eliminate Bukharin physically without first portraying him in court as a coconspirator in an attempt to assassinate Lenin.

There was a strange paradox in Stalin, unbelievable as it may seem. If the monster was at all capable of affection, then he actually loved Nikolai Ivanovich with some small part of his cruel heart. How could he, as he claimed, love his wife, Nadezhda Sergeyevna, yet viciously make fun of her and drive her to her grave? How could he love his daughter

Svetlana, yet at the same time torment her, like the despot he was, and doom her—though he could hardly peer that far into the future—to suffering that would follow her to the end of her life? Could Koba have not loved Nikolai in the same way—loved him but murdered him—because love and hate born of envy for Bukharin's shining personality fought with each other in the same breast?

How, considering everything I've written about Stalin so far (and everything that follows), did his affection for Nikolai Ivanovich manifest itself? In light of my argument that all of his acts were political theater, inspired by the cultivated cunning of a "Jesuit," this is difficult to explain. Simply put, Stalin obviously felt a certain intimacy in his relationship with Bukharin, a closeness that had nothing to do with political calculation or acts motivated by political considerations. Granted, this intimacy was a drop in the ocean, negligible in comparison with the insidious game he initiated against my overly trusting husband.

For example, not long before Bukharin's theory that class warfare would dwindle was subjected to criticism in the late 1920s, Stalin had essentially agreed with Nikolai in a private chat. As socialism evolves toward a classless society, he theorized, class warfare might intensify at certain periods, but over the long run conflict between classes would have to become increasingly less acute. In that conversation, Bukharin told me, Stalin had said, "But the kulak is not Kolchak"—in other words, the curve would indeed veer toward the waning of class warfare.

Thus, at the April 1929 plenum, Bukharin took issue with the directly opposing view put forward by Stalin at that time. "This strange theory of Stalin's," he argued, "raises the actuality of our current intensification of class warfare to something like an inevitable law for our development. It turns out now, we are told, that the farther we advance toward socialism, the more difficulties accumulate, the more class warfare intensifies—and, finally, at the very gates of socialism, we shall either have to start a civil war or waste away from hunger and drop dead." At this, Stalin began raving and ranting. History will decide who was right!

As I've already noted, Stalin smoothed the way to removing the most prominent Party figures from the political arena by using Bukharin, a naturally brilliant polemicist and agitator, to oppose the various types of leftist opposition. That achieved, he turned 180 degrees and went after Bukharin, Rykov, and Tomsky, laying a firm foundation for one-man rule.

From mid-1924 to the end of 1927, I frequently encountered Stalin at Bukharin's place. I was a young girl then, and perhaps my impressions of him could be mistaken, but Nikolai Ivanovich told me many things. He had ready access to Stalin's home and went often, though he did not enjoy the large meals and neither smoked nor drank. But even without wine, he was the life of the party. Koba talked with Nikolai about his youthful exploits and recalled (in vulgar language) how furiously his temper raged in those years.

Stalin's wife, Nadya, was exceptionally warm toward Nikolai Ivanovich, always delighted to see him. Right in front of her husband, she complained about Stalin's crude, despotic character. Once, in his absence, when relations between the two men had begun to worsen, she opened up and expressed solidarity with Nikolai's views. Her daughter, little Svetlana, idolized Bukharin and would boisterously voice her delight: "Hurrah! Nikolai Ivanovich is here!"

For his part, Nikolai never much liked Stalin's character, though he was so close to the man and a favorite of his family. When Bukharin's fortunes began to sink and his political differences with the despot caused sharp personal conflicts between them, these intimate experiences in Stalin's home inevitably instilled in his unconscious mind a hope of salvation.

At the government box at the theater one night in 1934, we ran into Stalin, who latched onto Nikolai Ivanovich right away. They went outside the box to an anteroom where the privileged could spend intermission and talked so long that they missed an entire act.

When we got home, I learned that Koba had bemoaned the loss of Nadya, speaking bitterly about how much he needed her. Stalin would hardly have started up such a conversation at the theater, more than a year after his wife's death, with anyone else. Evidently, his friendship with Nikolai Ivanovich while Nadezhda Sergeyevna was still alive had left its mark on even his soul. Certainly, nothing was really dear to him . . . and yet?

I've discussed these things in order to try to explain, at least partially, the psychology of the executioner in regard to his victim, as well as something of Bukharin's psychology. In the contest between the forces of love and hate arose the unparalleled duplicity Stalin had always exhibited. This duplicity continued during the investigation of Nikolai Ivanovich before his arrest and, apparently, even after he was imprisoned.

[Bukharin's Confrontation with Sokolnikov]

In those first days after coming home from Tashkent, Nikolai Ivanovich spent the major part of his time in his Kremlin study, terrified of missing the telephone's ring. Ah, how he waited for a call from his "benefactor"! Finally, the long-silent apparatus gave a ring, and Nikolai Ivanovich lunged for the receiver. It was Karl Radek, then a member of the *Izvestiya* editorial board, himself also under investigation. Having learned that Bukharin had cut short his vacation and returned to Moscow, he wanted to know why he was staying away from the newspaper.

Nikolai Ivanovich snapped back, "So long as the press does not print a retraction of the vile slander, I will not set my foot in the editorial offices!"

Radek reported that a Party meeting of the editorial board would be held sometime in the next few days and that the Party bureau expected Bukharin to be there without fail. Nikolai Ivanovich refused to attend, arguing that nothing substantial could be decided about this affair on the level of the editorial board; besides, his attendance would only put an additional strain on his nerves. Finally, Radek said that he wanted to get together, but Nikolai Ivanovich refused this request, too, because he did not want to complicate the investigation (he was still hoping for an honest one). He added that, much as he wanted to, he had not called or made any effort to see Aleksei Rykov.

"Nothing bad is going to happen to you," Radek said.

"That remains to be seen," Bukharin countered.

Thus, under stress, passed the first days of September.

Once, I made an incredible blunder: I asked Nikolai Ivanovich quietly—quietly, in case the walls were listening—whether he really thought that Zinoviev and Kamenev could have been involved in Kirov's assassination. His face dropped; he went pale and looked at me with eyes full of desperation. I understood then that it was improper to put such a question to him. Deep in his unconscious he had buried the suspicion, perhaps even the certainty, that the crime could not have been committed without the guiding hand of Stalin. My question had reminded him of the likely shape of his own future. If it had been possible to force his Party comrades to incriminate themselves and implicate others, then surely it would be possible to force him, Radek, and others to do the same. This prospect, however, was too painful for Nikolai Ivanovich to face in the beginning. What an onlooker might easily have understood and what should have been particularly obvious to Bukharin, since he knew Stalin both personally and politically and could well gauge his potential for treachery, remained beyond my husband's grasp, for he was still in shock.

To my startling question, he answered, "But these bastards, these low-life slanderers are killing me and Aleksei [Rykov]! They've already killed Tomsky; that means they're capable of anything! The NKVD is not the Cheka. It's been perverted into an organization of officials without ideology. They win medals for themselves; they play on Stalin's morbid suspiciousness—they should all be driven out, starting with Yagoda!"

Perhaps some would assume that Nikolai Ivanovich did not want to reveal his hand to me in terms of actually suspecting Stalin at this point, because he wanted to shield me—but, no, this was not at all the case. He was too emotional not to give himself away entirely in such a dreadful moment. It took a few days for him to recover from the blow he had sustained, to begin to think over things, and to tell me frankly that the NKVD had not degenerated without pressure from Stalin. Yet he wavered in this opinion, and the remark he repeated most often was something like this: "I don't understand anything, I absolutely can't understand anything. What is going on?"

Several days after Radek's call, the telephone rang again. Some functionary told Nikolai Ivanovich to go to Central Committee headquarters to meet with Lazar Kaganovich, its secretary. Why Kaganovich? Bukharin was puzzled and tried once again to phone Stalin. He got the same answer as before: "Iosif Vissarionovich is in Sochi." He went to see Kaganovich. I waited for his return with great trepidation, although at the time, for some reason, I was not afraid that he wouldn't come back at all. My presentiment did not fail me. Nikolai Ivanovich returned quite soon, extremely distressed. As he walked in, he said:

"You can't imagine what I've gone through. It's unimaginable; actually, it's inexplicable!"

He told me that he had had a face-to-face confrontation with the arrested Grigory Sokolnikov, as Kaganovich watched. Grisha Sokolnikov, a friend of his youth, a comrade who had set out together with him on his revolutionary path, testified against him, lying all the way. Grisha concocted the story that there was a "parallel" Trotskyist center, parallel to the "united" center that had already been "uncovered" and tried in the Zinoviev-Kamenev show trial. This center, which he had supposedly joined, was committed to wrecking, sabotage, and terror against members of government and to the assassination of Stalin. Supposedly, too, the Bukharinist "Rights" had shared its aims and had worked for the overthrow of the government and the restoration of capitalism in the USSR. Sokolnikov claimed that he had spoken personally with Bukharin on the latter point, and Nikolai Ivanovich had advised him to move as quickly as possible. Grisha even described when, where, and in whose presence these negotiations had taken place—a completely imaginary event. Nikolai Ivanovich would have to undergo more than one of these confrontations before his arrest, but this one was, if I may put it this way, his baptism by fire.

No normal person can take all of this in. You have to have an impossible operation, a reason transplant. Well, this reason transplant was successfully performed behind the walls of the NKVD by means of the techniques of the "investigation."

I asked Nikolai Ivanovich how he had refuted Sokolnikov's allegations.

"Is it really possible to refute such raving?" he replied. "I looked at him the way a ram looks at a newly installed gate and said, 'Grisha! Can you have lost your reason and not be responsible for your own words?' But he said calmly, 'No, I answer for them, and you will soon answer for yours.' "

(By this last remark, Sokolnikov was apparently hinting that what had happened to him would happen to Bukharin.)

Nikolai Ivanovich got lost trying to figure out what was going on. He simply could not explain it. The familiar eyes of his friend were looking at him; Grisha's face was pale, but not tortured. In fact, it was obvious that he had given in right away, for Nikolai Ivanovich had heard about his arrest just before the trip to the Pamirs, and rumors of such sensational downfalls spread like wildfire. In this case, the rumor, as I noted earlier, had suggested to Bukharin that Sokolnikov could not have been arrested on political grounds.

Kaganovich, Bukharin, Sokolnikov: the three men were alone in the office the whole time. The guards waited outside; the NKVD man in charge of Sokolnikov's case was not present. It would seem that Kaganovich had the power to take his place and ensure the prisoner's proper conduct, but I am not certain about this. Kaganovich took the role of an impartial observer, neither pressuring Sokolnikov nor supporting Bukharin. Finally, time was up; the guards came and led Grisha away.

And then, according to Nikolai Ivanovich, something quite surprising happened. Kaganovich exploded:

"He's lying, the whore, from beginning to end! Go back to the newspaper, Nikolai Ivanovich, and work in peace."

"But why is he lying, Lazar Moiseyevich? We should get to the bottom of this."

"We'll find out, we'll find out for sure, Nikolai Ivanovich," Kaganovich replied.

I do not remember whether Bukharin discussed with Kaganovich the incriminating testimony given against him at the Zinoviev-Kamenev trial. Nikolai Ivanovich may still have been trying to assimilate the profound impression left by his confrontation with Sokolnikov and let the moment slip by.

But he did respond directly to Kaganovich's suggestion about his work: "So long as the state prosecutor does not publish an announcement in the press dismissing the slander of me and announcing an end to the investigation, because there's no corpus delicti, I will not go to work."

Kaganovich promised that this would be seen to without fail.

On September 10, 1936, an announcement from the USSR Prosecutor's Office did indeed appear in the papers, but somewhat different in content from what Nikolai Ivanovich had demanded. The investigation of the case of Bukharin and Rykov had been halted, not because there was no corpus delicti but because there was no juridical evidence of criminal culpability. To Bukharin this meant: Not a thief until caught! Still, since the case was reported closed, it was possible to breathe more easily. Unquestionably, Stalin dictated this outcome to the confrontation with Sokolnikov. Further events would reveal that it was a tactical move on the Boss's part designed to demonstrate the "objectivity" of the investigation.

Nikolai Ivanovich phoned *Izvestiya* and told Semyon Lyandres, who heartily congratulated him on his rehabilitation, that he would be returning to work in a few days but wanted to use up the rest of his vacation first by just relaxing. He was so depressed by his confrontation with Sokolnikov that he got the naive idea of talking to Stalin about it, but he was not sure this would succeed.

We decided to spend several days at the dacha. Before we left Moscow, Nikolai Ivanovich received a telegram from Romain Rolland congratulating him on his rehabilitation and a similar letter from Boris Pasternak; he was deeply touched. After resting a few days at the dacha, he set off for *Izvestiya;* I stayed at Skhodnya with Yura. Usually, Nikolai Ivanovich would return from work after midnight; this time, he came back early to the dacha. He told me that he had been warmly greeted by the newspaper staff, but when he walked into his office, he found Boris Tal sitting behind his desk. Tal, press director of the Party Central

Committee, was acting as chief editor of the paper. Bukharin growled at Tal, who would later share his fate, that he had no intention of working under a political commissar. He walked out of the office, slamming the door. This was the only time Bukharin visited the newspaper after his vacation; he quit without doing a lick of work, even though *Izvestiya* continued to list him as editor for several months.

He brought back some foreign newspapers he'd picked up at the office. In one—I do not remember which—he read that Radek would be arrested very soon, then Bukharin and Rykov. Another paper reported that the confessions of the accused at the Zinoviev-Kamenev trial had been obtained by means of hypnosis and torture.

Nikolai Ivanovich was driven to total despair by these reports and by the situation at *Izvestiya*. At night, he raved in his sleep, repeating, "You are traitors yourselves, you are traitors yourselves!" Now that he'd been to the paper, he understood that not only would he not "work in peace," to quote Kaganovich, but he would not work at all at *Izvestiya*.

Did Kaganovich deceive Bukharin, or was he, too, not aware of Stalin's further plans? Nikolai Ivanovich had no way of knowing. There at the dacha, toward the end of that September, he would frankly speak with me yet again, and again, about Stalin as the criminal who organized the terror. And then, on the same day or the next, he would instead put the blame on Stalin's morbid suspiciousness, on the tendency of the Boss to believe rumors started by others; thus Bukharin spared himself the realization that his position was inescapable.

[Radek's Arrest and Testimony]

A classic example of the psychology of a doomed man clutching at a straw in the hope of saving his life: Karl Radek in his last days of freedom. Despite Bukharin's perfectly justifiable desire not to see him, Radek showed up at our dacha two to three days before his arrest that September. He begged forgiveness for barging in but explained that he wanted to say farewell to Nikolai Ivanovich. Since the prosecutor's office had not made a declaration ending the investigation in his case, Radek assumed that he would very shortly be in jail. (He was arrested between September 17 and 20.) He was optimistic, however, about Bukharin's situation, convinced that Stalin would not let him be arrested. Because Radek assumed he would never see Nikolai Ivanovich again (in which he was mistaken, as I shall explain later), he wanted to take this final opportunity to tell his side of the story and have his old colleague believe him. Radek swore that he had broken with Trotsky long, long before and had had nothing to do with the exposure of the secret Trotskyist organization. The last phrase is exactly how he put it, as if there really did exist at that time a secret conspiratorial organization that shared Trotsky's views. Neither with Zinoviev nor with Kamenev, he further asserted, had he had any contact, although he did add, "I'm sorry for Grigory [Zinoviev]." (As I would later tell Beria, I overheard this conversation from the adjoining room through open doors.)

What struck me most at the time, and amazed me even more later when I fully grasped the horror of events, was Radek's last request. Should he be arrested, he wanted Bukharin to write Stalin about it and ask the Boss to take charge of the matter personally. The letter should also remind Stalin that Radek had not concealed the sole letter he had ever received from Trotsky in exile, the one brought to him by the former Left Social Revolutionary Yakov Blyumkin, but had immediately forwarded it to the GPU without even opening it.*

"Karl Berngardovich," Nikolai Ivanovich asked, "why can't you write Stalin yourself, right now, before your arrest? Do you really need help from me?"

"Because, Nikolai Ivanovich," Radek explained, "my letter to Stalin wouldn't get there. It would be forwarded to the NKVD, since I'm under investigation. A letter from you would be delivered directly to Stalin."

"I'll think about it."

Before leaving, Radek repeated an earlier plea: "Nikolai! Believe me, believe, *no matter what happens to me,* I am not guilty of anything!"

Having spoken with strong emotion, Karl Berngardovich went closer to Nikolai Ivanovich, said farewell, kissed him on the forehead, and left.

Is it even imaginable that Radek, a man with a brilliant mind, a politician to the core, an essayist who analyzed both the national and the international political situation with a sensitivity all his own, could actually have expected salvation from Stalin? Did he really fail to understand that the case he strove to place in the tyrant's hands had been whipped up by those very hands? And that no one would lift a finger against him without an order from the Boss? Finally, consider where he turned with his absurd plea: to a person who himself feared the next day's dawn.

---

*Yakov Blyumkin, who killed Count von Mirbach, the German ambassador to the USSR, and helped organize the Left SR revolt, went over to the side of the Bolsheviks and worked in the Cheka-GPU. He was a follower of Trotsky and, while abroad on assignment, met with him in 1929, after which he was shot.

So then, did Karl Radek understand the actual situation, or not? He understood, all right, but hid this understanding from himself. In moments when he faced the truth, he pitied Grigory Zinoviev; when he could not bear the reality, he felt it necessary to swear that he had had no connection with Zinoviev's supposed secret organization. Here is the psychological state of a doomed man overwhelmed by incredible, fantastic accusations.

If I had not witnessed this conversation myself but had heard about it from someone else's lips, I would have considered the source a crackpot or witless fantasizer. Yet Radek was quite serious, and he was insistent. A few days afterward, Karl Berngardovich's wife, Roza Mavrikieyevna, came to our dacha in distress and repeated her husband's plea, for he had been arrested.

After some hesitation, Nikolai Ivanovich decided to comply. As requested, he wrote that Radek wanted Stalin to handle the case himself, and he reminded the Gensek that Radek had turned the unopened Trotsky letter over to the GPU. (I assume that Radek suspected the letter had a provocational purpose; otherwise, would he not have wanted to know what it said, even though he did not share Trotsky's views at that time?)

Nikolai Ivanovich also wrote that it was his impression that no connection existed between Radek and Trotsky, but his last remark—"But then, who the hell knows!"—robbed the letter of any value. The letter would not have helped Radek anyway, but that remark shocked me.

It reflected the atmosphere of distrust between one person and another that prevailed in that period, an atmosphere that is crucial to understanding everything that happened.

Radek was arrested in his Moscow apartment, but the *Izvestiya* dacha he used was searched as well. Afterward, Dusya, a young maid there, ran over to tell us that secret criminal documents had been discovered in the hollow core of a tubular coat rack. "What monsters!" she said. "And to think, Nikolai Ivanovich, that they wanted to drag you into it!"

This news greatly unnerved Bukharin. He reasoned that Radek would have destroyed any documents he did not want made public in the month following the press announcement about his investigation. Therefore, either Dusya had heard a fabricated rumor or documents had been planted in Radek's absence.

"So they could find whatever they want at my place, too!" Nikolai Ivanovich exclaimed, in total desperation.

Toward evening that day, we bid farewell to our dacha in Skhodnya and returned to Moscow. No one at the newspaper phoned to invite

Nikolai Ivanovich back to work. Until the celebration of the October Revolution, on November 7, he did not leave the apartment. On the holiday, having received a guest pass from the newspaper, he decided to greet this nineteenth anniversary in Red Square with me at his side. His place on the reviewing stand turned out to be on the lowest level, closest to the Mausoleum, where Stalin caught sight of him. Suddenly, I noticed a sentry coming our way and took fright. I assumed that he was either going to ask us to leave or, worse, arrest Nikolai Ivanovich. But the sentry saluted and said, "Comrade Bukharin, Comrade Stalin asks me to convey to you that you are not standing in the right spot. Come up onto the Mausoleum." Thus we found ourselves atop the Mausoleum, but Nikolai Ivanovich did not succeed in having a talk with Stalin, who stood some distance away and was the first to leave the rostrum.

Not far from us, I saw Anna Sergeyevna Redens (Alliluyeva), the older sister of Stalin's late wife, Nadezhda Sergeyevna.* Seeing me, she said, "Ah, how we loved Nikolai Ivanovich, Nadya and I." For some reason, she included herself in the past tense, and, in point of fact, everything was already in the past. She, too, had been alarmed by the appearance of the sentry, as she candidly told me. But now, heartened by Stalin's gesture toward Bukharin, which she took to be sincere, and in light of the declaration from the prosecutor's office, Anna Sergeyevna concluded that Nikolai Ivanovich's troubles lay behind him.

After the October festivities, about a month passed in relative quiet. Nikolai Ivanovich did not even rule out the possibility that he would be asked to "work in peace" again at the newspaper, but neither *Izvestiya* nor the Central Committee sent any word about work. Trying to occupy himself, he read and wrote out passages from the German books he had purchased in Berlin. The authors were fascist theoreticians; he dreamed of writing a major work attacking the views and arguments of these ideologists. But the more time passed after that noteworthy November 7, the greater the anxiety that took hold of him. By the end of the month, the nervous strain was so severe that he could not work at all. Confining himself to our apartment, he lurched back and forth like a caged beast. Every day he looked at *Izvestiya* to see whether the paper listed another editor, but he would invariably read on the last page: editor in chief, N. Bukharin. He would shrug his shoulders in bewilderment. He had not

*Stanislav Redens, Anna Sergeyevna's husband, held the post of chief of the Moscow Cheka in the early 1930s. As I heard, he tried to curb Stalin's pressure on the NKVD by making use of his family ties with him. With the arrival of Beria, Redens was transferred to work in Kazakhstan and then arrested. Later, Anna Sergeyevna herself was persecuted. According to eyewitnesses, she returned from exile half-mad.

even crossed the threshold of the newspaper since the day in September when he had found Boris Tal sitting in his office.

Finally, the Central Committee Secretariat notified him by telephone that a plenum of the Party Central Committee would be convened in December. He was given no agenda. Whether this session was reported in the papers, I do not recall for certain, but I believe it was not made public. The plenum met for only one evening.*

Coming home from this session, Nikolai Ivanovich burst out in exasperation, "Allow me to present myself! Your most humble servant, the traitor-terrorist-conspirator!"

Yezhov, the new people's commissar of the NKVD, had taken the floor. Galling as it is now to recall the fact, this was the man upon whom Bukharin had placed his hopes after Yagoda's removal. With terrifying force, according to what Nikolai Ivanovich told me that night, the new, all-powerful people's commissar railed at his predecessor. Twice, he declared that Yagoda had transformed the prison into a sanatorium for Zinoviev and Kamenev, had been several years late in exposing them, and had acted only when pushed, so two trials (three, actually, for Kamenev) had been necessary in order to exterminate them.

Listening to Yezhov rant, the wretched, downcast Yagoda, still a member of the Central Committee, remarked in a low, uncertain voice (as if to himself, according to Nikolai Ivanovich, who sat not far from him), "What a pity I didn't arrest you when I still could!"

Next, Yezhov attacked Rykov and Bukharin, accusing them of having connections with counterrevolutionary Trotskyists, of organizing a conspiracy, and, sounding the leitmotif of all three trials, of taking part in the assassination of Kirov.

"Shut up!" Bukharin shouted, insulted and enraged by the reference to Kirov. "Shut up! Shut up!"

All heads turned toward him, but no one uttered a single word.

After Yezhov's diatribe, the meeting broke for several minutes. Rykov took the opportunity to come over to Nikolai Ivanovich.

"We have to mobilize all our forces for a battle against this slander," he said. "Tomsky's suicide is an aggravating circumstance."

"Our one hope," Bukharin answered, "is to win Stalin over to our view. Otherwise, we'll gain nothing."

"Nikolai! You're wrong. We have to make the members of the

---

*Izvestiya TsK KPSS, no. 5, 1989, p. 75, states that the plenum was held December 4–7. Nikolai Ivanovich was there only one evening; I know of no other sessions.

Politburo and the Central Committee believe us, and go against Koba," Rykov hissed, in a voiceless whisper.

After the break, Kaganovich delivered a brief but vicious speech. Evidently, he had "reconsidered" and begun to believe not only the "whore" Sokolnikov instead of Bukharin but also the forced testimony of Zinoviev and Kamenev. Molotov competed with Kaganovich in the ardor of his attacks on Rykov and Bukharin.

No one rose to defend the two. Sergo Ordzhonikidze did interrupt Yezhov to ask questions, trying to make sense out of the ongoing nightmare, thereby becoming the one person to indicate a certain distrust in the new people's commissar. The conduct of the rest may be summed up in Pushkin's words in his drama *Boris Godunov:* "The people unspeechified."

Finally, Stalin took the floor. I report from memory what Bukharin told me:

> No need to make a hasty decision, Comrades. Look, the investigative organs also had material against Tukhachevsky, but we sorted it out, and Comrade Tukhachevsky may now work in peace.
>
> I think Rykov might have known something about the counterrevolutionary activity of the Trotskyists and did not inform the Party. But in respect to Bukharin, I still doubt this. [Here, he was purposely splitting Bukharin off from Rykov.] It is very painful for the Party to speak of the past crimes of comrades as authoritative as Bukharin and Rykov were. Therefore, we will not hurry with the decision, Comrades, but continue the investigation.

The Leader had planned everything in advance. And how deftly Iosif Vissarionovich knew how to deceive! For the benefit of Comrade Tukhachevsky, a candidate member of the Party Central Committee, present there at the plenum, he secured within several months not "work in peace" but eternal peace. For Bukharin, instead of the promised work at the newspaper, he ordered a renewal of the investigation, which, I have to think, had not actually stopped for a day since the September 10 announcement by the prosecutor's office. Incriminating materials were being fabricated against Bukharin and Rykov by the NKVD at a feverish tempo. Evidently, this was the real meaning of the Leader's speech, which was much more moderate than the preceding ones.

In fact, after such a short but most promising statement, Nikolai

Ivanovich decided to go up to Stalin. I transmit their conversation with maximum faithfulness, as my husband related it to me afterward.

"Koba!" he said. "You have to check the work of the NKVD, create a commission to find out what's going on there. Before the revolution, during the revolution, and in the hard days after it was achieved, we served only the revolution. So now, when the difficulties are already behind us, you believe slanderous testimonies? Do you want to toss us onto the filthy garbage pile of history? Come to your senses, Koba!"

Stalin replied in an indifferent tone. "If you want to talk about your past merits, no one can take them away from you. But Trotsky had them, too. In fact, speaking between ourselves, speaking between ourselves," he said twice, "few had as many merits before the revolution as Trotsky." He wagged a threatening index finger at Bukharin, evidently warning him not to blab to anyone in this life that he had praised Trotsky. (But Bukharin did manage to blab it in this life, to me.) Then Koba turned aside and walked off, not wanting to continue the conversation.

Nearly three months of agony passed until the February–March 1937 plenum. Bukharin spent them mainly in a small room. It was Stalin's former bedroom, since, after his wife's death in 1932, Stalin had asked Bukharin to exchange apartments with him.

The furnishings were quite modest: two beds with a night table in between, a broken-down couch with dirty upholstery and springs poking out through holes, a little table. On the wall hung a dark gray loudspeaker for the radio. Since the room had a sink with a water spigot and a small water closet, Nikolai Ivanovich found it convenient to set himself up there permanently, almost never leaving it.

On December 25, he listened on the radio to the speech Stalin gave at the Eighth Extraordinary Congress of Soviets about the new Stalinist constitution, which had been adopted December 5. Since Bukharin had taken a major role in discussing and writing this document but was now an outcast, he felt keenly his absence from the congress. But he was still weighed down even more heavily by what he had experienced at the December plenum. Evidently, only he and Rykov had asked Stalin to create a commission to investigate the workings of the NKVD. All the others at the session had maintained their silence. "Perhaps the time will come," he said, "when they will also prove to be inadequate witnesses to crimes and will also be destroyed!" But he knew, of course, that under Stalin's absolute dictatorship anyone who might come out in his or Rykov's defense would face immediate punishment. All the same, it was an incredible hardship for him to endure the silence of his comrades.

He recalled an ancient Egyptian tale: A pharaoh was being interred, and at the funeral ceremony not only his friends but also his foes assembled. The foes expressed their hatred for the deceased by throwing stones at the corpse. It lay still. Then one of the pharaoh's supposed friends also cast a stone. Suddenly, the deceased turned his head toward the false friend and began to moan loudly.

"And so with me! My soul is moaning, moaning so bad I can't stand it!"

Nikolai Ivanovich said this with such anguish, and with such a pathetic look, that at that instant it did seem to me that I heard a soulful moan.

In a little while, closer to the end of December, the testimonies against him, Rykov, and Tomsky began to pour forth. Obviously obtained by torture, these documents were distributed to all members and candidate members of the Party Central Committee as materials for the upcoming February–March 1937 plenum, in order to create the appropriate mood. And they had been skillfully supervised by a good director: they did not contradict one another. For example, the testimonies named the same dates for alleged conspiratory rendezvous, the same places for supposed gatherings of "confederates." Some of these secret meetings were described as taking place with Bukharin present, others in his absence, but at the latter someone would be sure to pass along a directive from him or Rykov. (Tomsky was mentioned, too, but more rarely; since he had departed life on his own, what was the point of wasting time on extorting testimony against him?) Directives from Bukharin or Rykov stated that the conspirators must hasten to bring about the overthrow of the Soviet government, the assassination of Stalin, and the "palace revolution" required before restoring capitalism; no other phrases satisfied the ends of the tyrant-monarch.

"A nice stew!" Nikolai Ivanovich commented. "If I were not I, but someone unknown to myself, I would believe it all."

So far, the majority of those tortured into giving incriminating testimony were either little known or totally unknown—not only to me but also to Bukharin. Many of them were Party officials from the provinces who had no relation to the Opposition.

Apropos of this situation, Rykov would state at the trial that counterrevolutionary groups had been formed from 1928 to 1930 in the territories of the Soviet Union but that "a precise enumeration, what groups were formed, where, in what quantity—this I cannot say."* And when the general prosecutor asked him to explain which part of the Bloc

---

Court Record in the Case of the Anti-Soviet "Bloc of Rightists and Trotskyists," p. 149.

of Rightists and Trotskyists Yenukidze had belonged to, he answered, "He must have belonged to the right part." With both of these comments, Rykov obviously strove to emphasize that the trial was nothing but monstrous insinuation.

When Nikolai Ivanovich read the testimonies sent to him, he sounded a familiar refrain: "I don't understand anything!" Then he whispered softly in my ear, "Could it be that Koba has lost his mind?"

I could not calm him. On the contrary, I alarmed him all the more by saying, "Next, expect testimony from Radek. After all, you wrote and petitioned on his behalf."

"Well, that can't happen!" he declared. But immediately afterward, he changed his mind: "No, no, you're right. Everything can happen!"

It was becoming all the more obvious what goals the so-called investigation sought and whose directions it followed. All the same, Nikolai Ivanovich sent several letters to Stalin, always addressing him as "Dear Koba" and rebutting the slanders, giving his alibi, and so forth. The only explanation for these efforts is that they sprang from those moments when Bukharin would convince himself that Stalin was only suffering from a morbid suspiciousness and could be argued out of it. There is no point in my repeating all of the testimonies that initially arrived; they did not differ from each other in any particular. The connection made to the "Parallel" Trotskyist Center presupposed wrecking as well, but attention was not focused on this aspect. The main subject was terror; the supposed organization of attempts on Stalin, and on Molotov and Kaganovich, was by no means forgotten—in short, the "palace revolution." Bukharin and Rykov were encompassed by inconceivable accusations, as if by the ring of a blockade.

"It smells like a grand bloodbath," Nikolai Ivanovich remarked. "They'll imprison people who did not even stand together with Aleksei [Rykov] and me!"

I stayed at my husband's side constantly, save for those minutes when I ran off to see the baby. Once, coming back from Yura, I saw that Nikolai Ivanovich was not in our room and became alarmed. I found him in the study, sitting at his desk, a revolver in his right hand, his left balled into a fist and supporting his head. I screamed. He shuddered, turned, and began to calm me:

"Don't be upset, don't be upset! I wasn't able to do it yet! When I thought that you would see me without breath, and the blood at my temple, when I pictured that. . . . Better it happen away from you, out of your sight."

My frame of mind at that moment is impossible to relate. But as I look back, I believe it would have been easier for Nikolai Ivanovich if his life had been terminated right then.

We went back to our room. On the way, Nikolai Ivanovich grabbed a little book of poems by Emile Verhaeren. Enervated by nervous strain and sleepless nights, he immediately lay down and read me the poem "Humanity."

The blood from mortal wounds of evenings crucified
In purple splendor seeps into the bogs and marshes.
Into the bogs and marshes seeps from distant skies
The blood of peaceful evenings, and the mirror waters
Reflect the scarlet blood of evenings crucified.

New Christs are you, the pastors of men's hearts are you,
With suffering and love you save the entire world,
You lead the sheep toward the blessed crystal shores!
And yet the bloody skies of evenings crucified
Foretell an end to all now and forever more!

Upon black Golgothas the evenings crucified
Bleed from the crown of thorns and from the robes of clouds.
Alas, the time of shining hopes has passed, the time,
Now seep in cursed bogs of dried-up slime
On these black Golgothas the evenings crucified!

"There it is," Nikolai Ivanovich declared in a weak voice, "the blood-drenched history of mankind!"

But the most amazing thing is that, despite everything, the time of shining hopes had not passed for him. He would pay for these hopes with his head. Moreover, one reason for his preposterous confessions in the dock—incomplete, but sufficiently egregious confessions—was precisely this: he still hoped that the idea to which he had dedicated his life would triumph.

At this particular moment, however, I was not capable of delving deeply into the meaning of Verhaeren's lines. In my mind's eye loomed the revolver that Nikolai Ivanovich had just held and then put back in his desk drawer. I became obsessed with the idea of getting rid of it, for I knew I couldn't watch him all the time. Everything was topsy-turvy in my soul, for I knew very well what our prospects were, yet I thought, What if the tyrant suddenly raises his hand against Nikolai Ivanovich? "Suddenly" was the possibility that worried me. It would be dangerous for me to hide the revolver in the apartment, for it might be found during a sudden search. No better solution occurred to me than to take it to my mother. Bringing Yura over to distract him, I told Nikolai Ivanovich I wanted to visit her. By this time, our son could crawl and pronounce his first meaningful word: "Papa." I went into the study, took the revolver from the desk, put it in my briefcase, and went to my mother's place at the Metropol. I had not seen her since August, when I picked up the baby on my way to the airport. For her own safety, we had decided by mutual consent not to meet.

Now Mother thought I was crazy.

"What are you doing?" she gasped. "You're walking around with a loaded revolver at such a dangerous time? You're lucky they didn't stop you in the Kremlin. Listen, it's not beyond the realm of possibility that they'll come for me tomorrow, and unlike Nikolai Ivanovich, I have no permit to possess firearms."

I saw that I had blundered, and we decided it would be best to take the revolver to the NKVD and tell them truthfully how it came to be at my mother's place. This is what Mother did.

I hurried back home as fast as I could. The baby was asleep and sweetly sniffling, keeping warm next to his father.

At the end of December, the doorbell rang. By this time, our apartment had become a house of the dead. No one had visited us, except for Nikolai Ivanovich's secretary, Avgusta Korotkova, or "Penochka," who had come to say good-bye to him. (This state of affairs would continue for half a year, from the preceding August to the following February.) A ring at the door was therefore a bad omen, signifying either a new package of testimony or arrest. My heart sank as I went to open the door. A state courier handed over a package with five wax seals. Radek's testimony had come. Nikolai Ivanovich opened the package, glanced into it, and uttered one word: "Awful!" He asked me to read it aloud while he hid his head under a pillow, like a child listening to a horror story.

This is what I remember:

INVESTIGATOR: So far, you have spoken about the counterrevolutionary activity of the Trotskyists, but you have not divulged anything about the counterrevolutionary activity of the Rightists.

RADEK: Since I have spoken openly about the counterrevolutionary activity of the Trotskyists, then *all the more* [my emphasis—AL] do I not intend to conceal the counterrevolutionary activity of the Rightists.

Since this testimony came to us three months after Radek's arrest, and he would affirm at the trial that he had "kept mum" and given no testimony for three months, it would seem likely that he testified against Bukharin immediately after he incriminated himself. In his concluding speech in the dock, however, Radek made the following point:

> I confess one more fault. Having already admitted my guilt and exposed the organization, I steadfastly refused to give testimony against Bukharin. I knew the position of Bukharin was as hopeless as mine, because our guilt was the same, if not in the juridical sense, then in principle. But we had been close acquaintances, and intellectual friendship is stronger than other friendships. I knew that Bukharin was in the same shaky position as myself, and I was convinced that he would give honest testimony to the Soviet power. Therefore, I did not want to deliver him to the people's commissar of internal affairs bound and tied. When I saw the trial in front of my nose, I understood that I could not appear in court while concealing the existence of another terrorist organization.*

Since Radek was forced to lie from beginning to end at both the preliminary investigation and the trial, it is difficult to say what is the truth. Possibly, the methods used on him were such that he broke right away; in that case, he apparently resisted testifying against Bukharin for a long time—that is, three months. On the other hand, if he held back from giving any testimony for three months, as he claimed at the trial, yet we received his testimony against Bukharin exactly three months after his arrest, then he must have given this testimony immediately after breaking and slandering himself.

Radek's testimony stipulated that the Rightist organization operated in conjunction with the Trotskyists and made use of wrecking and terror, with the aim of undermining the Soviet state. His allegations in regard to the supposed decision to assassinate Kirov are etched especially deeply in my memory; they were abundant with details, with fine points. Radek claimed that, after the decision was approved by the Trotskyist center abroad, he informed Bukharin of it in the editorial office of *Izvestiya*, where he recalled that a green-shaded lamp was burning. Before Bukharin would agree to the assassination, the testimony went on, he hesitated, became agitated, nervously paced the office, and

---

Protess "parallel'nogo" trotskiskogo tsentra [Trial of the "Parallel" Trotskyist Center] (Moscow, 1937), p. 231.

then finally sanctioned the act in the name of the Rightist terrorist organization.

When I finished reading all this, Nikolai Ivanovich flung the pillow off his head. His face was soaked with cold sweat.

"I absolutely do not understand what's going on! Just a little while ago, Radek asked me to write to Stalin for him, and now he comes out with this raving!"

By this time, Nikolai Ivanovich certainly understood that the testimonies were being obtained by illegal means, possibly torture, yet the fantastic transformations of Bolsheviks into traitors and criminals struck him as some inexplicable witchcraft.

He would understand it all after his arrest. At the trial, Vyshinsky asked him whether he could explain why everyone had testified against him. "You cannot explain?" the chief prosecutor rejoiced, evidently because Bukharin had delayed his answer. "It's not that I cannot," he replied then, "but simply that I refuse to explain."

Sensing the end, Nikolai Ivanovich told me about an interesting incident that took place in the summer of 1918, when he had been sent to Berlin as a member of the commission delegated to draft additional accords to the Brest peace treaty. There he heard that a remarkable fortune-teller, able to make exact predictions from the lines in one's hand, lived outside the city. Piqued by curiosity, he and Grigory Sokolnikov, also a member of the commission, decided to pay her a visit. I cannot recall what this palmist said about Grisha, but this is what she said about Bukharin:

"You will be put to death in your own country."

"What, do you believe the Soviet power will collapse?" Nikolai Ivanovich asked, seeking a political prediction as well from the palm reader.

"Under which power you will perish, I cannot say, but in Russia for certain. In Russia, there will be a wound in the neck and death by hanging!"

Rattled by her prediction, Nikolai Ivanovich exclaimed, "How can that be? A person can die from only one thing, either a wound in the neck or hanging!"

But the fortune-teller repeated, "There will be both the one and the other."

"So then," Nikolai Ivanovich explained, as he told me this story, "the anticipation of terror on a grand scale is choking me. In the language of the palm reader, presumably, this is the wound in the neck. Later will come the death by hanging; it doesn't matter that it's from a bullet."

["I Have Returned from Hell."—Bukharin, January 1937]

And the materials of the investigation kept coming and coming.

The testimony of Vasily Yakovenko, asserting that Bukharin had sent him to Siberia to foment kulak revolts, I have already discussed, and I have described my husband's reaction: before his arrest, he considered it an egregious lie, but at the trial he confirmed it.

Prior to his arrest, Nikolai Ivanovich received no testimony from such prominent Party figures as Nikolai Uglanov, head of the Moscow Party organization, or Vasily Shmidt, former people's commissar of labor, both of whom shared his views in the period of the Opposition from 1928 to 1930. Nor did he receive testimony from such protégés as Dmitry Maretsky, Ivan Kraval, and Aleksandr Slepkov. But he did receive testimonies from some other disciples: Aikhenvald, Zaitsev, and Saposhnikov, all of whom talked about the "palace revolution."

But I particularly remember the testimony of Bukharin's protégé Yefim Tsetlin. While Maretsky, Slepkov, and many other former protégés were sent to work outside Moscow after 1929, then expelled from the Party by a decree of the Central Control Commission "for assisting the counterrevolutionary group of Ryutin and spreading its program" and arrested afterward, this Tsetlin continued to work in the Scientific Research Section of the Commissariat of Heavy Industry as Bukharin's secretary and remained in close contact with him. At the end of 1933 or possibly in 1934, Tsetlin was arrested. Nikolai Ivanovich, convinced that he could not have been involved in anti-Stalinist activity, wrote Stalin pleading for his release. The Boss pondered for a long time. Tsetlin was sentenced and shipped off on the way to a place of confinement, but then Stalin ordered him taken off the transport and returned to Moscow. Unaware that Nikolai Ivanovich had interceded, Tsetlin sent a biting letter rebuking him for not lifting a finger to help. For that reason, he wrote, he refused to work with Bukharin; he was breaking relations and setting off for the Urals. Once there, however, Tseltin was arrested again, apparently no later than 1936. His forced confession declared that Bukharin had directed him to commit a terrorist act against Stalin. Furthermore, Nikolai Ivanovich had given him a revolver and told him when Stalin would be riding down Herzen Street. Supposedly, Tsetlin lay in wait there, ready to fire, but, alas, the Gensek's car did not come down Herzen Street.

After reading this testimony, Nikolai Ivanovich wrote Stalin again, trying to convince him that he truly had no terrorist intentions. And once again he urged Stalin to investigate why the arrested were smearing themselves and betraying others. Naturally, this request produced no result.

Once, Nikolai Ivanovich turned to me and said, "Actually, there is only one way out. To commit suicide and free myself from this appalling reading."

"No, it won't work now," I answered and told him what I had done with his revolver.

He did not even have the strength to get angry with me. He could only look at me in surprise and say that all was not lost; he had another. Indeed, he fetched a rather large revolver out of his study; engraved on the handle was the inscription "To the Leader of the Proletarian Revolution from Klim Voroshilov." He put this firearm in the drawer of the nightstand by the bed.

"If they come for me," he said, "I won't let them take me!"

His relations with Voroshilov had been rather warm in the past. Sometimes, at Voroshilov's request, he had written speeches for him. The inscription on the revolver stirred old memories, and in these trying moments he decided to write a few words of farewell. Bukharin did not ask for anything, knowing that even if he wished to help, Voroshilov was powerless. He wrote only one sentence: "Know, Klim, that I did not take part in any crimes. N. Bukharin."

I sent this note to Voroshilov, along with the letter to Stalin refuting Tsetlin's testimony, via a courier.

The reply came the next day: "I beg that there be no further correspondence with me. Whether you [*vy*] are guilty or not [he usually addressed Nikolai Ivanovich as *ty*) will be shown by the investigation. Voroshilov."

The degree of moral indignity my husband had to endure in those days is indescribable.

We assume that man is endowed with the greatest good in the world: human reason. But one wanted to be free from this "good" back then. To cease being human! To turn into something simple and brainless, perhaps some amoeba! The reality was that Nikolai Ivanovich and I were incarcerated together in a prison cell inside the Kremlin. He isolated himself even from his family. He did not want his father to drop in on him, walk into his room, and see his suffering. "Go away, go away, Papa!" he would cry feebly. Once Nadezhda Mikhailovna, with her affliction, literally crawled into the room to find out what new testimonies had been given and only with my help made it back to her bed.

Nikolai Ivanovich grew thin and old, and his ruddy goatee turned gray. (I became his barber; otherwise, in half a year, he might have grown a full beard.)

During this six months of waiting before his arrest, Bukharin's mail included little more than two short missives from Boris Pasternak, one of which I described earlier, and a letter that, as I think about it now, strikes me as rather strange. The correspondent was an old Bolshevik, the famous journalist Lev Sosnovsky, who had belonged to the Trotskyist Opposition for a long time and been expelled from the Party in 1927. Before that, he had been a regular contributor to *Pravda,* enjoying the reputation of a talented columnist. Eventually, he was reinstated in the Party and, if I am not mistaken, sent to *Izvestiya* in 1935 on orders from Stalin. In his letter, Sosnovsky explained that his financial situation was extremely strained because he had been fired from the paper. I do not know why he would turn to Bukharin, of all people: Nikolai Ivanovich, only nominally listed as editor in chief on the masthead, could not possibly help him. In actuality, Bukharin had himself been kicked out of work. The only thing he could do was help Sosnovsky materially, but this wouldn't be easy. Nikolai Ivanovich had never been paid a salary by *Izvestiya;* he'd turned it down. He had usually received a remittance from the USSR Academy of Sciences; these payments continued during the first months of the investigation, then stopped. Nevertheless, with Ivan Gavrilovich's help, he was able to send a small sum to Sosnovsky.

Not long before the trial of the "Parallel" Trotskyist Center, which took place on January 23, Nikolai Ivanovich was invited to the Central Committee. There, in front of every member of the Politburo, with Yezhov taking part, he was subjected to face-to-face confrontations with his accused conspirators.

The lexicon of the confrontations did not depart one iota from that of the testimonies we had received, for the accused called themselves "traitors, restorers of capitalism, wreckers, terrorists," and on and on. Any one testimony differed from the others only in details.

The first to stand before Bukharin was Lev Sosnovsky. His unique detail was his letter asking for help, now said to have served conspiratorial purposes. Supposedly, the two correspondents agreed upon this ploy in advance, prior to a meeting at the newspaper. Sosnovsky testified that the letter signified that the Trotskyists had decided to unleash terror; the money sent by Bukharin was a signal that the Rightist terror organization agreed with this decision and would act in accord with it.

"You transferred money to Sosnovsky?" Yezhov asked.

"Yes, I did," Bukharin answered and told how it had come about.

"It's all clear," Stalin observed, and Sosnovsky was led away.

(When Nikolai Ivanovich came home, he surmised that Sosnovsky was already under arrest when the letter was written; it had been sent in order to stage this episode.)

Second to face Bukharin was Yury Pyatakov. For his adherence to the Trotskyist Opposition in the past, he had been briefly expelled from the Party. Later, at the Sixteenth and Seventeenth Party congresses, he was elected to the Central Committee and served until his arrest. In recent years, Pyatakov had worked as Sergo Ordzhonikidze's assistant in the Commissariat of Heavy Industry. Since the work there was by definition concerned with industrialization, Pyatakov's unique detail, and chief point, was the accusation of wrecking.

But his physical appearance unsettled Bukharin far more than his preposterous charges. He looked like a walking corpse. As Nikolai Ivanovich said to me later, this was "not Pyatakov, but his shadow, a skeleton with its teeth knocked out." In his "Letter to the Congress," Lenin had characterized Pyatakov as a person not only of outstanding qualities but also of outstanding willpower. Evidently, the latter attribute had brought him to such a state: great efforts must have been required to break Pyatakov. During his confrontation with Bukharin, Yezhov sat close by, a living reminder of what had been done to him. The people's commissar undoubtedly feared that Pyatakov might break step and renounce his testimony. He did not. He confessed to being a member of the counterrevolutionary Center connected with Bukharin; this connection, he claimed, was facilitated by their working together in the Commissariat of Heavy Industry.

Pyatakov spoke with lowered head, trying to cover his eyes with his palm. Bitterness was evident in his tone: bitterness, so Nikolai Ivanovich believed, toward all those who witnessed this absurd spectacle without interrupting it, without calling a halt to this phenomenal abuse of power.

"Yury Leonidovich, explain, what has forced you to impugn yourself?" Bukharin asked.

There was a pause. Then Sergo Ordzhonikidze, peering intently at Pyatakov in amazement, distressed by the tortured look and improbable confessions of his hardworking aide, put his hand up to his ear (Sergo was hard of hearing) and asked, "Can your testimony really be voluntary?"

Pyatakov answered, "My testimony is voluntary."

"Absolutely voluntary?" asked Ordzhonikidze in still greater amazement, but there was no reply. Yet, at the trial, Pyatakov did manage to say in his concluding speech, "Any punishment you inflict will be easier than the very fact of my confession." In this way, he let it be known that his testimony had been extracted from him.

Why in that moment, before all of the members of the Politburo, did Pyatakov fail to reveal the truth and tell what had been done to him, how he had been brought to such a state that he could barely stand on his own two feet? Ultimately, this is impossible to fathom. Yet, Pyatakov understood that he would not be going home after the confrontation but rather to the dungeons of the NKVD, where the tortures of hell would begin all over again. And it is possible that drugs helped paralyze his outstanding willpower.

The third and last person led in for a confrontation was Karl Radek. According to Nikolai Ivanovich, his appearance was not so woeful as Pyatakov's; he was only unusually pale and much more agitated than the other two accusers. He said the usual stuff: the underground counterrevolutionary organization of the Trotskyists was connected through Bukharin to a like organization of the Rightists. And he confirmed the testimony we had read from his preliminary investigation: he had discussed the planned assassination of Kirov with Bukharin at the *Izvestiya* offices. His unique detail was that he had made an agreement with Bukharin to assassinate Stalin. (This is exactly the way he put it.) Without the murder of Stalin, Radek explained, the restoration of capitalism would be impossible. Through all of this, the Politburo members sat unmoved: not one tried to ask Radek a question, let alone express any misgiving about his confessions. Stalin gave the appearance of regarding it all as the truth. Radek's testimony suited him perfectly. Sergo Ordzhonikidze also kept silent, having apparently counted on being able to elicit the truth from Pyatakov and failed, but his expression was extremely disturbed and his eyes were full of perplexity and alarm.

Finally, Bukharin had his chance to speak:

"Tell me, Karl Berngardovich, when were you lying? Now, in your fantastic testimony, or then, at the dacha, when you asked me to write Stalin about your innocence? You know, I carried out your request."

Radek said nothing.

"I ask you to give an answer to my question. Did you ask me to write to Stalin about your innocence?"

"Yes, I did," Radek confirmed, then broke out in sobs. "Water!" he begged. "I feel bad."

Stalin poured water from a carafe and carried it over to him. Radek's hand trembled so violently that water splashed out of the glass.

With this, the confrontation ended. Radek was led out. Stalin asked Bukharin to explain why all three had testified against him.

"You can explain that better than I," Nikolai Ivanovich answered, again demanding that a commission be formed to investigate the work of the NKVD. No one responded to this proposal.

When he told me all this in detail at home, Nikolai Ivanovich said, "I have returned from hell, a temporary hell, but there can be no doubt that I will fall into it for good; they might arrest me today. Obviously, only then will I be able to explain to myself what is going on."

To repeat, it was the first confrontation of all, the one with Grigory Sokolnikov in the office with Kaganovich, that produced the most shattering effect on Nikolai Ivanovich, despite the apparently favorable result. During the half year of the investigation, he was steadily worn down psychologically and began to adapt himself to the situation, gradually reacting more calmly to the epithets "terrorist," "wrecker," "conspirator." Numbed to the horror, he would at times become indifferent and detached, then suddenly flare up and fly into an indescribable rage.

All of this happened just after agriculture had taken a turn for the better, rationing was discontinued, industry grew by leaps and bounds, and, whatever the hardships, new productive forces were being created. Never glancing backward, Nikolai Ivanovich had always looked ahead as these tremendous changes took place. In addition, the Soviet Union had become the bulwark of peace in the face of advancing fascism. In mid-1935, the Seventh Comintern Congress called upon all Communist and Socialist parties to join in a united front against fascism; to ensure the success of this endeavor, it was necessary to maintain the hard-won authority of the country. By the end of the year, our national prestige in the international arena had reached an all-time high. In January 1936, for example, in an address called "To My Soviet Friends," Romain Rolland wrote, "May the idea you serve triumph over mankind, the faith embodied in you!"

Yet, literally within months, the most flagrant injustice in history occurred. The Great Terror, an absurdity without precedent, as Nikolai Ivanovich put it, throttled the Party and its bright ideals, its majestic hope for the humanization of society. "What we want is socialist humanism," he said in his appearance at the Sorbonne, his last public speech. But the infernal flame of terror had begun to spread. Nikolai Ivanovich both understood and refused to understand; he could not make his way through the course of these events, for human thought is considerably more methodical than the swift flow of time.

Several days after the confrontations before the Politburo, the trial of the so-called Parallel Trotskyist Center was held. Several persons were tried, including Karl Radek, Yury Pyatakov, Grigory Sokolnikov, Leonid Serebryakov, and Nikolai Muralov. Bukharin tossed aside the newspapers covering the trial, refusing even to look at them.

"I can't read that raving; their statements at the confrontations were enough for me," he said in complete despair. When I told him that Sokolnikov and Radek had been sentenced to ten years each, not death, he assumed that they had saved their skins by maligning him. Even so, he knew, of course, that they had been forced to defame themselves as well. My own opinion is that these sentences were a lure for Nikolai Ivanovich, Rykov, and the others yet to be tried, intended to demonstrate that they, too, could save their lives by incriminating themselves and impugning their comrades. I believe that Stalin calculated this ruse, especially since it cost him nothing: once Nikolai Ivanovich could no longer find out about it, Radek and Sokolnikov were both destroyed.

"Who could have foreseen such a thing? Maybe only Nostradamus!" Nikolai Ivanovich exclaimed at the end of this trial. He was totally mystified.

The trial lasted from January 23 through January 30. Scarcely a month remained until the arrest of Bukharin.

This last month was the most difficult. Nevertheless, Nikolai Ivanovich had some relatively bright moments when he held out hope for life. After all, the "case" of Bukharin and Rykov had been drawn out too long; arrest was long overdue.

"What if they send me way out in the sticks? Will you come with me, Anyutka?" he asked with childish naïveté. "Will Koba really put on a third medieval inquisition in front of the whole world? For me, it's only expulsion from the Party that will be unbearable, that will be hard to endure. But I can find something to occupy myself anywhere. I'll take up the natural sciences and poetry; I'll write a novella about what I've lived through. My dear wife will be beside me; my son will grow up. What can I wish for in the present circumstances?"

"I'll go with you way out in the sticks, but I'm afraid these are only pleasant daydreams," I said, unable to console him.

Nor did these glimmers of optimism last long, for the true prospect was only too clear.

Nikolai Ivanovich continued to sit in his room as in a trap. In the last days, I found it difficult to get him even to go wash in the bathroom. He was afraid of running into his father—not only because he did not want to upset him with his appearance but more because he dreaded the question "Nikolai! What's going on?" He found relief only in the thought that his mother, who died in 1915, had not lived to see his sufferings. Lyubov Ivanovna, knowing that her son was drawn to the natural sciences, had dreamed of his becoming a biologist. It grieved her when he got involved in revolutionary activities, and it frightened her when the tsarist police came to search the apartment. "How would it be with her now? It's hard to imagine!" Nikolai Ivanovich said again and again.

Yet, in this dark age, biologists did not fare any better than old Bolsheviks.

In February, the last days of our life together were being counted off. Suddenly, the telephone rang. Ivan Gavrilovich cracked open our door and asked me to come pick up the receiver. To my surprise, it was Kolya Sozykin calling. This was the incident I had not wanted to reveal to Beria, but he had revealed to me. My former classmate and Komsomol organizer was inviting me to visit him at the Moskva Hotel. As I've noted before, Nikolai Ivanovich immediately suspected that my Kolya was a plant but eventually decided that nothing untoward would happen if I went to see him.

"Just don't say anything unnecessary," he warned. "But get a whiff of fresh air. Go, go, relax a little bit."

I stayed at Sozykin's only a short while but somehow managed to tell him everything "unnecessary" I possibly could: details of the December Central Committee plenum, of the face-to-face confrontations, of Bukharin's absolute denial of involvement in any of the crimes. I showed caution only by not mentioning Stalin's name, even though I had a very negative view of this inglorious figure. And when Sozykin asked what Stalin thought about events, how he personally regarded Nikolai Ivanovich, I replied with the conjecture that our dull-witted philistines liked to prate back then—namely, "The NKVD is deceiving Stalin."

Thus I poured out my heart to Sozykin, "got a whiff of fresh air," and hurried back. Nearing home, I saw Sergo Ordzhonikidze coming out of the entrance next to ours, the one closer to the Troitsky Gates. As he headed for his car, he noticed me and stopped. But what could I tell him at that moment? For several seconds, we stood silent. Sergo looked at me with eyes so full of grief that it is impossible for me to forget that gaze to the present day. Then he squeezed my hand and said two words: "Stand firm!" He got in his car and left. At that moment, I would never have guessed that his days, too, were numbered.

Back at home, I told Nikolai Ivanovich about this encounter, and although the advice to "stand firm" was cold comfort, he was touched. How little was needed in those days, how uplifting was even one kindly word! Right then and there, Nikolai Ivanovich wrote Ordzhonikidze, hoping he would not answer as Voroshilov had. I did not memorize this letter, as I did the material I will relate later, so I can give only a brief account of its contents. Nikolai Ivanovich suggested that since Sergo was well aware of the false testimonies cooked up against him and had been present for the monstrous and unaccountable confrontations, he, Sergo, must certainly appreciate Nikolai Ivanovich's condition and understand what he would expect. From everything that was happening, he went on, he was himself persuaded to think that a powerful force was active in the NKVD that neither he nor Sergo could fully grasp, at least not until one found oneself in a prison dungeon. Nonetheless, Nikolai Ivanovich continued, it was becoming more and more obvious to him that this force was operating with confidence and no fear of failure, because it had been able to compel all those who had dedicated their lives to the people and to the revolution to smear themselves and malign their comrades in the Party. One part toward the end, I can recite verbatim: "I am beginning to fear that if I am arrested I may find myself in the position of Pyatakov, Radek, Sokolnikov, Muralov, and the others. Farewell, dear Sergo. Believe that I am honest in all my thoughts. Honest, whatever may happen to me from this point on."

This statement reminded me of Radek's last words at our dacha: "Nikolai! Believe, no matter what happens to me, that I am not guilty of anything!"

Nikolai Ivanovich ended his letter with an appeal to Ordzhonikidze to look after his family in the event of his arrest. Specifically, he asked Sergo to take the baby for at least the first days, until I could recover, gain strength, and find work. This request made me put off sending the letter. Although it seemed unlikely that Ordzhonikidze would be able to take in Yura even for a short while, my maternal instinct feared the possibility. It seemed to me that with my mother's help in the beginning, then by myself, I would best be able to bring up my own child. But the problem solved itself. A short while later, there was no one to receive the letter.

Sergo Ordzhonikidze could not bear to be a passive observer of the unprecedented abuse of power, let alone a direct participant. For him, there was only one way out—to leave the scene forever. The question is, who chose this way out for him? Rumors say different things, contradict each other.

Now, after all my son and I have gone through, Bukharin's plea to Ordzhonikidze to help his family seems naive, even if Sergo had stayed alive. But how could Nikolai Ivanovich have foreseen that within three and a half months after his arrest I would be taken away from my child and denied the opportunity to concern myself about his daily bread?

[Reunion with Yura in 1956]

I was parted from my son when he was a year old and did not see him again for nineteen years. In the summer of 1956, the twenty-year-old man came to see me in my last place of exile: Tisul settlement, Kemerovo Region, Siberia.

I hope the reader will forgive me—if indeed I ever have a reader one day—for momentarily digressing from my recollections of dreadful days to skip ahead almost two decades. I will return to the Kremlin again to say good-bye to Nikolai Ivanovich. The history of our parting will not drop into the river Lethe, for it lives in my soul, in my memory.

But I feel the need for a little bit of happiness, and could the meeting with Yura I had dreamed about so long be anything but happiness after such an extended separation? Sergo Ordzhonikidze could not save him, but one way or another the boy's relatives saved him, each in turn, and he did not perish in the children's home. Praised be the people for that! But let me tell about this reunion with my son.

By that time, I had a new family. Actually, that statement is a bit misleading. I met the man who would become my second husband, Fyodor Dmitriyevich Fadeyev, in a camp. Before his arrest, he had headed the agro-production department of the Commissariat of State Farms in Kazakhstan. After his release and rehabilitation, he was not an exile but stayed in Siberia on my account. Because of this connection with me, he was arrested three times on various pretexts. Therefore, for the better part of our life together, Fyodor Dmitriyevich was either in prison or working far away and could come see me only on vacations. After my release from camp in 1945, I scraped out a living in various places of exile with our two small children. Since my husband had been educated at the Agricultural Academy in two departments, agronomy and animal husbandry, and had worked in agriculture for many years, he could always find work in my latest place of exile. State farms were all around; it was not hard to get a job. But no sooner did he start work than he was arrested, or I was sent off to another place of exile.

These years form a separate chapter of my life, also filled with drama, but this memoir is not the place to give it full treatment. When the political climate warmed in 1956, it seemed that Fyodor Dmitriyevich and I might settle down permanently together, but he died prematurely. Exhausted by eight years of confinement, plus an investigation that used torture to extract a self-indictment, he was unable to withstand the subsequent strains of life associated with me. As I say, this story deserves its own telling. I touch on it here only to explain that in 1956 there was a whole family eager to meet Yura.

Tisul settlement was located some forty to forty-five kilometers from the nearest train station, Tyazhin, and there was no regularly scheduled transportation between them. We set out on the road in a motorcycle with a sidecar. We had to take the children—Nadya, not yet ten, and Misha, six—because they were determined to see their brother right away. For them, this event was simply an enjoyable adventure. They had to squeeze into the sidecar, producing a drag on the vehicle that caused an accident and nearly got us all killed. But we finally made it to the station.

It is difficult to convey my state of mind. I was about to see my son, but he was an unknown young man. What kind of person would he be, after being brought up in a children's home? Would we find a common language? Would he be able to understand me? Would he consider my having other children a betrayal to himself, and reproach me? Finally, he would certainly ask me about his father, who the man was. Indeed, this was my main concern. Must I reveal that secret, would it not prove too great a burden for a youthful spirit? This was after the Twentieth Party Congress, where Khrushchev had given his secret speech against Stalin's crimes, so I had armed myself with newspaper clippings about "Stalin's cult of personality." It seemed to me then, and still does now, that the phrase hardly does justice to the crimes he committed, or adequately conveys that time to later generations, or explains the horror experienced by our country, but it was at least a step toward the truth, toward the future, and it lightened my task. Also, not long before Yura's arrival, I managed to buy a copy of Lenin's testament, his 1923 "Letter to the Congress," in which he had mentioned Bukharin so warmly. It had just been published for the first time as a separate booklet and was available at newsstands. In short, I tried to be well fortified. Dozens of questions occurred to me that I could not answer until I had made the acquaintance of my son.

As my new family and I walked along the station platform, I saw the train approaching from the distance. I became so excited I thought I might fall down at any moment; I walked over to a little hedgerow beside the platform and fainted. As it happened, this was not Yura's train, and by the time the one with him aboard drew into the station, I had "come to." I tried to take in the entire trainload of passengers with one glance, fearful I would miss my son. Since I had had nothing but his baby pictures all these years, I had no idea how he would look. Suddenly, I felt an embrace and a kiss. Yura had rushed up to me from the side while I was intently examining the last cars of the train.

I could recognize nothing but his eyes, the same shining eyes from his childhood. How he had picked me out, I do not know. He had not seen my photograph since he was a child; my look of anticipation must have given me away. He was indescribably thin, his bony hips hardly held up his pants, and every rib of his chest could be counted. The very image of Mahatma Gandhi. I peered into his face, searching for the family features so well known to me. The moment he spoke, my heart stopped: the timbre of his voice, his gestures, and the expression of his eyes were all exactly like his father's. But the color of his eyes was more like mine, dark brown, though they had been quite light when I last saw him.

"Well, well, Yurochka! Well, well!"

At first, I could think of nothing else to say. And he:

"Now I know where my skinniness comes from."

Indeed, I was not much stouter than Yura.

We got back to Tisul by evening, thoroughly worn out by a bumpy ride on the motorcycle.

The next day passed quietly. Yura was happy. He sang songs, he ran with the children to the vegetable garden for pea pods. That morning, when we had a breakfast of farina with raspberry jam, he asked Misha, "Well, now, tell me, who used to eat farina with raspberry jam?" Misha thought a moment and answered uncertainly, "It must be Lenin." We laughed. And Yura told his little brother that it was Pinocchio [in the Russian version by Aleksei Tolstoi].

Thus passed the first day of our life together—a happy, bright, remarkably easy day. As if a stone had been lifted from my heart.

I got to know my son, asked what interested him, inquired why he had gone to study at the Novocherkassk Waterworks Institute. I wondered whether it was because of an interest in the natural sciences or in mathematics. I told him that his grandfather Ivan Gavrilovich was a mathematician who once taught in a girls' school. I did not mention his father's enthusiasm for the natural sciences, not wanting to bring up the subject of Bukharin yet. I was curious to know what proclivities my son might have inherited.

Yura explained that he was studying at the waterworks institute purely by chance. The boys from the orphanage had gone to take the entrance examination, and he just went along. He passed and enrolled but really had no interest in the subject, which had to do with irrigation, draining of swamps, and other water-related projects. He mentioned that he had taken the exam barefoot.

"Why barefoot?" I asked in surprise. "Didn't they give you shoes in the children's home?"

"They did, but it felt freer and easier without them."

So it seemed that neither the natural sciences nor mathematics interested him. Instead, he liked drawing and dreamed of becoming an artist, an ambition he would eventually realize. But, still wary of topics connected with his father, I kept to myself the thought that Yura had inherited his love of art from Nikolai Ivanovich.

Still, the following day I could not avoid the painful question, although I had intended to put off as long as I could a conversation that would undoubtedly be difficult for me. I would have to tell my son not only who his father was but also, or so I assumed, where he was. Yura insistently kept asking:

"Mama, tell me, who is my father?"

"Well, what do you think, Yurochka? Who could your father be?"

"He must be some professor," Yura responded. This surmise amused me.

"Not a professor, but an academician."

"An academician even! My father's an academician, and I'm an idiot," said Yura.

Yura was by no means "an idiot"; on the contrary, considering the circumstances in which he had grown up, his level of development astonished me.

"But mainly," I said, "he was not an academician." (After all, I had mentioned that Nikolai Ivanovich was an academician only because Yura had guessed that his father was "some professor.") "Mainly, he was a famous political figure."

"Tell me his name."

"That I'll tell you tomorrow."

I imagined that if I pronounced the name, Yura would cry, "So it's Bukharin, that enemy of the people!" I became afraid.

"If you don't want to tell me now," Yura said, "let's do it this way: I'll try to name him myself, and you'll tell me if I get it right."

On the assumption that he would never guess correctly, I agreed, taking his proposal for a funny little game that would delay the inevitable. But Yura surprised me:

"I suppose that my father is Bukharin."

I looked at my son in amazement.

"If you knew, why did you ask me?"

"I didn't know; honestly, I didn't know."

"Then how were you able to guess?"

"I did it by the process of elimination. You said my grandfather was Ivan Gavrilovich, my father was a prominent political figure. So I started thinking: Which one of the leading political figures had the patronymic Ivanovich? And I came to the conclusion that it was Bukharin—Nikolai *Ivanovich.*"

I was impressed that he knew the given names and patronymics of the major political figures, Lenin's comrades-in-arms, and could name them all (except Aleksei Rykov, who was also *Ivanovich*). He did not know that Bukharin had been the youngest of them, which would have given him another clue. The difference in age between Nikolai Ivanovich and myself, in fact, did not occur to him. Difficult as it may be to believe, this scene occurred exactly as I have described it. Yet I do not rule out the possibility that his infant memory had registered his father's name when some relative or other mentioned it, then in this moment of nervous tension an echo of the name had popped into his head.

I showed Yura the newspaper clippings and Lenin's testament. I spoke a bit about his father, and for his own good avoided going into too much detail. Before Yura left us, I asked him not to disclose his real family name, fearing this would only bring additional difficulties to a life that was already far from easy.

At the children's home, he had been given a passport in the family name of the relatives from whom he had been taken. Thus he had become Yury Borisovich Gusman, even though he had not been officially adopted. After meeting with me, however, he found it hard to keep his background secret. Not long before his graduation at officer's rank from the waterworks institute, Yura had to fill out a very detailed questionnaire. He was troubled, because it struck him now that to maintain silence about his father was intentional withholding of information. He wrote me asking permission to reveal the truth; he also needed his father's year of birth, as well as mine, neither of which he knew. The questionnaire had to be filled out within two weeks, no later, but Yura's letter had taken so long to arrive that I sent him a telegram in order to meet the deadline. I gave him his father's family name, given name, patronymic, and year of birth, along with the year of my birth, thereby granting him permission to reveal his heritage.

The rest of that story, I hope, will someday be told by Yura himself. But now I must return to the Kremlin, to the infant Yura, ten months old, and to the doomed Nikolai Ivanovich, in order to part from him forever.

[The Last Plenum and Bukharin's Hunger Strike]

The letter to Ordzhonikidze still lay on the desk in our room. For several days in a row, Bukharin reminded me to send it, or, better yet, carry it myself to Sergo's apartment, which was more difficult for me than to send it by courier. The baby was spending more time with us now. He had no toys besides a rattle his father had brought to the dacha before the trip to the Pamirs, so he took the stuffed blue-gray birdie Nikolai Ivanovich had shot, made it hop across the floor, and tossed it up and down. He crawled over and stood up, holding on to his father's bed, then tottered toward him to get a kiss. Ouch! How piercing his scream was, and he got red in the face from the strain: "Papa, Papa, Papa!" Unconsciously, intuitively, he showed special affection for his father in the last days before the separation.

The doorbell rang. Alarmed as always, I went to open the door. This time it was a notice that the Central Committee plenum would be convened. Nikolai Ivanovich had been waiting for this event, since all of the testimonies had been labeled "Materials for the Plenum." But he had not ruled out the possibility of arrest beforehand. This notice arrived several days before the meeting and originally set the date, as best I remember, for February 17 through 19. In the event, it entered history as the February–March plenum.

Two points were listed on the agenda: (1) the question of N. I. Bukharin and A. I. Rykov; and (2) organizational questions.

Reading this notice, Nikolai Ivanovich stated categorically, "I will not go to that plenum. They'll have to deal with me on their own."

At once, he decided to go on a hunger strike. He wrote a declaration to the Politburo to be read at the meeting. I memorized it and can vouch for the accuracy of my recollection now: "In protest against the outrageous accusations of disloyalty, treason, and so forth, I am announcing a hunger strike to the death, and I will not break it until I am cleared. Otherwise, my last request is to leave me alone and let me die where I am."

He asked me to help him find a note written by Stalin that he wanted to destroy before any search could take place. He had happened upon this note quite innocently late in 1928 or early in 1929. After a Politburo session, he discovered that he had lost a little pencil, the one he most liked to use for taking notes. He returned to the empty meeting room and spied his pencil on the floor, but when he bent over to pick it up, he noticed a scrap of paper lying nearby. This he picked up, along with the pencil. A note in Stalin's hand read, "Must destroy Bukharinist disciples!" Evidently, the Boss had put his intention down on paper, accidentally dropped the note, and then forgotten about it. In this way, a document revealing his sinister plans found its way into Nikolai Ivanovich's hands and lay in his desk for many years. He decided to rid himself of it, so as not to be accused of even more crimes: theft, forgery, and so on. This note was the only document we destroyed before the search.

Did Bukharin's protégés know about it? I don't know about all of them, but I can say for certain that Dmitry Maretsky and Yefim Tsetlin did. I destroyed the note with my own hands, but it troubled me, and in writing (the reader can understand why) I put this question to my husband: "That means you knew about Stalin's plans?"

"At that time," he wrote in reply, "I did not suspect that Stalin could be thinking of shooting my former pupils. I thought he intended to destroy my school by isolating them from me. [In fact, Stalin began by sending Nikolai Ivanovich's disciples into remote areas, as I noted before.] Now I no longer rule out the possibility that he might physically destroy them."

The study was in complete disarray. The two lovebirds, dead, lay still in the enclosure. The ivy Nikolai Ivanovich had planted had withered. The stuffed animals, the paintings on the wall, were all covered with dust. Whenever I crossed the threshold, I experienced an especially acrid sensation of death.

We were sitting on the couch. Above it, my favorite watercolor still hung: *The Elbrus at Sunset*. I could stand the filth no more and wiped the dust from the glass with a rag. At once, the two-headed icy blue peak of the Elbrus was revealed, radiating in the rosy glow of sunset.

"Anyutka," Nikolai Ivanovich said, "poor Nadya died in this apartment. [He was referring to Stalin's wife.] And in this apartment I, too, shall die."

He was firm in his intentions: he would not go to the plenum, and if worse came to worst, he would starve himself to death on his bed. The plenum might not heed his protest, but at least Koba would let him die by himself at home.

Writing these lines decades later, I have the advantage over Nikolai Ivanovich in that I know step by step how things will turn out. He could not possibly have known, of course; he could only presume, and his presumptions were formed in large measure by his ardent joie de vivre.

Even though he knew what Stalin was worth, his hope for life compelled him at times to trust the monster.

Suddenly, while we were still sitting together in the study, three men walked in. We had not heard the doorbell; Ivan Gavrilovich had let them in. They abruptly informed "Comrade Bukharin" that he was about to be moved out of the Kremlin. Before Nikolai Ivanovich could react, the telephone rang. Stalin was on the line.

"What's with you there, Nikolai?" asked Koba.

"They've just come to move me out of the Kremlin. I don't care about the Kremlin, but I do want to ask that a place be found to hold my library."

"You just send them to the devil's mother!" said Stalin and hung up.

Standing beside the telephone, the three unknown men heard the Boss clearly. They packed off immediately to "the devil's mother."

Obviously, it was no accident that Stalin should call at precisely the moment Bukharin was being told to quit his apartment. Even without calling, Koba should have found it easy to imagine Nikolai Ivanovich's life inside his Kremlin "prison," but he could not resist playing his malevolent game. But this call, which took place several days before the February–March plenum, was not the only remarkable thing about this incident. I was struck more strongly by the fact that at such a terrible moment, with his letter to the plenum about his hunger strike still lying unsent on his desk, Nikolai Ivanovich was worried about being moved to a place large enough to house his huge library. Did he see a glimmer of hope for life? I think not. More likely, he calculated that he could draw Stalin into a conversation by bringing up the problem. But Koba had not called to converse.

It really made no sense to move Nikolai Ivanovich out of the Kremlin when only days remained before Stalin would guarantee him an apartment in prison. On the other hand, they did find the time to move Rykov out of the Kremlin before his arrest.

Having endured Stalin's latest stunt, as inexplicable as all the rest, we started back to our room, but Nikolai Ivanovich suddenly ducked into the adjoining storage room. Dusty, loaded with junk, more a cell than a room, it had vaulted ceilings and a window covered with an old-style grating in the shape of a rhombus, with bulges on the cross-pieces. Bukharin crashed to the floor, put his head on some dusty old boots, and cried out, "Vandals! Barbarians!" and burst into tears.

"What are you doing, Nikolasha! Why are you writhing in this dirt? Get up at once! Come on into our room!"

"No, I want to get used to a cell; prison is waiting for me! No, I won't come out! I can't stand it, Anyutka! *I can't stand it!* Besides everything else, I'm suffering because you have to go through all of this with me. If only I had known; if only I had been able to foresee! Then I wouldn't have loved you, or if I hadn't been able to suppress this feeling for you inside me, I would've run away from you, to the ends of the earth! But no, I was even eager to have a child on the eve of such a catastrophe."

I barely managed to talk him into returning to our dwelling place.

Toward evening, I sent the Politburo Bukharin's declaration of a hunger strike, addressed to the plenum of the Central Committee.

The next morning, Nikolai Ivanovich bid farewell to his father, his son, and Nadezhda Mikhailovna. He wanted also to telephone Svetlana (he called her Kozechka), his daughter by Esfir Gurvich. But the girl had just turned thirteen, and Nikolai Ivanovich was so despondent that he was afraid she would be traumatized. He didn't call her. His hunger strike was being imposed upon an organism strained by a half year's "investigation," or rather a half year's shameful mockery. Nikolai Ivanovich began to lose strength with catastrophic speed.

Two days into the strike, he felt particularly bad. He looked ashen, drawn, with sunken cheeks and dark hollows under his eyes. Finally, he could hold out no longer and asked for a drink of water. For Nikolai Ivanovich, this was a moral crisis: his hunger strike prescribed refusal of liquid as well as of food; it was a "dry" hunger strike. His condition frightened me so much that on the sly I squeezed an orange into the water in order to pick up his strength. But when Nikolai Ivanovich took the glass from my hand, he detected the aroma of orange juice and flew into a fury. The glass with its life-giving liquid sailed across the room and shattered in the corner.

"You're making me fool the plenum! I won't fool the Party!" he yelled. Never had he spoken to me with such wrath.

I poured another glass of water, without juice, but Nikolai Ivanovich pointedly refused it.

"I want to die!" he said. "Let me die here, next to you," he added, in a faint voice.

Feeling the energy draining from my body, I lay down beside him. At that moment, I had the sensation that we would die together; I felt us falling into a bottomless chasm. I had held together staunchly for all these months, but right then I started sobbing. And my tears drove

Nikolai Ivanovich to even greater despair. He thought of calming me down with a song.

"Let's sing a song together, Anyutka; the one we loved to sing with Klykov."

And he started off softly:

> *The moonlight, magic, shines o'er the river,*
> *All is held in the stillness of night.*
> *In this world I need nothing but you, dear,*
> *My beloved always, forever in sight!*

Nikolai Ivanovich's singing made me laugh and momentarily distracted me from my dark thoughts.

"Poor Klychini," he said, recalling the chauffeur. "What is he thinking about me now? That is, if they haven't raked him in, too."

I have no idea what eventually happened to Nikolai Nikolayevich Klykov.

After Bukharin's listing as editor in chief was finally removed from *Izvestiya,* on January 16, he very rarely looked at the papers and almost never turned on the radio, especially after he heard someone's speech accusing him of having sold himself to the enemies of the Soviet state for thirty pieces of silver. Even Yura's nanny, a Byelorussian, spoke up with indignation:

"What nasty things those skunks are saying! That Nikolai Ivanovich, poor as a church mouse, sold himself for thirty pieces of silver? He has no need of that!"

But on February 19, I believe, the day the plenum was to begin, Nikolai Ivanovich asked me to switch on the radio for news about the meeting he refused to attend. Funereal music was playing. We became anxious: Who could have died? A moment later, the announcer said that Sergo Ordzhonikidze had died from a stroke the day before. We believed this report.

Nikolai Ivanovich's condition now became indescribable. Banished from life like a leper, he was even deprived of the right to go next door and say good-bye to Sergo, a man he deeply respected.

"He couldn't take it, poor Sergo," he said in utter despair. "He couldn't take this horror."

Ah, if only Bukharin had known that death had by no means come by stroke! Yet, it is good that he did not know. By this time, he understood that under Stalin's absolute rule Sergo was powerless to change the situation, but his very presence in the hall of the plenum back in

December, his aroused and agitated look, his single word of distrust to the accusing orators, his single phrase to Pyatakov ("Is your testimony voluntary?")—all these things had warmed Nikolai Ivanovich's heart. Now Ordzhonikidze's death traumatized him to such a degree that at moments he seemed to lie in a state of prostration. He worried that his hunger strike and desperate protest against fantastic accusations, if not hidden from Ordzhonikidze, had possibly hastened his end.

Nikolai Ivanovich knew that Sergo loved and respected him; he had given bright expression to such feelings whenever possible. In 1925, for example, at the Fourteenth Party Congress, when Nikolai Ivanovich found himself the chief target for attacks from the Zinoviev-Kamenev Opposition, Ordzhonikidze had said:

> Comrades, we all know Bukharin, but Vladimir Ilyich [Lenin] knew him best of all. He valued Bukharin very highly and considered him the most important theoretician in our Party. I think in this matter we should remain on Ilyich's side. Bukharin is one of the best theoreticians; our dear Bukharchik, we all love him and will support him. Comrades, if our other leaders had that magnificent trait of Bukharin's, by which he not only has the valor to express his thoughts even when they run counter to the whole Party but also the valor to admit his mistakes when he becomes convinced of them, if our other leaders had this fine quality, how much easier it would be for us to eliminate our disputes.*

Ordzhonikidze's powers were greatly reduced in 1929, but in spite of this (according to Nikolai Ivanovich), he tried with all his might, as chairman of the Party's Central Control Commission, to smother the continuing discord. Bukharin, after being expelled from the Politburo, fired as chief editor of *Pravda* and removed as secretary of the Comintern Executive Committee, worked from 1930 to the beginning of 1934 in the Commissariat of Heavy Industry. During this time, Sergo, who headed the commissariat, retained his respect for him and made a point of being considerate. Semyon Lyandres told me that whenever he entered Ordzhonikidze's office with Nikolai Ivanovich, Sergo would invariably stand up to greet Bukharin and give him a friendly handshake right away, even when other people were present. Sergo also paid close attention to Nikolai Ivanovich's opinions and helped him in many ways during the 1930s. For example, he supported Bukharin's initiative to organize scientific research, which mobilized the most important scientists in the country and elevated the work of the scientific research insti-

*Stenographic Record, Fourteenth Congress of the VKP(b), p. 231.

tutes. In short, Nikolai Ivanovich and Sergo Konstantinovich were linked by profound mutual respect and affection. And so Ordzhonikidze's death hit Nikolai Ivanovich like a physical blow. He lay without rising from the bed—unconscious, as far as I could tell. In fact, this apparent stupor was a state of intense concentration: he was composing a poem dedicated to Sergo's memory, an expression of shock and grief at his heavy loss. Weakening as he starved, he wrote while reclining. I typed this poem in triplicate. The first copy was sent off to Sergo's widow, Zinaida Gavrilovna. The second, much as I regret to report it, was sent to the person responsible for his death. I kept the third.

Unfortunately, I did not memorize the verses, since I could never have imagined they would be taken during the search, despite my insistent pleas to leave them with me. Now I recall only the final two lines:

> *Solid as granite in the flaming sea,*
> *He cracked like lightning in the foamy waves.*

Because of the death and state funeral of Stalin's latest victim, the plenum was postponed a few days, until February 23. When the notice for the rescheduled session arrived, the agenda added a third point (number 1):

1. The question of N. I. Bukharin's anti-Party behavior in regard to the hunger strike he has announced to the plenum.
2. The question of N. I. Bukharin and N. I. Rykov.
3. Organizational questions.

The additional point exasperated Nikolai Ivanovich. How could one speak of anti-Party behavior in respect to the plenum, he wondered, when the accusations brought against him were more criminal than anti-Party in nature and could more reasonably be brought against a highway robber than a political figure? "This type of thing is not done in public life," he would manage to slip in at his trial.

But no matter how offended he was by this response to his desperate protest, Nikolai Ivanovich was at the same time perplexed that this point was added to the agenda. Perhaps things were not so bad, he decided, and Koba would again surprise everyone, turn into a human being, distrust the shameful investigation, and spare both Bukharin and Rykov. Ah, how naive these speculations seem now! Although, taking the circumstances into account—the psychology of the doomed Bukharin together with the character of Stalin—perhaps this speculation contained an element of good sense.

For one reason or another, considering this new point on the agenda, Nikolai Ivanovich made a new decision: to go to the plenum after all, but without breaking his hunger strike.

By February 23, therefore, he had fasted for seven days and nights and was so weak he had to practice walking in the room before undertaking the trip to the meeting. Even though it was only a short distance away, since the plenum was being held in the Kremlin, I decided to accompany him there. But I lacked the strength to wait for the end of the session or to come back at its approximate conclusion. Besides, I could not be sure that Nikolai Ivanovich would not be arrested immediately after this first session. I trudged home and waited there anxiously. This time, he was allowed to return.

He told me what happened: In the vestibule, by the coat rack, he ran into Rykov. Aleksei Ivanovich, himself haggard and ravaged by suffering, regarded his friend with a pained expression, so greatly had Nikolai Ivanovich changed. Then he said, "Tomsky proved to be the most farsighted of us."

Let me remind you that two months earlier, at the December plenum, Rykov had considered Tomsky's suicide a complicating factor in the investigation and had censured it. Now he realized that the investigation was such in name only; in reality, as he put it, "it is persecution."

At the entrance to the hall where the Central Committee session was to be held and where Stalin was already present, Bukharin was met by two men (and they would be the only ones) who shook his hand with compassion: Iyeronim Uborevich and Ivan Akulov, then secretary of the All-Union Central Executive Committee. (Both of them, as the reader knows, were later shot.) Akulov even said, "Courage, Nikolai Ivanovich." Everyone else who encountered Bukharin looked past him.

As he entered the hall, he could no longer stand on his own two feet. His head started to swim; he sank down and remained sitting on the floor of the aisle leading to the Presidium. Stalin walked over to him and said:

"So who did you tell about your hunger strike, Nikolai, the Party Central Committee? Just look at yourself, you've wasted away to nothing. Ask the plenum to forgive you for your hunger strike."

"Why is that necessary," Bukharin asked, "if you are preparing to expel me from the Party?"

Expulsion was the very worst punishment Nikolai Ivanovich could imagine, although at times he was ready to head "out to the sticks," if that would save his life.

"No one is going to expel you from the Party," Stalin answered. Thus he continued to lie, undeterred by the Central Committee members sitting within earshot. Evidently, they believed him, too. "Come, come, Nikolai, ask forgiveness from the plenum. You did a bad thing."

How the "Jesuit" loved for everyone to submit to his will! These words, after all, were spoken just four days before Bukharin's arrest, when, undoubtedly, the Boss had already decided not only to arrest him but also to execute him.

But once more Nikolai believed Koba, perhaps because it was hard to imagine that anyone would lie so senselessly. Barely managing to get up off the floor, he walked to the rostrum. There, he begged forgiveness for his hunger strike, explaining that he had acted because of extreme agitation over unfounded accusations, all of which he positively denied. He said he would end the strike in hopes that the monstrous charges would be dropped. And, yet again, he demanded that a commission be formed to investigate the work of the NKVD. Bukharin lacked the strength to deliver a long speech; besides, there was no point. He descended from the rostrum and sat back down on the floor, not because he had succumbed to weakness again but because he felt himself to be an outcast.

No one present at the plenum, except those who happened to overhear Bukharin's exchange with Stalin, suspected that his willingness to break his hunger strike and beg forgiveness was based on the Gensek's promise not to expel him from the Party—a promise that led him to assume also that the charges against him would be dropped.

But immediately after Bukharin spoke, Yezhov stepped up to deliver an accusatory speech about the bloc of Rightists connected with the Zinoviev Trotskyist Center and the bloc of Rightists connected with the "Parallel" Trotskyist Center, sentenced the month before. In other words, all of the accusations of wrecking, organizing kulak rebellions, planning the dismemberment of the USSR, espousing terror, plotting a "palace revolution," making numerous unsuccessful attempts on Stalin's life, and taking part in Kirov's assassination remained in full force.

Nevertheless, Nikolai Ivanovich still assumed that Koba, having made his "promise," would give the plenum a pleasant surprise by voicing his misgivings about the slanderous accusations. Surely, this was the secret import of Koba's "promise." Indeed, why else would he need to make it? What, in fact, did he get out of it? And what was the point of his mysterious telephone call?

When he got home, Nikolai Ivanovich took a bite of food for the first time in a week, "out of respect for the plenum," and seemed to calm down a bit. But he slept only fitfully that night, constantly imagining that someone was knocking on the wall from the deceased Ordzhonikidze's apartment, banging holes through it, and stuffing them with antirevolutionary documents to be found during a search of his own apartment, much as had been done at Radek's dacha (if the maid Dusya is to be believed).

In a miserable state, Nikolai Ivanovich returned to the plenum the following day. Molotov and Kaganovich gave speeches in which, as at the December plenum, they attacked him ferociously.

As Molotov spoke, Bukharin screamed, "I'm not Zinoviev and not Kamenev! I won't lie about myself!"

"We'll arrest you, then you'll confess," Molotov answered. "The fascist press reports that our trials are provocational. If you deny your guilt, you'll prove you're a fascist hireling!"

When he told me about this exchange, Nikolai Ivanovich remarked, "There's the catch!"

One of the orators, I don't recall which, brought up Bukharin's confrontations with Radek, Pyatakov, and Sosnovsky at the Politburo and asserted that they confirmed the existence of a bloc of Trotskyists and Rightists, making it clear what Bukharin and Rykov had been up to. Stalin interjected, "Bukharin sent me a letter, deciding to take Radek under his protection. Just look what a clever conspiratorial step that was!" (I'm quoting Nikolai Ivanovich's account.)

The accusation was floated that Bukharin, Rykov, and Tomsky had been involved in the Ryutin Platform. Bukharin and Rykov steadfastly disavowed any knowledge of the platform beyond that available in the press. Nikolai Ivanovich added that if he had had a particular point of view he would have written it himself; he would not have needed Ryutin.

"You did write it," Stalin stated flatly. "It is called Ryutin's for conspiratorial purposes."

But what shook Nikolai Ivanovich most was the contribution of Mikhail Kalinin, whom he rated incomparably higher on the moral scale than either Molotov or Kaganovich. Kalinin's speech provided a glaring example of the intensity of Stalin's pressure on the Politburo, for he spoke sluggishly, squeezing out each word, and, as Bukharin said to me, "dragged his butt." In fact, the impotent all-union elder and nominal chief of state spoke with such evident spiritual pain that Nikolai Ivanovich could not feel hatred for him and indeed sincerely pitied him. Let me remind the reader that it was Kalinin who had said to Bukharin a few years earlier, in private conversation, "You, Nikolai Ivanovich, are two hundred percent right, but we have let the power slip through our hands, and there is nothing more worthwhile than Party unity."

During this second session, according to Nikolai Ivanovich, the Central Committee members were distraught and dispirited. Lenin's sister, Mariya Ilyinichna, who had remained on friendly terms with Bukharin, wiped away her tears with a handkerchief.

After the first two sessions, the plenum may have discussed the case of Bukharin and Rykov on the morning of February 25, as well. (I do not recall exactly, but this is not so important.) To prevent a general vote by all members of the Central Committee, Stalin proposed the election of a commission to make the final decision in the case. In addition to all the Politburo members, it included Iona Yakir to represent the military, as well as Mariya Ilyinichna and Nadezhda Konstantinovna, Lenin's widow, in order to disguise the Boss's naked abuse of power in the name of his predecessor. The two women had already personally experienced Stalin's power when they had gone to his office to stand up for Zinoviev and Kamenev and emerged from the confrontation barely alive. There can be no doubt that Stalin had already decided the results of the commission's deliberations.

The February–March 1937 plenum went on with its work, but for the next three days, until the proclamation of the special commission's decision, Bukharin and (I think) Rykov did not attend the sessions. (Thus, it was only the February plenum for them.) Although Nikolai Ivanovich was now psychologically prepared for arrest and the inevitability of parting with life, he was collected as at no other time during these agonizing months of the investigation. Giving up hope for vindication in his lifetime, he turned to posterity: he decided to write a letter to the future generation of Party leaders, declaring his innocence of the criminal charges and asking for posthumous reinstatement in the Party.

I was twenty-three years old now; my husband was convinced that I would live until the day when I could personally deliver his letter to the Central Committee. But, certain that any writing of his would be confiscated during the routine search, fearful that any such discovery would cause me to suffer repressions, he asked me to memorize his valedictory statement word for word so that the actual letter could be destroyed. (He did not imagine that I would be persecuted anyway, letter or no.) Again and again, Nikolai Ivanovich read his letter in a whisper to me, and I had to repeat it after him. Then I read and reread it myself, softly repeating the phrases aloud. Ah, how he griped when I made a slip! Finally, convinced that I had completely memorized the text, he destroyed the letter. This last address to the Party, his last address to the people, he had written on a little table in our room. On that same table lay a folder containing the letters Lenin had sent him over the years. With great emotion Bukharin reread these letters in the final hours before his arrest.

[*The Last Good-bye and the First Search*]

The fateful day of February 27 arrived. Stalin's secretary Poskryobyshev telephoned that evening and informed Nikolai Ivanovich he was required to appear before the plenum.

We began to say farewell.

Ivan Gavrilovich was in terrible condition. Debilitated by suffering for his son, the old man lay in bed most of the time. At the moment of parting, he began to have spasms, his legs involuntarily jerking up, then falling back to the bed, his hands shaking, his face turning blue. He looked as if he were about to give up the ghost. But the trembling subsided, and he once again asked his son in a weak voice:

"What's going on, Nikolai, what's going on? Explain it!"

Before Nikolai Ivanovich could respond, the telephone rang again.

"You're holding up the plenum," Poskryobyshev snapped, executing his master's command. "They're waiting for you."

I cannot say that this caused Nikolai Ivanovich to hurry up very much. He found time to say good-bye to his first wife, Nadezhda Mikhailovna. Then it was my turn.

The tragic moment of our terrible separation, the pain that lives still in my heart to this very day: I cannot do them justice. Nikolai Ivanovich fell to his knees before me. With tears in his eyes, he begged forgiveness for my ruined life. He urged me to raise our son as a Bolshevik—"A Bolshevik without fail!" he said twice. He asked me to fight for his vindication and to remember every single word of his testimonial letter, then to deliver it to the Central Committee when the situation should change. "And it definitely will change," he said. "You're young, and you'll live to see it. Swear that you will do this!" I swore.

He got up from the floor, embraced me, kissed me, and said finally, with great emotion, "See that you don't get angry, Anyutka. There are irritating misprints in history, but the truth will triumph!"

A nervous chill went through my body, and I felt my lips trembling. We understood that we were parting forever.

Nikolai Ivanovich put on his leather jacket, his hat with ear flaps, and turned to the door.

"See that you don't lie about yourself, Nikolai!"

That was all I could say in farewell.

Having seen my husband off to "purgatory," I hardly had time to lie down before they came for the search. Now there was no doubt. Nikolai Ivanovich had been arrested.

A whole squad came, a dozen or so persons, including a doctor wearing a white smock over his NKVD uniform. A search with a physician in attendance! An unprecedented event! Just see how humane they are!

The leader of the search party was Boris Berman, chief of the NKVD Investigative Department. He would be shot later. He came to my search as if to a banquet, wearing a stylish black suit, white shirt, and a fine ring on his finger, and sporting an elongated little fingernail. His smug expression revolted me. The instant he entered my room, he asked, "Any weapons?"

"Yes," I replied and gestured toward the drawer of the nightstand. I wanted him to retrieve the revolver with the inscription "To the Leader of the Proletarian Revolution from Klim Voroshilov."

Berman suddenly seized me by the hand in an overbearing manner, exactly as if stopping me from grabbing the gun to shoot him. Then he took the revolver from the drawer, read the inscription, and smirked, evidently because he had found an unexpected trophy for the Boss.

"Any more?"

"Yes."

There was a German hunting rifle that Rykov had brought back from Berlin as a gift for Nikolai Ivanovich.

Then Berman wanted to know where Bukharin's archive was kept. I asked for clarification: What exactly did he mean by "archive"? Absolutely everything, it turned out. To reach the study, we had to pass through Ivan Gavrilovich's room; there, the physician was sitting beside the old man. In the study, I found a crowd of men and two women, all hard at work. From the safe, they pulled out the minutes of Politburo sessions and the stenographic records of Central Committee plenums; they were emptying out all of the drawers of the desk, as well as the cabinets that held documents related to Bukharin's many years of work at *Pravda*, *Izvestiya*, the Comintern, and the Scientific Research Center. They were also clearing out all of his publications: books, pamphlets, speeches. Meanwhile, from the room where we had spent the last, tortured months together, they took the folder with Lenin's letters and the rough draft of the Party program (the proposal passed at the Eighth Party Congress, in 1919). In one desk drawer, they discovered several letters Nikolai Ivanovich had written me in my childhood, mostly descriptions of nature, and the handwritten manuscript and typed copy of his poem in memoriam of Sergo Ordzhonikidze. These letters and manuscripts were seized, too, despite my protests to Berman that they were "documents unrelated to the investigation." (But, then, what could actually be related to such a scandalous "investigation"?) In fact, everything was cleared out, down to the last scrap. It was all heaped into a huge pile in the study, a mountain of paper that was then labeled "the archive." Like barbarians, the search party destroyed Nikolai Ivanovich's honest and energetic life's work, in order to wipe the true portrait of Bukharin from the face of the earth and replace it with the defiled one to be presented at his trial (if not quite as besmirched as Stalin and his sycophants would like). Then a truck pulled up to the back door. As I watched from the kitchen window, they filled it to overflowing and drove away, evidently to the NKVD.

But Berman remained behind with the two women and a few of the men. Then began the demeaning procedure of the personal search.

They lifted Ivan Gavrilovich up from his bed. Stunned and depressed, he stood shaking in agitation while they rummaged through his pockets and turned them all out on the bed. I did not see the search of Nadezhda Mikhailovna. They entered the baby's room, but Nanny Pasha was in a fighting mood and would not let them frisk her. She shoved one of the NKVD women aside and shrieked, "Get back! Get back! You won't find anything here, you shameless louts!" Yura slept on, undisturbed. When they tried to go to his bed, I determinedly blocked their path, but they did search his cradle.

I was spared a personal search since I was in my nightgown; in fact, I stayed in it to the end. But both my bed and Nikolai Ivanovich's were subjected to meticulous probing.

Going on midnight, I heard a sound in the kitchen and went to take a look. I was overwhelmed by the scene that greeted my eyes. It seems the "officials" had worked up a hunger and had fixed themselves a feast. Since there were too few places at the kitchen table, they were sitting on the floor. Newspaper was laid down as their tablecloth, and thereupon sat an enormous ham, and some sausage and eggs were being fried on our stove. In horror, I rushed back to my room. Immediately, I recalled a sentence I had recently memorized in Bukharin's testament: "At the present time, the so-called organs of the NKVD are in the main a degenerate organization of unprincipled, dissolute, well-kept functionaries." True, these are the people who execute these outrages, but who corrupted them? I could hear them laughing merrily in the kitchen.

Then Berman popped into my room to invite me to share their supper. "You're not eating anything, Anna Mikhailovna. Could it be that you've decided to follow Bukharin's example and announce a hunger strike?" he asked.

I boldly replied, "I'm not about to announce a hunger strike, but I won't eat at the same table with you or sit on the same floor."

Berman smiled ironically and informed me that he was leaving and that only the "worker lads" would remain.

I asked where I could find out about Nikolai Ivanovich. "From me," he answered readily and gave me his name (which I had not known until then) and telephone number.

Soon the "worker lads," having eaten their fill, began to sing. Ivan Gavrilovich's room was closest to the kitchen, and I wonder what he thought, hearing all this. Afraid that this merry group would awaken the baby, I went to the kitchen to quiet them down. These NKVD "officials" had no intention of apologizing but, to my delight, said that they were leaving, anyway. A hush fell over the apartment. Not everyone left, however; the women remained behind. They were under orders to turn the pages of all of the books in Bukharin's huge library in hopes of finding something compromising. This page turning lasted for days. Several times, I went into the immense somber room with arched ceilings and shelf after shelf of books that was the study, and there the women kept turning, turning, turning the pages of books. I cannot believe they were able to turn them all. When they left, they sealed the glass doors of the bookcases.

For several days afterward, I lay in bed like a dead person. This was the reaction that set in after such prolonged nervous tension. And for a long time, the imaginary rustle of turning pages tormented me.

Nadezhda Mikhailovna, wearing the medical corset without which she could not move from place to place, crawled into my room. Neither of us could realistically console the other as we shared our impressions of the search, made gloomy prognoses of the fate of Nikolai Ivanovich and Rykov, and, with pain in our hearts, watched over Yura. He crawled around the room looking for his father, calling out for him.

Eventually, though drained of energy and spirit by many months of torture, I tried to gather up my strength. I had to look after the baby, who had been deprived of a proper mother's care for half a year. And I had to work fast to learn what was happening to my husband before the *vertushka* telephone was disconnected. Berman's number could be dialed directly only from this device. A week after the arrest, I decided to phone.

A man's voice, which I recognized as his, answered, but when I identified myself, he said, "Berman is not at work." I began phoning daily. Coming to recognize my voice, the chief of the NKVD Investiga-tive Department would not even bother to ask who was calling but immediately answer that he was not in. Eventually, I had enough of this and shouted, "Why are you lying? I recognize your voice!" Berman hung up immediately. But he phoned back the same day, undoubtedly after getting authorization from Yezhov. He read off a list of books Nikolai Ivanovich had requested from home, the German books of fas-cist ideology he had bought in Berlin in 1936. I was given permission to break the seal on the bookcase.

"Bring the books to Investigator Kogan," Berman said. "A pass will be ordered up for you."

Just as I was about to leave, Kolya Sozykin phoned and offered to go along with me. On the way, he bought some oranges for Nikolai Ivanovich, perhaps with funds appropriated for this purpose by the NKVD. He left me at the entrance to the famous building on Lubyanka Square.

Investigator Kogan was sitting in a small but long and narrow room, more like a coffin than an office. He greeted me with conspicuous civility.

"Well now, Anna Mikhailovna, just last evening I had a chat with Nikolai Ivanovich in this room. He has a sweet tooth, your husband. When we had tea, he took six lumps of sugar in his glass."

"That's funny. He never did that at home. Evidently, he has devel-oped a longing for sweets because of his bitter life."

I handed over the oranges and the books.

"What do you mean, a bitter life? We treat Nikolai Ivanovich well, so there's no need for you to bring oranges. Better to give them to the child."

But I did not take them back.

Kogan handed me a little note written in Nikolai Ivanovich's hand:

"Don't worry about me. They are looking after me, and watching after me, in every way. Write how you are there. How is the boy? Take some photographs of yourself with Yura and send them to me. Your Nikolai."

"Exactly as if Nikolai Ivanovich were in a sanatorium here," I ven-tured timidly, so struck was I by the phrase "looking after me, and watching after me."

"He even has the opportunity to work," said Kogan, holding out to me a manuscript page from a chapter of Bukharin's book *The Degrada-tion of Culture under Fascism*.

Noting the title, I remarked, "Doesn't it seem paradoxical to you that the fascist hireling Bukharin is writing an antifascist book?"

Kogan turned red. "That's not for you to decide! If you insist on discussing matters related to the investigation, today will be the last time we meet. If not, then I will permit you to call me from time to time, and to come here to find out how Nikolai Ivanovich is doing."

The investigator reminded me to answer my husband's note. I wrote briefly that we were all feeling "not bad," and said a thing or two about Yura. I promised to bring photographs. Kogan insisted that I add that we were still living in our apartment. I refused, since I could not divine the hidden significance of this, and told him that I was only waiting for the day when I could get out of the Kremlin.

I was still sitting down as we said good-bye; the investigator firmly pressed my hand. I glanced at his face and was surprised to see unspeakable remorse in his eyes.

I got up to leave.

"My telephone number, the telephone, Anna Mikhailovna, write it down!"

But he wrote it down himself on a little piece of paper. He asked me not to abuse the privilege, to call no sooner than two weeks from that day and be ready to bring along the photographs.

On that date exactly, with the photos in hand, I tried to contact Kogan. I was unsuccessful, and after many more telephone calls, his successor informed me, "Investigator Kogan has been sent on a long trip. There is no point in telephoning for him any more."

Anyone who survives from that time will recall what was meant by "a long trip." I was no longer permitted to telephone for information about Nikolai Ivanovich or to give him the photographs.

[Bukharin's Arrest]

Let us go back to the February–March 1937 plenum for the last time. I would no longer hear my husband's version of events after February 27, the day he failed to return home from the plenum because he was arrested on the spot with Rykov.

I learned some further details from women whose husbands had attended the plenum, then been arrested after Bukharin, but shot before he was. Most of my information came from Sarra Yakir, Nina Uborevich, and Lyudmila Shaposhnikova, the wife of Mikhail Chudov. Their stories agreed with each other, so I assume my account is basically correct.

At the February 27 session, the decision of the special commission was read out as Bukharin and Rykov listened. Immediately afterward, they were arrested and led from the plenum under guard. The text of the decision, in effect a command rather than a recommendation for debate and a vote, was succinct: "Remove from the Central Committee, expel from the Party, arrest, continue the investigation."

Thus charged with treason, Bukharin and Rykov were probably not given an opportunity to say a final word. I doubt they were even given access to the rostrum. As they were taken off to jail, they did nothing but protest their innocence, or so I was told.

Many people have wanted to know whether any speeches were given in defense of Bukharin and Rykov at the February–March plenum. Nikolai Ivanovich told me himself that there were none when he was present.

I do not know how the Central Committee members acted when the two accused men were absent from the plenum, waiting at home for the decision of the special commission. Nor do I know how they behaved after the arrests.

After my return to Moscow more than twenty years after these events, however, rumors leaked out from various sources that both Pavel Postyshev, then secretary of the Ukrainian Communist Party, and Grigory Kaminsky, people's commissar of public health for the Russian Republic, had defended Bukharin and Rykov. Reportedly, they also demanded that Grigory Sokolnikov and Karl Radek, who were still alive though they had been found guilty at their recently concluded trial, be brought before the plenum and subjected to a cross-examination, a face-to-face confrontation with my husband and Rykov. But Stalin objected that it was superfluous to call condemned "enemies of the people" for testimony and noted that, besides, Bukharin's previous confrontations with Sokolnikov and Radek had been witnessed by many Politburo members. (In fact, Sokolnikov had not been called before the Politburo to confront Bukharin. Where and with whom Rykov had confrontations, I do not know.) In these confrontations, Stalin went on, the condemned men had confirmed their accusations against Bukharin; repetition of the confrontations was unnecessary, if the Central Committee members trusted their Politburo. In this way, the Boss rebuffed the demand from Postyshev and Kaminsky.

I hesitate to assess the accuracy of this account. At the time, the moment had already been lost; the majority of the Central Committee members were doomed; Postyshev and Kaminsky themselves had not long to live. I heard the story of Kaminsky's arrest from the persecuted wives of former NKVD officials. As he was being led off to interrogation, he yelled at the top of his voice, "Comrades, it's provocation!"

Iona Yakir's courageous act of abstaining from the special commission vote on the fate of Bukharin and Rykov was reported to me by his wife, Sarra, Chudov's wife, and Iyeronim Uborevich, whose husband had heard the story from Yakir himself. Considering the situation, Yakir's action could be regarded as a statement in defense of the two accused.

Sarra Yakir and Iyeronim Uborevich did not know anything about how Lenin's sister and widow had acted in the deliberations, but Chudov told his wife that neither one even made an appearance at the special commission. I have no confirmation of this, but it seems more than likely. Both women could surmise very well—indeed, they knew for a fact—that it was impossible to change a decision made by Stalin.

The commission's vote was recorded by name, according to the wives who told me about it, but I am convinced that any record preserved for history would be preserved only in the form demanded by the Boss.

For precisely this reason, I distrust the document recently cited by Gennady Bordyugov and Vladimir Kozlov in their article "Nikolai Bukharin: Episodes in a Political Biography," and also by Dmitry Volkogonov in his study "Triumph and Tragedy: A Political Portrait of Stalin," both published in 1988.* Supposedly, the document accurately gives the composition of the commission and reports its discussion of the charges. To judge from it, the commission was far more populous than Bukharin told me. On the other hand, it is possible that he remembered only the chief members, or perhaps members not part of the Politburo were added after he and Rykov left the plenum.

All the same, my suspicions are aroused by the document's portrayal of Yakir's actions.

Supposedly, the commission discussed three alternatives:

1. *Yezhov's* (the most severe)—To remove Bukharin and Rykov as candidate members of the Central Committee and turn them over to the court of the Military Tribunal for enforcement of the supreme penalty, execution by shooting.
2. *Postyshev's*—To turn them over to the court, but not for execution.
3. *Stalin's*—Not to turn them over to the court but to send their case to the NKVD for additional investigation.

*"Nikolai Bukharin: epizody politicheskoi biografii," *Kommunist*, no. 13, 1988, p. 108; "Triumf i tragediya: politicheskii portret Stalina," *Oktyabr'*, no. 12, 1988, p. 114. [The latter title was published as a four-volume work in 1989 by Novosti Press.]

Ultimately, all subscribed to Stalin's proposal. According to this document, Yakir originally supported Yezhov. In fact, using material evidently drawn from the same source, Volkogonov asserts in his work that even after Stalin's suggestion, which seemed at first blush more humane, Yakir and Aleksandr Kosarev continued to push for the death penalty. But if Yakir really was "bloodthirsty" in this case, what prompted Yakov Matusov, a senior officer in the NKVD Investigative Department, to tell me in the Lubyanka inner prison, as I explained earlier, "You thought that Yakir and Tukhachevsky would save your Bukharin! But we do good work. That's why they didn't succeed!"?

In any event, many who sat on the commission, Kosarev among them, did not have long to live. Yakir had slightly more than two months. Therefore, it would have been easy to leave a record pleasing to the dictator. Incidentally, Nina Uborevich brought up Yakir's role without any prompting from me: "He was the only one who abstained from voting."

In his recent work *On Stalin and Stalinism*, the Soviet historian Roy Medvedev apparently relies upon another document, although there can, of course, be only one authentic one.* He writes that the voting was done by name (as the wives told me) in alphabetical order. Consequently, all who voted before Stalin supported the death penalty; those who voted after him voted for his proposal. If that's true, fortune smiled on Yakir, whose name begins with the last letter of the Russian alphabet.

Where lies the truth? I've made my opinion sufficiently clear and leave the matter to the reader's deliberation.

The notice that appeared in the press at the time did not accurately report the commission's decision (which was, as I've made clear, Stalin's decision): "The plenum considered likewise the question of the anti-Party activity of Bukharin and Rykov and moved to expel them from the ranks of the Communist Party."†

For one thing, this notice does not even mention the charges brought against Bukharin and Rykov based upon the forced testimony given at the first two show trials. Furthermore, the phrase "anti-Party activity" fails to convey the monstrous abuse Stalin heaped upon them, such as the following:

A couple of words about the wreckers, saboteurs, spies, and so on. Now, I think, it is clear to all that today's wreckers and saboteurs, no matter what flag they use to mask themselves,

Znamya, no. 2, 1989, p. 206.
†*VKP(b) v rezolyutsiyakh i postanovleniyakh*, pt. 1 (Moscow, 1940), p. 653.

Trotskyist or Bukharinist, have long ceased to be a political force in the workers' movement, that they have turned into an unscrupulous and unprincipled gang of professional wreckers, saboteurs, spies, murderers. It is understood that these gentlemen must be blasted and uprooted without mercy as enemies of the working class, as traitors to our motherland. This is clear and needs no further explanation.*

Thus, in only "a couple of words," as if merely in passing, Stalin blasted and uprooted the Bolshevik Leninist guard.

I assume that he spoke these "couple of words" at the February–March 1937 plenum just after Bukharin was arrested, so as not to lose the opportunity of rubbing it in.

[Bukharin's Testament]

For many long years, I kept Nikolai Ivanovich's letter-testament engraved in my memory. After my release from camp, but still in exile, I wrote it down several times. Each time, becoming afraid it would be discovered, I would destroy it. Only in 1956, after the Twentieth Party Congress, did I decide not to destroy the text I had written most recently. I have kept it to the present day. Its pages are yellow with age.

Here is the full text of Nikolai Bukharin's letter-testament:

TO A FUTURE GENERATION
OF PARTY LEADERS

I am leaving life. I bow my head, but not before the proletarian scythe, which is properly merciless but also chaste. I am helpless, instead, before an infernal machine that seems to use medieval methods, yet possesses gigantic power, fabricates organized slander, acts boldly and confidently.

Dzerzhinsky† is no more; the wonderful traditions of the Cheka have gradually receded into the past, those traditions by which the revolutionary idea governed all its actions, justified cruelty toward enemies, safeguarded the state against any counter-

---

Court Record in the Case of the Anti-Soviet "Bloc of Rightists and Trotskyists," p. 149.

†Head of the secret police, or Cheka, under Lenin.

revolution. For this reason, the organs of the Cheka won a special trust, a special honor, an authority and respect. At the present time, the so-called organs of the NKVD are in the main a degenerate organization of unprincipled, dissolute, well-kept functionaries who, enjoying the former authority of the Cheka, seeking to satisfy the pathological suspiciousness of Stalin (I fear to say more), pursuing rank and glory, perform their foul deeds without, incidentally, understanding that they are simultaneously destroying themselves: history does not tolerate the witnesses to dirty deeds!

These "wonder-working" organs can grind any member of the Central Committee, any member of the Party, into dust, turn him into a traitor-terrorist, saboteur, spy. If Stalin doubted in himself, confirmation would follow in an instant.

Storm clouds hang over the Party. My head alone, guilty of nothing, will implicate thousands more of the innocent. For, after all, an organization must be created, a "Bukharinist organization," that in reality not only does not exist now, when I am in my seventh year without a shadow of disagreement with the Party, but did not exist then, in the years of the Right Opposition. I knew nothing about the secret organizations of Ryutin and Uglanov. Together with Rykov and Tomsky, I expounded my views openly.

Since the age of eighteen, I have been in the Party, and always the goal of my life has been the struggle for the interests of the working class, for the victory of socialism. These days the newspaper with the hallowed name *Pravda* prints the most contemptible lie that I, Nikolai Bukharin, wanted to destroy the achievement of October, to restore capitalism. This is an unheard-of obscenity. This is a lie that in its obscenity and irresponsibility toward the people could be matched only by the story that [Tsar] Nikolai Romanov devoted his entire life to the struggle against capitalism and the monarchy, to the struggle for the realization of the proletarian revolution.

If I was more than once mistaken regarding the methods of building socialism, may my descendants judge me no more severely than did Vladimir Ilyich. We were the first to pursue the same goal by an as yet untrodden path. The time, the mores were different. *Pravda* would print a page for discussion, then everyone debated, sought the right path, argued, and made up and proceeded onward together.

I turn to you, the future generation of Party leaders, on whom will fall the historic mission of clearing the monstrous cloud of crimes that in these terrible days is growing more and more grandiose, spreading like wildfire and smothering the Party.

I address myself to all Party members!

In what may be the final days of my life, I am certain that sooner or later the filter of history will inevitably wash the filth from my head.

I never was a traitor; I would have unhesitatingly traded my own life for Lenin's. I loved Kirov and never undertook anything against Stalin.

I ask the new, young, and honest generation of Party leaders to read my letter aloud at a plenum of the Central Committee, to vindicate me, and to reinstate me in the Party.

Know, comrades, that the banner you bear in a triumphant march toward communism contains a drop of my blood, too!

I delivered this letter to the Central Committee of the Communist Party in 1961. The Bolshevik trials of the 1930s were being reexamined by the Party Control Commission, and I was summoned a number of times to be told that the question of Bukharin's rehabilitation would be decided in the near future. For whatever reasons, this did not take place at that time.

Repeatedly, I sought his rehabilitation from senior Party leaders and in the highest Party echelon, the presidiums of Party congresses, but without result.

Finally, in a letter addressed in 1986 to Mikhail Sergeyevich Gorbachev, general secretary of the Central Committee, Presidium of the Twenty-seventh Congress of the Communist Party, I wrote the following:

What have you done about Bukharin? He has been forced into a procrustean bed that differs from the famous mythological one in its technical perfection. This is the Stalinist bed! Like a magnet, it caught Bukharin and stripped everything from him that bound him to the Communist Party and to Leninism; it castrated his revolutionary spirit, severed him from socialism. It cut away all his virtues, besmirched all his moral and intellectual qualities, for which he was loved in the Party. It, this Stalinist bed, removed from Bukharin the love of Vladimir Ilyich. "Lenin's favorite son" is what Bukharin's comrades called him, knowing Lenin's partiality for him. "The Golden Boy of the Revolution" is what Lenin called Bukharin. This was known in Party circles, and I myself heard it from the lips of Vladimir Ilyich. It, this Stalinist bed, took away from Bukharin his feeling of boundless love, commitment, profound respect, and esteem for the genius of Lenin, for Lenin the leader, for Lenin the man and personal friend.

It, this Stalinist bed, left Bukharin with only a dry catalog of mistakes, real and imagined, which he committed on his long (thirty years) and honest revolutionary path. Down this path, he boldly hauled the "cartload of history," openly expressing his thoughts out loud for discussion, for polemics among his comrades, in the name of a united goal, in the name of the triumph of the idea linking him with Lenin.

The words of Lenin are written on your Party cards: "The Party is the mind, honor, and conscience of our epoch." Act as befits those attributes!

I think that you, as Party leaders, can give but one possible answer to my appeal—a positive one.

It cost me a great effort to carry the text of Bukharin's letter "To a Future Generation of Party Leaders" through the long years of prisons, camps, and exiles. I want to believe that this future generation will be you.

The distance of half a century separates me from the dramatic events described in this book. I conclude this account with the news that Nikolai Ivanovich has finally been exonerated and reinstated in the Party. I am glad I lived to see the day. Justice has triumphed.

But nothing has dimmed my memory. And to the present moment the words that Bukharin addressed to the future live in my soul: "Know, comrades, that the banner you bear in a triumphant march toward communism contains a drop of my blood, too!"

EPILOGUE:

I Always Believed That the Truth Would Triumph

[From Anna Larina's speech at a conference commemorating the centenary of Nikolai Bukharin's birth, given before the Institute of Marxism-Leninism of the Communist Party Central Committee on September 30, 1988.]

Not too long ago, it would have been hard for me to imagine that I would be speaking to you here in this building, in this "temple," which I have opposed for almost thirty years in my many written appeals for the rehabilitation of Nikolai Ivanovich. In the final reckoning, it was precisely from here—to be sure, on instructions from above during the period of the Stalin cult, and by inertia afterward—that the falsification of Party history emanated, that famous Stalinist *Short Course* that has traveled a distance of no mean extent. For this reason, we had an image of Nikolai Ivanovich Bukharin and of Lenin's other close colleagues that was defaced beyond all recognition.

The historian Vladimir Naumov told me that one of my appeals made an especially strong impression on him. It was yet another appeal for Nikolai Ivanovich's rehabilitation, but one in which I made a critical analysis of the introductions to the stenographic records of several Party congresses, republished in Khrushchev's time. Reissuing the stenographic records could itself be regarded only as a progressive development, a step toward a truthful history. But the introductions could not bear critical scrutiny; the stamp of dogmatism and falsification lay too heavy upon them, and this disturbed me. Presumably, the stenographic records of Party congresses and conferences are read by highly qualified people such as historians, but perhaps also by people like me, interested in grasping the reality they convey rather than a falsified history of the Party. They make it possible for any reader to learn what views were held by each speaker. These introductions I mentioned were firmly imprinted with the authoritative stamp of "The Institute of Marxism-Leninism under the Central Committee." That is why, at the outset, I used the phrase "in this temple."

I intended to send my appeal to Nikita Khrushchev, but I studied these congresses so zealously that the work went on for almost a year, and, alas, I was too late. I had to send my appeal instead to Leonid Brezhnev, along with copies for every member of the Politburo. To Anastas Mikoyan, in addition to the appeal, I sent a personal letter asking that he, as the oldest member, who knew Bukharin well, tell the truth about him. A short time later, his secretary, Aleksandr Barabanov, telephoned me to ask, "Anastas Ivanovich wonders whether you sent your appeal only to him or to all the members of the Politburo." "To all of them," I answered. I had failed to consider the possibility that after Khrushchev's removal Mikoyan would lose influence in the Politburo, then be expelled in 1966. Thus there is little chance he did anything about my letter. One way or another, the appeal remained unanswered. I had turned to Mikoyan because I knew that in him Khrushchev had found a true support for his policy of unmasking Stalin's crimes. I was aware of Mikoyan's exceptional concern for family members of comrades who had been posthumously rehabilitated as well as for those people who had returned from the camps and exile, including my son and me, although Nikolai Ivanovich had not as yet been rehabilitated. I also knew that relations between Mikoyan and Bukharin had been cordial. And I was able to imagine what incredible pressure must have been brought to bear upon Mikoyan to make him carry out Stalin's criminal orders.

Most of my appeals were addressed to Brezhnev. Eventually, I sent an appeal to Mikhail Gorbachev, at the Twenty-seventh Party Congress, in February 1986. It was long, historically grounded, and, to my great joy, proved to be the last. I did not have to write another.

It is difficult to convey my reaction, my excitement and delight. I had always believed in the rehabilitation of Nikolai Ivanovich Bukharin, Aleksei Ivanovich Rykov, and Mikhail Pavlovich Tomsky. These figures should not be considered separately; they are one entity. Although I believed that the truth would triumph, it was detained too long on the road. I had already lost hope that I would live to see the rehabilitation. Almost every time before writing a new appeal, I talked on the telephone with Rykov's daughter, Natalya Alekseyevna. We could not refrain from writing to the congresses, but at the same time we gave a heavy sigh. Our hopes were slight, very slight.

Yet we lived to see the day!

Words fail to communicate my feelings. Possibly, I am like an astronaut beyond the force of gravity. A terrible oppressive weight has been lifted from me, from my mind. It's as if I were weightless, but the problem is I can't come back down to earth. Recently, I have had many occasions to give talks, to recall and recall again the one whose shining image I have carried all through my painful life, the one who has remained alive in my memory and been impossible to forget. What a bitter thing it is that Nikolai Ivanovich cannot rejoice along with me and realize along with us that his prophecy has finally come to pass and that the "filter of history," as he put it in his letter to posterity, has washed the filth from his name at last! Back in that tragic moment when Nikolai Ivanovich wrote his testament, he assumed that he had made a great discovery when he foresaw that even after his death (by shooting, on the basis of horrendous, unfounded charges of treason) he could be called a Bolshevik once again and be reinstated in the Party posthumously. But it so happened that during Khrushchev's time many prominent and rank-and-file figures were reinstated ahead of us, while we went on waiting. All those relatives in the same position as I had to wait more than thirty years.

I would like to devote more attention to the question of how the campaign for Nikolai Ivanovich's rehabilitation was waged. It was lengthy, and opposition was strong. The question of rehabilitating Bukharin and Rykov and revoking the bogus trials was already an issue back in Khrushchev's time. A commission was formed with Olga Shatunovskaya as chair, working in the Party Control Commission. I spoke both with her and her colleague Kolesnikov. The latter encouraged my hopes by saying, "The rehabilitation of Nikolai Bukharin will take place in the very near future." But as you know, it did not occur until February 4, 1988.

My struggle for Nikolai Ivanovich's rehabilitation can be divided into two stages.

First, there was the struggle to preserve in my memory the letter he had addressed "To a Future Generation of Party Leaders." This was not easy to do under the conditions of prison, camp, and exile. I wrote it down for the first time in 1945, but, fearing it would be discovered, I destroyed it. This happened a number of times. Finally, I wrote it down one last time in 1956, following the Twentieth Party Congress. This manuscript I have kept to the present day. It is now on display in the Museum of the Revolution in an exhibition commemorating the centenary of Nikolai Bukharin's birth.

Second, after returning to Moscow from exile in 1959, I wrote numerous appeals for Nikolai Ivanovich's rehabilitation, both to the Party congresses and during the periods in between. I wrote them in my own name and at Nikolai Ivanovich's behest. In response, I heard only the silence of the grave or official telephone calls informing me that there were no grounds for reconsideration. I do not say that I alone deserve the credit for Nikolai Ivanovich's rehabilitation. My son Yury Nikolayevich joined with me in the struggle. He also appealed more than once to the Central Committee for the rehabilitation of his father. In 1978, he sent an appeal to the general secretary of the Italian Communist Party, Enrico Berlinguer. In response, a conference was held in Rome at which representatives of socialist and communist parties from many countries looked into aspects of Bukharin's theoretical thought. Also, an invaluable contribution to the understanding of Bukharin as a person, and hence to his rehabilitation, was made by the American scholar Stephen Cohen. He literally lifted the lid off the coffin when, in 1973, he published *Bukharin and the Bolshevik Revolution,* which was in actuality the political biography of Bukharin.* Professor Cohen revealed Bukharin to new generations who previously had known about him only as an enemy of the people or an enemy of the Party. I say this even though I do not agree with this author on every point. I can say, however, that I have never read a more profound work on Nikolai Ivanovich. My son Yury, who did not know English, translated this book into Russian with a dictionary in his hands and the help of Yevgeny Aleksandrovich Gnedin, who had known Bukharin and spent many years in camp and exile.

Also involved in the campaign of rehabilitation were Komsomol workers at the Kama auto factory in Naberezhnye Chelny. Their political club, led by the Komsomol organizer Valery Pisigin, played an active role. When the working class rose up, it had an enormous political significance. The ongoing program of perestroika, together with the elimination of "blank spots" in the field of history, helped the rehabilitation of Bukharin, Tomsky, and others. (I think that in respect to Bukharin, Rykov, and other major political figures it was not a matter of "blank spots" but rather "dirty spots" in the history of the Party.) All this became possible because of the course the Party has taken in restoring

---

*A Russian-language edition of Cohen's book, published in the United States in 1980, circulated in the Soviet Union for a number of years. A Soviet edition was published in Moscow in 1989.

its true and unfalsified history. We have lived to see the rehabilitation of Nikolai Ivanovich and his intellectual kin, Aleksei Rykov, Mikhail Tomsky, and other close companions of Vladimir Ilyich Lenin.

But in order to grow a crop, you must first prepare the soil. And I am happy to have given all that I could in the triumphant campaign.

In conclusion, I propose that this conference address a petition to either the Central Committee's Politburo or the Moscow City Executive Committee (I do not know which is relevant here) to perpetuate the memory of Nikolai Ivanovich Bukharin. I suggest placing memorial plaques at the building where *Pravda*'s editorial offices were once located and where he worked for more than eleven years, on the site of *Izvestiya*'s editorial offices, and at the building where the Comintern was once located.

BUKHARIN'S PRISON LETTER TO ANNA LARINA— DELIVERED 54 YEARS LATER

The story of Nikolai Bukharin and Anna Larina is not over—even after the end of the country he helped create. Historical documents that could reveal the full truth about what happened to Bukharin during his year of isolation in Stalin's prisons, his efforts to save his family from the murderous terror, and his conduct at the 1938 Moscow trial remain hidden in Russian archives, particularly the Kremlin (Presidential) Archive and that of the former KGB. Slowly and elliptically, however, some documents are emerging, one way or another.

The letter translated below, excavated from the Kremlin Archive, was delivered unofficially to Anna Larina in June 1992, fifty-four years after Bukharin wrote it to her in prison on the eve of his trial and execution. Readers of these memoirs can imagine her reaction—joy over hearing so unexpectedly from her husband one more time, but also lacerating depression caused by renewed memories of the events that had destroyed their lives. As usual, Anna Mikhailovna found her balance. She allowed Bukharin's letter to be published, along with her present-day response, in the newspaper *Izvestiya* (October 13, 1992) and the journal *Rodina* (No. 8–9, 1992). Publication reopened discussion of Bukharin's fate for a second time—now in a Russia whose government no longer honored him as a founding father.

In important respects, Bukharin's letter speaks for itself. His deep concern for the safety of Anna and their baby son, Yuri, his invalid first wife, Nadya (Nadezhda Lukina), and elderly father who lived with him and Anna, and his young daughter, Svetlana, by a second marriage confirms beyond any doubt that Stalin used the family as hostage to compel Bukharin's participation in the show trial. But as he would do systematically at that bizarre spectacle two months later, even in this letter Bukharin had to convey his full meanings guardedly, reminding his wife to "read between these lines." Here too readers can guess the horrible choices, torment, and deceit inflicted on him in prison by Stalin's agents.

Bukharin was right, of course, to suspect that his tormentors might not actually give the letter and other items mentioned here to Anna, as clearly they had promised to do. Everything went instead to the terror's architect, Stalin, in whose private archives they remained buried for more than half a century. Indeed, as readers know, Stalin's men lied to Bukharin about his family's well-being. Anna was not at home "with the little one" in January 1938, but already deep in the Gulag. His infant son had already begun his twenty-year odyssey through foster homes and orphanages. And Nadya, unable even to stand without a spinal corset, was soon arrested, tortured, and dragged to her place of execution.

There is, however, a happier postscript. Bukharin's letter confirmed our long-standing suspicion that this most irrepressibly intellectual of political leaders had somehow written manuscripts in prison. They too remained hidden until the summer of 1992, when, with help from three top political and archive officials in the Yeltsin government, Anna Mikhailovna finally received them from the Kremlin Archive— one thousand pages of philosophy, autobiographical fiction, and poetry written in Bukharin's small script. The book he began just before his arrest, about which he expresses such concern in the letter, is still "lost." But the search for it, and other revealing pages from this quintessential case of what Russians call "living history," goes on.

SFC
November 1992

To Anna Mikhailovna Larina

Dear Sweet Annushka, My Darling!

I write to you on the eve of the trial, and I write to you with a definite purpose, which I emphasize three times over: No matter what you read, no matter what you hear, no matter how horrible these things may be, no matter what might be said to me or what I might say—endure *everything* courageously and calmly. Prepare the family. Help all of them. I fear for you and the others, but most of all for you. Don't feel malice about anything. Remember that the great cause of the USSR lives on, and *this* is the most important thing. Personal fates are transitory and wretched by comparison. A great ordeal awaits you. I beg you, my dearest, muster all your strength, tighten all the strings of your heart, but don't allow them to *break*.

Do not talk carelessly with anybody about anything. You will understand my position. You are the person closest, dearest to me, only you. In the name of everything good that we have shared, I beg you to use all your strength and spirit to help yourself and the family *endure* this terrible phase. I think that father and Nadya should not *read the newspapers* during the days in question: let it be *as though they are asleep.* But you will know best what to do and what to say so that it will not be an unexpected horrible shock. If I ask this of you, believe me when I say that I have come to it through great suffering, and that everything that will happen is demanded by bigger and greater interests. You know what it costs me to write you such a letter, but I write it in the deep conviction that I must act only in this way. This is the main, basic, and decisive factor. You yourself understand how much these short lines say. Do as I ask you, and keep a grip on yourself—be *like a stone,* a statue.

I am very worried about YOU, and if they allow YOU to write to me or to send me some reassuring words about what I have said above, then THIS weight would fall somewhat from my soul. I ask you to do this, I beg you, my dearest friend.

My second request is an immeasurably lesser one, but for me personally very important. You will be given three manuscripts:

a) a big philosophical work of 310 pages *(Philosophical Arbesques);*

b) a small volume of poems;

c) the first seven chapters of a novel.

Three typed copies should be made of each of them. Father can help polish the poems and the novel. (A *plan* is attached to the poems. On the surface, they seem to be chaotic, but they can be understood— each poem should be retyped on a separate sheet of paper.)

The most important thing is that the philosophical work not be lost. I worked on it for a long time and put a great deal into it; it is a very *mature* work in comparison to my earlier writings, and, in contrast to them, *dialectical* from beginning to end.

There is also that other book *(The Crisis of Capitalist Culture and Socialism),* the first half of which I was writing when I was still at home. Try to *rescue* it. I don't have it here—it would be a shame if it were lost.

If you receive the manuscripts (many of the poems are related to *you,* and you will feel through them how close I feel to you), and if you are allowed to pass on a few lines or words to me, *don't forget to mention my manuscripts.*

It is not appropriate for me to say more about my feelings right now. But you can read between these lines how much and how deeply I love you. Help me by fulfilling my first request during what will be for me a very difficult time. Regardless of what happens and no matter what the outcome of the trial, I will see you afterward and be able to kiss your hands.

Good-bye, my darling,
Your Kolka

January 15, 1938

P.S. I have the small photograph of you with the little one. Kiss Yurka for me. It's good that he cannot read. I am also very afraid for my daughter. Say a word or two about our son—the boy must have grown, and he doesn't know me. Hug and kiss him for me.

LETTERS FROM
SOVIET READERS

---

[1]

2 October 1988

Dear Anna Mikhailovna:

Thank you for your memoirs. Before such people I bow down in respect.

By nature I am a sociable person and if I may say so a peace-loving one, but I simply hate the Stalinists. Perhaps I react the same way only to anti-Semites, but often one and the other correspond.

From the years of my youth, the name of your husband has been linked in my mind with a certain tragic incident.

Before the war, we lived in a forest district of the Sokolnikov region. The families of foresters living there were very friendly with one another, but especially my parents—Aleksandr Petrovich Grachov and Valentina Timofeyevna Grachova. They were friendly with the family of the Spitsyns. I recall Ivan Yakovlevich Spitsyn as a skinny middle-aged man (he was fifty-five years old at the time), with a wedge-shaped gray beard. His wife, Galina Demyanovna, was the daughter of the forester Mochalsky, who had done a lot in his time to maintain the forests outside Moscow. Up to recent times, there was a street named after Mochalsky in the area of metro station Semyonovskaya. (Now it is named after Ibrammov.) A close friend of the Mochalsky family was [the famous writer] Vladimir Korolenko. Galina Demyanovna had an excellent knowledge of French. (She had studied at the Sorbonne before the revolution.)

(For goodness' sake, forgive me for describing everything in such detail. But from childhood the tragedy of this family made the strongest impression on me and exerted a certain influence on my views.)

Spitsyn was a very nice man, one of the intelligentsia, unusually modest, and, as it seems to me, completely removed from politics. Ivan Yakovlevich was absorbed in his work. Galina Demyanovna "kept house," raised their daughter (theirs was a late marriage, and at that time their daughter was nine years old, the same as I), and read French novels.

Everything changed on the eve of 1 May 1940. In the morning, it was noticed that Ivan Yakovlevich had disappeared somewhere. He often went for a walk in the woods in the mornings, but this time two things were worrisome: first, he had left the house much too early and, second, all his footwear remained at home (only his slippers were gone). The daughter got upset and started rummaging through his footwear: "Mama, here are Papa's shoes, and these are here too." After taking her daughter to school, Galina Demyanovna ran over to our place. It turned out that my mama was the first to look up in the attic. (The Spitsyns lived in a one-story wooden house.) She saw Ivan Yakovlevich hanging there. (After this, my mama had a nervous condition and even went to a psychiatrist for treatment.) The official version of the suicide went like this: sudden derangement. He left behind a "banal" note: "I beg that no one be accused of my death."

Years passed, and my parents told me the truth. It turned out that "the clouds had begun to gather" over Ivan Yakovlevich at that time. The last straw was that he was told officially: he should not take part in the May Day demonstration (he was not worthy). Obviously, there was something else, but I do not know what it was. Now I have no one to ask (my parents died ten years ago). Saving his wife and daughter, Ivan Yakovlevich took leave of life. And he did truly save them: no one "touched" them. True, having lost their breadwinner, they fell into terrible poverty (they might not have survived, had it not been for the help of relatives and friends). Ivan Yakovlevich's main "sin" was his close acquaintance (nearly a friendship!) with Nikolai Ivanovich Bukharin.

Dear Anna Mikhailovna, does this name mean anything to you—Ivan Yakovlevich Spitsyn? Most likely not. Because Nikolai Ivanovich's acquaintance with Spitsyn evidently dates from the twenties, when you were a child . . .

Please answer this question for me. This "detail" in the life of a friend of my parents very much interests me. But answer me only in the event that you know something about Ivan Yakovlevich: I understand, after all, how many readers' letters you must be receiving (and will keep on receiving)—you can't answer them all.

Respectfully yours,

Olga Aleksandrovna Grachova,
Library Assistant, Lenin Library
Party member since 1966

Moscow

[2]

6 October 1988

Dear Anna Mikhailovna:

Thank you for your memoirs *This I Cannot Forget* published in issue no. 10 of the journal *Znamya*. I am fifty-eight years old and by nature a not very sentimental muzhik from Vyatka. But I'll tell you straight out, I cried when I read the pages of Anna Mikhailovna's "road to calvary." For what, for what "sins"? These oprichniks, be they three times cursed, these dregs and nonhumans mocked and murdered the best and noblest people of our country. You have gone through the horrors of prisons and camps, you were not broken, you withstood it, and now you have brought the truth about yourself and N. I. Bukharin to the people—you have given him back to us alive.

I recalled those terrible years when people feared to say the name of N. I. Bukharin out loud. Only in the form of cursing was it possible to speak of him. But not everyone believed the monstrous lie about him. I, for example, after the Twentieth Party Congress, was certain that sooner or later the truth would triumph. And so it has. I could not believe that the friend and comrade-in-arms of Lenin could have been an enemy. What a word that is—"enemy." It was said first of all by the one who killed him, the most accursed hangman and abomination in human form. In truth, Stalin cannot even be compared with any tyrant. There had never been any like him in existence before. All those Atillas, Neros, and Sullas are also nonhumans, but in treachery and cruelty they are to him like common little mice to a man-eating crocodile.

We must write and write about those terrible years. The more memoirs there are, the better. They are the guarantee that something like this never will happen again.

Thank you also for writing in *This I Cannot Forget* not only about the monsters but also about the families of the persecuted. Thanks for the mother of Tukhachevsky. Yes, the poet will come who will write about that mother. But they will also write about Anna Mikhailovna. About her courage, spirit, endurance and the power of a wife's loyalty. Can your deed really be compared with that of others, for example, the wives of the Decembrists? It is a hundred times greater! Here is the kind of woman we have in our Rus!

I hope, Anna Mikhailovna, that [in the next issues] you will write everything you remember and all the details about yourself and especially about Nikolai Ivanovich. No one can do it better than you. God grant you the health and the years ahead necessary for this work, which the people need so much. Good health to you, or as we say around Vyatka—the health of a wild boar, so you can bear every adversity and the weather.

I bow down to a true Russian woman and tell everyone, everyone here to read *This I Cannot Forget*. I am certain that our state will take care of Anna Mikhailovna, that it will surround you with heartfelt attention. The name of N. I. Bukharin is always next to Lenin. And we shall live to see the day when Lenin's faithful friend will have a monument built in Moscow.

Where is the grave of N. I. Bukharin? Can it be that there is none? But surely there must be archives? And perhaps there are witnesses . . . ?

I await the next issue of the journal with great anticipation. *Znamya* is read by us until the pages fall apart. The editors have chosen good writers. They have a good man there in Chief Editor Georgy Baklanov. He's also a fine fellow for the speech he gave at the Nineteenth Party Conference. That will be remembered. Well done!

In three days it will be N. I. Bukharin's one hundredth birthday. If only he had lived seventy years . . . Who can guess what he would have done? Even in his short life as an outstanding Bolshevik he did [so much]. A great humanist and philosopher will live through the ages. And next to him is Anna Mikhailovna. Also for the ages.

With all my heart and a bow down to Mother Earth,

Anatoly Andreyevich Demakov

Darovskoi Settlement
Kirovskaya oblast

[3]

25 October 1988

Dear Anna Mikhailovna:

I read your *This I Cannot Forget* in the journal *Znamya,* and my own "This I Cannot Forget" arose before my eyes. I was arrested on 23 June 1941, article 58 section 1A and p.sh. [suspicion of espionage] I was seventeen years old at the time. You write about Blyuma Savelievna Gamarnik, I saw her in 1941. After my arrest I was put in a cell in the Butyrka prison occupied only by Gamarnik, I spent half a year in there with her, she looked very bad, very pale, thin, and toothless. She was very kind to me in the autumn I was sent away on a transport to the Saratov prison, and Blyuma Savelievna remained in Butyrki, I never saw her again. You write about Lyudmila Kuzminichna Shaposhnikova in 1942–43 I don't remember precisely the year they put Shaposhnikova Lyudmila Kuzminichna in a cell with us in the Saratov prison, but she was not with us long they took her away with her things, maybe they shot her in the Saratov prison. What we have lived through is impossible to forget and it's very insulting to see people avidly reading about the sufferings of another without even a trace of sympathy on their faces. And many even say, "Ah, how interesting!" Lord, what is interesting here! I don't have to tell you what I have gone through in my life, I got my rehabilitation in 1956, now what color is there in my life? Well, there is none—my pension is seventy-two rubles, I work in order to earn a living and at work I am still a rare bird, and the misery I lived through in the past is a matter of such indifference to my co-workers that at the first little run-in they try to needle you with it. Not long ago the assistant secretary of our Party organization shamelessly tossed this in my face: "Too bad Beria didn't beat you to death." My God whom did we tell about the unforgettable horror we had to endure? Not once has anyone asked me how I am doing, how can I manage to live out my days after such an emotional trauma on the contrary they try to humiliate me to show their superiority over you. Have we really earned such an attitude toward us, so they can read stories about the horrors of the camps and prisons in which we innocents were tortured and murdered, so they can say "oy, how interesting" and pass the journal from hand to hand.

Only the person who has lived through this himself can understand our unforgettable experience and cry over it, but so little sympathy remains for us.

I wish you good health dear Anna Mikhailovna! Forgive me for writing you. After my release, I have not met with any of the b/z [former zeks] like myself, but you are close to me, you knew those people with whom we had to share our pain.

With great respect for you.

Valentina Gavriilovna Donskaya-Krylova

Moscow

[4]

17 November 1988

Memoirs. Archives. Testimonies.
Response to *This I Cannot Forget* by A. M. Larina (Bukharina)
Journal *Znamya* 10, 11, 12, 1988.

In my fifty years of labor (including the Soviet Army and the war), I have given forty years to school, to children. Teacher. Director. Twenty years devoted to boarding schools. I have cared for orphans, children wronged by fate . . .

When I read *This I Cannot Forget* by Anna Mikhailovna Larina (Bukharina), I could not contain myself: many times the tears welled up, a lump rose in my throat, I sobbed. . . .

What a degree of endurance and suffering was visited upon her pure, trusting heart, her candid, noble, and proud soul! It seems to me that if she had not written this now, all the same something would have remained in our world, among the people. Such human power does not die! It is the power of light, truth, and goodness!

I am a pedagogue, a teacher. All my life I have grown close to children, become like kin to them, like one of them. And clearly this is why I was physically unable to read what was said about children, their miseries and sufferings, and mainly—how the Stalinist law, the Stalinist sword of punishment, was applied to children. . . .

A grown man can bear anything, tolerate anything. Everything not sent by the Lord. We know many examples of this, we are apprised of this.

But it happens that the children, who cannot answer back, can bear more and give no complaint. Here the Stalinist experiment has no equal, it is unrivalled!!! For its cruelty, blasphemy, villainy, hypocrisy.

Hangman! Tyrant! Lunatic! Paranoiac! . . .

As the strangler of children, old men, women, "his subjects," Stalin surpasses Hitler.

You don't have to think, guess, weigh, doubt what kind of a man Stalin was. He was a man of one word only: *ubyu!* [I'll kill you!]

"I'll kill you," he said in the ear of Sasha Kosarev. And he killed him.

"I'll kill you," he threatened his wife, Nadya Alliluyeva. And he killed her.

"I'll kill you," he whispered in fury and suspicion, whether it be children, old men, women. And he killed, killed, killed. . . . Tormented. Tortured. Trampled. Shed blood. . . .

I bow my gray head down low to Petya Yakir, a boy, the son of the glorious Yakir family and the son of our motherland. His image shone and will never dim. May this image always live next to his father, next to Iona Emmanuilovich Yakir, Nikolai Ivanovich Bukharin, and Anna Mikhailovna Larina-Bukharina. . . .

While paying our respects to the countless victims of Stalin's repressions, we will always remember and never forget the children who shared the same fate with their parents, guilty without guilt.

May the image of the children find its reflection in the universal Monument to the victims of the repressions.

May there never again descend to our earth and never again appear the Unclean Power.

May there always be Joy! May there always be Mama! May there always be Children!

> Pyotr Mitrofanovich Chaplin, veteran of labor,
> invalid of the Great Patriotic War,
> member of the CPSU since 1944

Mytishchi

Please publish this.

I thank all of you, dear ones, for a great and difficult work, incalculably necessary for our people. I wish you good health and success.

> Sincerely yours,
> P. Chaplin

[5]

29 December 1988

Good day, dear Anna Mikhailovna!

I read your *This I Cannot Forget* in the journal *Znamya*. I'm shaken, I can't get over it. It's already a month later, and I simply can't come back down to earth, to our reality. I am still living your life, I hear your voices, the voices of your tormentors. How did you manage to live through all that? It's incomprehensible, the mind can't take it all in. And yet what a great reserve of endurance there is in the human organism! Your reminiscences made me cry, and understand a lot in life. *Many thanks to you.* You have revealed to us Nikolai Ivanovich Bukharin and many people connected with his work, with state service. You are the living history of our motherland. Thank you for being. When I finished reading your memoirs, my first desire was to get down on my knees before you and kiss your hands and feet. To beg for your forgiveness, although it's not my fault that you endured inhuman sufferings, but the motherland is guilty before you, and I am a part of our motherland. And I beg your forgiveness for the torments which innocently fell to your lot. I well remember that time when the trials went on. I remember the turmoil inside me when our teachers told us we had to scratch out some portraits, cut them out of our textbooks. (I was born in 1923.) And what happiness for you, and for all of us, that you lived through these inhuman torments and told us the truth about that time. You are a lucky woman. You were the wife of N. I. Bukharin—the favorite of the Party and V. I. Lenin. I bow down before you, I firmly press your courageous hand.

Respectfully,
Anastasiya Stepanovna Silvestrova

Baku

[6]

6 January 1989

To the Editors of *Znamya:*

The memoirs of A. M. Larina about N. I. Bukharin, published in nos. 10, 11, and 12 of your journal, make a painful impression. These memoirs force one to reflect again and again: Who was ruling our country over a period of thirty years? A "paranoiac with a withered hand" or the cruelest despot of the twentieth century, the skilled inquisitor, the semiliterate politico by the name of STALIN? Around him, especially up to the ill-fated year of 1937, there were high-minded politicians of major status, evidently, honest people of N. I. Bukharin's sort, who one way or another facilitated Stalin's rise to power, facilitated the creation of a fascist-style dictatorship in our country. Why were such intellectuals and experienced politicians as Trotsky, Kamenev, Zinoviev, Rykov, Bukharin, and many other representatives of the Leninist Guard (as it is now customary to call them) unable to resist a semiliterate scoundrel, a mentally unbalanced man? And if we assume that Trotsky, Kamenev, or Zinoviev could have "overthrown" Stalin and deprived him of power, and possibly of life, who then would have come to power? Might the same situation as with Stalin be repeated, only with a different name? Could it be that the appearance of Stalinism after the October Revolution was a logical consequence of the attempt to build socialism in such a backward country as the Russia of that time?

It occurs to me that if we had not had the most brutal so-called Red Terror immediately after October, when we exterminated the better part of the Russian intelligentsia or forced it to abandon Russia, and simultaneously exterminated or expelled the technical specialists, the progressively minded bourgeoisie, when we destroyed anyone who was "not with us," when we savagely shot the entire family of Romanovs, including the children, if we had not had that, we would not have had Stalinism. Our tragedy consists in the fact that when the new government was being formed the leaders of the October Revolution, especially after the death of Lenin, carried on a fierce struggle for power among themselves and had no thought for collective leadership. From the memoirs of A. M. Larina and other recently published materials it follows that almost all the politicians after Lenin's death were constantly intriguing against each other, forgetting state interests, and they frequently changed their convictions in the effort to preserve their positions as leaders.

1937 might not have happened, had democratic aspects of power been created in our country after October, if the Constituent Assembly had been convened and a political opposition been retained. This was not done, and the politically illiterate crowd shouted, "Away with the Uchredilovka!" [A pejorative term for the Constituent Assembly.] Today the question comes up again: Is it possible to build socialism in the conditions of a backward semiliterate Russia?

At the present time, it is urgently necessary for us to create democratic institutions and to revive a political opposition, perhaps to form an alternative party or parties—for example, the party of the liberal intelligentsia or the party of the "greens."

Returning to the problem of Stalinism, I would like to say that I completely share the idea of the writer A. Adamovich: Stalin and his right-hand men, such as Molotov, Zhdanov, Kaganovich, Voroshilov, and the like, should be judged for the evil deeds they committed against their own people. Neither I nor my relatives, thank God, suffered repressions in Stalin's times, so the voice of "blood vengeance" does not sound in me. But reading the memoirs of victims of Stalin's repressions, I feel my blood "run cold" and involuntarily there come to mind the atrocities of the German fascists, whom we properly judged (alive and dead) with the full severity of the law.

Respectfully,
Professor Yevgeny Samsonovich Stanislavsky
Moscow

[7]

January 1989

To the Editors:

In October, November, and December your journal printed *This I Cannot Forget* by Anna Mikhailovna Bukharina.

Only now, in mid-January, have I been able to get these issues in the library.

Judging by the memoirs of Bukharina, she will be seventy-five on January 27.

I think that you must be in contact with her.

Therefore I ask that you convey our greetings on her birthday, our wishes for her good health. We bow down before her courage.

It is impossible to read her memoirs without tears. It may be a troubled history, but it is the history of our motherland. A feeling of pain and simultaneous pride fills us, people of the older generation, that we had such contemporaries, people devoted to the motherland, yet slandered and destroyed. I remember, although I was a pupil of the lower classes in Kiev, when the trials were held, many did not believe in the guilt of the "enemies of the people."

Now in our time there are also people who want to seek out "enemies of the people," those who are supposedly hindering perestroika. They form fascistic organizations like Pamyat [Memory], Otechestvo [Fatherland], Karabakh.

One cannot help taking offense when their words turn to threats of physical extermination for those people who do not share their views. Can one really get reconciled to this?

Only the feeling that they will not be punished enables them to carry on like this. Such people cannot be changed by persuasion, education. More decisive measures are needed.

Member of the CPSU, Party group organization. Center of Civil Aviation of the SEV [Warsaw Pact] countries.

Faina Vladimirovna Penker

Ulyanovsk

[8]

February 1989

Hello dear Anna Mikhailovna!

Yesterday I finished reading your memoirs. I confess, I was overwhelmed.

Anna Mikhailovna, you are a very courageous woman. What you have lived through is difficult for me even to imagine. I was born and grew up in another time. People now call that time the period of stagnation. For me your life is a legend. Not everyone has the strength to live through such things. Nevertheless, you preserved your dignity, your love of life.

We were brought up to be indifferent. In school we were taught to believe our Party, our government. And God forbid we should ever express any distrust of them! Life turned out completely different. I was very naïve for a long time. I could not believe that it was possible to do something which was considered forbidden in school. I didn't listen to the speeches of Leonid Brezhnev, because they were uninteresting and boring to me.

We knew almost nothing about how people lived in other countries. On television they showed only negative examples. And the thought arose then, how good that I was born and live in the USSR! And how bad it is for people abroad!

With the coming of Mikhail Gorbachev to power, the coming of glasnost, I was truly in a state of shock for a while. The world had turned upside down.

I subscribed to many publications. Now you begin to live life anew. Sometimes it is awfully hard, I don't know why. But I will never understand people who can have such a calm attitude toward Stalin. And many absolutely approve of his horrible regime. I can't read about all this calmly. Sometimes you just lay the journal aside, because you feel your heart squeezing tight.

My generation did not know Stalin; for us he's the past. But how can people keep silent about this? Feed us falsehood, lie about how good we are while robbing the country?

Anna Mikhailovna, I respect and love you a lot. God grant you good health.

Respectfully,
Svetlana Gennadiyevna Lukyanova
A nurse, thirty-five years old

P.S.

I would like, of course, to receive an answer.
My address:
Raigorodok Settlement
Donetskaya oblast
Slavyansky raion

[9]

20 March 1989

Dear Anna Mikhailovna:

In the name of thirty Communists of our Party organization, the most thanks for your book, *This I Cannot Forget.* It cannot be read without getting upset, and what a marvelous person we saw Nikolai Ivanovich Bukharin to be from your memoirs. And yet in the past this name was mentioned only with "Trotskyists-Bukharinists." And how many young people did not know the beloved friend and comrade-in-arms of Vladimir Ilyich Lenin—Nikolai Ivanovich Bukharin.

Dear Anna Mikhailovna, thanks to you for bearing all the horrible burdens in your life, for surviving despite everything, for bringing to our Party and people the letter-testament of N. I. Bukharin. We read it at a Party meeting.

Many residents of our community read your memoirs, *This I Cannot Forget.* And from your memoirs we learned about many wonderful people of our country and about their fates. Everything published in the press about N. I. Bukharin we faithfully collect, only it's a pity nothing that N. I. Bukharin wrote has come to us yet, but people are interested in this.

We bow down in respect to your endurance, courage, and honesty. We hope that poets and writers will be found to glorify the heroism of Anna Larina and others like you.

Anna Mikhailovna, we want in a few words to share with you about perestroika. It has come to our community only in the form of glasnost. In the press we read about everything we could not have read about in the past. But as for actions little has been done. We agree that perestroika depends on each and every person. That is, if even before perestroika this person was a good worker, honest and not shiftless. There have been a lot of those, but they didn't change anything in life, and they still don't. Change still depends more on directors at the local level and higher, on the leaders. Don't you agree?

But how many enemies perestroika has. How much filth of every kind has sprung up: grafters, bribe takers, scammers, bureaucrats of every stripe. How hard it will be to force them out of their warm cushy spots. But we will believe and work for a better future.

Anna Mikhailovna! We would love to receive from you just a few lines in answer, so that we know that our letter reached you.

Once again many thanks to you for the book and the best-best health to you, may you live to the day when Truth and Justice finally triumph, that is what N. I. Bukharin, his comrades-in-arms, and millions of Soviet people gave their lives for.

Writing at the request of Communists,

Valentina Nikolayevna Zelenets

Stantsionny Settlement
Krasnodar territory
Apsheronsky raion

[10]

14 April 1989

To the Editors of *Literaturnaya Rossiya:*

I ask you, your staff, to forward a not very large letter sent in answer to the article *This I Cannot Forget* by A. M. Larina (Bukharina), written by her in the journal *Znamya*, December 1988. A. M. Larina. How do you do! With sincere respect a former sailor addresses you. Been abroad many times. Advise you to read the journals *Politicheskoe obrazovaniye* [Political education] nos. 12, 15, and many others. Where our historians describe: the Doctors of Historical Sciences, Professors P. Podbolotov, B. Starkov, O. Volobuyev, S. Kuleshov. "Know the past in the name of the present." A. M. Larina, I and my com. always believe and listen to our historians, they alone describe only the truth and accuracy of our history. And to our children and grandchildren. Say thanks to the historians, that from their pen we learned the real truth of our time. A. M., I never write unnecessary things to the newspapers, since I am a technical person and connected with automation, I have something to think about. Yet your article touched me, since there is a lot of untruth in it, and I don't feel like stirring up the past. N. I. was rehabilitated: so pray to God and live out your old age. Believe the people know well that N. I. was a Left Communist, and in a difficult moment quit the CC. Didn't go to work, even though V. I. Lenin asked him to, and he knew well that the revolution might

fail. V. I. Lenin (vol. 36, p. 285). They, along with N. I. Bukharin (etc.), have little that is proletarian, but a lot that is bourgeois with the attitude "of the lord and nobleman" (vol. 36, p. 288). A. M. you praise L. B. Rozenfeld-Kamenev a lot. *You shouldn't. The people know* that he was thrice expelled from the Party and thrice admitted, but he didn't stay. *But how many of their organizations did remain?* Once the Great Patriotic War began, *these people put on the fascist uniform. They became policemen, agents, began to mock the Soviet people.* I had occasion, A. M. Larina, to experience myself how the enemies of the people mocked us, tens of millions of completely innocent Soviet people. The war found me on the outskirts of Leningrad. They took us away in special trains to Germany. But our partisans fought back some of them. And then the forests, winter, and we were kids four to five years old. That's *what the childfolk did,* but how many died. A. M., I can't write any more, but I'll say I had occasion to be in Germany as a specialist. I talked a lot with German Communists, they spoke poorly of *N. I.,* of Bronstein-Trotsky. Worked a lot, then quit. A. M. Nicolaevsky thirty years later wrote reminiscences, the whole truth was written, since I was connected with scholars, and they said it was written accurately. They are Admiral Kim Alekseyevich Reshetov, Colonel Yury Nikolayevich Solntsev, the chairman of a department of Lobachevsky University. And K. A. Reshetov is second in command of the northern submarine fleet. Address: City of Leningrad, Petrograd district, Lodeino-polskaya St., house 8, apt. 24. A. M., the mother of my wife was sent away to the city of Zima, Irkutsk oblast, since she is an assistant professor. My uncle worked for *ten* years building Komsomolsk on the Amur. They were sent not for their politics but to work (they were engineers). On this, that's all. Respectfully yours, Viktor.
Trudy Settlement
Gorkovskaya oblast
V. I. Epifanov

[11]

23 April 1989
To the Editors of *Znamya:*
　　　One cannot read calmly and without agitation *This I Cannot Forget,* the story of our tragic past by Anna Mikhailovna Larina (wife

of Bukharin), published in your journal. This is the pure truth about what millions of Soviet people have lived through, and I hope you will print it as a separate little book, which will surely be bought and bring profit to your publishing house, for honestly earned money, after all, is perestroika.

But one thing bothers and irritates me. Why do writers and scribblers of all ranks show their *cowardice* by writing about those Stalinist executors of the terror who have already died, but about those who are flourishing today and who in return for repressions have received ranks, rewards, high pensions, who have grown fat paunches and red physiognomies, who still put on dress coats on the Day of Victory and march in columns alongside real veterans of the Great Patriotic War—about them you don't write a thing. This is an outrage.

And when you read in the press about *evildoers* of the Soviet people, but they are already dead, then one can only call such scribbling *"playing with corpses"*—no more, no less. Write and don't be afraid, this is the truth, but you are writing half-truth, not everything openly, and if you are not permitted to write the truth that way, then you should also confess to your impotence, and not incur the reader's wrath. Why, why??

And one more question. In the press I read that after the revolution there was a society of "old Bolsheviks," which later was routed by Stalin, but perhaps in our time it would do some political good to create a society or committee of "former political prisoners" of the Stalinist repressions, which would unite people and provide a lot of material for history and the press, though now the former political prisoners are scattered and act alone, but are they not many, many?

Veteran of the war and prisoner of the jails and camps of Vorkuta 1947–1955.

Nikolai Andreyevich Krasnov

Ulyanovsk

And one more personal opinion: I cannot pray to God and turn my soul inside out, since I am not a believer, but I pray to fate that the rotten hands of Pavlenko, my KGB investigator from the city of Kuibyshev, swell up so that they never raise a pistol against an unarmed man, for with his cruelties he beat all resistance out of me and wrote what he wanted.

And a second one: May our government not waste money on searching for German criminals, but only deal with its own colleagues. That would command more respect.

[12]

27 April 1989

Dear Anna Mikhailovna:

I read and together with you lived through the shattering story of
your life, and likewise the life and death of Nikolai Ivanovich Bukharin.
I was especially moved by the last months and days of his fight for life,
for human dignity.

Today we know a lot about the baseness and villainy of Stalin and
his henchmen, about how they got rid of undesirables. You have
described shocking scenes in which their methods were used on
Bukharin. It's the way a wolf is hunted: they close in on him from all
sides with little flags, chase him, demoralize him, and then kill him.
With Stalin this method was worked out into a fine science. Apparently
this was a need of his black nature: not simply to eliminate a man he
found unsuitable, but from the start to tease him, toy with him,
humiliate him, and then kill him. Thus it was with Mikhail Koltsov,
Aleksei Kuznetsov, Aleksandr Kosarev, and others. What good was his
hypocritical remark "We shall allow no harm to come to Bukharin, the
favorite of the Party!"—when already he knew that he would kill him.

I was shaken by the words of Kalinin you quoted: "You, Nikolai
Ivanovich, are two hundred percent right, but we have relinquished the
power and there is nothing better than Party unity." Party unity—at
such a price! Excuse me, Nikolai Ivanovich, he seems to say, but we
are forced to murder you in order to preserve Party unity. And this was
said by one of the kindest men—Mikhail Ivanovich Kalinin (so we
always imagined him)!

These words of Kalinin—"we have relinquished the
power"—could serve as an epigraph to the thirty-year reign of Stalin. It
is clear now that after Lenin the power could not have fallen into other
hands. For the nucleus of the Party, from which a worthy successor to
Lenin's cause should have come, was comprised of men with highly
developed minds and bright personalities. They could never have
imagined that some Koba or other would actually twist them all around
his finger. They took him seriously, on an equal basis, while he (an
alien among friends!) unerringly pursued the goal he had already set
himself (even back in Lenin's time), seizing on their mistakes, their

vacillations, expertly guiding them and setting them against one another. It's painful to read this and to become aware of all this. Today, after fifty years, it's all so obvious, so easy to understand, but then . . .

In the history textbook N. I. Bukharin, I recall, is accorded little space. Something about the Bloc of Rightists and Trotskyists, etc. I had never before read anything about Bukharin, and certainly nothing by him. What I have managed to read in recent years has revealed the man.

What a man!—I exclaim along with those who knew him in life. If the power after Lenin had come into the hands of *humane* and honorable (despite all their errors, which were unavoidable) people, would we really be in the situation we are in today? But alas!—it came into the hands of a nonentity not by the will of fate, nor by the will of chance, but by the will of that nonentity himself. Since that time the stream of "gray men" in power has not ceased flowing. Since that time bright and honest people, people of excellence, people of the intelligentsia, have been killed, if not physically, then morally, they have been excluded from society or absented themselves. A glaring example of this is Andrei Sakharov. Dozens of well-known persons could be named. But how many are there who are not well known, who vegetated, who were constantly "enticed," who were expelled from the Party, etc. The Stalinist traditions have prospered.

You have had to wait a long time, Anna Mikhailovna, for the situation to change. Fifty whole years—half a century!

I am happy for you, that despite what you experienced you maintained your spiritual loyalty to N. I. Bukharin through all your life, fulfilled his last wish, bore his spiritual testament to his posterity. Higher justice has triumphed.

I know that you have seen not a few years (I saw you on television), but in your memoirs you appear as a beautiful young woman (even a girl), happy in love. That's the way I see you in my imagination. You say that "the pain lives on in my soul to this day." I can believe you. It's easy to understand.

Some writer said about Pushkin, "Imagine Pushkin in our time! He's a true man of perestroika! How he would delight in everything now! How he would work! What joy and enthusiasm he would show in various television discussions—and just plain discussions!"

The same thing could be said about Bukharin, even their characters are similar, in my view. Each had an overflowing joy of life, an optimistic outlook, and a good heart. A human charm, the desire and ability to labor for the good of the motherland.

Anna Mikhailovna, in closing I want to congratulate you on your birthday; I wish you good health and many more years ahead. You should see the renewed society and live in it. I believe you will.
P.S.

I was born in 1935. Grew up in a village. In school I learned [Ukrainian] verses about Stalin:

> *Stalin will come to our parade,*
> *And give us his good greeting,*
> *For all the children, all of us,*
> *He's our own true father. . . .*

I first heard the words "cult of personality" in 1955, when I was studying in the city. I recall that I could not comprehend what this meant. . . . I remember Odessa deep in mourning, lowered flags, soul-stirring music, people walking down the street silently crying. I cried too. The leader and teacher had died, "our true father." But my father had died in 1944, not far from his own area. They say they hadn't even time to put on a military uniform before they rushed into battle.
PPS.

Recently they showed a scene from the film *The Fall of Berlin,* in which the great Leader and Commander in Chief, the Generalissimo, supposedly flew to Berlin to celebrate the victory, and there was supposedly greeted with banners by the peoples of Europe whom he had liberated.

In reality this never happened, he was not in Berlin, and the scene was ordered by Stalin himself after viewing the completed film. The scene was "for history." This example and many others show that Stalin, despite all his "genius," did not have a far-reaching mind. Else how can one understand his fervent desire to revise history, to remain in it the way he wanted, and not the way he was. An intelligent person could not fail to understand that this does not happen.

Do-svidaniya.

Raisa Yakovlevna Rezanova

Odessa

INDEX

_____

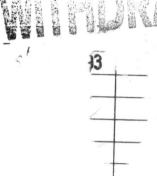